Healthcare Ministry

Refounding the Mission in Tumultuous Times

Gerald A. Arbuckle, S.M.

A Liturgical Press Book

THE LITURGICAL PRESS
Collegeville, Minnesota

Cover design by Greg Becker

1   2   3   4   5   6   7

Library of Congress Cataloging-in-Publication Data

Arbuckle, Gerald A.
    Healthcare ministry : refounding the mission in tumultuous times /
Gerald A. Arbuckle.
        p.   cm.
    Includes bibliographical references and index.
    ISBN 0-8146-2570-3 (alk. paper)
    1. Medicine—Religious aspects—Christianity.   2. Religious health
facilities.   3. Pastoral medicine.   I. Title.
R725.56.A73   2000
261.8'321—dc21   99-16139
                                                                        CIP

In memory of Cardinal Joseph Bernardin,
Eileen Vera Arbuckle,
and William Gerard Kerslake:
refounders of Christian healthcare ministry.

Contents

Part II: Refounding Christian Healthcare

Acknowledgments

My special thanks to Ms. Gillian Paterson for her encouragement to write this book; to Mark Twomey, managing editor of The Liturgical Press, for his ready willingness to publish the book; to my colleagues Michael Mullins, S.M., and Ms. Patricia Moroney for their constant support and willingness to share with me their experiences of organizational consultancies; to Ms. Catherine Duncan for her detailed reading and commenting on the text; to Sr. Teresa Stanley, C.C.V.I., for first introducing me to the Catholic healthcare ministry; to the many people who have shared their experiences and love of the healing ministry. These people, however, are in no way responsible for the book's inadequacies.

Gerard A. Arbuckle, S.M.
January 1, 1999

Introduction

The crown of wisdom is to fear the Lord:
she makes peace and health flourish.
—Sir 1:18

At no previous period has healthcare in the Western world faced a more chaotic and threatening environment.[1] It struggles to move from a hospital to a community focus, from an emphasis on illness to one of wellness, from a bio-medical to a holistic model, from simple to complex technologies, from patient passivity to collaborative interaction. Costs are rising and populations are aging, bringing difficulties never before experienced with such intensity. There are increasingly complex medico-ethical challenges, the administrative burden of coping with changes in funding sources, the closing of many once-flourishing hospitals. Healthcare institutions will not survive and respond to people's needs simply by imitative refining of existing assumptions, structures, and traditional methods of leadership.

In the midst of these transitions and turmoil Christian healthcare has a particular problem of discovering how best to continue its ministry within a secularizing and fast-changing society. There is an urgent need for Christian healthcare to refound itself, that is, it must invent new ways to bring Christ's healing gifts to cultures in ever-increasing change. Otherwise the healing mission of Jesus Christ may not survive into the twenty-first century.

---

[1] See W. Jack Duncan and others, *Strategic Management of Health Care Organizations* (Oxford: Blackwell, 1995) 6.

How different all this is from the achievements of the past! The Christian healthcare ministry, particularly hospital services, had become successful beyond the dreams of its founders. Now it is in the chaos of change. The words of the psalmist can be applied here: "Your favour, Yahweh, set me on impregnable heights, / but you turned away your face and I was terrified" (Ps 30:7).

Yet one fact of human experience is that chaos, the radical breakdown of the predictable, can be a creative experience both personally and organizationally: "Now the earth was a formless void [chaos], there was darkness over the deep, with a divine wind sweeping over the waters" (Gen 1:2). Like the Israelites of old, we can use the chaos we experience to refound the healthcare ministry in ways that respond creatively to the most urgent needs for healing today, in forms that we cannot even imagine at the moment. Chaos can be God's gift to us.

Purpose of This Book

Christian healing ministries can be creatively refounded in a postmodern world in which major cultural changes are expected to continue. However, methods of ministering suitable for a former cultural stability will rarely be effective in the turbulent change that healthcare is now experiencing.

The purpose of this book, therefore, is twofold: first, to provide anthropological insights; second, to provide a spirituality that will help to facilitate the refounding of healthcare as a ministry. The book is not concerned with issues such as contemporary bio-medical ethical problems or contractual relationships between healthcare organizations and governments or trade unions.

My ideas on reform processes in healthcare are developed by reviewing the thinking and records of different countries such as the United States, Britain, Canada, Australia, and New Zealand.[2] Throughout the book I draw on my own experience: I have been in healthcare consultancies to organizations in these countries since 1988. Since 1993 I have been a consultant at various times to healthcare systems in Australia and North America, including to the Catholic Health Association of the United States, whose 1995 annual national assembly was titled "Refounding the Ministry: Leadership in an Era of Profound Change."

[2] See Marshall W. Raffel, "Dominant Issues," *Health Care and Reform in Industrialized Countries,* ed. Marshall W. Raffel (University Park: Pennsylvania State University Press, 1997) 303.

My keynote address[3] to this assembly on refounding healthcare ministry forms the heart of this book. The address was subsequently given to similar associations in Canada, Australia, and New Zealand. In October 1995 the late Cardinal Joseph Bernardin of Chicago built his pastoral letter on the future of Catholic healthcare on this central message, namely, the challenge in these chaotic times to refound the Christian healing ministry.[4]

The book is written for people who are specifically responsible for maintaining Christian values in healthcare, for example, ecclesiastical authorities, trustees, religious congregational leaders, members of boards of management, CEOs, mission leaders, managers, educators. While my research has focused primarily on healthcare ministries of Roman Catholic institutions, I believe the major problems are common to healthcare institutions of all denominations. Given the fact that greater co-operation is developing between Catholic institutions and those of other denominations, it will also be useful for problems particular to Catholic institutions to be more widely known. National and local governments are involved more than ever in these facilities, and a deeper appreciation on their part of Christian healthcare values and challenges can further collaboration.

The book will be helpful to care-givers not working in Christian healthcare institutions but who reverence the core values of compassion, justice, mercy, and concern for the poor. Part II particularly will demonstrate the origins of these values and the cultures of healing inspired by them that were formed over generations.

The inspiration to write this book has come from listening to many who are committed to the healing mission of Jesus Christ, such as Dame Cicely Saunders of St. Christopher's Hospice, London. Her holistic approach has helped refound the hospice movement throughout the world, and my meeting with her in 1997 reassured me that healthcare can be refounded on truly Christian principles no matter how great the challenges. Likewise my contact with Jean Vanier, founder of L'Arche communities for people with disabilities in many countries. And there are others whose devoted lives are unknown to the public, such as Maria, a cleaning lady who helped turn an entire hospital back to its original concern for the poor (see Chapter 6).

---

[3] For a summary of the address see Gerald A. Arbuckle, "It's Time to Refound Health Care Ministry," *Human Development* 17:2 (1996) 24–30.

[4] See Cardinal Joseph Bernardin, *A Sign of Hope: A Pastoral Letter on Health Care* (Chicago: Archdiocese of Chicago, 1995).

Structure and Style of the Book

This book is divided into two parts:

Part I, "Understanding Contemporary Healthcare Challenges," summarizes the dramatic changes impacting on healthcare and the problems they have generated. Thus, chapter one describes the complex relationship between culture, health, illness, sickness, and disease. Chapters two and three analyze the reasons for today's chaos in secular and Christian healthcare. The reform of Christian healthcare ministry is impossible without this knowledge.

Part II, "Refounding Christian Healthcare," describes in particular the anthropological insights and spirituality that can assist the refounding of the healing mission of Jesus Christ. Thus, chapter four concentrates on the nature of chaos and its implications for leadership; chapter five clarifies the biblical foundations of the vision and mission of Christian healthcare. Subsequent chapters explain what leaders in healthcare (for example, trustees and CEOs) can do to assure that Christ's healing mission continues, as well as a spirituality suited to this task.

Though the book draws on several disciplines—Scripture, theology, management studies—its main foundation is cultural anthropology, the study of culture and cultural change. This discipline has been called by anthropologist Raymond Firth "an inquisitive, challenging, uncomfortable discipline, questioning established positions . . . peering into underlying interests, if not destroying fictions and empty phrases . . . at least exposing them."[5] Like a surprising move on a chessboard, anthropology offers a new way of looking at contemporary healthcare issues. It helps widen and deepen a non-medical perspective on health, sickness, and healthcare. In particular, it enlightens us, as no other discipline, about cultural implications of the chaos of contemporary healthcare, for example, why people resist change, and why many hospital mergers fail.[6] Anthropology lays bare the cultural forces that motivate people, of which they are often unconscious.[7]

---

[5] Raymond Firth, "Engagement and Detachment: Reflections on Applying Social Anthropology to Social Affairs," *Human Organization* 40 (1981) 200.

[6] See Cecil G. Helman, *Culture, Health and Illness,* 4th ed. (Oxford: Butterworth-Heinemann, 1985) 338–83; Arthur Kleinman, *Writing on the Margin: Discourse between Anthropology and Medicine* (Berkeley: University of California Press, 1995).

[7] For an introductory overview of the role of social anthropology, see James L. Peacock, *The Anthropological Lens: Harsh Light, Soft Focus* (Cambridge: Cambridge University Press, 1986).

Handbook

The book has a handbook format to aid readers who are not specialists in cultural anthropology or other disciplines to use its material in practical ways. Sometimes significant conclusions are summarized in accessible guidelines. References are given throughout the text to support the arguments and as a resource for people wishing to go deeper into the points discussed.

Case Studies

Frequent use is made of case studies because healthcare workers have to relate to highly complex situations which are not readily open to solution through the application of general rules. Case studies are ideal because they present accounts of such real-world situations which can be analyzed, interpreted, and discussed with fellow workers.[8] Where it was necessary to preserve the anonymity of people and places, incidental details have been changed.

Overview of the Book

My aim in the following pages is to summarize the major themes of the book and to give some preliminary definitions of terms commonly used in the text.

Contemporary Healthcare Challenges

The mid-twentieth century was a time of triumphalism for medicine, and the health industry is still to some degree enjoying the successes of the great medical breakthroughs that permitted us to dream of the day when there would be a pill for every ill. However, with the onslaught of HIV/AIDS and the possible return of drug-resistant diseases such as tuberculosis and malaria, we have become less sanguine.

In the United States, the richest nation on earth, medical services are the best in the world, that is, *if* you can afford them. In contrast to some other industrial democracies, the United States has yet to decide that healthcare is a public good and that every person has a right to it. Consequently and scandalously, forty million people without insurance must depend on charity, the chance of help in emergency clinics, or the grudging assistance of Medicare or Medicaid, if they qualify. On the other hand, governments

---

[8] See Alan B. Thomas, *Controversies in Management* (London: Routledge, 1993) 7.

of countries such as Canada, New Zealand, United Kingdom, and Australia, which subsidize universal healthcare insurance, are so burdened by spiraling costs, inexorably increased by the healthcare demands of an aging population and expensive, sophisticated technology and drugs, that their economies risk breaking under the strain.

Politicians and economists argue that people must face more rigorous rationing of resources and/or higher taxes if the demands on healthcare are to be met. Both options are politically unpopular. Rarely does a day go by without stories in the national mass media in Australia, Britain, and New Zealand complaining about the long lists of people waiting months or longer for elective surgery and the fact that some people die before their turn comes. There are accounts of elderly people living in shocking conditions because services to help them are inadequate. Rationing of treatment has been a mixture of queuing and arbitrary decisions by authorities,[9] but the well-off are able to avoid waiting for services by means of private health insurance (see Chapter 2). No government has a satisfactory answer to the problems of aging populations, the speed of change in procedures and drugs, and the necessity to ration the supply of services in the midst of potentially unlimited demand.

What Is Health?

The considerable theoretical and practical problems in healthcare reform are not assisted by a mistaken understanding of health itself.[10] Many medical professionals have a "medical" model of health and illness. It is a politically unpopular model as it monopolizes an undue amount of funding. According to this model, there are two aspects of illness (see Chapter 1). First, it is commonly caused by pathological processes in the biochemical functions of the body. Specific pathogens cause particular diseases which are, as it were, "hosted" by the patient's body, which is viewed as a kind of machine. Second, the task of the medical person as an agent of healthcare is to reengineer the machine back to normal by identifying and removing the cause of the disease. In this model, outside forces and the individual's mind and spirit are seen as unimportant.

In recent years medical professionals have tended to modify this model somewhat. Individuals are now encouraged to "take care of their health"

---

[9] "Social Insurance Survey," *The Economist* (October 24, 1998) 19.

[10] See David Seedhouse, "Theory or Practice?" *Reforming Health Care: The Philosophy and Practice of International Health Reform,* ed. David Seedhouse (Chichester, N.Y.: John Wiley, 1996) 230.

and exhorted to alter unhealthy lifestyles. Yet even this advice still ignores the impact of the wider environment and cultural factors that cause or contribute to poor health.[11]

Holistic Health and Healthcare

There is growing disillusionment with the limitations of scientific medicine, particularly in such disciplines as mental health, social anthropology and sociology, environmental studies and systems thinking, and theology and spirituality that view the rightful functioning or harmony of the body as intimately related to psychological, cultural, environmental, and spiritual factors. For example, to understand stress necessitates appreciating the complex interplay between the body's immune system and such non-biological aspects as culture, social support, and sense of self-worth. And so a new model of health has emerged—the "holistic" model, which the World Health Organization rather idealistically defines as "a state of complete physical, mental and social well-being and not merely the absence of disease or infirmity."[12]

In addition to the active participation of individuals themselves, holistic healthcare involves not only medical professionals (many of whom are reluctant or refuse to accept this model) but a wide range of agencies and disciplines. Governments must seek to develop a just society in and through which people can achieve harmonious well-being. Difficult political decisions must be made, such as resisting the excessive demands of the medical profession to have exclusive rights to determine public healthcare policies, or controlling economic rationalists who, in order to balance the books, would favor the rich to the disadvantage of the poor.

The mission of the healing Jesus commits us to is a holistic understanding of health and healthcare (see Chapter 5): "Look, I am making the whole of creation new" (Rev 21:5). Healing is a process whereby humankind individually and collectively struggles to be restored to the divine image in which it was originally formed. According to this way of thinking, where there is injustice, there is ill-health; where there is suffering without meaning, there is ill-health; where there is oppression of the poor by the rich, there is ill-health. Therefore, healthcare that confines itself to a

---

[11] See John J. MacDonald, *Primary Health Care: Medicine in Its Place* (London: Earthscan, 1992) 30–7.

[12] Cited by Fritjof Capra, *The Turning Point: Science, Society and the Rising Culture* (London: Flamingo, 1983) 119.

medical model of health is deficient from a theological and spiritual point of view. Healthcare must contribute to the new creation of the world.

Throughout this book "health" and "healthcare" should be understood as *holistic* health and healthcare, except where the context indicates that they are to be used in the restricted sense of *medical* health and healthcare.

Culture, Health, and Healthcare

If Christian healthcare is to continue, there must be sensitive under-standing of culture and culture change. For this reason, emphasis is given to these issues throughout this book. Health and healthcare are related to culture. In fact, culture determines our way of life, down to what we eat, how we work and recreate. Hospitals and other healthcare facilities have their own distinctive cultures, as do the medical and nursing professions. These traditional healthcare institutions are under significant stress today, necessitating profound cultural shifts within a short time. The resulting cultural chaos, while potentially destructive, can with the right leadership be the occasion of considerable creative action for the good of society.

Cultural change is potentially devastating because cultures are systems of *felt* meanings, operating usually at a subconscious level, and providing us with a much-needed sense of order and predictability. In the healthcare industry today there are massive restructurings, downsizing, closures, and mergers of institutions, and they are often not smooth, let alone successful. Commonly the reason for trouble is simply the failure to be attentive to the purpose and power of culture. When a culture is interfered with, people's feelings are deeply affected, often leading to distress and resistance.

Structures can change easily, but people's feelings cannot. In the rush of change (for example, a merger or acquisition), corporate managers can be so concerned with the financial aspects that they neglect the emotional re-actions of the employees involved. When failures occur, managers often look back and admit they were inattentive to cultural and human factors, but in the meantime people have suffered unnecessarily and their organi-zations have possibly been irremediably destroyed (see Chapter 8).

Refounding Christian Healthcare Ministry

Traditional Ministry: Involvement in Hospitals Questioned

In the past, Christian Churches committed their resources to hospital ministry, with outstanding success. Often they began hospitals with scant financial resources in the harsh frontier worlds of the goldmines and forests of North America or in the typhoid-ridden mining camps of Western Australia. It is a story of courage, faith, and hope. However, if Christian organizations were to confine themselves to hospital ministry, the healing ministry could end because acute care hospitals are less and less the vehicle of healthcare.[13] There is a strong move away from acute care hospitals to community care. For example, in Australia the average length of a hospital stay in 1985/86 was 6.6 days, but in 1993/94 this figure had fallen to 4.5 days.[14] People are being discharged from hospitals earlier, and often too soon, because of technological changes and financial pressures. The community is then expected to care for these people.

The financial investment in acute care hospitals by Christian denominations remains considerable. In the United States the fifty-nine Catholic healthcare systems in the Catholic Health Association form the largest non-government non-profit healthcare sector in the nation.[15] However, moral theologian Fr. Richard McCormick, S.J., contends that many non-profit hospitals will find it impossible to support themselves as competition for patients intensifies from for-profit facilities. It will be increasingly difficult to obtain funds to serve the poor because managed care organizations (that is, systems that attempt to manage the costs and quality of healthcare) will resist subsidizing the uninsured, and cutbacks in Medicare and Medicaid will continue. He ends with the question: "How do we save the souls of these institutions as they maneuver through a competitive minefield?"[16] This question is at the heart of this book.

Christian denominations in Canada[17] and Australia conduct government-assisted public hospitals, and are therefore particularly subject to governmental planning decisions. While there are significant benefits to be gained in this system—for example, the hospitals are open to all socioeconomic groups—it has particular challenges for the churches. Governments can

---

[13] See Richard A. McCormick, "The Catholic Hospital Today: Mission Impossible?" *Origins* 24:39 (1995) 648; and Richard A. McCormick, "The End of Catholic Hospitals," *America,* 179:1 (1998) 5–11.

[14] See Marilys Guillemin, *A Woman's Work Is Never Done: The Impact of Shifting Care Out of Hospitals* (Melbourne: Health Issues Centre, 1997) 13.

[15] See Arthur Jones, "Huge Nonprofit System Feels Pressure to Cut Costs, Merge and Get Bigger," *National Catholic Reporter* (June 16, 1995) 12.

[16] McCormick, "The Catholic Hospital Today," 653.

[17] See Peggy Leatt and A. Paul Williams, "The Health System of Canada," *Health Care and Reform,* ed. Raffel, 5.

withdraw their financial support for these hospitals with little warning and close them down or merge them with other facilities.

In Australia,[18] however, denominational hospitals are mainly private and must compete in an increasingly competitive and costly environment. Can they afford to continue? Even if the hospitals are financially viable should the churches continue to sponsor them when there may be other more urgent pastoral needs, such senior care facilities? How are sponsors to reconcile their often expensive and exclusive services with the gospel call to respond preferentially to the poor? These are urgent questions (see Chapters 3 and 6).

Religious Congregations and Healthcare

Traditionally in the Roman Catholic Church, religious congregations through their ministry safeguarded the "souls" of the institutions of healing. Religious, who were never paid for their work, staffed most key administrative positions and as nurses they were very visible in their distinctive habits throughout the facilities. Today, however, the culture of religious life has almost disappeared. Since Vatican II ended in 1965, the decline in vocations to religious life has been so swift that many religious congregations today face extinction.

The involvement of lay people in healthcare management has been rapid and extensive, though religious often still remain as trustees. The challenge to lay people is a daunting one. At a time when many care-givers have no affiliation to a Christian Church or practice no religion, they need to discover radically new methods of continuing the healing mission. Is this possible? Is it possible to continue to foster healthcare ministries in an environment in which healthcare delivery is increasingly seen as an economic commodity, subject to the market forces and the profit motive, not as a fundamental right? This book attempts to answer these critically important questions (see Chapters 6–9).

Need for Refounding Healthcare Ministries

Refounding is the process of retelling the original story of a culture or organization and reinterpreting it in creative ways in view of the changing needs of the contemporary world. Healthcare in the Western world must

---

[18] See Ann Wall, "Australia," *Health Care Systems in Liberal Democracies,* ed. Ann Wall (London: Routledge, 1996) 29–31.

undergo this process at all levels. For example, the move from a medical to a holistic model of healthcare demands a quantum-leap in thinking and action, not modifications of existing structures, which is renewal. The right people are needed to lead this process, that is, people of above-average imagination and creativity, with the drive to take the risks necessary to build new cultures of healthcare within and beyond hospitals. They will be people who understand the political tensions involved in issues of justice and inequality, and the allocation or rationing of scarce resources.

The more so in Christian healthcare. Christ's healing mission will not be re-enacted merely by polishing up, superficially improving, or renewing old methods of ministry: there simply must be ongoing refounding. The Catholic Health Association of the United States summarizes the task confronting Christian healthcare ministries:

> The current revolution in healthcare presents [us] . . . with important opportunities and challenges. It calls for leaders in Catholic healthcare to *refound* the Church's healing ministry in light of the values that have shaped that mission. At the same time, the revolution challenges healthcare leaders to achieve a *transformation* in the way health ministry is carried out.
>
> To be successful, health leaders will need to shift from a *hospital system focus* on providing acute care, treating illness, and caring for individual patients, to a *health system focus* on coordinating a continuum of care, maintaining wellness, improving the health status of persons in their communities.[19]

For this process to begin and continue, we need people with the qualities of the founders of Christian healthcare, people with similar imagination and creativity, who first hear and live the healing mission of Jesus Christ and then devise ways to reinterpret it in the turbulent world of contemporary healthcare. They will go to the heart of the story of the healing Jesus, wisely discarding all accidental and historical accretions. They will know that traditional methods of ministry can no longer work; today's responses can become tomorrow's problems.

They will not be individualists, but team-oriented people who recognize that the task cannot be grasped or solved by one person alone. The servant-leadership of the listening and healing Jesus is their model. They will be carriers of Christ's mission, committed to building and rebuilding cultures of Christian healing by such measures as developing community-based

---

[19] Catholic Health Association of the United States, *A Workbook on Redesigning Care* (St. Louis: CHA, 1995) 9.

programs, advocacy pressure groups to protect respect for life, political action campaigns for the rights of the marginalized, educational projects for wellness, and so on.

Mergers, Affiliations, Alliances

Traditionally, hospitals of different denominations were self-supporting and self-managing, with minimal relationships with other healthcare facilities or government agencies. In the world of managed care and rising costs this is increasingly impossible. In a survey of a cross-section of hospitals/systems in the United States, only 12 percent expected to remain independent by the year 2000.[20] In Christian healthcare mergers of hospitals within the same denomination or across denominations are increasing. There is even some controversial collaboration with for-profit organizations.

Where mergers succeed—and this is less common than generally recognized—it is because people have been patient enough see whether or not their organizational ethics, philosophies, and cultures were compatible. Healthcare reformers need to realize that the development of a new culture through an organizational merger is a slow and humanly perilous adventure. They cannot neglect the emotional or grieving reactions of their employees, or the organizational cultures from which they come.[21] Nor should they lose sight of the fact that the fulfillment of the healing mission of Jesus Christ is the goal of all decision-making (see Chapter 8).

A Spirituality of Healthcare

Spirituality is a way of bringing the healing message of Christ into everyday life. A spirituality of reconciliation is needed that seeks to draw the "whole creation" (Rom 8:22) back to justice, love, and harmony with God. An essential quality of such reconciliation is the willingness to let go of the familiar and all that holds us back from holistic healing. One day a ruler asked Jesus

> "Good Master, what shall I do to inherit eternal life?" And when Jesus heard this he said, "There is still one thing you lack. Sell everything you own and distribute the money to the poor. . . ." But when he heard this he was overcome with sadness, for he was very rich (Luke 18:18, 22-23).

[20] See Barry S. Bader, "Look Before You Leap," *Trustee* (March 1997) 18–19.
[21] See William H. Miller, "Costly Inattention: Ignoring Employee Impact Can Ruin Mergers," *Industry Week* (September 29, 1986) 28.

The lesson for healthcare personnel is this: there must be a willingness to let cherished structures and processes die when they no longer serve the healing mission of Jesus. To let go is to be poor in spirit, open in faith to risk and to the unknown. This is not easy. It demands courageous leadership born of an inner detachment because, as Peter Drucker comments:

> [Few] service institutions [such as healthcare] attempt to think through the changed circumstances in which they operate. Most believe that all that is required is to run harder and to raise more money. Precisely because results in service institutions are not easily measured, there is need for organized abandonment. There is need for a systematic withdrawal of resources of money, but above all, people—from yesterday's efforts.[22]

Spirituality is not a quality of individuals only, but also of organizations or cultures.[23] Leaders in Christian healthcare will have a sensitive awareness of the need for cultural as well as individual grieving, and that the rights of individuals and groups are oppressed if this is neglected (see Chapter 9).

[22] Peter Drucker, *Managing in Turbulent Times* (London: Pan Books, 1982) 46.
[23] See Walter Wink, *Engaging the Powers: Discernment and Resistance in a World of Domination* (Minneapolis: Fortress Press, 1992).

Part I

Understanding Contemporary Healthcare Challenges

Chapter 1

Culture, Health, Illness, Sickness, and Disease: Clarifying Terms

Culture is not only a means of representing disease, but is essential to its very constitution as a human reality.[1]

—Byron J. Good

Health and illness are fundamentally a consequence of the way societies are organised and function.[2]

—Jake M. Najman

This chapter explains:

- the meaning of culture: symbols, myths, and rituals;
- some initial guidelines for healthcare workers seeking to understand organizational cultures;
- the distinctions between illness, sickness, and disease;
- the relationship between culture and disease;
- the inadequacy of the medical model to explain disease;
- the postmodern and paramodern critique of the medical model.

[1] Bryon J. Good, *Medicine, Rationality and Experience: An Anthropological Perspective* (Cambridge: Cambridge University Press, 1994) 53.

[2] Jake M. Najman, "Health and the Australian Population," *A Sociology of Australian Society,* ed. Jake M. Najman and John S. Western (Melbourne: MacMillan, 1993) 332.

Healthcare and culture are intimately related. First, healthcare organizations, for example hospitals, are themselves cultures and they are under considerable pressures from many sides. This chapter clarifies the complex anthropological meaning of culture and provides initial practical guidelines for healthcare workers who are committed to lead cultural change. Organizational planning that neglects the power and inner dynamics of culture will inevitably fail.

Second, this chapter explains the historical interplay between culture and health, because it is impossible to define the meanings of the words "health," "illness," "sickness," and "disease" without reference to the culture. Culture intimately affects the health even of those insensitive to their cultural heritage and unconcerned about their health. If Christian healthcare ministry is to be refounded within a multicultural setting, such as we find in the countries of contemporary North America, Europe, and Australasia, we must be sensitive to this powerful interconnection.

Understanding Culture

"Culture" is a difficult term to define. Often, especially in management texts,[3] it is loosely used to mean "what people do around here." But culture is better defined as a pattern of shared meanings and values, embodied in a network of symbols, myths, and rituals, created by a particular group as it struggles to adjust to life's challenges and educating its members about what is considered to be the orderly and correct way to feel, think, and behave.[4] Culture significantly shapes people's emotional reaction to the world of people and things. The word "emotional" is important: a culture penetrates the deepest recesses of the human group and individuals, in particular their feelings. Hence, it is more accurate to define culture not as "what people *do*," but rather "what people *feel* about what they do."

While this understanding of culture assumes the importance of factual history and visible phenomena, it emphasizes first the developmental, or ever-evolving, survival role of culture for a people in a world of change, prejudice, and discrimination. Second, it emphasizes that culture is not

---

[3] See the discussion by Allan Williams and others, *Changing Culture: New Organisational Approaches* (London: Institute of Personnel Management, 1993) 11–38; for a fuller explanation of culture see Gerald A. Arbuckle, *Earthing the Gospel: An Inculturation Handbook for the Pastoral Worker* (Maryknoll, N.Y.: Orbis Books, 1990) 26–61.

[4] This is an adaptation of a definition by Clifford Geertz, *The Interpretation of Cultures* (New York: Basic Books, 1973) 89.

one facet of life along with, for example, religious, political, or economic activity, which is a view particularly popular among contemporary management writers. On the contrary, culture is the complete set of feelings affecting all behavior of individuals and groups in varying degrees.

"Subculture" is a term for groups whose special interests and sense of belonging set them apart from the wider culture, for example, youth subculture or ethnic subculture. In a hospital there may be many subcultures, such as administrative, medical, housekeeping, and patients. Subcultures may differ on various measures, such as the rigidity of separation or distance from the main culture; the level of exclusivity; the degree of overlap with other subcultures; diversity of access to political power. For example, medical professionals hold considerable power over other subcultures in a hospital. When their sense of superiority is questioned they may react to protect their elitist status preventing other workers, such as nurses, from making significant contributions to healthcare.

Symbols, Myths, and Rituals

For most of our lives we are rarely aware of the degree to which culture, through its constituent elements of symbols, myths, and rituals, influences our thoughts, emotions, and actions. Each of them operates most powerfully at the level of the unconscious, giving us that all-important sense of experienced or felt meaning and order.

Rituals are the visible expressions of symbols and myths. These, unlike symbols and myths, are obvious to an observer in a culture. No one who watches the inauguration ceremonies for a president of the United States will miss the special emphasis the presidency has in the nation's mythology.

A *symbol,* for example, a flag or a crucifix, is any reality that by its very dynamism or power leads to (that is, makes one think about, imagine, get into contact with, or reach out to) another deeper and often mysterious reality through the sharing in the dynamism of the symbol itself and without additional explanations.[5] A symbol is more than just a sign. Signs only point to the object signified, but symbols by their very dynamism *re*-present the object. The stop sign down the road used to be just a sign indicating that I must stop the car to allow other traffic to pass. This week, however, it became for me a symbol because I accidentally hit it to avoid a major collision with another car. Every time I see the notice, I *relive* the accident.

---

[5] I am grateful to Fr. Adolfo Nicolas, S.J., for this definition.

A symbol has the two particular qualities of meaning and emotion. It can have many meanings at the same time, thus making it difficult for people to know which meaning is intended by a speaker, especially if that person belongs to a different culture. A symbol's emotion charge causes people to react with negative or positive feelings. For example, when I see a stethoscope that symbol evokes in me feelings of trust and respect for the professional person who wears it, but it also causes me to feel uneasy as I recall the time a doctor used one to diagnose that I had a weak heart.

Contrary to popular beliefs, *myths* are not fairy tales or fallacies. Myths, along with symbols, form the very heart of every culture. A myth is a story or tradition that claims to reveal in an imaginative or symbolic way a fundamental truth about the world and human life. The truth is regarded as authoritative by those who accept it. Myths (sometimes called "cultural stories") are symbols in narrative form; for example, the creation stories of the book of Genesis or the arrival of the Pilgrim Fathers in the founding of the United States, giving meaning to life. Without myths we are unable to know what things are, what to do with them, or how to relate to them. The original meaning of myth is story. It is only the modern use of the word as a synonym for error that has given myth a negative connotation.

A culture does not continue if it lacks myths, especially its creation or founding myth operative down through time. Creation myths like to speak about *first* causes; in them people express their primary understanding of humankind, the world, their nation, their organization, like the creation stories in the book of Genesis. On a far less exalted level, there are creation stories of why and how a healthcare facility was formed. Rollo May describes founding myths: "[They] are like the beams of a house: not exposed to outside view, they are the structure which holds the house together so people can live in it."[6]

Myths: Clarifications

Several clarifications need to be made about myths because an understanding of their purpose and power are crucial to this book.

Myths Speak to Hearts

Myths speak primarily to the hearts and feelings of people, even though they also have a cognitive or intellectual dimension. Because it is difficult

[6] Rollo May, *The Cry for Myth* (New York: Delta, 1991) 15.

to articulate feelings, people frequently identify their myths by describing individuals (for example, heroes/heroines) who embody the qualities of the myths. These risk-takers venture out into the unknown world where they battle against evil and articulate the tensions we feel. For example, in the eighteenth century St. Marguerite D'Youville, foundress of the Grey Nuns in Quebec, would discover resources for the poor even when situations were most desperate. Florence Nightingale (1820–1910), in the midst of the perils of the Crimean War, fought against the deadly lack of hygiene in the military hospitals. She, like Marguerite, embodies the courage of countless people through the ages who have risked their lives to aid the suffering.

Myths Contain Values

Myths enshrine a people's *values,* that is, the action-oriented priorities or convictions that they hold dear; values motivate people to act, even if action demands sacrifices. But myths do not set out how values are to be reconciled when they appear to be in opposition. Many Christian hospitals have core values such as mercy, compassion, hospitality, and justice in their founding myth, but the myth does not explain how to reconcile the demands of justice with mercy. (This point will be further examined in Chapter 5.)

Myths Define Organizational Types

Myths articulate the particular type of organization needed in a culture. For example, the founding myth of a hospital will indicate that its organization must differ from that of a supermarket. The primary aim of healthcare delivery should be "a cured patient, a comforted patient and a healthier community, not to earn a profit or a return on capital for shareholders,"[7] as is the case of a supermarket. The organizational structures of a hospital and a supermarket should differ accordingly.

Myths Are Changeable

Myths can change over time. For example, the founding myth of hospitals for decades assumed they had to be large to cope with surgery aftercare. That is no longer necessarily the case, since improved technology

[7] Cardinal Joseph Bernardin, "The Case for Not-for-Profit Health Care," *Origins* 24:32 (1995) 540.

cuts down or completely eliminates the need for extended hospitalization after surgery.

At times myths drift; that is, they change or degenerate without any deliberate planning on the part of individuals or groups. Sometimes the dominant myth is distorted because a secondary myth assumes an exaggerated position.[8] For example, Christian hospitals founded primarily to serve the needs of the poor can over time shift their priorities to the wealthy. The reevaluation of priorities is not easy, for the simple reason that myths reside in a group's feelings, which are not easily challenged or changed.

Myths Inspire People

Myths provide an inspirational vision for people who hold them, an overall view that inculcates a sense of pride, direction, purpose, or simply an *esprit de corps*. When organizations lack myths they have no vision to animate people and eventually disintegrate: "Where there is no vision the people get out of hand" (Prov 29:18). Sociologist Peter Berger comments:

> It is through myths that men are lifted above their captivity in the ordinary, attain powerful visions of the future, and become capable of collective actions to realize such visions. . . . By definition, myth transcends both pragmatic and theoretical rationality, while at the same time it strongly affects them.[9]

CASE STUDY ▬▬▬▬▬▬▬▬▬▬▬▬▬▬▬▬▬▬▬▬▬▬▬▬▬

Myths in Conflict

Following several radical internal structural changes the morale of a hospital dropped alarmingly. Staff, feeling the organizational culture was no longer supportive of them or the patients, became cynical about the core values: respect for patients, justice, compassion.

The trustees, faced with the crisis of survival because of outside pressures, employed key managers whose basic philosophy is economic rationalism, that is, struc-

---

[8] See Gerald A. Arbuckle, *Out of Chaos: The Refounding of Religious Congregations* (London: Geoffrey Chapman, 1988) 68–77.

[9] Peter L. Berger, *Pyramids of Sacrifice: Political Ethics and Social Change* (Harmondsworth: Penguin, 1974) 32.

tural change at all costs for financial advantage. "Get the finances right and the vision/mission will be guaranteed," they stated. The trustees had accepted this axiom. The staff and patients, however, recognized that this philosophy was in fundamental conflict with the founding story of the hospital, but were unable to be heard by either the managers or the trustees, which caused the drop in morale.

The trustees erred because they did not understand that business and mission could be creatively interrelated, as it had been over the century when the hospital had been directly administered by religious sisters. If they had insisted that the managers respect the mission and values from the beginning, a way might have been found to overcome the financial problems. The staff believed this, but the trustees did not. Hence, the widespread cynicism.

This case study highlights the clash between two myths—one which places profit at the service of patient care, the other assuming healthcare is primarily an economic commodity. These two myths will be examined more fully later in Chapters 5 and 8.

Myths Are Not Primarily About History

Myths can contain or have solid foundations in historical realities, but the purpose of myth and history differ. Myth is concerned not so much with a succession of events as with the moral significance of these happenings. A myth is a "religious" commentary on the beliefs and values of a culture.

The creation account in the book of Genesis is a myth enshrining fundamental values. For example, God freely created the world and so loves humankind that men and women are to be stewards of this creation. It is not primarily about history, but an evaluation of the event of creation. Mother Teresa of Calcutta can be viewed historically or mythologically. As seen from the historical perspective, she is depicted as fitting into a definite time period, influencing and being influenced by events around her. If, however, she is evaluated as a person who exemplifies the virtues of zeal for the rights of the poor, commitment to Jesus Christ the healer, then we are measuring her by the founding story of Christian healthcare.

Some Practical Implications for Healthcare

Guideline 1

Culture is resistant to change. Culture protects us from the awesome insecurities of chaos. It is "an area of meaning carved out of a vast mass of meaninglessness, a small clearing of lucidity in a formless, dark, almost ominous jungle."[10] For this reason every culture has a built-in resistance to change, primarily because people fear a breakdown of felt order or predictability. Healthcare facilities contain a further source of resistance to change because people see them as protectors against death itself. Little wonder that there is such resistance to change in healthcare cultures.

It can happen that members of a healthcare facility can agree with considerable enthusiasm to new mission directives for change, but then do nothing about them. At workshops participants commonly assure me that they are certainly open to change, and are even offended that I dare to question them on the issue. I then ask them where they sat before the coffee break and invariably the majority reply: "In the seats we are now sitting in!" I do not have to press the point any further. When change hits culture, culture wins! Research into failures of organizational re-engineering projects supports this insight: "Estimates of the number of 'failures' [of re-engineering efforts] range to as high as 70 or 80 per cent of all initiatives. . . . The people-related issue of 'culture' has been shown to be the major inhibitor to re-engineering progress among US and European organisations."[11]

This guideline is further explained in Chapter 4.

Guideline 2

Customs evoke strong feelings and reactions. Because symbols contain strong feeling, healthcare professionals working in a cross-cultural facility need to be sensitive to the customs of cultures other than their own. In some cultures, for example, male doctors are forbidden to examine women patients. Failure to know this can cause unnecessary communication problems and harm to patients. Customs must be respected, and where they conflict

[10] Peter L. Berger, *The Sacred Canopy: Elements of a Sociological Theory of Religion* (New York: Doubleday, 1969) 23.

[11] Mike Oram and Richard S. Wellins, *Re-Engineering's Missing Ingredient: The Human Factor* (London: Institute of Personnel and Development, 1995) 4.

with sound hygiene there needs to be well-prepared briefings of the patients and their families by sensitive counselors with multicultural experience.[12]

Guideline 3

Cultures/subcultures define social purity/impurity. Ethnocentrism is a dynamic at work in every culture and subculture. In its mild forms, ethnocentrism is normal, reasonable, and serves a useful purpose. Cultural identity requires that people feel pride in their group's achievements, that other cultures have something to learn from their group. But unchecked, this group pride can go over the brink into prejudice and discrimination against people who are different, and then it ceases to be a positive value. It can frustrate attempts to build a healthy society across cultural boundaries. Nationalism—an expression of ethnocentrism—makes culture an object and a thing of worship.

The assumption is that "our way of life is *the* way to live" and must be protected at all costs. "Members of other subcultures have nothing of value to offer us!" Pejorative and divisive expressions such as "dirty,"[13] "unreasonable," "uppity," and "crude" are used of them; the often unspoken assumption is that the speaker is "clean," "reasonable," "polished." I have sometimes heard such emotive terms used of one another by people of different subcultures in hospitals. Unless these barriers of ethnocentrism break down, intersubcultural communication at any worthwhile depth is impossible.

CASE STUDY ▰▰▰▰▰▰▰▰▰▰▰▰▰▰▰▰▰▰

Ethnic Groups and Healthcare

A group of Australian aborigines explained why they would not go to the local public hospital: "We do not

---

[12] See Geri-Ann Galanti, *Caring for Patients from Different Cultures: Case Studies from American Hospitals* (Philadelphia: University of Pennsylvania Press, 1997); Gary L. Kreps and Elizabeth N. Kunimoto, *Effective Communication in Multicultural Health Care Settings* (Thousand Oaks, Calif.: Sage Publications, 1994); Kathryn H. Kavanagh and Patricia H. Kennedy, *Promoting Cultural Diversity: Strategies for Health Care Professionals* (Newbury Park, Calif.: Sage Publications, 1992); Malcolm MacLachlan, *Culture and Health* (Chichester: John Wiley, 1997).

[13] See Mary Douglas, *Purity and Danger: An Analysis of Concepts of Pollution and Taboo* (Harmondsworth: Penguin, 1970) 41–53; and Arbuckle, *Earthing the Gospel,* 147–66.

feel wanted. To go inside the door we must have great courage. Often it is impossible, because white people there think us no good, they laugh at our customs. They say they are dirty, primitive and useless. They have taken away all our land, our hope."

For two hundred years these people have suffered cultural and economic oppression from the dominant white population and these tragic reactions are to be expected. When an ethnic group makes contact with a dominant culture, the contact of cultures is not an abstract concept, but a high order of human drama accompanied by a ghostly cast of prejudice, discrimination, physical and mental ill-health, longing, and fear.

The case study illustrates how the ethnocentric attitudes and behavior of people of one culture can gravely affect the physical and mental health of another people. The intensity of ethnic identity, or ethnicity, generally depends on the attitudes of the dominant group toward non-members in its midst. The ethnic identity of oppressed groups, such as aboriginal peoples in this case study, is called "involuntary" or "ascribed":[14] there is little or no escape from negative labeling and oppression.

In these circumstances the "we/they" dichotomy is strong. The dominant group or subculture, often out of a sense of fear of losing its position of power, pejoratively stereotypes the "they" and institutionalizes the oppression so that in key areas of life, such as employment, access to health services, education, and social relationships, the oppressed are excluded from equality with the "we." To develop and "legitimate" this discrimination, the out-group is frequently branded as racially or culturally inferior, as has happened to aboriginal peoples in Australia, with disastrous impact on their personal and collective health.[15] Such is also the fate today of many

[14] See Gerald A. Arbuckle, "Understanding Ethnicity, Multiculturalism, and Inculturation," *Human Development* 14:1 (1993) 5–10; Benjamin B. Ringer and Elinor R. Lawless, *Race, Ethnicity and Society* (New York: Routledge, 1989) 18–27.

[15] See Ernest Hunter, *Aboriginal Health and History: Power and Prejudice in Remote Australia* (Cambridge: Cambridge University Press, 1993) 76–199; Henry Reynolds, *This Whispering in Our Hearts* (Sydney: Allen and Unwin, 1998); Peter Khoury, "Aboriginal Health as a Social Product," *Second Opinion: An Introduction to Health Sociology,* ed. John Germov (Melbourne: Oxford University Press, 1998) 57–74.

economically poor migrants to rich western nations; for example, African migrants to France and Turkish migrants to Germany.

Guideline 4

When creation myths are retold they become regenerative. Whenever a creation or founding myth is ceremoniously retold it becomes a regenerative myth for a group. The sacred time of the founding of a culture or nation is lived again, providing people with a renewed sense of identity, belonging, and energy. For example, the Exodus event, the creation myth of the Israelite people, is also a regenerative myth; whenever the Israelites feel lost they retell, and are regenerated by, the founding story of the nation, and express it in ritual (see Psalm 78). If the reliving of the founding story is to be authentic, people are expected to undergo a deep interior and exterior change; they cannot be mere spectators (see Chapters 5 and 9 for a fuller explanation).

CASE STUDY

Hospital Managers are Re-energized

Another consultant and I were asked to help managers adjust to significant organizational cultural restructuring in an Australian hospital. We began by inviting the managers collectively to draw the history of the hospital since its founding early last century. At first they were reluctant to do so, but they grew enthusiastic as they became increasingly involved in the task. Some drew the five founding sisters arriving by sailing ship in 1838 from Ireland, having survived the dangers of the long journey. Others depicted them working with the poor. Others sketched a bishop who was angry with the sisters' concern for the poor of all denominations. Still others highlighted the financial risks that the congregation took in building a hospice and facilities for the destitute.

When they had finished the task we asked them to describe what they felt as they reflected on the composite drawing. Representative replies were: "The courage and faith of the sisters in the midst of impossible pressures are amazing!" "There is the tradition of concern for the needy and that must continue." "This hospital has a long

history of financial crises, yet each time the faith of the
sisters and staff has triumphed. With the same faith we
will get through this present threat and be stronger than
ever!" In the space of an hour the group had moved from
depression to hope.

In the above case study the participants of the workshops commonly
were historically inaccurate about the details of the history of the hospital.
But historical accuracy was not the point of the exercise. More importantly
the managers were recounting the hospital's founding myth and this energized them.

Guideline 5

One enters into a culture through feelings and myths. The way into a
culture is to be in touch with a people's feelings by listening to their myths
or stories. It is in stories that one is able to sense what people are passionate about: their values, beliefs, frustrations. For decades, leaders, managers, and employees have been wrongly told to leave their feelings at the
door. But if one is not in touch with one's own feelings there is no way one
will be able to connect with the feelings of others (see Chapter 8).

Illness, Sickness, Disease, and Healing: Cultural Insights

Disease describes the scientifically or medically endorsed breakdowns
of a physiological and biological nature, whereas *illness* is the subjective
experience of the individual or the knowledge that one is ill.[16] The act of
being ill is the result of efforts on the part of the sick person, and their as-
sociates, to make sense of what they are experiencing. *Sickness,* on the
other hand, "is the ascription of ill health to a person by others, an ascription that may be made in the absence of the subjective awareness of illness
(e.g., in some forms of mental illness)."[17] These words are also applied by
extension to cultures; for example, the Israelites are perceived by YHWH as

---

[16] See Arthur Kleinman, *The Illness Narratives: Suffering, Healing and the Human
Condition* (New York: Basic Books, 1988) 3.

[17] Alastair V. Campbell, *Health as Liberation: Medicine, Theology and the Quest for
Justice* (Cleveland: Pilgrim Press, 1995) 45; see comments by Bryan S. Turner, *Medical Power and Social Knowledge* (London: Sage Publications, 1995) 2–3.

metaphorically diseased and sick when they break the covenant, and meta-phorically healthy when harmony exists (Jer 30:17).

The words, namely "disease," "illness," and "sickness," have different meanings in different cultures as will be explained in the analysis of four culture models.[18] In practice, a culture may well have elements of all four models, though one model will predominate at a particular time. An an-thropological model is not a perfect representation of the real world at all, but a highlighting of major emphases of a culture. Nuanced explanations or details are omitted to allow us to grasp key features of what is in reality a highly complex situation. Any particular culture may then be compared with the model to see to what extent the model resembles it.

Each culture model shows a preferred way of mediating between hu-mankind and disease; for example, through magic, through religion/com-passion for suffering, by rejection of the abnormal, through technical control of disease, or by a holistic response.

Model 1: Premodern Culture: Early Holistic Societies

Summary

Mental, physical, and social health are profoundly interrelated. Good health exists when people live in harmony with each other, their gods or spirits, and the environment. Health can be recovered through the use of a wide variety of folk medicines, but these are useless if social relationships and events are not renewed, and evil spirits ritually ejected, for it is they which are the primary causes of illness and sickness. Sickness is not merely physical but mirrors the social circumstances of the individual. This model of health is holistic in the sense of viewing sickness as related to the whole person and the social and natural environment.

Hippocrates, a physician in the fourth century B.C.E., emphasized holis-tic health when he insisted on the indivisible connection between a healthy mind and a healthy body. Plato in the same century agreed:

> As you ought not to attempt to cure the eyes without the head, or the head without the body, so neither ought you to attempt to cure the body without the soul . . . for the part can never be well unless the whole is well and, there-fore, if the head and body are to be well, you must begin by curing the soul.[19]

---

[18] See Gerald A. Arbuckle, *From Chaos to Mission: The Refounding of Religious Life Formation* (Collegeville: The Liturgical Press, 1996) 42–57.

[19] Plato, as cited by Gareth Tuckwell, "Christian Healing: A Ministry to the Whole Person," *Catholic Medical Quarterly* 42:2 (1991) 13.

Explanation

This culture type, found commonly in Asia, Africa, parts of North, Middle, and South America, and the South Pacific, and throughout Europe up to the Reformation, is one in which behavior is highly traditional. One's identity is inseparable from the group into which one is born, such as the extended family, clan, or tribe. Ask South Pacific migrants in Britain or the United States who they are and they will begin to describe an extensive range of relationships. When the evangelist Matthew wanted to define who Jesus is, he started by listing a long genealogy (Matt 1:1-17). Many peoples of the world would understand his logic.

Founding myths exalt stability and the sacredness of tradition, not change; the culture is a gift of the gods/ancestors so it must not be questioned. The fear of being mocked, laughed at, or punished by spirits if one goes against tradition enforces conformity to the group's norms. Because tradition is pivotal, harmony and unity must be maintained in the group at all costs, even if the objective norms of justice are broken in the process. To be expelled from the group, as Cain found after murdering Abel (Gen 4:10, 12-13), is the severest form of punishment possible, because the individual then loses all sense of identity and rights. Respect for patriarchal values is also a strong force in maintaining the healthy status quo. If women misbehave, then men, the guardians of tradition and stability, experience shame; to avoid such shame and maintain a sense of male honor, women must be kept in inferior status and fully under men's control.

Illness, Sickness, and Healing

Thinking is far less compartmentalized than is the case in Western societies. One facet of life is generally intertwined with many others, not only situationally, but in people's thinking.[20] Thus illness cannot be reduced to one physical cause such as a germ; rather, it is a form of evil that has complex social implications and causes. Evil destroys life, health, good status, and prosperity.

Premodern cultures recognize there are immediate and rational causes for misfortune; for example, cancer causes death. For every misfortune

---

[20] See Peter Morley, "Culture and the Cognitive World of Traditional Medical Beliefs: Some Preliminary Considerations," *Culture and Curing: Anthropological Perspectives on Traditional Medical Beliefs and Practices,* ed. Peter Morley and Roy Wallis (London: Peter Owen, 1978) 2–18; Alice B. Child and Irvin L. Child, *Religion and Magic in the Life of Traditional Peoples* (Englewood Cliffs, Calif.: Prentice Hall, 1993) 129–39.

there is always a physical or natural cause. However, a further and far more important question, namely "Why?" must be answered in other ways. Often people believe that the ultimate cause of evil, in the form of sickness or death, is that ancestors punish the living for not showing them respect or for breaking tribal taboos. The living can also harm others through the intentional or unconscious use of magical forces, such as sorcery and witchcraft. Sorcery is the conscious use of magic to harm some person or group, whereas witchcraft is seen as a malign quality innate in a person. Witches, unlike sorcerers, are generally unaware that they have this quality or are exercising it. For many peoples, for example, among the aboriginal Yolngu community in Australia, when there is a death it is generally believed to be the result of sorcery.[21]

CASE STUDY

Death Without Physical Cause

A Maori man in New Zealand had been sentenced to a lengthy jail term. After a short time he called his Maori friends together and told them he would die shortly, even though he was physically very fit. His offense, he believed, would be punished by sorcerers at the instigation of the dead man's relatives. Within a week he had died, but it was impossible to find any medical cause of the death. His friends said he had died from *mate Maori* ("Maori sickness") of mystical origins.

Traditionally, Maori people ascribed any departure from normal health to attacks by malignant spirits.[22] Anthropologist Joan Metge provides further background to this case study: "[Fear] of sorcery [among Maori in New Zealand] is dormant most of the time, becoming dominant only under stress and in the face of the unaccountable. A diagnosis of sorcery usually

---

[21] See Janice Reid, *Sorcerers and Healing Spirits* (Sydney: Australian National University Press, 1983) 152.

[22] See Peter Buck, *The Coming of the Maori* (Wellington, New Zealand: Whitcombe and Tombs, 1958) 404–13.

involves attributing responsibility to some particular person . . . known to envy or have been offended by the victim."[23]

CASE STUDY ▮▮▮▮▮▮▮▮▮▮▮▮▮▮▮▮▮▮▮▮

Spirit Possession

In a contemporary Samoan village it was reported that a man had become deranged and was thought to be possessed by an *aitu* ("spirit"). A member of the man's family eventually admitted that he had not properly looked after his aunt when she was alive. The extended family met and concluded that her *aitu* was punishing them so they pushed a pipe into her grave and filled it with scalding hot water. The man was restored to good health.[24]

This case study helps to explain some illnesses of Samoan migrants in the United States. Ineke Lazar records that in Samoan society culture-bound disorders *(ma'i aitu)* included a severe form of hysterical psychosis, other neurotic symptoms, and certain physiological conditions. She notes that a common complaint in the Los Angeles Samoan community she researched is that, in the words of her informants, "Samoan illnesses do not show up on X-rays. So, the doctor does not know what to do." The people turn to traditional Samoan therapists specializing in *aitu* ("spirit") related illnesses, who use what they believe is spirit medicine. They must first find out where the spirit comes from and why it is troubling the living.[25]

[23] Joan Metge, *The Maoris of New Zealand* (London: Routledge & Kegan Paul, 1976) 92.

[24] See Richard A. Goodman, "Some *Aitu* Beliefs of Modern Samoans," *The Journal of the Polynesian Society* 80:4 (1971) 463–79.

[25] See Ineke M. Lazar, *"Ma'i Aitu:* Culture-Bound Illnesses in a Samoan Migrant Community," *Oceania* 55:3 (1985) 161–81. For analyses of witch doctors and health see Aylward Shorter, *Jesus and the Witchdoctor: An Approach to Healing and Wholeness* (London: Geoffrey Chapman, 1985); E. Fuller Torrey, *Witchdoctors and Psychiatrists: The Common Roots of Psychology and Its Future* (New York: Harper & Row, 1972); Philip Rack, *Race: Culture and Mental Disorders* (London: Routledge, 1991) 120–3; Susan Fernando, *Mental Health, Race and Culture* (London: Macmillan, 1991) 150, 166.

Traditional healing techniques in this type of culture serve four main functions. They are: *diagnostic,* to discover not only what the cause of the sickness is, but also *who* is causing it; *curative,* that is, they aim to heal the person and restore peace to the community; *preventive,* particular rituals to defend people from attacks of evil spirits or sorcerers; *causative,* that is, magical rites used to turn events in one's favor.[26]

Shamanism and Health

Tribal cultures, as is evident in the above case studies, have a variety of specialists (e.g., shamans, diviners) and methods to discern precisely which spirit or person is causing the evil, the reasons why, and the necessary remedies.

Shamanism is a term for an intricate mixture of religious and ethno-medical beliefs and practices found among cultures in Asia, Africa, and aboriginal America. It claims, as does witchcraft, the use of spiritual powers to counter the influence of enemies and cause or cure disease. While illness may have several causes, the most important is due to the loss of the soul through evil forces. The shaman's skill, exercised through a trance-like state, is to find the missing soul in some hidden section of the cosmic world and restore it to the sick person.[27]

Illness and Sickness in Gospel Times

The culture that Jesus belonged to was premodern, so the disciples accepted without question the causal link between illness and the breaking of a cultural norm. When they "saw a man who had been blind from birth" they asked Jesus: "Rabbi, who sinned, this man or his parents, that he should have been born blind?" Jesus refused to accept the causal link, replying: "Neither he nor his parents sinned" (John 9:1-3). People such as lepers and the blind were defined by the community as sick, dangerous to society, and marginalized. The sick would have felt desperately alone, their self-image gravely affected. Jesus refused to accept the culturally-assigned cause of illness, but concentrated on the physical and social healing of the sick by restoring them to community life.

[26] See Willem Berends, "African Traditional Healing Practices and the Christian Community," *Missiology: An International Review* 21:3 (1993) 275–88.

[27] See Mircea Eliade, *Shamanism: Archaic Techniques of Ecstasy* (Princeton, N.J.: Princeton University Press, 1964); Arthur Kleinman, *Patients and Healers in the Context of Culture: An Exploration of the Borderland between Anthropology, Medicine, and Psychiatry* (Berkeley: University of California Press, 1980) 203–58.

For centuries in the Western world illness was believed to be caused by God as a punishment because of people's immorality 'or their breaking of cultural taboos. Cholera, of epidemic proportions in the nineteenth century, was often thought to result from a life of sin. This belief still lurks in the background and can emerge quite suddenly depending on the nature of the disease. For example, in the early stages of the epidemic of HIV/AIDS (1982–85) a moral panic erupted, with public hysteria evident in society and the mass media that people had succumbed to the disease because God was punishing them for their immoral lifestyle.

In brief, premodern cultures have an appreciation of health that with its limitations is holistic. They distinguish between illness, which is an impairment of the body, and sickness, which is the breakdown of social relationships and the inner affliction that results from sickness. Sickness is not so much "a biomedical matter as it is a social one. It is attributed to social, not physical, causes. Thus sin and sickness go together. Illness is a matter of deviance from cultural norms and values"[28] affecting all aspects of the community. Healing involves not just the individual but also social or community relationships that have been fractured in consequence of a person's sickness.

Model 2: Modern Culture: The Medical Model

Summary

The dramatic development of scientific knowledge about causes of illnesses led to the increasing professionalization of medicine and the establishment of teaching hospitals and medical institutes committed to the study of the human body. This gave rise to what is called the "medical (or biomedical) model" of healthcare, which diverges from the previous model with the introduction of two factors: the *disease* and the *engineering* factors.

Disease is a biological abnormality in a particular part of the body: the emphasis is now less on symptoms provided by the patient, now seen as subjective, and more on signs that could theoretically be objectively calculated, often with the use of instruments, by the doctor.

The human body is likened to a machine that can be restored to health through correct scientific detection of disease and treatment. This is the engineering factor of the model. The structural, environmental, and cul-

---

[28] Bruce Malina and Richard L. Rohrbaugh, *Social Science Commentary on the Synoptic Gospels* (Minneapolis: Fortress Press, 1992) 210.

tural aspects of healthcare are downplayed because society's health is assumed to be mainly dependent on the quality of medical expertise and the availability of medical resources. Economic rationalism applied to healthcare management is a more recent effort by devotees of modernity to assess human behavior and health in terms of objective statistical criteria.

Explanation

Since about the sixteenth century, reinforced by the writings of the Enlightenment and the nineteenth century, the pivotal concept of modern culture became the *self,* not the group as in premodern culture.[29] The preeminent position of the person and the belief that human progress is inexorable found support in the emergence of classical physics. Matter was thought to be the foundation of all life and the material world was assumed to be an orderly machine consisting of elementary parts. These assumptions of classical physics were adopted by scientists and Western society in general, and they deeply affected the thinking of politicians, social commentators, economists, philosophers, and the developing medical profession.

Rene Descartes: Influence. Rene Descartes (1596–1650), French philosopher and scientist, profoundly influenced the evolution of this culture model in at least two ways.

First, with his axiom "I think, therefore I am," it was concluded that individuals must equate their identity with their rational mind. The idea of an integrated body, mind, and spirit lapsed. This encouraged people to overlook their bodies as avenues of knowing and, unlike the premodern culture model, to separate themselves from the natural environment.

Living organisms were thought to be machines built from parts; so also cultures. The latter could be divided up and sections destroyed without any guilt because of this mechanistic view. Such a view supported ruthless colonialism, extreme capitalism, and eventually even Social Darwinism. Social Darwinism assumed that societies evolve through natural conflicts between social groups. The best adapted and most successful social groups survive these conflicts, raising the evolutionary levels of society. Government intervention, in healthcare for example, wrongfully interferes with this dynamic.

[29] See Daniel Bell, *The Cultural Contradictions of Capitalism* (New York: Basic Books, 1976) 16; Richard Tarnas, *The Passion of the Western Mind* (New York: Ballantine, 1991) 224–47; Brian Morris, *Anthropology of the Self: The Individual in Cultural Perspective* (London: Pluto, 1994) 1–22, 118–98.

Second, given Descartes' stress on rationality, forms of knowledge that did not fit norms of precise thinking were not considered to be valuable. Hence, knowledge through symbols and myths is not considered valid. In other words, feelings do not provide any valid insight to reality. Patriarchy was a powerful force in the evolution and maintenance of this culture, since it was believed that only men could undertake logical, rational, or emotionless thinking.

Cult of Self-fulfillment. The emphasis on rationality affected people's views of God. To some, Isaac Newton's view of the cosmos as an orderly entity pointed to God's omnipotence and wisdom. As the cosmos was so neatly ordered, so also would society be if things were left to God; the deity would reconcile conflicting interests of individuals, just as the Creator keeps the planets at peace with one another. This viewpoint, however, eventually gave way to an assumption that the predictable behavior of the natural world showed there was no need for a God. Materialism and secularism thus became acceptable.

With the "death of God," sin lost its scriptural meaning: the breaking of one's relationship with God. The focus moved to self and the imperative of personal (or national) self-fulfillment in order to be healthy; sin became synonymous with the failure to get ahead in life through using one's own initiative and resources. It was a small step then to such racist actions as isolating or exterminating minority ethnic groups, the handicapped, or the elderly. Minority people were "sinful" or "weak" through their own fault and needed to be punished and destroyed (for example, aboriginal peoples in Australia, Jews in Nazi Germany) and their resources used in ways to foster an "orderly," "healthy" world.

Disease, Illness and Healing

Over the period of the modern culture two quite opposing views of disease, illness, and healing emerged: a holistic approach, with its roots in Scripture and Christian tradition, and what came to be called the "medical model," the latter becoming the dominant force with its roots in scientific rationalism described above.

Holistic Care. The Christian tradition has always seen suffering as mysterious. Ultimately, Christians seeking to answer the question "Why suffering?" seek meaning in faith. Jesus Christ died for our sins and our pain must be related to the redemptive suffering of Christ who freely submitted to suffering and death. Suffering has significance when related to Christ's mission (1 Pet 4:12-13). In this tradition, as in the premodern culture, the person who is physically sick also experiences inner affliction, for example the inner pain of loneliness resulting from the breakdown of one's predictable lifestyle and relationships.

Early Christians organized themselves to take care of suffering patients, inspired by the example of Christ (1 Cor 12:26-27), emphasizing the unity of soul and body. The early Christian hospice was open to poor members of the community and it developed by the fourth century into the hospital, where the sick poor were given assistance. Monastic orders continued the tradition for centuries, but in the nineteenth century more and more religious congregations were established with the primary task of caring for the poor sick, most often regardless of their church affiliation.[30] In his history of Catholic healthcare in United States, Christopher Kauffman emphasized the holistic concern of these congregations: "Catholic nurses and chaplains brought prayer, ritual, and symbol to those suffering on the limits of existence; in this sense both the sick and their care givers dwelt in an environment conducive to perceiving the ultimate horizon as a religious experience. . . . The religious meaning permeated Catholic health care. . . ."[31]

The Sisters of Charity were founded in the early nineteenth century by Mary Aikenhead. She, like many foundresses of healthcare facilities at this time, described the person-centered ministry that should characterize the work of her sisters:

> to attend to the comforts of the poor, both spiritual and temporal; to visit them in their dwellings and in hospitals, to attend them in sickness, to administer consolation in their afflictions, and to reconcile them to the dispensations of an all-wise Providence in the many trials to which they are subject.[32]

No division between soul and body in this instruction!

[30] See Joseph H. Fichter, *A Sociologist Looks at Religion* (Wilmington: Michael Glazier, 1988) 71–2; Turner, *Medical Power,* 157–61; Norman Vetter, *The Hospital: From Centre of Excellence to Community Support* (London: Chapman and Hall, 1995) 4–9; Timothy S. Miller, *The Birth of the Hospital in the Byzantine Empire* (Baltimore: Johns Hopkins, 1997) 118–66.

[31] Christopher J. Kauffman, *Ministry and Meaning: A Religious History of Catholic Health Care in the United States* (New York: Crossroad, 1995) 2–3.

[32] Quoted by Margaret M. K. O'Sullivan, *"A Cause of Trouble?" Irish Nuns and English Clerics* (Sydney: Crossing Press, 1995) 7.

CASE STUDY ███████████████████████████████████████

Evangelicalism Challenges Medical Dominance

As the medical profession developed in the nineteenth century it became increasingly difficult to maintain the emphasis on holistic care of patients. Leonard Sweet, in his history of Evangelicalism and healthcare in the United States, described the nineteenth century scene: "Some physicians looked askance at clergy stirring up 'religious excitements.' They especially condemned the 'disastrous effects' of sickroom shedding of tears for sins. Some physicians tried to keep clergy out of the sickroom for precisely this reason."[33] One clergyman insisting on the principle of equal access to the sickroom by both doctor and clergy wrote in 1884 that often the clergy's "visit will be as beneficial, sometimes more so. Indeed, we ought to be as ready to send for the minister to pray, as for the physician to prescribe. . . . Many owe their lives to answered prayer, offered in the sick room."[34]

The Medical Model: Explanation. Given the philosophical and scientific trends from the seventeenth century, the development of the science of medicine was understandably based on the dualism of body and mind. One's body was to be treated separately from one's mind (and social relationships). In fact, the mind was quite unimportant in medical diagnosis and treatment. As a logical consequence of Cartesian dualism, bodies, not persons, were cases to be studied. Thomas McKeown summarizes what emerged:

> Nature was conceived in mechanistic terms . . . a machine which might be taken apart and reassembled. . . . In medicine, the same concept lead further to the belief that an understanding of disease processes and of the body's response to them would make it possible to intervene therapeutically, mainly by physical (surgical), chemical, or electrical methods.[35]

[33] Leonard L. Sweet, *Health and Medicine in the Evangelical Tradition* (Valley Forge, Pa.: Trinity Press International, 1994) 144.

[34] James Erwin, as cited by Sweet, *Health and Medicine,* 143.

[35] Thomas McKeown, as cited by Robert Kane, *The Challenges of Community Medicine* (New York: Springer, 1974) 103.

During the Middle Ages and the Renaissance the institutional Church's assumption that the Church alone should have concern for the soul unwittingly and indirectly supported the view in the secular world that the body was but a machine. Spiritual matters were the sacred preserve of clerics, which further encouraged doctors to neglect the spiritual dimensions of illness. This, together with Descartes' philosophy of the mind-body dichotomy, contributed to the rise of medical notions of disease.

The following are the characteristics of what has become known since the nineteenth century as the "medical" or "biomedical model" of disease, diagnosis, and curing:

- A body is sick because it has a disease, that is, an abnormality caused by a particular noxious agent, such as a virus, parasite, or bacterium. This is known as the "germ theory" of disease or the "doctrine of specific aetiology."

- The patient needs to be passive, since medical science is concerned only with the body as a kind of machine and not with a person within a set of complex social relationships, as was the case in the premodern culture. It is no longer so important to ask patients their symptoms since the doctor's role is to discover through laboratory testing the germ causing the disease. Social and psychological factors are unimportant in disease diagnosis.

- Illness or inner affliction, as defined in model 1, is of no concern in the biomedical model.

- The restoration of health is to be achieved through medical technology and scientific processes.[36]

While the benefits of this biomedical model are not denied, enthusiasm for it has far exceeded its achievements. Though disease has been increasingly described in scientific terms, until very recent times doctors have been unable to control it by adhering to this model. David Locker summarizes the findings: "The main conclusion . . . is that patterns of health and disease are largely the product of social and environmental influences. Although health and illness may involve biological agents and

---

[36] See Nicholas Abercrombie and others, *The Penguin Dictionary of Sociology* (London: Penguin, 1988) 153; Sarah Nettleton, *The Sociology of Health and Illness* (Cambridge: Polity Press, 1995) 3.

processes, they are inseparable from the social settings in which people live."[37]

Historian Jonathan Miller contends that therefore "Medicine did not make an effective contribution to human welfare until the middle of the twentieth century"[38] through the introduction of antibiotics. Until the latter part of the nineteenth century doctors had few particular medicines other than quinine for malaria, digitalis for dropsy, and lime juice for scurvy. One medical historian believes that 1912 was possibly the first year when a visit to a doctor was likely to be helpful to the patient because of advances in medical knowledge.[39]

The reality is that technical responses to diagnosis and curing of disease has led to:

- excessive concentration on acute hospital services to the detriment of primary care facilities and reduced attention to the socioeconomic causes of disease. Resources have become focused on patients who are attractive from a technical point of view, while the handicapped, elderly, and mentally ill are often left to survive in inappropriate conditions.

- the development of a monopoly for doctors in determining the allocation of resources in healthcare services. In 1934 the American Medical Association declared its policy: "All features of medical service . . . should be under the control of the medical profession. No other body or individual is legally or educationally equipped to exercise such control."[40]

Though Descartes' body-mind dualism was the significant condition for the development of the biomedical model of diagnosis and treatment of sickness, it also laid the foundation for the creation of several contemporary schools of psychology, possibly the best known of which is psychoanalysis.

---

[37] David Locker, "Social Causes of Diseases," *Sociology as Applied to Medicine,* 4th ed., ed. Graham Scambler (London: W. B. Saunders, 1997) 30.

[38] Jonathan Miller, *The Body in Question* (New York: Random House, 1978) 9.

[39] See Sweet, *Health and Medicine,* 145.

[40] Cited by Edward Rayack, *Professional Power and American Medicine: The Economics of the American Medical Association* (New York: World Publishing, 1967) 164–5. See explanatory comments by David G. Green, *From Welfare State to Civil Society* (Wellington: New Zealand Business Roundtable, 1996) 148–51.

Economic Rationalism and Healthcare

Another powerful support of the modern culture model in healthcare services has emerged in recent times, namely the philosophy of "economic rationalism." This thinking insists on "small-government" and market-managed policies, for example privatization, deregulation, lower taxation, and reduced government spending.

Economic rationalism, along with its operational wing managerialism, assumes that healthcare is primarily an economic commodity and is subject to the principles of supply and demand of the market place. In its extreme form economic rationalism is a return to an excess of capitalism. Robert Alford[41] identifies a new group of people in healthcare who are committed to this philosophy; he terms them "corporate rationalizers." They are to be found among hospital administrators, hospital insurance executives, corporate executives and bankers, medical school directors, and city and state public health administrators. Thus:

- The dramatic rise of for-profit hospitals in the United States in recent years is an example of economic rationalism: the *primary* aim of healthcare management is a financial return to shareholders, not the quality of service to patients.
- In the 1990s the planners of healthcare reform in many countries, such as Australia[42] and New Zealand,[43] are more commonly now economists or accountants, not people with a background in healthcare delivery.

Model 3: Postmodern Culture: Questioning Modernity

Summary

The postmodernist view is that the "human mind now appears to be anything but a neat thinking machine that—when properly operated—

---

[41] See Robert Alford, "The Political Economy of Health Care: Dynamics without Change," *Readings in Medical Sociology,* ed. David Mecanic (New York: Free Press, 1980) 459–60.

[42] Michael Pusey, *Economic Rationalism in Canberra: A Nation Building State Changes Its Mind* (Cambridge: Cambridge University Press, 1992) 59–75.

[43] See Jane Kelsey, *The New Zealand Experiment: A World Model for Structural Adjustment?* (Auckland: Auckland University Press, 1995) 215; Robert H. Blank, *New Zealand Health Policy: A Comparative Study* (Auckland: Oxford University Press, 1994) 134.

poses right questions and prints out right answers."[44] In recent decades the biomedical model of sickness and curing with its controlling domination by the medical profession has been severely criticized. Health is now becoming as much a socially defined idea as a physical one. Sickness is not an individual, haphazard event, but something affected by levels of power and wealth. The answer to curing sickness is to be found primarily in changing the structures and attitudes of society so people can liberate themselves from social and economic poverty. Individual efforts alone cannot break unjust socioeconomic systems.

Explanation

The term "postmodernism" emerged in the 1930s, but its meaning remains unclear and at the same time highly controversial.[45] However, it is possible to identify a model of culture which could be called postmodern, based on events that emerged in the 1950s and 1960s. This model rejects the assumptions that reality is ordered in a way that can be laid bare by the human mind and that it is possible to build a universal human culture upon a foundation of rational thought. Nor is it assumed any longer that human progress is inevitable. The genocides of World War II and the explosions of the atomic bombs over Japan put that belief to rest.

Postmodernism connotes an extensive cultural malaise notable for its cynicism, deconstructionism, pragmatism, narcissism, skepticism, relativism, and nihilism. Critical realist assertions such as truth and ethics are considered to be without foundation and instead there is a relativistic construction of the world through language and narrative. That is, the major theme of postmodern culture is the decline of "*meta*narratives," such as foundational theories legitimating a universal morality and social progress. There is a massive breakdown of certainty, writes Jean-Francois Lyotard, "a loss of a central organizing principle governing society and a unitary standard of cultural excellence or morality, and a decline in the belief of a unitary, coherent self."[46]

---

[44] Walter T. Anderson, "Epilogue," *The Truth About the Truth: De-Confusing and Re-Constructing the Postmodern World,* ed. Walter T. Anderson (New York: Putnam, 1955) 240.

[45] See Paul A. Komesaroff, "Introduction," *Troubled Bodies: Critical Perspectives on Postmodernism, Medical Ethics, and the Body,* ed. Paul A. Komesaroff (Melbourne: Melbourne University Press, 1955) 9.

[46] Jean-Francois Lyotard, "The Postmodern Condition," *The Postmodern Turn: New Perspectives on Social Theory,* ed. Steven Seidman (Cambridge: Cambridge University Press, 1994) 27–38.

Several factors have influenced this rejection of modernity and consequent cultural chaos. For example:

- As physicists reflected on the random behavior of atomic and subatomic phenomena it became clear to them that the emphasis of classical physics on an orderly world could no longer be accepted.

- There was also a growing disillusionment among many people, especially in the 1960s, with the belief that more and more technological achievements must mean progress. There broke out in the Western world what can be called the Revolution of Expressive Disorder. It was a middle-class revolt against all certainties and boundaries— political, moral, sexual, educational, artistic, medical, and social. It was an intense effort to enshrine the rights of the individual as a feeling, free person rejecting all impersonal bureaucracy, political and medical manipulation.

Sociologist Bernice Martin notes that the most common feature of this revolution was the symbolism of "anti-structure," "anti-order."[47] Little wonder, therefore, that the postmodern culture model assumes that it is impossible to achieve consensus on any values, such as the sanctity of human life. Any consensus smacks of order, a taboo word in postmodernism.[48]

Disease, Illness, and Healing

Postmodernism has had a profound impact on healthcare. It has generated criticisms of the medical model and it has also contributed to human problems that cannot be resolved through this model.

Critiques of the Medical Model. Significant writers, research reports, and political movements, in a questioning postmodern style, have critiqued the biomedical model of disease/curing, demonstrating that it is impossible to define disease, illness, and healing without constant reference to cultural factors. Here are some examples:

Talcott Parsons: Affirmation of the Total Human Individual. In the 1950s sociologist Parsons critiqued the biomedical model to the extent

---

[47] See Bernice Martin, *A Sociology of Contemporary Cultural Change* (Oxford: Basil Blackwell, 1981) 53–246.

[48] See Steven Connor, *Postmodernist Culture: An Introduction to Theories of the Contemporary* (Oxford: Basil Blackwell, 1989) 8.

that he reaffirmed the pivotal importance of the "total human individual."[49] He believed that injury and sickness among individuals should be assessed not only in biological and economic ways, but also according to their psychological and social aspects.

But Parsons at the same time reinforced the medical profession's monopoly in defining the nature of sicknesses and their cures. Others challenge him on this. Parsons viewed the sick role as a kind of deviance or social abnormality and the doctor as legitimating the sick role and freeing the patient from normal social duties (e.g., exemption from work). In the Parsonian model the dangerous assumption is that the doctor is selfless and objective and that patients should be passive, compliant, and grateful to the doctor, who has the superior knowledge.

There are other criticisms of the Parsonian position.[50] Sometimes the sick role may be assigned to people when in fact it should not be. For example, a worker under stress cannot have the problem "solved" by medicine when a radical change in working conditions is needed. Others also disagree with the model because it gives to the medical profession power to apply diagnostic labels to people that have serious moral, social, and individual consequences. This can occur, claims Graham Scambler, "most consciously when the conditions being diagnosed are personally or socially stigmatizing. Stigmatizing conditions can be defined as conditions that set their possessors apart from 'normal' people, that mark them as socially unacceptable or inferior beings."[51] For example, in the past, people who were hearing impaired or mentally ill were often declared deviant and tragically marginalized. In the 1980s AIDS/HIV patients suffered the same victimization.

Michel Foucault: Critique of the Medical Profession. Foucault challenges the assumption that knowledge leads to liberation; on the contrary, knowledge is most often a way to gain new control over people. In recent times his sociology[52] has been used to critique the medical model and its definitions of disease and healthcare.

---

[49] Talcott Parsons, *The Social System* (London: Routledge & Kegan Paul, 1970) 431.

[50] See Margaret Stacey, *The Sociology of Health and Healing* (London: Routledge, 1988) 160–76; Sharyn L. R. Anleu, "Medicalisation of Deviance," *Second Opinion,* ed. Germov, 96–120.

[51] Graham Scambler, "Deviance, Sick Role and Stigma," *Sociology as Applied to Medicine,* ed. Scambler, 49.

[52] See, for example, Michel Foucault, *Madness and Civilization: The History of Insanity in the Age of Reason* (New York: Random House, 1965); Michel Foucault, *The*

Foucault, aiming to trace the historical development of medical interest in the human body, claims that the "body is the ultimate site of political and ideological control . . . and regulation,"[53] and that modern medicine has developed considerable political power in society through a process of "clinical gaze" or surveillance of the human body, labeling it as "deviant or normal, as hygienic or unhygienic, as controlled or needful of control."[54] Foucault writes: "[Medicine] set itself up as the supreme authority in matters of hygienic necessity. . . . (It) claimed to ensure the physical vigour and the moral cleanliness of the social body; it promised to eliminate defective individuals, degenerate and bastardized populations."[55]

Evan Willis: Critiques of the Medical Monopoly. Willis writes of Australia but his comments are applicable throughout the Western world. Medical dominance in Australia was obtained, he claims, in two historical phases. Practitioners of orthodox medicine first united to protect themselves from other health workers and formed themselves into an exclusive elite group. From this position they have been able to monopolize the medical developments ever since. The second period began late last century when, primarily through their political power, medical practitioners were able to develop an image of illness and curing most helpful to themselves and to persuade governments to exclude various therapies (e.g., chiropractic) from legitimate practice, and "to limit others such as optometry and dentistry to certain parts of the body, and to subordinate the work of nurses, midwives and other allied health-care workers to the power and authority of medicine."[56] Nurses, despite their upgrading of skills through

---

Birth of the Clinic: An Archaeology of Medical Perception (New York: Vintage Books, 1975); Michel Foucault, *An Introduction,* vol. 1, *The History of Sexuality* (London: Penguin, 1979). For a critique of Foucault's contributions see Alan Peterson and Robin Burton, eds., *Foucault: Health and Medicine* (London: Routledge, 1997); and Nicholas J. Fox, *Postmodernism, Sociology and Health* (Buckingham: Open University, 1993) 27–37.

[53] Deborah Lupton, *Medicine as Culture: Illness, Disease and the Body in Western Societies* (London: Sage Publications, 1994) 23.

[54] Ibid.

[55] Foucault, *An Introduction,* vol. 1, *The History of Sexuality,* 23.

[56] See Julianne Cheek and others, *Society and Health: Social Theory for Health Workers* (Melbourne: Longman, 1996) 152. See also Evan Willis, *Medical Dominance: The Division of Labour in Australian Health Care,* 2d ed. (Sydney: Allen and Unwin, 1989). In 1990 the New Zealand government restored the right of midwives to sole charge in birth situations and gave them the right to prescribe drugs. See Elaine Papps and Mark Olssen, *Doctoring Childbirth and Regulating Midwifery in New Zealand: A Foucauldian Perspective* (Palmerston North, New Zealand: Dunmore, 1997).

university training, are still subordinate to the medical profession.[57] Nurses must keep to their traditional role of caring, not curing.

Ivan Illich: Critique of the Medicalization of Society. Ivan Illich's radical and basic thesis is that development is enslavement to need, not liberation from scarcity. Applied to healthcare services, this means that the medical profession exists to serve its own needs for social status and financial reward, not the needs of patients. He begins his book: "The medical profession has become a major threat to health. The disabling impact of professional control over medicine has reached the proportions of an epidemic."[58]

This epidemic is called "iatrogenesis," that is, the fostering of a professional mystique that hides the fact that doctors are partly the cause of a large amount of the sickness which they claim to cure. There is "clinical iatrogenesis," which is false diagnosis resulting in sickness, even death; "social iatrogenesis," that is, doctors' control over our bodies is so great that it helps to make our own bodies foreign to us (for example, the natural act of childbirth has become a medical process). Then there is "cultural iatrogenesis," which means that doctors have made the natural experiences of pain and death forbidden topics for others. By encouraging us to deny these experiences doctors hinder us from fully and naturally living: "The medicalization of society has brought the epoch of natural death to an end. Western man has lost the right to preside at his act of dying. Health, or the autonomous power to cope, has been expropriated down to the last breath."[59]

Paulo Freire: Critique of Healthcare Education. Freire sees education systems as major vehicles for perpetuating unjust structures in society. Education suffers from "narration sickness," where all the power resides with teachers, and students must meekly become receptacles to be filled with information to be mechanically memorized. Critical reflection is discouraged. Through a process of "conscientization," however, people become aware of this oppressive process and claim their authority to question information imposed on them and the world around them.[60]

---

[57] See Evan Willis, *Illness and Social Relations: Issues in the Sociology of Health Care* (St. Leonards, N.S.W.: Allen and Unwin, 1994) 17–18; Margaret Sargent and others, *The New Sociology for Australians* (Melbourne: Longman, 1997) 140–2.

[58] Ivan Illich, *Limits to Medicine: Medical Nemesis—The Expropriations of Health* (London: Penguin, 1990) 11.

[59] Ibid., 210.

[60] See Paulo Freire, *Pedagogy of the Oppressed* (London: Penguin, 1973) 45, 47.

To encourage the learner as subject, Freire suggests a structured dialogue method in which all participate as co-learners to create a collectively
understood reality. His educational method, when applied to health education, empowers patients to question the medical model, with its neglect of
the socioeconomic and cultural causes of disease, and to challenge medical professionals when they insist that patients are to be passive receivers
of information in their presence.[61]

Feminist Critique: Male Dominance Critiqued. Research shows that the
medical profession has tried to "medicalize" the experiences of women
and consequently take power from them, for example in childbirth and
mental illness. Medical practitioners have long advised and controlled
women as to when and how they are to give birth. The mother has relatively little control over the process as it has been transformed from a natural event into a medical event.[62] Women are more likely to be categorized
as suffering from clinical depression than men, but rarely are the oppressive cultural causes identified. Describing the British situation, a review
states that women as patients "suffer rather than benefit from views which
presume their physical and/or psychological weakness. . . . The sexual
stereotypes of women as potentially sick . . . and emotionally unstable
have militated against a rational approach to women's illnesses."[63]

Feminist studies also critique the patriarchal power in the medical profession, a characteristic of the modern culture model. In Britain, for example, women still suffer from inequality of job opportunity, low status
positions, and poor pay within the healthcare service.[64] In Australia women
as specialists are confined to certain areas considered to be "women's
work," areas of medicine of relatively low status, such as gynecology, pe-
diatrics, or plastic surgery.[65] It has also been found that women are shoul-
dering the burden of patients discharged from hospitals before they are

[61] See John J. Macdonald, *Primary Health Care: Medicine in Its Place* (London:
Earthscan, 1992) 158–61; Nina Wallerstein and others, "Freirian Praxis in Health
Education and Community Organizing," *Community Organizing and Community for
Health,* ed. Meredith Minkler (New Brunswick, N.J.: Rutgers University Press, 1997)
195–211.

[62] See Papps and Olssen, *Doctoring Childbirth,* 55–81.

[63] Sheila Hillier and Graham Scambler, "Women as Patients and Providers," *Sociology as Applied to Medicine,* ed. Scambler, 133, 126.

[64] See ibid., 131–3.

[65] See Sargent and others, *The New Sociology,* 141–2.

sufficiently recovered.[66] The pattern can be expected to be the same elsewhere in Western societies.

Research Reports: Critique of the Medical Model. Research studies prove beyond doubt the inadequacy of the biomedical model of disease and healing. The assumption that biomedical skills have caused dramatic changes in disease patterns has been shown to be inaccurate. The evidence is that very little decrease in mortality rates in the Western world by the 1940s can be assigned to improvements in medical care; rather, the decrease can be attributed to cultural factors (political, environmental, socioeconomic forces) influencing the improvement in food and hygiene.[67]

Though sickness may well involve biological agents, it is inseparable from the cultural environment. For example, in Britain there is a direct relationship between the possibility of dying at any age and social class; the lower people are in the class hierarchy the greater the chance of early death. Lower socioeconomic groups have poorer diet, suffer more overcrowding and stress, and are less likely to seek medical aid than members of middle and upper classes.[68]

CASE STUDY

Health of Indigenous Peoples

The importance of stressing cultural influences in patterns of sickness and health is especially obvious when we review the life expectancy rates for indigenous and non-indigenous populations in several Western countries in the 1980s. In Australia, life expectancy of indigenous people is 54.0 years, non-indigenous, 72.8 years; in the United States, 67.1 and 70.1; in Canada,

---

[66] See Marilys Guillemin, *A Woman's Work Is Never Done: The Impact of Shifting Care Out of Hospitals* (Melbourne: Health Issues Centre, 1977) 5–8.

[67] See Ray M. Fitzpatrick, "Society and Changing Patterns of Disease," *Sociology as Applied to Medicine,* ed. Scambler, 3–17.

[68] For example, see Douglas Black and others, *Inequalities in Health: The Black Report and the Health Divide* (London: Penguin, 1992) 104–26, 227–63; Richard G. Wilkinson, *Unhealthy Societies: The Afflictions of Inequality* (London: Routledge, 1996) 55–109; Jim Chandler, "The United States," *Health Care Systems in Liberal Democracies,* ed. Ann Wall (London: Routledge, 1996) 163–6; David Blane, "Inequality and Social Class," *Sociology as Applied to Medicine,* ed. Scambler, 104–20.

64.0 and 72.4; in New Zealand, 65.2 and 70.8. Indigenous peoples have been subjected at times to horrendous oppression by the non-indigenous population with the inevitable impact on morale, diet, and access to medical services. Unless oppressive structures are addressed we cannot expect an improvement in life expectancy for indigenous peoples.[69]

Health Problems of Postmodernism. The medical model is increasingly unable to respond to the human problems of postmodernism. Postmodernist philosophy leads to a radical breakdown of personal and social meaning, a "deep malaise of futurelessness,"[70] a dramatic rise in destructive narcissism that no amount of medication can resolve. Psychoanalyst Neville Symington comments that the "therapists are fighting an uphill battle against narcissism. . . . The stresses of a fast-changing society cause psychological problems to become more common and narcissism is one of them."[71] The philosophy of postmodernism contributes to the problem.

According to the postmodernist mind, the self is no longer the coherent self of the modernists, but instead the creative story-teller; one has as many potential selves as one is able to tell innovative stories. The idea of self as "continuously revised biographical narratives"[72] is an attempt to achieve meaning in a world where it is assumed that reality cannot be known to any degree. There is a constant search for personal identity, but one is always aware that even when it is achieved to some degree, it ultimately remains a fiction because there is no way to prove its objective truth. Mary Jo Leddy says that in postmodernism meaning is something that happens from time to time,[73] that is, a particular incident in life offers a fleeting insight into one's identity. One may keep retelling what happened in an effort to reassure oneself that life does have meaning. Life

[69] See Jake M. Najman, "Health and the Australian Population," *A Sociology of Australian Society*, ed. Najman and Western, 322–4.

[70] Jerome Bruner, as cited in Unni Wikan, "The Nun's Story: Reflections on an Age-old, Postmodern Dilemma," *American Anthropologist* 98:2 (1996) 280.

[71] Neville Symington, as cited in *The Australian Magazine* (October 25, 1997) 14; and *Narcissism* (London: Karnak Books, 1993).

[72] Anthony Giddens, *Modernity and Self-Identity* (New York: Polity Press, 1991) 5.

[73] See Mary J. Leddy, "Formation in a Post-Modern Context," *The Way Supplement* 65 (1989) 10–12.

becomes a series of often disparate, unsatisfying meaning-giving episodes which lack an underlying, uniting, and objectively knowable foundation giving meaning to everything that happens.

So there is ongoing, even manic, search for new experiences in the hope that ultimately some persuasive meaning will emerge, but there is the feeling at the same time that this is impossible. Inevitably the ongoing search by individuals for sustained meaning in life in the midst of a rapid change produces many very fragile, insecure, highly narcissistic and depressed people for whom antidepressants offer no solution. Little wonder that the suicide rate rises dramatically.

CASE STUDY

Postmodernism and Suicides

New Zealand is a country that is affluent and culturally committed to postmodernism. Between 1991 and 1993, 40 out of every 100,000 young males committed suicide. This rate was close to twice that of the United States, Canada, Ireland, and Austria; more than three times that of Britain. One reason commonly given is that young people become psychologically exhausted with the constant and impossible pressure to achieve a satisfying meaning in life.[74]

Theologian Fr. Richard McCormick, S.J., argues that the contemporary rise in support for physician-assisted suicide is in part a consequence of absolutizing individual autonomy, a postmodern phenomenon, leading to an intolerance of dependence on others: "Given the canonization of independence in our consciousness, 'death with dignity' means to die in my way, at my time, by my hand."[75]

[74] See Mike Moore, *Children of the Poor: How Poverty Could Destroy New Zealand's Future* (Christchurch: Canterbury University Press, 1996) 53–4; Philip Shenon, "Macho New Zealand Leads World in Teen Suicides," *The Denver Post* (July 28, 1995) 22A; Wilhelmina Drummond, *Suicide in New Zealand: Adolescents at Risk* (Palmerston North, New Zealand: Nagare Press, 1996).
[75] Richard McCormick, "The Consistent Ethic of Life under Challenge: Can Catholic Health Care Offer Leadership?" *Theology Digest* 42:4 (1995) 325.

The significant rise in the interest in astrology and magic in affluent countries is linked to the malaise of postmodern culture. Astrology places the meaning of life into a large universal overview; personal meaning and universal meaning could now fit neatly into one system of thought. Molly O'Neill comments on magic in *The New York Times:* "Americans are increasingly enchanted with products and notions that promise a simple route to transformation, salvation or cure. More and more marketers are imbuing foods and forms of exercise, cosmetics and folk cures with magical powers to fight aging and disease."[76]

Model 4: Paramodern Culture: Holistic Health

Summary

This is a culture model that is very slowly and hesitantly emerging, in which "we glimpse new ways of thinking about ourselves, new possibilities for coexisting with others—even profoundly different others."[77] In this model people move away from the medical model toward developing a holistic approach to healthcare both at the personal and community levels. With the rising level of sickness now clearly the product of humankind's own actions, and with the necessity to place a ceiling on the financial costs of medical services, more people are accepting the holistic model, the antithesis of the dualism of Descartes.

Explanation

This model reflects evolving trends in a wide range of scientific, philosophical, and social thinking that critique, on the one hand, the excessive optimism in modern culture about human progress and, on the other hand, the in-built pessimism of postmodernism. The questioning of postmodernists can easily evoke a sense of hopelessness. If human perfectibility is impossible, why bother to struggle for excellence? If the cultural causes of sickness are so complex, why should we waste energy when little positive results can be expected?

---

[76] Molly O'Neill, "As Life Gets More Complex, Magic Casts a Wider Spell," *The New York Times* (June 13, 1994) 1B. Fads endowed with magical properties flourish historically in times of social chaos. See Arbuckle, *Refounding the Church,* 84–6.

[77] Walter T. Anderson, *The Truth about Truth: De-confusing and Re-constructing the Postmodern World* (New York: Putnam, 1995) 11.

Among the factors that have influenced the as yet tentative development of this culture type are people such as Teilhard de Chardin,[78] philosopher Jacques Derrida, the new physics, a yearning for a spirituality, feminism, the growing concern to protect the environment, the dissatisfaction with the impersonality of the biomedical model of healing, the desire for holistic health, and the rising demand among minority peoples for multiculturalism.

For example, Derrida's deconstructionism seeks to uncover oppressive ways of thinking and encourages people to restructure their way of life and that of society. Deconstructionism in management studies,[79] for example, exposes the way patriarchal values dominate organizational life and make it very difficult, often impossible, for women to assume leadership. Once these values are identified, then action can be taken to allow women to enter organizations to counter masculine dominance. The more space that can be given to "feminine virtues" of mutual responsibility, compassion, gentleness, and love, the more collaborative or healthy a society will emerge.

A second example is that scientists during this century have become increasingly aware that the classical physics of the modern culture model no longer has categories for what they are finding. Instead of the machine-like universe of modern culture, they are discovering a world that is a harmonious indivisible whole, a pattern of dynamic relationships that include the human observer in an essential way. All organisms, from the smallest bacteria to humans, are integrated wholes and living systems, interdependent and interrelated (see Chapter 4). The greater whole is the biosphere itself, a dynamic and highly integrated web of living and nonliving forms. Recognition of these realities has helped foster the concern of people to protect the environment.

Disease, Illness, and Health

In the paramodern model of health there is a clear shift away from the modernistic optimism that scientific medicine has all the answers. People distrust the belief that doctors have superior knowledge of the causes of disease and they demand a more active role as patients in decisions relat-

---

[78] See comments by Fritjof Capra, *The Turning Point: Science, Society and the Rising Culture* (London: Flamingo, 1983) 331–2.

[79] For example see William Bergquist, *The Postmodern Organization: Mastering the Art of Irreversible Change* (San Francisco: Jossey-Bass, 1993); and John Hassard and Martin Parker, eds., *Postmodernism and Organizations* (London: Sage Publications, 1993).

ing to their health. The increase in medical malpractice lawsuits and the consequent call by the mass media for more public accountability from the medical profession have fostered growing distrust of scientific medicine. People who favor paramodernism call for an end to the "passive patient" and "deference to experts in society at large . . . [and] a greater sense of personal responsibility for health promoted by health education [to supplant] obedience to doctor's orders."[80]

In brief, paramodernism emphasizes holistic health, which has the following qualities:

- "The unity of the psyche and soma and the need to get beyond the presenting of symptoms to explore the history and circumstances of the patient's life."[81]

- The recognition that the causes of disease are far more complex than germs: cultural factors are of critical importance.

- Prevention—through changes in individual and community behavior patterns—is more important in reducing disease in the long term than the biomedical approach.

- Radical political and socioeconomic policies are required to reduce unemployment and levels of poverty,[82] a position that is particularly distasteful to economic rationalists.

- There is a growing acceptance in society (though with little support from the medical profession) of "alternative healing" practices;[83] for example, meditational systems, reflexology, acupuncture, Native American and other indigenous peoples' healing methods.

- The focus is primarily on care within the community, not the hospital.

- The patriarchal hold over healthcare services is being increasingly questioned.

- In reaction to the dehumanizing influences of postmodernism, political and social campaigns that respect the dignity of life are

[80] Mary A. Elston, "The Politics of Professional Power: Medicine in a Changing Health Service," *The Sociology of the Health Service,* ed. Jonathan Gabe and others (London: Routledge, 1991) 77.

[81] Nettleton, *The Sociology of Health,* 230.

[82] See Basiro Davey and Jennie Popay, *Dilemmas in Health Care* (Milton Keynes: Open University Press, 1993) 184–99.

[83] See Nettleton, *The Sociology of Health,* 212.

developing, often across traditional denominational boundaries; for example, anti-euthanasia and anti-abortion campaigns, the hospice movement.

• There is a growing yearning among people, who despair of the narrowness of the medical model of healing and the poverty of postmodernism, for a holistic personal and community experience of the healing Jesus, but they reject the deadening rigidity and impersonality of much that they perceive in institutional Christianity.[84]

The switch to paramodernism is evident in publications of the World Health Organization (WHO). In 1948 WHO, in its definition of health, recognized the basic distinction between health and disease when it stated that health is "a complete state of physical, mental and social well-being and not merely the absence of disease and infirmity." Disease pertains to the world of biology and pathology, but health to the realm of the fully human, including feelings, behaviors, and quality of life. The disciplines of theology, spirituality, political theory/praxis, sociology, and psychology are as essential as biomedical science for good health. WHO's definition of health in 1984 further developed the paramodern notion of health: health is "a resource for everyday life, not the object of living; it is a positive concept emphasising social and personal resources, as well as physical capacities."[85] In this sense, individuals are unhealthy when they have no employment, poor community relationships, no meaning in their lives.

Summary

Culture is not primarily an entity but a process that is actively or persuasively at work, particularly in the unconscious of the group and individuals. It is a pattern of shared meanings and values expressed in symbols, myths, and rituals. Its fundamental function is to provide a *felt* meaning or a sense of order. Every culture has a built-in resistance to change because people fear a breakdown of predictability.

People's understanding of health, illness, sickness, and disease is intimately linked to their culture. In the premodern culture health is understood in holistic terms. It is primarily about maintaining good relationships, par-

[84] Meredith B. McGuire, *Ritual Healing in Suburban America* (New Brunswick, N.J.: Rutgers University Press, 1988) 3.

[85] WHO's definition as cited by David Locker, "Prevention and Health Promotion," *Sociology as Applied to Medicine,* ed. Scambler, 244.

ticularly with members of one's extended family—living and dead. Illness (and even death) is caused by the breakdown of these relationships.

Modernity means that all human problems can be converted into technical problems, and if the techniques to solve problems do not as yet exist, then they will have to be invented.[86] Economic rationalism is a contemporary return to the competitiveness and rationality of the modern culture. It judges the worth of any delivery of healthcare in monetary terms.

The medical model, which is characteristic of the modern culture (and particularly popular in Western societies), focuses on the human body and emphasizes two aspects: "disease" and "engineering." The body is like a machine and disease is a breakdown of this machine; the doctor's role is to engineer it back to good shape again through medical technology grounded in exact scientific laboratory procedures. The spiritual, structural, environmental, and cultural (or relational) causes of illness are considered to be of little or no importance.

Postmodernism and paramodernism question the dominance of the medical model. The paramodern culture with its new physics and systems view of living organisms is a return to holistic thinking of the premodern culture, to the insights of "mystics and of many traditional cultures, in which knowledge of the human mind and body and the practice of healing are integral parts of natural philosophy and of spiritual discipline."[87]

Christian healthcare is about holistic health. Healing is not to be understood in purely physical terms, but it is a process involving body, mind, spirit, emotions, and relationships with God, people, and the environment.

[86] See Berger, *Pyramids of Sacrifice*, 36.
[87] Capra, *The Turning Point*, 333.

Chapter 2

Healthcare Services and Policies in Chaos

Unless there is radical change within ten years, there is a good chance that our health care system [in the United States] will collapse of its own weight. . . . Currently, most countries are in turmoil about health policy.[1]

—Victor R. Fuchs

Most people in Britain think that the National Health Service is on its knees.[2]

—*The Economist*

More . . . agree . . . that the [healthcare] system [in Australia] is a ticking time bomb.[3]

—*Australian Health and Aged Care Journal*

This chapter explains:

- the nature and causes of contemporary chaos in healthcare services and policies;

- the principles that should guide healthcare reform;

- the meaning and complexity of rationing in healthcare;

[1] Victor R. Fuchs, *The Future of Health Policy* (Cambridge, Mass.: Harvard University Press, 1993) 11.

[2] "How to Pay for the NHS," *The Economist* (March 15, 1997) 16.

[3] *Australian Health & Aged Care Journal* 8:3 (1996) 19.

- examples and evaluation of healthcare reform;
- the strengths and weaknesses of managed care, particularly Health Management Organizations (HMOs);
- the impact of economic rationalism on healthcare policies;
- the urgent need for Christian healthcare reformers to have the appropriate professional knowledge and communication skills.

Healthcare is in chaos, the most obvious sign being the ever-increasing demand for more and more funds. Today in the United States 13.6 percent of the gross domestic product is spent on healthcare services; 10.3 percent in Canada; 7.1 percent in Britain; 9.4 percent in France;[4] and 8 percent in Australia. In the United States and elsewhere, efforts have been made to control costs by making healthcare facilities more efficient and urging medical staffs to be more cost-conscious, but costs have still continued to rise. However fast spending grows, demand for treatment seems to increase faster.[5] Little wonder that healthcare is in turmoil.

Since no economy can continue to allow unrestrained increases to their healthcare budget, the question grows daily more urgent: How can healthcare expenses be controlled in ways that are just and politically acceptable? This question has generated considerable conflict; for example, about the values of private and universal insurance coverage, about constraining the power of the medical professions, about controlling the rising costs of medicine, and about quality and efficiency of services.

If Christian thinkers are to contribute in a refounding way to this debate and influence healthcare policies at the political level, and themselves develop appropriate practical responses, they must thoroughly understand the issues involved. Thus this chapter focuses on the causes of the chaos in healthcare, the principles that should guide the development of healthcare policies, and an overview of the ways in which various governments are trying to control costs.

Healthcare Services: Costs and Frustration

The following are significant factors contributing to the rising costs of, and general exasperation over, healthcare services.

---

[4] See Ray M. Fitzpatrick, "Organizing and Funding Health Care," *Sociology as Applied to Medicine,* ed. Graham Scambler (London: W. B. Saunders, 1997) 275.

[5] "Curing the NHS's Ills," *The Economist* (October 18, 1997) 55.

Aging Populations

In Western countries populations are significantly aging, inevitably increasing demands on healthcare services. There is a dramatic drop in recent years in the birthrate, while at the same time people are living longer. Hence, as Professor Robert Blank writes, it is estimated that within a few years Western countries will "on average be faced with total health expenditures some thirty percent higher [than today] and per capita expenditures some twenty percent higher than current figures, solely as a result of population aging."[6]

In Britain almost half the total healthcare budget is spent on people aged sixty-five or over, though they account for only 16 percent of the population. It is estimated that by the middle of the next century the numbers of people aged sixty-five and over will have almost doubled.[7] The average person between the ages of sixteen and forty-four costs Britain's National Health Service about four hundred pounds per year; however, people aged eighty-five or over cost three thousand pounds per year.[8]

In the United States thirty-six million people who are now served by Medicare are already straining the allotted finances; early in the next century seventy-six million will be requesting Medicare benefits. Current expenditures are exceeding revenues at such a speed that by the year 2000 Medicare's resources will be $53 billion in arrears.[9]

Rising Costs of Medical Technology

Henry Aaron argues that "medical technologies that did not exist two or three decades ago account for the bulk of medical expenditures and explain most of the rise in health care spending."[10] High-tech medical facilities and services are increasingly costly. The three main categories of high costs are diagnostic (e.g., entire body scanners [CAT scans]), surgery, and

[6] Robert H. Blank, *New Zealand and Health Policy: A Comparative Study* (Auckland: Oxford University Press, 1994) 30.

[7] See "Safe in Whose Hands?" *The Economist* (October 26, 1996) 67.

[8] See "Curing the NHS's Ills," 55.

[9] See editorial "Time for Nation to Face Medicare Reality," *South Bend Tribune* (June 12, 1996) 10A; John R. Wolfe, *The Coming Health Crisis: Who Will Pay for Care for the Aged in the Twenty-first Century* (Chicago: University of Chicago Press, 1993).

[10] Henry J. Aaron, *Serious and Unstable Condition: Financing America's Health Care* (Washington: The Brookings Institution, 1991) 26. See also Blank, *New Zealand and Health Policy,* 34–41.

prescriptions. Just one example of the dramatic rise in expensive "super drug" prescriptions aptly illustrates the point. Interferon beta, a recently-marketed drug for multiple sclerosis, costs approximately ten thousand pounds (about $16,000 U.S.) per year per patient. It is estimated that if everyone who would benefit actually received the drug, it would increase Britain's national drug account by 10 percent.[11]

Impact of Violence and Drugs

In the United States there has been a fivefold rise in medical emergencies over recent years, many the result of violence and drugs. This places severe financial strains on hospitals "because trauma patients consume vast amounts of resources."[12]

Rising Expectations and Demands for Services

The more knowledge that is gained about diseases and their origins, the more demand is generated for professional healthcare services. In some circles there is an expectation that extraordinary means must be used to prolong life, at enormous monetary costs, even if only successful for very short time periods. Politicians are wary about thwarting people's unrealistic expectations because this could cost them their jobs.

Ultimately, at the heart of these expectations, there is a fantasy that death can be avoided. The medical profession has encouraged these expectations, despite the fact that people's trust in medical intervention as the answer to every sickness is misplaced. As was mentioned in the previous chapter, the drop in death rates over the last hundred years has been the result primarily of improvements in nutrition and sanitation, rather than by formal medical actions.[13]

Waiting lists for hospital services in countries such as New Zealand, Australia, and the United Kingdom continue to rise, often at an alarming rate. In Britain over a million people are awaiting operations; the number of people waiting for more than a year has also started to rise. The fact is that people with an arthritic hip are no longer prepared to wait eighteen

---

[11] See "Safe in Whose Hands?" 67.

[12] W. Jack Duncan and others, *Strategic Management of Health Care Organizations* (Cambridge, Mass.: Basil Blackwell, 1995) 536.

[13] See evaluation by the New Zealand Public Service Association, *The New Zealand Health Care System* (Wellington: New Zealand Public Service Association, 1985) 13.

months for help; they are also less willing to sit for hours in a hospital casualty department waiting for medical services.[14]

Questionable Management of Resources

There is a widespread opinion that resources are not being adequately or appropriately used in healthcare services. The following comments would support this view, at least in the countries referred to:

The influential international weekly review *The Economist* argues that Britain's National Health Service "has turned muddling into an art."[15] And this "muddling" is financially costly.[16]

In the United States healthcare services absorb more resources than are required. The extravagance occurs in two areas, argues Victor Fuchs, professor of economics and health research at Stanford University: "Administration (including marketing, billing, and collecting) and excess capacity of facilities, equipment, and specialized personnel."[17]

For example, the United States spends as much as 22 percent of its health resources on administration costs, compared with only 6 percent by the National Health Service in Britain.[18] There are ten thousand mammogram machines in the United States, when two thousand would fill present demand; five thousand would in fact screen the whole population.[19] Facilities for open heart surgery far exceed demand. So also for other medical facilities. Despite the fact that Americans spend about twice as much as Europeans on healthcare, they live no longer. There is simply uncontrolled

---

[14] See "The National Health Service: Prognosis—Poor," *The Economist* (May 3, 1997) 55.

[15] "Safe in Whose Hands?" 68.

[16] See Judith Allsop, *Health Policy and the NHS: Towards 2000* (London: Longman, 1995) 188.

[17] Fuchs, *The Future of Health Policy,* 160. See also Daniel Callahan, *False Hopes: Why America's Quest for Perfect Health Is a Recipe for Failure* (New York: Simon & Schuster, 1998). Callahan argues that the potential of future contributions of technology to the advancement of healthcare is gravely limited. Finance should be directed away from cost-expensive technology to health education and palliative care and the development of "sustainable medicine."

[18] See Fitzpatrick, "Organizing and Funding Health Care," 279; Eli Ginzberg, *The Road to Reform: The Future of Health Care in America* (New York: Free Press, 1994) 49–50.

[19] See Chris Hackler, "Health Care Reform in the United States," *Reforming Health Care: The Philosophy and Practice of International Health Reform,* ed. David Seedhouse (Chichester: John Wiley, 1966) 16.

growth resulting in "fragmentation, chaos, and disarray . . . pluralism verging on anarchy."[20]

This expensive chaos will not change until American healthcare systems accept some kind of macromanagement by governments or other agencies.[21] Until this happens the rampant dispersal and duplication of sophisticated, high-cost medical technology will continue.

Controversial managerial reform has been attempted in recent years with varying degrees of success in several countries, such as Britain[22] and New Zealand.[23] Comments on these efforts will be made later in this chapter. One immense obstacle to reform is the lack of well-researched information on the effectiveness of healthcare services. In 1988 the Social Services Select Committee of the British House of Commons stated:

> The last major weakness of the National Health Service is that it is not possible to tell whether or not it works. There are no outcome measures to speak of other than that of crude numbers of patients treated. . . . As a result, the correct level of funding for the NHS (National Health Service) cannot be determined and the public and politicians cannot decide whether or not they are getting value for the resources pumped into the National Health Service.[24]

The same absence of well-researched evaluation into the effectiveness of healthcare services is to be found throughout Western society. In any case research would rarely be acceptable to professional vested interests, especially medical personnel and associations. As Angela Coulter finds in Britain: "Evaluative research is essentially a subversive activity. . . . Arguments about the sanctity of clinical freedom and the inability of nonspecialists to understand clinical issues are invoked in order to discredit such research."[25]

---

[20] Arthur R. Somers, "Who's in Charge? Alice Searches for a King in Mediland," *The New England Journal of Medicine* 287:5 (1972) 849.

[21] See Thomas S. Bodenheimer and Kevin Grumbach, *Understanding Health Policy: A Clinical Approach* (Stamford, Conn.: Appleton & Lange, 1995) 119.

[22] See Norman Johnson, ed., *Private Markets in Health Welfare: An International Perspective* (Oxford: Berg, 1995) 17–38.

[23] See Toni Ashton, "From Evolution to Revolution: Restructuring the New Zealand Health System," *Reforming Health Care,* ed. Seedhouse, 85–93.

[24] Social Services Committee, *The Future of the National Health Service* (London: HMSO, 1988) xi.

[25] Angela Coulter, "Evaluating the Outcomes of Health Care," *The Sociology of the Health Service,* ed. Jonathan Gabe and others (London: Routledge, 1991) 133.

The Primary Task of Reform Is Unclear

In Australia, hospitals account for approximately half of all healthcare expenditure, despite the fact that cultural factors (that is, political, economic, and social processes) are the major causes of illness.[26] This imbalance in the distribution of resources is common throughout the world. Healthcare analyst David Seedhouse, after reviewing efforts to reform healthcare systems in several countries (United States, Britain, New Zealand, Holland, South Africa), concludes that the fundamental weakness preventing success in all cases was the failure to begin "from theory rather than convention."[27] He argues that to attempt to restructure a health system along rational lines at present is certain to fail for two reasons. First, the definition of what health systems means is often arbitrary. For example, the popular image is that healthcare is synonymous with hospital services, which is a too narrow view. Second, "there is no proper account of the purpose of health systems."[28]

Seedhouse, a paramodernist, is correct. Far too often healthcare reform begins with two assumptions: a narrow modernistic definition of ill-health, namely physical/mental disease and injury, and belief that financial costs of caring for or curing people so afflicted must be reduced. But there can be no authentic reform *unless* it starts with a broad definition of ill-health; that is, people have ill-health when they lack a range of necessary opportunities in life, are unable to develop creatively, and/or have a greatly disabling life obstacle.[29] Healthcare reform will involve, in addition to re-assessing medical and associated services, structural and economic reform to allow people to obtain jobs, be defended against discrimination, live in unpolluted air, drive on safe roads, etc.

Hospitals: Cultural Implications of Rapid Change

Any reform, however well-intentioned, necessitates cultural changes. These changes inevitably evoke resistance and at times the disturbing symptoms of cultural chaos. The human cost of reform is rarely appreciated (see Chapter 3).

---

[26] See Jake M. Najman, "Health and the Australian Population," *A Sociology of Australian Society*, ed. Jake M. Najman and John S. Western (Melbourne: MacMillan, 1988) 333.

[27] David Seedhouse, "Theory Before Practice?" *Reforming Health Care*, ed. Seedhouse, 233.

[28] Ibid., 230.

[29] See ibid., 231.

For example, over the past thirty years hospitals have gone through immense organizational changes with dramatic consequences for their cultures, staffs, and budgets. An insight into the speed of change is provided by Dennis Pointer and Charles Ewell when they identify four stages in the evolution of hospitals in the United States.[30] In the *refuge stage* (mid-1700s to late 1920s) hospitals were little more than refuges for the destitute and transient sick. In the *physician stage* (early 1930s through to the mid-1960s) power moved from trustees and community control to medical staff. With the discovery of powerful new drugs hospitals were now able to focus primarily on curing patients rather than just caring for them. Physicians controlled the knowledge and technologies, giving them considerable organizational and political power over larger and more complex hospitals. In the *business stage* (mid-1960s through the mid-1980s) hospitals under administrators became more businesslike to provide the resources required by modern medicine. The *corporate stage* began in the mid-1980s in the response to the need for hospitals to survive financially in the face of intensifying competition. This is the stage where economic rationalism began to flourish.

Healthcare Policy: The Paramodernist Approach

According to Antonio Gramsci, "A main obstacle to change is the reproduction by the dominated forces of elements of the hegemonic ideology. It is an important and urgent task to develop alternative interpretations of reality."[31]

Paramodernist Vincente Navarro, professor of health policy at Johns Hopkins University, speaks of healthcare reforms in the United States in recent times as an "ideological avalanche." Economic rationalists have developed with minimal opposition anti-welfare state positions and have weakened the humanitarian principles of the New Deal of the Roosevelt presidency. The severe cost-cutting policies of the 1980s became "the most influential policies not only in the United States but—because of the government's great influence on other countries—in most of the Western developed capitalist world."[32] People who would normally have supported

[30] See Dennis D. Pointer and Charles M. Ewell, *Really Governing: How Health System and Hospital Boards Can Make More of a Difference* (Albany, N.Y.: Delmar, 1994) 4–8.

[31] Antonio Gramsci, as quoted by Vincento Navarro, *The Politics of Health Policy: The U.S. Reforms, 1980–1994* (Oxford: Blackwell, 1994) 1.

[32] Ibid., ix. See also his book *Dangerous to Your Health: Capitalism in Health Care* (New York: Monthly Review Press, 1993).

a welfare state's concern for distributive justice have been politically seduced into accepting brutal capitalist reforms.

Navarro uses the philosopher Antonio Gramsci to support his analysis. Gramsci calls this seduction "hegemonic ideology." By *hegemony* Gramsci means the ability of a class or social group to develop its own world view into a politically dominant way of life. The triumphs of the medical model and contemporary economic rationalism are examples of the dangerous hegemonic ideology of professional, political, and socioeconomic elites. Navarro urges reformers to help people become conscious that they are being manipulated by politicians and pressure groups to accept unethical policies of economic rationalism in healthcare. Such consciousness, he claims, will lead people to dream of alternative ways of healthcare.

Bryan Turner, reflecting on the Australian situation, agrees with Navarro: "[The] social struggle over . . . disease is a political conflict over the distribution of power. . . . The dynamics of welfare distribution, for example of health-care arrangements, are the outcome of conflicts between elite groups for the control of . . . resources."[33]

To appreciate the significance of this kind of analysis, I will first clarify the types of existing healthcare services, and then define what is meant by holistic healthcare reform.

Focus of Healthcare Services[34]

Three major orientations of healthcare services can be distinguished. The first type is termed *primary healthcare:* ambulatory services, availability of general practitioners, health education programs such as anti-smoking campaigns, and political action to remove job/housing/education/age/gender discrimination. The second type is *curative healthcare:* acute-care hospitals, community and hospital outpatient services. The third type is *chronic healthcare:* long-term care, hospice facilities, nursing homes.

Since the 1950s and 1960s healthcare concern has moved from primary to curative services as a consequence of the medical model, medical technology, and economic rationalism. In the United States this swing, to specialist services in particular, is especially marked: only 13 percent of physicians are general or family practitioners, a remarkable drop from 75 percent in the 1940s. In Britain, on the other hand, two-thirds of all

---

[33] Bryan S. Turner, *Medical Power and Social Knowledge* (London: Sage Publications, 1995) 84.

[34] Adapted from Blank, *New Zealand and Health Policy,* 68.

physicians are general practitioners.[35] Since the 1970s there have been some efforts to return to primary services—from cure to prevention—for reasons discussed in Chapter 1, namely that it is more effective to promote good health than to treat illness, but the hard political decisions that favor the poor are rarely made. Rising demand for chronic care services due to the increase in elderly patients is also demanding a readjustment in the way finances are allotted.[36]

A Philosophy of Holistic Healthcare

Holistic healthcare embodies four principles, which can be summarized as follows:[37]

The Principle of Beneficence

According to this principle it is the duty of healthcare providers to respond to people in need.

CASE STUDY

The Poor in the United States

Among the world's industrialized countries, the United States alone gives its citizens no rights to healthcare. Since the principle of beneficence is not set down by federal and state governments,[38] healthcare providers are under no obligation to accept it. Americans must depend on various forms of insurance, such as private or employment-based, to protect themselves. The majority of the forty million uninsured Americans are the most socially and economically vulnerable. For example, of people under sixty-five, 24 percent of African-Americans and 39 percent of Hispanics are uninsured, compared

---

[35] See Bodenheimer and Grumbach, *Understanding Health Policy,* 59, 61.

[36] See Sarah Nettleton, *The Sociology of Health and Illness* (Cambridge: Polity, 1995) 228–33.

[37] See Tom L. Beauchamp and James F. Childress, *Principles of Biomedical Ethics* (New York: Oxford University Press, 1994) 120–394.

[38] See William J. Curran, "The Constitutional Right to Health Care: Denial in the Court," *The New England Journal of Medicine* 320:4 (1989) 788.

with 14 percent of whites. They must turn to the emergency rooms or clinics of under-financed public or non-profit hospitals, tolerating hours of waiting before receiving help. It is even possible that they could be turned away.[39] For-profit hospitals and clinics already have a history of growing non-beneficence.[40]

Policies exist to give access to healthcare to particular groups otherwise unable to pay for and receive care, such as the elderly (Medicare), poor children (Medicaid), poor adults (Medicaid and local/state general aid), the disabled (Medicaid and Medicare). However, many do not qualify or, if they do, the benefits they receive are limited. Less than half those with incomes below the nation's poverty line could receive Medicaid. Even if people have access to special services there is no certainty that they will be helped. In 1991, 26 percent of the country's physicians refused to accept Medicaid patients and a further 35 percent restricted the number of Medicaid patients they would assist.[41]

The Principle of Nonmaleficence

This principle obliges healthcare providers not to cause harm. This is not easy for medical personnel committed to the biomedical model. For example, a worker under considerable occupational stress can be prescribed antidepressants over a lengthy period of time, when in fact the person needs counseling to decide to change jobs. The failure of the doctor to suggest this counseling is an act of maleficence.

The Principle of Autonomy

One has the right to decide what one wishes to undertake as healthcare, provided it is within the law and respects the rights of others. A patient with inoperable cancer has the right to choose not to submit to extraordinary means in order to prolong life. Doctors have an obligation to keep the

---

[39] See Bodenheimer and Grumbach, *Understanding Health Policy,* 22, 26.

[40] See Robert Kuttner, "Columbia/HCA and the Resurgence of the For-Profit Hospital Business," *The New England Journal of Medicine* 335:5 (1996) 363.

[41] See Bodenheimer and Grumbach, *Understanding Health Policy,* 27.

patient fully informed in order that the person may make a free decision in such matters.

The Principle of Justice

This principle—that people should have equal access to healthcare services—is the most controversial of all the principles and generally the most neglected. Distributive justice is about two contentious issues: the equitable *access* to healthcare and the *allocation* of resources in an equitable manner.[42]

CASE STUDY ▰▰▰▰▰▰▰▰▰▰▰▰▰▰▰▰▰▰▰

The Paradox of Healthcare in the United States

All industrialized democracies accept the principle of justice in healthcare except the United States, which has the best medical technology in the world, but the most wasteful. Americans spend almost twice as much on doctors, drugs, and up-market brain scanners as Europeans, but live no longer. Chinese children are more likely to be vaccinated against disease than Americans, despite the fact that health spending per head in the United States is about 150 times higher than in China. The United States has an over-supply of beds and medical specialists, but it lacks the political will to accept the right of all people to an equitable share of healthcare resources.[43]

As regards the equitable distribution of healthcare resources, disadvantaged peoples commonly find it difficult, if not impossible, to obtain justice. The hegemony of the powerful, referred to above, blocks the less powerful from receiving justice in healthcare in many nations. In Australia, writes sociologist Margaret Sargent, "Women have more disorders than

---

[42] See Richard A. McCormick, *Health and Medicine in the Catholic Tradition* (New York: Crossroad, 1987) 75.

[43] See "Health Care in America: Your Money or Your Life," *The Economist* (March 7, 1998) 14.

men, working-class people more than middle-class, Aboriginal people and non-English speaking immigrants more than Anglo-Australians, older people more than younger."[44] The principle of justice, its roots, and implications for healthcare will be considered more fully in Chapter 4.

Healthcare Policies

Fundamental to this book is the assumption that healthcare is a larger category than medical care; it embraces health education and socioeconomic and political structural change to provide people with opportunities to develop their human potential and overcome discrimination. Public health policy, therefore, means those government measures which aim to develop a balance between the different dimensions of healthcare.

Types of Policies

Historically, one can distinguish four theoretical types of public health policy:[45]

Traditional Public Healthcare Policy

This type of healthcare policy originated last century when, with the rapid development of industrialization and urbanization, governments in Europe and North America legislated to improve sanitation and housing conditions. From the 1870s, government medical officers emphasized the need for individuals to be immunized against diseases and to take care of their personal hygiene.[46] Nineteenth-century temperance campaigns belong to this model, along with the anti-VD propaganda in World War I and "better-eating" literature on the home-front during the last war.

Individual Responsibility Policy

In this type the obligation is on the individual to opt for a healthy way of life. In 1974 the Canadian government issued a report which, having identified four elements in health—human biology, the environment, life-style, and healthcare organization—stressed the need for people to adopt a healthy

[44] Margaret Sargent and others, *The New Sociology for Australians* (Melbourne: Longman, 1977) 145.
[45] Ibid., 138–40.
[46] See Nettleton, *The Sociology of Health and Illness,* 232.

life-style.[47] The British government published a similar report two years later.[48] Public health policy, according to this type, is restricted to providing the public with information about the need to act responsibly in order to be healthy. This policy is criticized for several reasons.

First, it assumes that the individual is free to decide on a healthy lifestyle. It overlooks the fact that cultural factors (e.g., socioeconomic class structures, employment discrimination) deeply affect how people live. They may have little or no control over these factors. Totally ignored in this policy type is the seductive power of advertising, such as that undertaken by tobacco companies, impacting on the lifestyles of individuals.

Second, the type of policy lends itself to scapegoating individuals or classes of people by blaming them for their poverty—a very popular approach for New Right politicians and their supporters. It serves little purpose to blame the poor for their smoking habits, when in fact it is the impoverishment of their lives through various forms of oppression that must be addressed.

Third, in the exercise of this type of policy there is a definite slant against women. Much advice is directed toward women, and especially mothers. Social policy analyst Sarah Nettleton argues that the assumption that "women ought to take responsibility for not only their own health but that of others is . . . reinforced."[49]

Finally, this type of policy naively assumes that because people receive information they will automatically change their behavior.

New Public Healthcare Policy

This type of policy emphasizes a more equitable distribution of healthcare resources in order that all citizens can be both socially and economically productive. The type has received particular impetus from the World Health Organization in its emphasis on health for all through primary health care by 2000. However, while WHO assumes there is a connection between health, lifestyles, and the socioeconomic environment, there is no encouragement in the literature for local or global governments to chal-

---

[47] See David Locker, "Prevention and Health Promotion," *Sociology as Applied to Medicine,* ed. Scambler, 248.

[48] Cited by Locker, "Prevention and Health Promotion," 248. The document is: Department of Health and Social Security, *Prevention and Health: Everybody's Business* (London: HMSO, 1976).

[49] See Nettleton, *The Sociology of Health and Illness,* 237.

lenge the unjust structures that compel people to live poorly and in unhealthy ways.[50]

Holistic Healthcare Policy

Holistic healthcare policy is built on the assumption that most health problems are associated with cultural or class-related factors: people are poor and unhealthy primarily because they are powerless to do anything about it. Few governments wish to embrace this model fully. In fact, given the current popularity of economic rationalism there are deliberate moves to reinforce existing unequal power structures in society, as the following examples illustrate.

Policies in Action

United Kingdom

The first and third types above remain especially favored by recent governments. David Locker supports this conclusion: "Attempts to control the 'manufacturers of illness' or to deal effectively with health-related issues such as poverty, housing and the environment, have been much less evident."[51] The philosophy of the former conservative government is seen as inimical to any significant effort to alter the power structures in favor of the poor, and therefore of their health.

John Mohan concludes that the government's policies have given priority to the "'productive,' who produce goods and services that can be profitably marketed, and marginalised the 'parasitic,' who are either dependent on state benefits or whose economic activities are deemed 'unprofitable' in narrowly conceived terms."[52] It is claimed that over the past seventeen years the "health gaps between the rich and poor, between social classes, between north and south, and between the inner city and shire counties have all widened."[53]

Australia

Australian health policy-makers have gradually shifted their concern from equity and social justice to cost containment and, more recently, to

---

[50] See Sargent, *The New Sociology,* 237–8.

[51] Locker, "Prevention and Health Promotion," 253.

[52] John Mohan, "Privatization in the British Health Sector: A Challenge to the NHS?" *The Sociology of the Health Service,* ed. Gabe, 40.

[53] Fabian Pamphlet, *Health Crisis—What Crisis? Proceedings of the Fabian/Socialist Health Association Conference 1996* (London: Fabian Society, 1996) 2.

cost-effectiveness.[54] Consequently, minority groups like the aboriginal people are increasingly overlooked.

CASE STUDY

Land Rights Fundamental to Health

The health of the aboriginal people is among the worst in the world. For example, aboriginal infant death rates are between two and five times the rates of white Australians, yet successive governments have either ignored or done little to relate to this problem. In recent years public health policies have followed the first three models listed above; namely, Traditional Public Healthcare Policy, Individual Responsibility Policy, and New Public Healthcare Policy. However, they have been ineffective because the real issues have not been addressed.

The legacy of being despised and rejected for over two hundred years in their own country lies heavily on the aboriginal people. It was only in 1967 that they were given citizenship in their own country. In 1992 the High Court acknowledged for the first time that aboriginal people could claim rights over land that was traditionally theirs. Land for the aboriginal people, as for most traditional societies,[55] is at the heart of their identities. Without their land they have no dignity, no sense of belonging or self-respect. The High Court's decision is the first major step toward the revitalization of aboriginal self-identity and a foundation for good health.

However, the present government, in response to the politically powerful farming and mining lobbies, seeks to overturn the High Court's decision, which will restrict or even extinguish aboriginal rights over land. Thus, the fourth model above is not to be applied to the aboriginal people, but there cannot be any lasting improvement to

---

[54] See Hal Swerissen and Stephen Duckett, "Health Policy and Financing," *Health Policy in Australia,* ed. Heather Gardner (Melbourne: Oxford University Press, 1997) 33.

[55] See Gerald A. Arbuckle, *Earthing the Gospel: An Inculturation Handbook for the Pastoral Worker* (London: Geoffrey Chapman, 1990) 49.

aboriginal people's medical health until they have the space to "stand tall" through legitimate rights over their land.[56]

United States

Recent welfare reform has been dramatic, even brutal. Americans will be entitled to a maximum of five years of welfare over their lifetime. Once this is finished, "it's a work or starve scenario. . . . Charity will be the only recourse in a downturn for jobless families who have used up their social assistance."[57] A group of New York City Church leaders complain that the reform is "akin to slavery,"[58] yet their voices have caused no concern either to legislators or to the mass of the population.

This anti-poor reform testifies to the fact that the United States is fundamentally unwilling to accept a holistic healthcare policy. The poor are increasingly marginalized. Why do Americans tolerate this? Eli Ginzberg argues that, unlike many other nations, the "poor [in the United States] and the near-poor have seldom, if ever, had the political clout to impel the public and government to act on their behalf."[59] Because of the lack of a publicly funded healthcare system, health benefits are mainly work-related and continue to be covered by collective bargaining agreements. The system strengthens, as Vincente Navarro points out, "inequalities and differentials among wage earners, favoring the strongest [the sector of labor with the strongest muscle at the bargaining table] and discriminating against and/or excluding the weakest."[60] Politically the poor have no muscle to battle against the hegemonic political and economic power of the rich, and the present welfare reform further reinforces their powerlessness. Consequently their health can only continue to decline.

New Zealand

Since the 1890s New Zealand has moved away from the laissez-faire theory of the state, firmly opting by the late 1930s for the paramodern

---

[56] See Chris McGillion, "Australia Down Under," *The Tablet* (December 13, 1997) 1595.

[57] Adele Horin, "Welfare Reform US-Style—With a Sting in the Tail," *Sydney Morning Herald* (November 1, 1997) 10.

[58] See *USA Today* (August 4, 1997) 8A.

[59] Ginzberg, *The Road to Reform,* 104.

[60] Navarro, *The Politics of Health Policy,* 184.

model. The consequences of state action in New Zealand over the decades was to establish an economically and socially egalitarian society, with a universal system of healthcare and a range of welfare structures that prevented discrimination against the poorer sections of the population.

However, between 1984 and 1992 this situation changed dramatically under the forces of economic rationalism. The right to welfare services (e.g., healthcare, unemployment relief) was removed through government legislation. Now services are provided only as a limited safety net for citizens in trouble, with dramatic consequences for the poor: "The important values such as human dignity, distributive justice, and social cohesion, have been given second place to the pursuit of efficiency, self-reliance, a fiscal balance, and a more limited state."[61]

Within a short space of time a new underclass of poor people has emerged which has little sympathy from the political system and the population in general. Unable to plead their case, the poor now show increasing signs of health deprivation. It has been estimated that one-third of all New Zealand children now live below the poverty line.[62] Between 1984 and 1993, the percentage of households living in absolute poverty has more than doubled, from 4.3 percent to 10.8 percent.[63] Social commentator Michael Moore points out that "it has become fashionable to blame the victims. Bad parents and lazy people are seen as the problem."[64]

Rationing Medical Resources: Balancing the Principles

"Rationing" is not a popular term, as it implies exclusion from or denial of a service, so some prefer expressions like "priority setting" or "resource allocation." Yet no matter what terms are used, the fact is that decisions are and have to be made, even within a holistic healthcare model, to exclude people from certain services. The reality is that unforeseen costs have developed, and will continue to do so, because of such things as AIDS, innovative drugs like interferon and erythropoietin, transplants. At the same time from the same budget broken legs have to be repaired and hips replaced. All nations directly

---

[61] Jonathan Boston and Paul Dalziel, *The Decent Society?* (Oxford: Oxford University Press, 1992) 88.

[62] See Mike Moore, *Children of the Poor: How Poverty Could Destroy New Zealand's Future* (Christchurch: Canterbury University Press, 1996) 15.

[63] See Paul Dalziel, "Reaping the Whirlwind of the Economic Reforms," *Tui Motu* (August 1998) 3.

[64] Moore, *Children of the Poor,* 11; also reported by Catherine Masters, "Caught in the Maze of Poverty," *The New Zealand Herald* (June 14, 1997) 3G.

or indirectly ration healthcare services according to the model of healthcare policy they choose, simply because they do not have unrestricted resources.

Any form of rationing can raise considerable tension within communities, as the following two case studies illustrate.

CASE STUDY

Dialysis Refused

In 1997 a man in New Zealand was refused kidney dialysis by a government health agency and this evoked a national outcry in the mass media lasting several days. One paper headlined: "Why Are They Letting Him Die?: Tears as Favourite Uncle is Refused Kidney Treatment."[65] The agency commented that "It's a question of weighing up all the values that go into that and it has never been easy."[66]

CASE STUDY

MS Sufferers Refused Treatment

In Saskatchewan, Canada, the provincial government refused to fund the drug Betaseron for multiple sclerosis sufferers. The reactions were strong, leading to protest movements. Critics said that it was the "start of a two-tiered health system . . . one for the rich and one for the poor."[67] The treatment costs nearly $17,000 per year.

The United States rations medical services by the capacity of people to pay, and this is a process, as has been explained above, which discriminates according to categories of race, class, and employment conditions.[68]

[65] *Sunday Star Times* (September 21, 1997) 1.
[66] Ibid.
[67] *The Leader Post* (October 20, 1997) 1.
[68] See Basiro Davey and Jennie Popay, eds., *Dilemmas in Health Care* (Buckingham: Open University Press, 1993) 34–5.

In 1991 the Oregon Legislature formally rationed services to Medicaid re-cipients by deciding that the state government would pay only for the first 587 items on a list. Medical services are rationed for the poor according to this plan, while the rich in the state can enjoy an abundance of services. (In March 1998 the legislature voted to include doctor-assisted suicide on the list of "services" that Medicaid covers, under the title of "comfort-care."[69])

In those countries in which universal healthcare exists, governments routinely decide where expensive technology is to be situated. In Canada hospital costs are much less than in the United States, mainly because the government rations hospital services according to the perceived need of particular patients, not on the basis of their ability to pay. In Canada and other countries like New Zealand, Australia, and Britain this policy some-times leads to lengthy waiting lists for medical services such as open heart surgery.[70] In New Zealand five-year delays for heart by-pass surgery fol-lowing a heart attack are common.[71]

However rationing is done, the real problem is to decide the criteria on which decisions are made. For example, should those who have unhealthy lifestyles be discriminated against in favor of those who regularly exercise or do not smoke? Should preference for surgery be given to people who have been waiting the longest, even if they are very elderly? Should ser-vices be provided to people because they claim that they need them to im-prove their quality of life? There are no simple ways to establish criteria. The phrase "quality of life" is so nebulous that it can mean anything.

The fundamental issue remains a philosophical or moral question, as David Seedhouse points out: What kind of society does a nation desire to have—one that maximizes the quality of life for the most productive *or* one that draws the weakest closer to the standards of the strongest? If the first is chosen, then medical services will tend toward, as in United States, expensive technology and medicine, while the second will focus on com-munity or the common good.

Unless this question is openly debated and addressed, then rationing will be directed according to pragmatic exigencies or a philosophy that may be destructive of the common good. Such a thinking is already creep-

---

[69] See Bodenheimer and Grumbach, *Understanding Health Policy,* 188–9; "John Kitzhaber's Prescription," *The Economist* (April 25, 1998) 35.

[70] See Keith J. Mueller, *Health Care Policy in the United States* (Lincoln: University of Nebraska Press, 1993) 159–64; for an analysis of criteria for rationing see Fitzpatrick, "Organizing and Funding Health Care," 284–5.

[71] See Blank, *New Zealand and Health Policy,* 99.

ing into places like Britain, New Zealand, and Canada, where once policy was firmly based on the four principles explained above. Christian reformers will begin with a philosophy founded on the healing mission of Jesus Christ and from that point clarify the criteria for rationing. This means rejecting economic rationalism.

Healthcare Policies under Strain: Case Studies of Reform

In 1987 the OECD (Organization for Economic Collaboration and Development) devised a threefold typology of healthcare systems, namely the Beveridge, Bismarckian, and Consumer Sovereignty types.[72]

The Beveridge type, as in Britain and New Zealand, is based on the right of each citizen to healthcare and involves services funded through taxes that are owned and controlled by the government.

The Bismarckian type, such as in Holland, is also built on the principle of universal coverage, but it is financed through government-regulated, non-profit-making insurance funds from contributions of employers and individuals.

In the Consumer Sovereignty model it is assumed that health is a commodity and ill-health an insurable risk. The stress is on private insurance bought either by the individuals or by employers, and on private ownership of services. It is a modified market in this sense that healthcare providers are accountable in varying degrees to governments, and services are given to people too poor to obtain insurance. This model aptly describes the healthcare system of the United States, so also to a lesser extent Australia's system.

The two thematic pillars of the present healthcare policies of Western governments are cost containment (through such actions as rationing services, placing limits on budgets, privatization, etc.) and maintaining access to services. The following case studies illustrate how particular governments today struggle to resolve the tension between holding costs down and maintaining access. Britain and New Zealand, because of reforms in the 1980s and 1990s, have in part moved away from the Beveridge type to embrace aspects of the modified market model.

Canada: Single-Payer National Insurance

In 1994 an American cartoon depicted two beggars in conversation, one saying to the other: "You know, there's one way to solve this healthcare

---

[72] See Ann Wall, *Health Systems in Liberal Democracies* (London: Routledge, 1996) 183–4.

problem. Marry a Canadian!" Canadians are rightly proud of their system, considering it one of their country's most valued institutions and integral to their identity as a nation.

Certainly the Canadian system is radically different from that in the United States, simply because it has a single-payer method of national health insurance conducted by the provincial governments and financed by provincial and federal taxes. Private health insurance to cover services which are funded by the provincial health policies is prohibited. Governments pay doctors a fee-for-service, and neither doctors nor hospitals are able to charge private insurers for services received in the government-approved health system. This policy thus avoids the development of a preferential service for the rich. Every Canadian, no matter how wealthy or poor, is entitled to receive the same healthcare service.[73] Of all industrialized nations Canada stands out as having possibly the most egalitarian healthcare system.[74]

Canada has been able to develop this system in contrast to the United States for two reasons. First, there are significant cultural differences between the two peoples: like Australia, the United Kingdom, and New Zealand, Canada has long had a political philosophy that encourages state intervention in society, whereas in the United States the emphasis on the rights of individuals is so strong that government action to control these rights is rarely tolerated.

Second, the medical profession in Canada, in line with the country's political philosophy, has been far more cooperative with the government than its counterpart in the United States. Doctors have been generally prepared in Canada to accept what would be unheard of in America—tight control over their fees and hospital expenditures. Administrative costs in Canada are far lower than in America because there are no overhead costs from multiple insurers and less paperwork required to reimburse fees since they are established beforehand.[75]

Canadians are now fearful for the future of their healthcare system. The problem is rising costs, the growing influence of economic rationalists, and

[73] See Bodenheimer and Grumbach, *Understanding Health Policy,* 199–202. For a review of the issues in rationing see Henry J. Aaron and William B. Schwartz, *The Painful Prescription: Rationing Hospital Care* (Washington, D.C.: Brookings Institution, 1984).

[74] See Theodore R. Marmor, "Patterns of Fact and Fiction in the Use of the Canadian Experience," *Reforming Health Care,* ed. Seedhouse, 60–70.

[75] See Mueller, *Health Care Policy,* 159–64; Andre-Pierre Contandriopoulos and others, "Canada," *Private Markets,* ed. Johnson, 39–63.

powerful interest groups. The political right and medical authorities are pushing for the introduction of private, profit-making services. The province of Alberta in particular is anxious to have a two-tier system in which the privately insured have access to preferential and speedy treatment while the uninsured can join queues. In 1995 the province already allowed fifteen private specialist clinics to charge the public system and to request extra expenses from patients. The privatization of healthcare and welfare services is far more than an economic or managerial issue. Since it threatens the distinctive cultural identity of Canadians we can expect significant social and political disruption the more it is championed by interest groups.

However, if Canada is to preserve its universal insurance and withstand the assaults from economic rationalists, ongoing cost control is essential. Saskatchewan, the originator of Medicare in 1947, has again set an example to the other provinces by converting fifty-two hospitals into less expensive health centers, and further developing home care and community services. Elsewhere in Canada hospitals are either being closed or merged, as in-patient stays shorten or are substituted by out-patient and home-care services, and doctors' incomes are becoming restricted. The reaction against these changes by staff most affected by them is increasingly negative. For example, in a survey some four-fifths of doctors expressed the desire to create a two-tier or public-private system, with patients paying more than the government-supported fees.[76]

The United States: Individualism Triumphs

The resistance of Americans to the New Deal social policies of Franklin Roosevelt, to the introduction of Medicare and Medicaid in 1965, and finally to the Clinton reform plan in the early 1990s, is understandable in light of the nation's founding myth which remains powerfully operative to this day.

America's founding myth is the belief that Americans are called to build a new land of peace, plenty, and justice; a land where, unlike the Europe the Founding Fathers left, no person or group (especially a government) will suppress the rights of the individual. The rights of the individual, not the well-being of the community, have priority.[77] Thus the individual has

---

[76] See "Canada's Medicare on the Sick-List," *The Economist* (September 23, 1995) 33.

[77] See Gerald A. Arbuckle, *Refounding the Church: Dissent for Leadership* (London: Geoffrey Chapman, 1993) 39; Robert N. Bellah and others, *Habits of the Heart: Individualism and Commitment in American Life* (San Francisco: Harper & Row, 1985) 275–96.

the unqualified right to own guns despite the tragic consequences to the community. It is a world made for capitalism and its expression—unrestrained competition, not collaboration for the common good. It is little wonder that interest groups such as the medical profession, through its professional associations and major corporations (e.g., insurance companies and the health industries), have been able to wield considerable unrestrained economic and political power.[78] Marginalized peoples must solve their own problems.

Any attempt by governments to redress the imbalance in favor of the common good is met with strong emotional opposition. Efforts at healthcare reforms are branded as "socialized medicine," "government meddling." Expressions of this kind are enough to condemn the most logical and justice-based plans! Healthcare analyst Lawrence Jacobs notes that even when programs such as Medicare and Medicaid have been introduced successive administrations have been unable to establish realistic controls on costs. This is again due to an abiding suspicion of government intervention.[79] In fact, claims Eli Ginzberg, the "U.S. health care system broke loose from dollar controls in 1965 and has operated substantially free of financial discipline ever since."[80] Left unchecked, over the next ten years Medicare will drain the treasury of $1.6 trillion.[81] The founding story's disdain of government intervention even for the sake of distributive justice haunts policy makers.

Competition in Order to Control Costs: Managed Care and For-Profits

Over the last decade in the United States there has been immense growth in managed care processes in response to the chaos of healthcare costs and the excesses of unrestricted "fee-for-service" medicine. Managed care aims to reduce costs by controlling the choice of doctors and hospitals for which the insurer will pay. Doctors and hospitals who join managed care plans are paid at lower rates, but benefit from a definite number of patients. Employers also benefit, because managed care re-

---

[78] See Alastair V. Campbell, *Health as Liberation: Medicine, Theology, and the Quest for Justice* (Cleveland: Pilgrim Press, 1995) 73.

[79] See Lawrence R. Jacobs, *The Health of Nations: Public Opinion and the Making of American and British Health Policy* (Ithaca, N.Y.: Cornell University Press, 1993) 233–6.

[80] Ginzberg, *The Road to Reform,* 86.

[81] Editorial, "Inevitable Surgery on Medicare," *The New York Times* (June 26, 1997) 26A. Also "Will Medicare Sink the Budget?" *The Economist* (February 1, 1997) 35–6.

duces the premiums that companies must pay. Almost 160 million people are now covered by managed care, a dramatic development over the ten years since it first began.

Managed care includes a variety of programs, two of which are Integrated Delivery Networks (IDNs) and Health Maintenance Organizations (HMOs).

Integrated Delivery Networks (IDNs). An IDN is a network of organized care offering integrated physician, hospital, and nursing services within a specified geographic market. These services are based on the following values: they are person-oriented, favor non-institutional care, provide universal access, offer a uniform benefits structure, and extend care in a simplified system into the community.[82]

Health Maintenance Organizations (HMOs). Approximately sixty million Americans, up from six million two decades ago, are enrolled in HMOs.[83] There are some 630 HMOs nationwide.[84] Columbia/HCA, the biggest and most aggressive of the HMOs, is now the country's tenth largest employer. Its 1995 profits were just short of $1 billion, but it and others are beginning to experience a downturn in profits.[85]

HMOs are businesses, medical providers, and a form of health insurance all in one. Employers and consumers pay HMOs a fixed amount per month to provide health care. Some HMOs employ doctors and pay them salaries, but most HMOs contract with doctors, hospitals, and other providers and pay them discounted fees to provide services. Enrollees choose a primary care doctor, who approves referrals to specialists.

The reactions to HMOs are not all positive: doctors complain because their incomes are down and patients are angry because their treatments are restricted. Politicians are vigorously seeking to control them—more than a thousand bills seeking to stop suspected abuses by medical profiteers have

---

[82] See Catholic Health Association of the United States, *Ministry Perspectives* 2:2 (1993) 1.

[83] See Jana B. Knol, *Surviving a Competitive Health Care Market: Strategies for the Twenty-first Century* (New York: McGraw-Hill, 1995) 120–7.

[84] See Steven Findlay, "Using HMO Study to Assess Your Plan," *USA Today* (October 8, 1997) 9D.

[85] See Robert Kuttner, "Columbia/HCA and the Resurgence of the For-Profit Hospital Business," *The New England Journal of Medicine* 335:5 (1996) 362; "Aetna Implodes," *The Economist* (October 4, 1997) 75; Sandy Lutz and E. Preston Gee, *Columbia/HCA: Healthcare on Overdrive* (New York: McGraw-Hill, 1995).

been tabled in state legislatures in the past year.[86] The increasing backlash is attributable to the following:

(1) The primary focus of HMOs is maximizing profits. HMOs have changed the way American health is run, for their primary focus is profit for shareholders, not the well-being of the patient. This is a most dramatic change with grave implications for healthcare services, especially for the poor. Up to this point, Robert Kuttner observes, hospitals have run their affairs on "explicit and implicit understandings that have allowed doctors and hospitals to balance professionalism, profitability, and service."[87] Voluntary or non-profit hospitals have historically accepted uninsured patients, been prepared to take Medicaid losses, not insisted that every action be measured in terms of its profitability, and supported research. But for-profit hospitals hold a radically different philosophy, namely the profit motive.[88]

In the old-style reimbursement health insurance plans, the people who paid the accounts assumed the financial risks. Providers treated patients as they thought appropriate and passed on the bills to insurers, employers, and patients. In HMOs, however, the risks have moved to others; now providers and insurers carry the risk in a way that encourages them to control costs. Healthcare buyers pay an HMO a fixed annual premium per patient; in turn, the HMO may pass on a similarly fixed per-patient amount to doctors. If costs for treating a patient rise above these fixed amounts, the HMO and/or its providers must pay the difference. Hence, HMOs are accused of refusing costly but necessary treatment and/or of sending patients home from hospitals before they are ready in order to cut costs and maintain profits.[89]

(2) Doctors in HMOs have lost autonomy. People have fewer choices among doctors and hospitals. HMOs shift decision making and power from doctors to managed care administrators; economic considerations may take precedence over doctors' professional authority in medical decisions.[90]

---

[86] See "American Health Care," *The Economist* (March 7, 1998) 21; Christine Gorman, "Managed Care 1998: Playing the HMO Game," *Time* (July 13, 1998) 22–32.

[87] Kuttner, "Columbia/HCA," 363.

[88] See Jan Greene, "Has Managed Care Lost Its Soul?" *Hospitals and Health Networks* (May 20, 1997) 36–42; Janice Castro, *The American Way of Health* (Boston: Little and Brown, 1994) 154–63.

[89] See Kutter, "Columbia/HCA," 365; Peter T. Kilborn, "Largest H.M.O.'s Cutting the Poor and the Elderly," *The New York Times* (July 6, 1998) 1, 9A.

[90] See George Silver, "Editorial: The Road from Managed Care," *American Journal of Public Health* 87:1 (1997) 8–9.

In addition, there are the alleged unethical "partnerships" between doctors and hospitals of HMOs, which allow doctors to obtain a stake in "their" hospitals and share in the particular HMOs' success. These agreements encourage doctors to refer patients only to specialists at the HMOs' hospitals, even when this may not be to the advantage of the patient.[91]

(3) The rhetoric of efficiency lacks substance. Voluntary or non-profit hospitals have often been criticized by investor-owned hospitals for being inefficient; they have even been called "social parasites."[92] In a comprehensive evaluation of this point, the Institute of Medicine of the National Academy of Sciences concluded that there was "no evidence to support the common belief that investor-owned organizations are less costly or more efficient than are not-for-profit organizations."[93] Neil Gilbert and Kwong Leung Tang also conclude that many researchers share this "cautiously balanced view."[94]

In summary, despite the rapid growth of for-profit hospitals, 85 percent of all hospitals remain under the control of non-profit organizations.[95] However, the critical problem is that HMOs are out to alter the ethic of healthcare—from one of service to the patient/community to a culture in which accountability is primarily to profit-oriented shareholders. However, there are legislative moves to make HMOs publicly more accountable and to give patients more rights to challenge decisions of HMOs.[96]

From a positive perspective, however, HMOs and other forms of managed care are providing a national benefit because they are forcing clinicians to accept pre-set remuneration for their services and to be more widely accountable for their services. Clinicians who want higher fees are severely critical of managed care firms.[97] Managed care also controls the excessive demands of patients. Under the old fee-for-service method, insured Americans could claim almost any treatment they desired, with little

[91] See "American Health Care," *The Economist* (August 2, 1997) 55.

[92] See comments recorded by Kuttner, "Columbia/HCA," 448.

[93] Institute of Medicine cited by Neil Gilbert and Kwong L. Tang, "The United States," *Private Markets,* ed. Johnson, 212.

[94] Ibid.

[95] See Emily Friedman, "Capitation, Integration, and Managed Care: Lessons from Early Experiments," *The Journal of the American Medical Association* 275:12 (1996) 957–62.

[96] See Wayne J. Guglielmo, "Roping Down Managed Care," *Medical Economics* (June 23, 1997) 106–19.

[97] See Friedman, "Capitation, Integration, and Managed Care," 957–62.

consideration given to costs or efficiencies. With managed care, they can
no longer do so. This is one reason why managed care is unpopular.[98]

Attempts at Government Reform: The Clinton Proposals

In September 1993 President Clinton formally identified six goals in his
administration's healthcare reform plan: security, simplicity, savings,
choice, quality, and responsibility.[99] In order to provide all Americans with
life-long healthcare security, he proposed:

1. a system of universal coverage to be based on the existing policy
   that employers must provide health insurance for their employees;

2. government assistance to help smaller businesses to develop this
   insurance system;

3. controls over the enormous costs of healthcare;

4. that Americans would be encouraged to take more responsibility
   for their own health;

5. that consumers would have a wider choice of physicians (something that many insurance policies had not previously permitted).

The plan, which was substantially supported by the Catholic Health Association of the United States, failed to pass Congress. Residual fears
about "creeping socialism" in government again surfaced and made it
impossible for a rational debate on the critical issues of the plan to take
place. Opponents of the plan argued that further government intervention was not necessary in the health insurance market because costs
could be controlled and good quality maintained through increased, not
less, competition.[100] Republican legislators in particular refused to accept the fact that the deregulated market provision of healthcare had led
to glaringly unjust health coverage at exorbitant costs to millions of individuals and the nation.[101]

[98] See "American Health Care," *The Economist* (March 7, 1998) 14, 21–4.

[99] See Ginzberg, *The Road to Reform,* 8–11, 185–203.

[100] See Wendy K. Mariner, "Business Versus Medical Ethics: Conflicting Standards
for Managed Care," *Three Realms of Managed Care,* ed. John W. Glasser and Ronald P.
Hamel (Kansas City, Mo.: Sheed and Ward, 1997) 93.

[101] See Hal Swerissen and Stephen Duckett, "Health Policy," *Health Policy in Australia,* ed. Gardner, 34–5.

In November 1997 Clinton proposed a very modified plan, which included a "patient's bill of rights" that would allow patients to receive emergency treatment and to choose a specialist without referral and the extension of Medicare to cover any "near-elderly" who were forced into early retirement. Republicans are outraged by these proposals, alleging they will result in more government control ("creeping socialism") and excessive costs.[102]

New Zealand: Economic Rationalist Revolution

Over the last decade New Zealand has consistently received international acclaim for the boldness of its economic revolution based on the principles of economic rationalism. It has, comments *The Economist,* "transformed itself from one of the great disasters of modern macroeconomics into an object lesson in the conduct of economic policy."[103] From the mid-1980s governments have increasingly emphasized an ideology of managerialism within departments, including healthcare services, placing more stress on business skill, financial accountability, and market competition.[104] For example:

- At all levels of the healthcare system managers are to make decisions, not doctors with the assistance of nurses and administrators; boards were to be appointed from the central government and placed under the control of business managers.[105]

- The democratic involvement by locally elected hospital committees/boards and clinicians ceased, to be replaced by managerial consultants.[106]

- A quasi-market with profit objectives has been constructed in which the state, private, and community providers compete for contracts from purchasers.[107]

---

[102] See "Health Insurance," *The Economist* (December 13, 1997) 31; Walter A. Zelman, *The Changing Health Care Market Place* (San Francisco: Jossey-Bass, 1996) 170–1, 216–7.

[103] "New Labour, New Zealand," *The Economist* (November 29, 1997) 18.

[104] See Christine Cheyne and others, *Social Policy in Aotearoa/New Zealand: A Critical Introduction* (Auckland: Oxford University Press, 1997) 124–45; Michael Jones, *Reforming New Zealand Welfare: International Perspectives* (Sydney: Centre for Independent Studies, 1997); Blank, *New Zealand and Health Policy,* 67–87.

[105] See Robert H. Blank, "Health Policy," *New Zealand Politics in Transition,* ed. Raymond Miller (Auckland: Oxford University Press, 1997) 270.

[106] See ibid., 274.

[107] See Cheyne, *Social Policy,* 218–40.

• The increase in private hospitals and private health insurance is now providing significant competition with the public sector for patients and medical staff; in a small country with limited resources the question is asked: Is such competition morally beneficial for the common good?

Fundamental to the managerial and market-oriented reforms was the radical social policy paradigm shift from universal access on the basis of need to assisting only particular groups close to or in absolute poverty. Benefits for these groups should be minimal, since poverty is now assumed to be the result of individual behavior. Thus the pre-existing right to income and unemployment relief was seen to foster unnecessary dependency and financial wastage.[108] On the basis of this policy shift, hospital inpatients and outpatients were to be charged a fee (eventually rejected on account of popular protest), something unheard of since the introduction of the welfare state in the 1930s.

As earlier noted, the human cost of the reforms has been immense, causing greater poverty and widening inequalities to the extent that for the first time in over a century an identifiable socioeconomic underclass is emerging.[109] The financial costs of the healthcare services continue to rise, so that there is as yet no proof that the managerial and market reforms have achieved their goals. Comprehensive evaluation is lacking.[110]

Britain: Managerial Ideology in Action

Like New Zealand's healthcare system, the National Health Service (NHS), as it was formed in 1948, was based on the following assumptions: universal coverage, the medical model of health, the dominance of the medical profession in decision making, the centrality of the acute-care hospital, and passivity of patients.[111] When compared with the healthcare system of the United States, the NHS is expense-effective, but by the early 1980s it became clear that rising costs could not be sustained unchecked.

---

[108] See Blank, "Health Policy," 271.

[109] See Jones, *Reforming New Zealand,* 120–9.

[110] See Claudia D. Scott, "Reform of the Health System in New Zealand," *Health Care and Reform in Industrialized Countries,* ed. Marshall W. Raffel (University Park: Pennsylvania State University Press, 1997) 183–4.

[111] See Oliver Morgan, *Who Cares? The Great British Health Debate* (Oxford: Radcliffe Medical Press, 1998) 17.

The chief aim of the reforms from the mid-1980s, therefore, was to contain costs and achieve greater value for money by introducing managerial principles and competition on the supply side. Thus, the reforms introduced in Britain since 1984 are not unlike those in New Zealand:

- Business practices and managerial hierarchies were introduced into the NHS; the traditional power of clinicians to decide policy was undermined.

- Quasi-market principles were adopted. For example, the NHS was divided into purchaser and provider groups to foster market competitiveness. Doctors in general practice could opt for "general practice fundholders"; that is, they could purchase for their patients various hospital services, such as elective referrals to hospitals, diagnostic assistance, etc. The aim was to make hospital administrations and hospital-based consultants more competitively responsive to doctors in general practice or at the level of primary care.

- The development of for-profit healthcare facilities has, as healthcare analyst Joan Higgins writes, "weakened the commitment to equal access to health services for all. . . . [It] has created a change in the moral climate of health service provision."[112]

- Only the most needy were to receive welfare assistance.[113]

It is difficult at this stage to provide an accurate evaluation of the success or otherwise of these reforms. On the positive side, it is said that they promote better primary and preventive care and the medical profession is being made more accountable to the public.[114] On the negative side, however,

- the internal markets are requiring more administrative costs and more managers;

- medical professionals feel that their expertise is increasingly ignored, to the detriment of patients;[115]

[112] Joan Higgins, as cited in Norman Johnson, *Reconstructing the Welfare State: A Decade of Change* (London: Harvester, 1990) 94.

[113] See Ian Holliday, *The NHS Transformed* (Manchester: Baseline Books, 1995); Judith Allsop, *Health Policy and the NHS,* 155–97.

[114] See "Recent Trends in Health Policy: Consumerism and Managerialism." *Sociology of Health and Health Care,* ed. Steve Taylor and David Field (Oxford: Blackwell, 1997) 214–34.

[115] See Bodenheimer and Grumbach, *Understanding Health,* 207.

- the authoritarianism and centralist aspects of the reforms paradoxically run contrary to the professed liberal values of free competition and private enterprise of the New Right;[116]

- though there is much political rhetoric about the value of the reforms, there has been denial by government of the need to monitor and evaluate them;[117]

- the reforms have produced greater socioeconomic inequality.[118]

Australia: A Mixed System under Strain

Australia's healthcare system belongs to the modified market model in which health is understood as a commodity to be purchased in the way and to the level that the individual chooses. The public sector under government control guarantees to a far more significant extent than in the United States universal coverage through Medicare, but there exists a small, vocal, competitive private hospital and private health insurance system. Australia's modified market system reflects, as health policy analyst Ann Wall notes, the country's "somewhat paradoxical cultural traditions in which a strong individualist underpinning is tempered by a commitment to the values of equity, access, equality and participation."[119]

Over the years the government has been successful in containing the costs of healthcare, but now the strain is showing.[120] Medical health spending per person is growing in excess of inflation, at an average annual rate of more than 2 percent. People are fleeing private health insurance at an alarming rate. In the early 1970s about 80 percent had private health insur-

[116] See David Cox, "Crisis and Opportunity in Health Service Management," *Continuity and Crisis in the NHS,* ed. Ray Loveridge and Ken Starkey (Buckingham: Open University Press, 1992) 29.

[117] See Ray Robinson, "Introduction," *Evaluating the NHS Reforms,* ed. Ray Robinson and Julian Le Grand (Newbury: King's Fund Institute, 1993) 1; David Gladstone and Michael Goldsmith, "Health Care Reform in the UK: Working for Patients?" *Reforming Health Care,* ed. Seedhouse, 71–84; John William, *A Better State of Health: A Prescription for the NHS* (London: Profile Books, 1998) 93–194.

[118] See Vic George and Stewart Miller, "The Thatcherite Attempt to Square the Circle," *Social Policy Towards 2000,* ed. Vic George and Stewart Miller (London: Routledge, 1994) 22–48.

[119] Wall, *Health Care Systems,* 199.

[120] See Vivian Lin and Stephen Duckett, "Structural Interests and Organisational Dimensions of Health System Reform," *Health Policy in Australia,* ed. Gardner, 46–62.

ance, but today the rate is under 30 percent; this proportion has been falling at a rate of about 2 percent per year in recent years[121] simply because it is too costly, thus placing an increasing burden on Medicare services. Waiting lists for elective surgery grow by the day.

Efforts at reform based on the principles of holistic healthcare are seriously hampered by several factors. For example, the Australian Medical Association has vowed to fight any moves to bring managed care into the country because this would challenge their autonomy;[122] some critics argue that the specialist medical practitioners are fearful of losing high fees.[123] There is a powerful lobby also which continues to stress the medical model of healthcare, thus discouraging efforts to develop a more holistic approach to healthcare. Primary care issues such as health promotion, education, and particular groups (the aged, aboriginal peoples, the mentally ill) are increasingly marginalized as they lack political power to be heard. The financial savings from the deinstitutionalization of mental health patients have not been redirected to mental health services in the community. These remain gravely underfunded.[124] At the same time, economic rationalism, with its emphasis on the importance of impersonal efficiency, is becoming an increasingly influential force that may ultimately destroy the present universal insurance system.[125]

Summary

The costs of healthcare in the Western world continue to escalate at an alarming rate. Some people, including governments, have turned to economic rationalism to legitimize the introduction of a business ethos into healthcare. The worth of any provision of healthcare is then judged *primarily* by a quantifiable outcome, a "how-much-healthcare-for-the-dollar"

[121] See Heather Gardner, "Political Parties and Health Policies," *The Politics of Health: The Australian Experience,* ed. Heather Gardner (Melbourne: Churchill Livingstone, 1995) 174, 287–8; Maura McGill, "Private Care Enhances Public Good," *The Sydney Morning Herald* (November 17, 1998) 15.

[122] See Wall, *Health Care Systems,* 45.

[123] See Marion Downey, "Insurers seek US-Style Health Overhaul," *The Sydney Morning Herald* (January 30, 1997) 3; and Mike Steketee, "A Case of Greed," *The Weekend Australian* (March 7–8, 1998) 31.

[124] See Pamela Barrand, "Mental Health Reform and Human Rights," *Health Policy in Australia,* ed. Gardner, 136–53.

[125] See John Kerin, "Push for Levy Rise in Medicare Overhaul," *The Australian* (January 8, 1998) 4.

rationale. This threatens the traditional value system of healthcare. While improved management and business procedures are necessary, they must not jeopardize the rights of people to share equally in healthcare services. Thus, there are now two languages in healthcare, that of economic rationalism and the holistic ethic, and they are fundamentally at odds.[126]

In light of the contemporary turmoil in healthcare, as explained in this chapter, it is imperative that Christian reformers:

- deepen their understanding of the vision, mission, and values of the healing Jesus, which must influence all decisions in healthcare; without this understanding it will be impossible to resolve the tension between mission and business (see Chapter 5);

- recognize that a new type of leadership is needed in Christian healthcare, one that is not only knowledgeable about the mission of the healing Jesus, but professionally trained to understand the complexity of contemporary healthcare, political agendas, resource issues, rationing, and be able to communicate with their counterparts in politics and government agencies (see Chapter 6);

- recognize the seductive forces of economic rationalism and the ways in which people can unknowingly be oppressed;

- understand that marginal groups such as the elderly, migrants, people needing chronic healthcare services, etc., are especially vulnerable in today's economic rationalist climate and continue to need skilled political and legal advocates;

- appreciate that rationing, even in a holistic healthcare environment, is a complex process. There needs to be an ongoing community debate in order to develop an informed consensus on basic ethical issues. Skilled and professionally trained Christian communicators are required to work in mass media and political circles in order to be able to influence public opinion.[127]

---

[126] See Joanna Rogers and Elizabeth Niven, *Ethics: A Guide for New Zealand Nurses* (Auckland: Longman, 1996) 35.

[127] See Max Charlesworth, *Bioethics in a Liberal Society* (Cambridge: Cambridge University Press, 1993) 107–59; anonymous, "Healthcare Rationing Is Inevitable but How Should It be Done?" *Catholic Medical Quarterly* 47:1 (1996) 3–4.

Chapter 3

Christian Healthcare Ministries in Chaos

Catholic hospitals as we know them today will not be recognizable in 2010 because they will have—mostly—disappeared. That is a saddening threat only if we lack imagination—and faith.[1]

—Richard A. McCormick, S.J.

Catholic health care organizations are responding to the competitive environment in which they find themselves and are already taking steps that will sustain their mission.[2]

—William J. Cox

This chapter explains:

- briefly the contribution of Christian healthcare ministries;

- external challenges threatening the future of Christian healthcare;

- internal challenges: different theologies of healthcare within the churches;

[1] Richard A. McCormick, "Hospitals Will Vanish and Evolve," *The Catholic Standard and Times* (June 8, 1995) 7.

[2] William J. Cox, "Christian Ethics Must Counter Market Forces," *The Catholic Standard and Times* (June 8, 1995) 7.

■ the decline of religious congregations and its implications for Catholic healthcare;

■ the urgency to evaluate all healthcare ministries by the criteria of the healing mission of Jesus Christ, the priority of people's needs, and available resources.

The volume, momentum, and complexity of change in healthcare is accelerating at an alarming and turbulent rate. This is the message of the first two chapters. Since there is a massive investment by the Christian churches in healthcare, particularly in acute care hospitals, the first part of this chapter concentrates on the implications of this change for Christian healthcare ministries.

These are tumultuous and dangerous times for Christian healthcare, but the greatest danger is a temptation to deny the reality of what is happening. Serious questions must be asked: Have we become over-committed to acute hospitals? Are there more urgent ministries in healthcare today? Is the culture of business and secularism in healthcare so powerful that it is wiser to direct our evangelizing resources elsewhere? Have we become so successful as business operations that we have lost our prophetic voice? My task is not to answer these questions but to highlight their urgency.

The second part of this chapter analyzes theological divisions in the churches themselves that threaten their ongoing commitment to healthcare. The Catholic Church's involvement in healthcare in particular faces an uncertain future. Religious congregations have traditionally been the primary carriers of the founding myth of healthcare. Their rapid decline, however, means that lay people must increasingly assume this responsibility. Are religious congregations adequately preparing for this transition? What structural and formation changes are necessary to guarantee this transition? I do not answer these questions immediately but focus on their relevance.

Christian Healthcare: Contribution to Society

The Christian Churches have made and continue to make an enormous contribution to healthcare in many countries. The following examples, with particular reference to the Catholic Church as a representative organization, demonstrate some aspects of their success in the United States, Canada, and Australia.

The United States

The Catholic Church sponsors more than 1200 healthcare systems, facilities, and related organizations. It supports the largest network of non-government, non-profit hospitals and nursing homes in the United States, serving over forty million people annually. Twelve of the top non-profit healthcare systems are Catholic. Analyst Arthur Jones estimates that the network produces annually thirty-two billion dollars in revenue, approaching the yearly gross domestic product of Ireland. The majority of Catholic healthcare facilities are owned by women; in fact, Catholic healthcare is the largest industry owned and run by women in the world.[3]

Christian substance-abuse programs are estimated to have a 70 to 80 percent success rate, whereas secular therapeutic programs report an average success rate of only 6 to 10 percent.[4]

Canada

The Catholic Church's involvement in healthcare in this part of North America goes back to the seventeenth century. In 1998 there were seventy-eight Catholic hospitals.[5] The level of involvement in healthcare by the Church is evident in its commitment to the province of Ontario, where there were thirty hospitals. Over thirty thousand people are employed in its healthcare ministry there, and its hospital sector accounts for $1.3 billion of the $7.5 to $8 billion spent on healthcare in Ontario.[6] Catholic hospitals are publicly funded and are run by semi-autonomous boards.

---

[3] See Arthur Jones, "Special Catholic Healthcare Report," *National Catholic Reporter* (June 16, 1995) 11–12.

[4] See Amy L. Sherman, "Cross Purposes: Will Conservative Welfare Reform Corrupt Religious Charities?" *Policy Review* 74:2 (1955) 58.

[5] Information supplied by Richard Haughian, Catholic Health Association of Canada; see also Michel Martin, "Catholic Hospitals Strive to Retain Religious Focus in an Increasingly Secular Country," *The Canadian Medical Association Journal* 148:1 (1993) 64–6.

[6] See Catholic Health Association of Ontario, *Brief to the Harris Government* (Toronto: CHAO) (June 26, 1995) 1.

Australia

The Catholic Church is the largest provider of non-government health-care services in the country. It sponsors fifty-eight hospitals, of which thirty-eight are privately operated and twenty-two are public. The public hospitals are owned by a diocese or a religious congregation, funded by state governments, and open to all. The boards and CEOs of these public hospitals are appointed by their owners.

In addition the Church directs many other ministries, e.g., five hundred aged-care services, involving seventeen thousand nursing home and hostel beds, hospices, primary and community care facilities, medical research institutes.[7]

Healthcare: Continued Involvement Questioned

There is growing concern that the churches cannot or should not continue to be involved in medical institutions, at least in their present form. Fr. Richard McCormick, S.J., moral theologian at Notre Dame University, writing about the future of Catholic hospitals in the United States, concludes that "the mission has become impossible,"[8] so great is the chaos that confronts them. He believes inter alia that Catholic hospitals have uncritically absorbed cultural aspects of the wider society:

> [Our healthcare institutions] reflect our American culture more than they reflect the fulfillment of a religious mission. The fact that we survive as . . . [institutions] only by limiting the percentage of Medicaid patients we treat— not to mention the severe limits on cost-free care—reminds us that we are fundamentally woven on the loom of United States, with its political and societal priorities, traditions, and patterns.[9]

William Cox, executive vice-president for government services of the USA Catholic Health Association, is more hopeful in the quotation heading this chapter about the future of Catholic healthcare organizations in the United States, but the tone of his observations is cautious. Catholic health-care, he comments, is needed, but it will survive into the next century only

---

[7] Information provided by Francis Sullivan, Executive Director of the Australian Catholic Health Care Association.

[8] Richard A. McCormick, "The Catholic Hospital Today: Mission Impossible," *Origins* (March 16, 1995) 649.

[9] Richard A. McCormick, *Health and Medicine in the Catholic Tradition* (New York: Crossroad, 1987) 76.

on two conditions: that Catholic healthcare leaders are managerially competent and that they have the "capacity to respond to today's markets with creative fidelity to the best in the Catholic tradition and community."[10]

Christian Healthcare: External Challenges

Why are McCormick and others skeptical about the future of Christian healthcare services, in particular hospitals? One can identify external and internal challenges that make it difficult, if not impossible at times, to carry on the mission of healing based on Christian values, at least in traditional ways. While I mainly focus on the United States' experience, much that is said can be applied elsewhere.

The following external challenges impacting on Christian healthcare is not exhaustive, and although I arrange them as separate items, in fact they are often interrelated (see Figure 3.1).

Complexity of Moral Issues

In the turmoil of contemporary healthcare, the greatest challenge, writes Joseph Califano (former secretary for health under President Carter), "may be to deal with the . . . ethical and moral issues that medical science serves up almost daily. Nowhere does our nation's inventiveness pose a greater challenge to civilized society with moral and ethical standards than in the arena of biomedical research."[11] Over the last few years Faustian dreams have entered the world of practical reality. Scientists are coming close to enhancing or decreasing all kinds of genetic odds. They will eventually be able to manipulate genes to improve scientific skills, athletic ability, and physical beauty. Some form of genetic engineering, possibly cloning, may be able to replace mating as a controlled manner of making humankind. The impossible becomes possible.

Califano rightly asks, "Do we have the ethical, moral and legal geniuses to prevent genetic clinics from becoming little shops of horror?"[12] Postmodernism does not make answering this question any easier. Through its denial of any universal truths it rejects also the possibility of ever finding unchallengeable criteria for judgment.

---

[10] Cox, "Christian Ethics," 7.

[11] Joseph A. Califano, "The Dangers of Discovery," *America* (January 14, 1995) 8.

[12] Ibid.

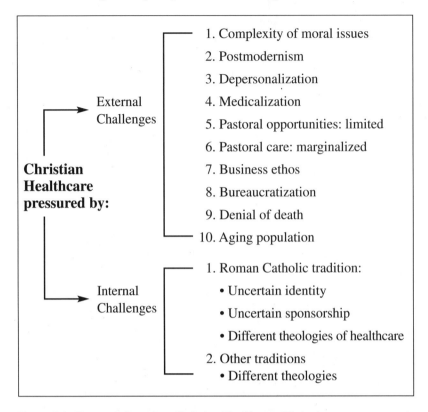

Figure 3.1: Factors Influencing Christian Healthcare Ministries

Thomas Shannon, a professor of religion and ethics, writes that bioethics "examines the ethical dimension of technology, medicine, and biology in their application to life."[13] It covers an area that is essentially broad. This, says Shannon, "is what makes bioethics as a discipline complex and exciting. It means that a revolution in thinking is called for. . . . Bioethics is teaching us the necessity of genuine interdisciplinary thinking and working."[14] Praxis-oriented biomedical research is urgent, but often it is beyond the resources of individual healthcare systems. In 1978 the United States Congress created the President's Commission for the Study of Ethical Problems in Medicine and Biomedical and Behavioral Re-

---

[13] Thomas A. Shannon, *An Introduction to Bioethics* (New York: Paulist Press, 1997) 4.

[14] Ibid., 4–5.

search.[15] The Australian government established a similar committee in 1988 to advise it on bioethical issues that might have a bearing on public policy.

These developments are fine, but the churches will need to enter this complex field more vigorously to ensure that public debate and policy respect the basic principles of the healing mission of Jesus Christ. By and large, however, the Churches seem reluctant to join the wider public debate. This is certainly the case in Britain.[16] Why this hesitancy? Have the churches lost their prophetic commitment? Some explanation emerges in the following section.

Postmodernism

As explained in Chapter 1, the Revolution of Expressive Disorder which marked the coming of the age of postmodernism in the late 1960s and early 1970s attacked traditional moral and cultural boundaries.[17] Not surprisingly, the role of the Churches in healthcare came under public attack: their commitment to universal moral values made them an easy target for the advocates of postmodernist morality.

Philosopher Alasdair MacIntyre claims that postmodern societies have no concept of virtue, of what it means to lead a healthy life or die a good death, because they do not agree to a common set of values on which an ethics of behavior can be built.[18] This is especially evident in the area of medical ethics. The Christian churches in their stand on the dignity of the human person and the sacredness of life before and after birth are increasingly isolated by society at large. Medical personnel can be particularly hesitant to join Catholic facilities fearing they will lose access to patients because of the limitation of reproductive services as a consequence of the Church's moral teaching.[19]

[15] See Kevin D. O'Rourke and Dennis Brodeur, *Medical Ethics: Common Ground for Understanding* (St. Louis, Mo.: Catholic Health Association of the United States, 1987) 19.

[16] See Charles Miles, "The Genetics Revolution," *The Tablet* (January 14, 1995) 38.

[17] See Gerald A. Arbuckle, *Earthing the Gospel: An Inculturation Handbook for the Pastoral Worker* (Maryknoll, N.Y.: Orbis Books, 1990) 119–27.

[18] See Alasdair MacIntyre, *After Virtue* (Notre Dame, Ind.: University of Notre Dame Press, 1981) 238–45.

[19] See David M. Semple, "From Ministry to Market," *Health Progress* 77:5 (1996) 21.

As a consequence of the postmodern revolution, therefore, questions such as the following are asked: Why should the churches be in healthcare at all when their values conflict with the values of society? What right do they have any longer to insist on a common set of ethical imperatives to be accepted by clinicians, staff in general, and patients?

Depersonalization of Healthcare[20]

The growth in medical technology threatens to weaken or destroy the personal relationship between clinicians and patients. Jerome Kassirer, editor of *The New England Journal of Medicine,* comments:

> These [technological] trends are likely to induce cultural changes in the delivery of care even more revolutionary than any restructuring that is going on today. On-line, computer-assisted communication between patients and medical data bases, and between patients and physicians, promises to replace a substantial amount of the care now delivered in person.[21]

Medical staff already feel that the development of managed care (see Chapter 2) is also eroding the traditional personal relationship between themselves and their patients. The sense of frustration is expressed by Ellyn Spragins, commenting on the American scene: "The revolution [in establishing HMOs] that has already shunted 53.3 million people from Marcus Welby—style medicine into the Wal-Mart model of health care [i.e., a supermarket model] will convert an additional 50 million by the turn of the century."[22] While some clinicians in the United States,[23] New Zealand, and Britain feel that the medical profession should be more accountable to outside evaluation, others believe this is interfering with their rightful independence to develop personal relationships with patients.

From a Christian perspective personalized healthcare and medical accountability are essential (see Chapter 5). But this raises critical questions for Christian ministries, particularly in acute hospitals: Is it possible to

---

[20] In this analysis I am particularly indebted to McCormick, "The Catholic Hospital Today," 649–50.

[21] Jerome P. Kassirer, "The Next Transformation in the Delivery of Health Care," *The New England Journal of Medicine* 332:1 (1995) 52, cited by McCormick, "The Catholic Hospital Today," 649.

[22] Ellyn Spragins, "Does Your HMO Stack Up?" *Newsweek* (June 24, 1996) 56.

[23] See McCormick, "The Catholic Hospital Today," 650.

resolve the tension today between these two qualities? If Christian institutions cannot resolve the tension should they withdraw from further involvement in healthcare?

Medicalization of Healthcare

Particularly through the influence of the medical profession and its emphasis on the biomedical model, healthcare services are dominated by the acute care hospital where technological resources are concentrated.[24] Huge sums of money are spent in the name of medical progress in hospitals, with only marginal improvements to the overall health of a nation. As explained in Chapter 1, most observers conclude that recent improvements in health in developed countries are due to better living standards and changes in lifestyle.

In the United States, of the 680 hospitals sponsored by the Catholic Church, 560 are acute care, making up 10 percent of the nation's total, and containing 14 percent of its acute care beds. Its commitment to the nursing home and residential care ministry is similarly impressive, but the question arises: Is the Catholic Church, given its large involvement in acute care hospitals, being seduced by the culture of the biomedical model when it should be giving more time, energy, and finance to other ways of improving health?[25]

Decline in Pastoral Care Opportunities in Acute Hospitals

Traditionally acute care hospitals allowed the churches to provide holistic pastoral care for patients over an extended period of time, but this is no longer the case. Technological improvements in healthcare have substantially lessened the time patients stay in hospitals today. For example, in the 1940s patients entering the hospital for myocardial infarction remained there for five to seven weeks, but today stay for only five to seven days. Groin hernia operations required a stay of about six weeks in the 1940s, about five days in 1985; today they require a one-night stay or are performed as out-patient surgery.[26] Acute care hospitals are a diminishing

[24] See Thomas McKeown, "A Historical Appraisal of the Medical Task," *Medical History and Medical Care,* ed. George McLachlan and Thomas McKeown (Oxford: Oxford University Press, 1971) 30.

[25] See Jones, "Special Catholic Healthcare Report," 11.

[26] See Myfanwy Morgan, "Hospitals, Doctors and Patient Care," *Sociology as Applied to Medicine,* ed. Graham Scambler (London: W. B. Saunders, 1997) 70.

focus of healthcare: in the United States in 1985, 25 percent of surgery was undertaken in day surgeries, but today that is now over 75 percent. In Australia in 1985/86 the average length of stay in hospitals was 6.6 days; in 1993/94 this figure had fallen to 4.4 days.[27]

Given these trends, it is not surprising that the late Cardinal Joseph Bernardin urged Catholic healthcare providers "to leave behind their attachment to acute care institutions and to forge a new future in the world of community-based networks."[28]

Marginalization of Pastoral Care

Christian pastoral care has been defined as

> that activity within the ministry of the Church which is centrally concerned with promoting the well-being of individuals and of communities. The ultimate aim of pastoral care is that of ministry as a whole, i.e. to increase love between people and between people and God. Its specific functions are healing, sustaining, reconciling, guiding and nurturing.[29]

Pastoral care as defined is far broader than the traditional ministry of a chaplain, which mainly focused on the administration of the sacraments to the sick and dying. However, the ministry of pastoral care is often marginalized within a hospital culture. When the biomedical model of healthcare is over-emphasized, pastoral care's focus on holistic health is seen as an anachronism. Economic rationalists, when faced with the need to cut costs in hospitals, either reduce the funding for the pastoral care departments or refuse to pay for them in the first place. In this atmosphere it is difficult for pastoral care to be taken seriously.[30]

Business Management Ethos

The introduction of business management processes such as productivity measures, marketing, strategic planning, cost-analysis systems, is es-

---

[27] See Marilys Guillemin, *A Woman's Work Is Never Done: The Impact of Shifting Care Out of Hospitals* (Melbourne: Health Issues Centre, 1997) 13.

[28] Cardinal Joseph Bernardin, "The Catholic Moment," *Health Progress* 76:1 (1995) 25.

[29] Stephen Pattison, *Pastoral Care and Liberation Theology* (Cambridge: Cambridge University Press, 1994) 14.

[30] See Lindsay Carey and others, "Health Policy and Well-Being: Hospital Chaplaincy," *Health Policy in Australia,* ed. Heather Gardner (Melbourne: Oxford University Press, 1997) 190–210.

sential for healthcare institutions. Good stewardship requires their use, but they must always be subordinate to Gospel values such as justice, compassion, mercy (see Chapter 5). However, given society's often excessive emphasis on the techniques of business management, it is possible that Christian-based services can be unwittingly corrupted by the values of economic rationalism.[31] This can come about in the following ways.

Unnecessary Competition

There needs to be competition, but not in a way that is contrary to an identity as a values-based institution. Unnecessary competition exists when Christian institutions refuse to collaborate in order to make the best use of limited resources. For example, Catholic sponsors have competed needlessly against each other at considerable cost to win contracts for healthcare facilities. Collaboration could have provided a better service to the public.

The Catholic archdiocese of New York undertook a feasibility study to see if the majority of their health providers could unite into one single delivery network for the best advantage of patients. Patricia Cahill, who was involved in this study, was saddened by what she found:

> I think the basic destabilizing truth . . . is that Catholic sponsors don't trust one another, and that sentiment also finds expression among the managements and medical staffs of our institutions and agencies. There is a great fear of giving something up to one another on the one hand and the almost naive willingness to cut the same deal with a non-Catholic entity. . . .[32]

CASE STUDY

Misunderstanding the Congregational Charism

In an American town two hospitals owned and administered by different religious congregations were in financial difficulties. Efforts to merge the facilities failed because one congregation claimed that their particular

---

[31] See George J. Annas, "Reframing the Debate on Health Care Reform by Replacing Our Metaphors," *Three Realms of Managed Care,* ed. John W. Glasser and Ronald P. Hamel (Kansas City, Mo.: Sheed and Ward, 1997) 92–104.

[32] Patricia Cahill, "Collaboration among Catholic Health Providers," *Origins* 24:12 (1994) 213.

charism must be preserved at all costs. The founder, it was said, would have wanted this. Their hospital was eventually forced to close but the other congregation was able to merge its hospital successfully with a Baptist hospital, to the benefit of the town.

In this case study the religious of the congregation that refused to merge their hospital, believing this would go against their founder's wishes, misunderstood the meaning of their founder's charism. Biblically a charism is a gift of God "to be used for the general good" (1 Cor 12:7), that is, for building the Christian community. In religious congregations we speak of the "charism of the founder," or the founding experience, that is, a gift of the Spirit transmitted to their founder's followers to be lived, to be preserved, deepened, and constantly developed in harmony with the mission of Jesus Christ. A true charism is always reflective and creative, stimulating people to find new ways to express its inner mission.[33] It is not a gift exclusively for the members of a religious congregation. The healing mission of Jesus Christ has priority and all charisms must serve this purpose. The congregation which refused to collaborate for fear of "losing its charism" failed to realize this biblical truth.

Uncritical Acceptance of Management Language

In recent times the language of non-profit healthcare administrations has changed significantly in favor of business management; for example, heads of hospitals are no longer "matrons," but "chief executive officers." Basil Mott, dean of health studies, University of New Hampshire, warns that there is a seductiveness about the new jargon of business and corporate cultures: "To caricature the scene, some of us may take an 'ego-trip' in the world of entrepreneurship and high finance, drawn by the glamour of the corporate office and the corporate jet whisking us around as we build new corporations and service networks."[34] He is concerned about the uncritical use of language antithetical to the values of service and caring. Un-

[33] See Antonio Romano, *The Charism of the Founders* (Middlegreen: St. Paul's, 1989).
[34] Basil J. Mott, "Whither the Soul of Health Care?" *The For-Profit Hospital,* ed. Richard M. F. Southby and Warren Greenberg (Columbus, Ohio: Battelle Press, 1986) 144.

less healthcare people are careful they can be seduced into adopting the competitive and patriarchal assumptions of management jargon: "I speak of such abstract and tough talk as strategy, tactics, market penetration, and product realignment—jargon that depicts a world of winners and losers, a macho world that is like war. It isn't a language that evokes the values of serving and caring for human beings."[35]

Some seduction has taken place. In the United States the rapid rise of hospital costs following the introduction of Medicare and Medicaid caused non-profit hospitals to cut back significantly on charity care; they introduced tight management practices aimed at budgets, expenditures, and surpluses. Many now resemble the for-profit hospital systems, so that their historic philanthropic mission has been seriously undermined, a point made earlier in this chapter by Father McCormick.[36]

Research: Uncritical use of Business Models

Research into hospitals by the York University Centre for Health Studies in the province of Ontario, Canada, found:

- Business practices are not necessarily efficient and effective; in fact, they can be more harmful than helpful.

- Hospital workers disliked substituting the word "customer" for "patient" because people in hospitals have little choice about being there and can rarely act as a customer is expected to act, simply because they lack the information to make choices about treatments.

- Care-givers objected to being told to use the expression "have a nice day" to patients; as hospitals now contained only the sickest people, wishing them a "nice day" seemed nonsensical.

- There is little examination of whether production-management techniques are really suited to hospitals; their introduction is often ideologically-led.[37]

---

[35] Ibid., 145.

[36] See Eli Ginzberg, *The Road to Reform: The Future of Health Care in America* (New York: Free Press, 1994) 28.

[37] See Jane Coutts, "Business Theory Seen as Failure in Hospitals," *The Globe and Mail* (May 9, 1966) 6A.

In one Catholic healthcare system a draft strategic plan consisting of seven chapters relegated the vision, mission, and values to chapter five. The business consultants were surprised when the wary trustees asked that chapter five be moved to chapter one, commenting, "Get the business up and running, then we can worry about the mission." They assumed that business and mission are separable.

Management: Priority over Leadership

The business management ethos, if adopted without question, will stifle what is most urgently needed in healthcare today, namely, leadership in the midst of the complexity and chaos. The primary task of the manager is to prevent the complexity of a modern organization degenerating into total chaos; they take details like financial planning, quality control, staffing, and market research, and then give them order and consistency. For managers, systems and structures are all, and change is not integral to their role. The transforming leader, however, challenges the status quo to face up to change in the environment; the manager bows to the status quo.[38]

But a word of warning. Transforming leaders need systems and structures behind them under the direction of some gifted managers, otherwise the leaders do not have the necessary space and time to clarify a much-needed vision for the group. Management *and* leadership, therefore, are necessary, but in the chaotic atmosphere of healthcare the second has priority and management exists to serve it (see Chapter 4 for a fuller explanation).[39]

Ignoring Valuable Expertise

CASE STUDY

Misplaced Arrogance

On one occasion I was asked to lecture in the United States to a particular statewide association of healthcare providers. On arriving in the auditorium to prepare mate-

---

[38] See Stephen Covey, *The Seven Habits of the Highly Effective People* (New York: Simon & Schuster, 1990) 101; John P. Kotter, *A Force for Change: How Leadership Differs from Management* (New York: Free Press, 1990) 3–18.

[39] See Gerald A. Arbuckle, *Refounding the Church: Dissent for Leadership* (Maryknoll, N.Y.: Orbis Books, 1993) 101–3.

rial for the lecture, I was approached by a representative of a nationwide for-profit healthcare organization who commented: "It is time non-profits realized that they have no expertise to be in healthcare. We will eventually 'do them in!'" This type of comment about the supposed lack of business efficiency of non-profit healthcare services has been so frequently repeated that people uncritically accept it. In a national survey in the United States, 59 percent felt for-profit hospitals were more efficient, compared with 34 percent favoring non-profit hospitals.[40]

The perception by the speaker in this case study of the overall inefficiency of non-profit healthcare facilities is incorrect. It is not uncommon for religious congregational leaders to share this perception. They hand over their authority to lead and to question business practices to consultants and others who have little or no sense of the founding vision, mission, and values of the healthcare institutions. Yet religious have no reason to develop an inferiority complex in business matters, because their predecessors built their healthcare facilities with brilliant business acumen and faith. History can repeat itself. I replied to the gentleman in the above case study: "You seem to have a rather simplistic view of history. Look around you. Who built these vast building complexes, beginning with the most slender of financial resources?" He saw the point.

Secularization

"Secularization" can connote "the preoccupation with factors peripheral to and distractive from holistic human care (competition, liability, government controls, finances),"[41] or substituting a business ethos for the values of healthcare as a humane service. Father McCormick identifies instances of this when physicians, for example, act as business people, picking and choosing whom they will serve on the basis of their own financial interests; or drop objective moral standards, being prepared "to do the patient's bidding for a price."[42]

[40] See Jane Hiebert-White, "Market Transformation: Will Not-for-Profit Providers Survive?" *Health Progress* 77:3 (1996) 10.

[41] McCormick, "The Catholic Hospital Today," 650.

[42] Ibid., 650.

Secularization can also mean a process by which sections of a culture are removed from the control or influence of religious institutions. This has happened in Canada. In Canada in 1968 there were 230 Catholic hospitals, but by 1998 the figure had dropped to 78. The most significant reason for this decline from the 1960s was the greater commitment by the provincial governments to providing their own healthcare facilities. Christian hospitals lost a significant degree of autonomy, particularly in the Quebec province (the number of Catholic hospitals in the province dramatically dropped from eighty-seven in 1968 to only one in 1998), because under Medicare (established in 1966) all hospitals were to be publicly funded. In these circumstances sponsors, such as religious congregations, long accustomed to their independence, are confronted with challenges never envisioned when their facilities were first established.

Bureaucratization

An ever-growing number of institutions, such as local and national governments, insurance companies, consulting firms, and managed care organizations, may be involved in any particular healthcare facility at the same time. Now "contractualism" is popular: in countries such as Britain, Australia, and New Zealand governments restructuring public hospitals (some managed by the churches) contract with private agencies to run various internal services.[43] While these different agencies may focus on the needs of patients, they have needs of their own which can conflict with those of patients. Considerable skills in cultural, organizational, and political analysis and theological reflection are needed in leaders to ensure that the rights of the patients are truly being served.

Denial of Death

Ernest Becker believes that there is in each one of us a deeply rooted denial of mortality: "The idea of death, the fear of it, haunts the human animal like nothing else; it is a mainspring of human activity . . . [which] is designed largely to avoid the fatality of death, to overcome it by denying in some way that it is the final testing of man."[44] The cultures of Western

---

[43] See Jonathan Boston, "The Limits to Contracting Out," *The State under Contract,* ed. Jonathan Boston (Wellington, N.Z.: Bridget Williams, 1995) 78–111; Kenneth L. Vaux, *Health and Medicine in the Reformed Tradition* (New York: Crossroad, 1984) 128–31.

[44] Ernest Becker, *The Denial of Death* (New York: Macmillan, 1973) ix.

societies reinforce this inner denial by further camouflaging death in its many expressions. In a kind of planned obsolescence death is being systematically removed from our consciousness through all kinds of cover-up rituals (see Chapter 9 for further explanation).[45] The healthcare culture has become one of the rituals through which mortality can be denied. Daniel Callahan, an ethicist, observes:

> Our toughest problem is not that of a need to ration health care. . . . It is that we have failed, in our understandable eagerness to vanquish illness and disability, to accept the implications of an insight available to all: We are bounded and finite beings. . . . We have tried to put that truth out of mind in designing a modern health care system, one that wants to conquer all diseases and stay the hand of death.[46]

The biomedical model of healthcare is itself a powerful culture encouraged by the medical profession and society to protect us from our most primitive fears and fantasies of death (as will be explained more fully in Chapter 4).[47] This culturally-supported denial of death (which will be further explained in Chapter 9) raises a critical question for Christian healthcare: Do their facilities collude in, and contribute to, this escapism?

Example: Colluding in Denial of Death

In 1991, about thirty-four billion dollars, or 28 percent of Medicare's budget in the United States, was spent on people in their last year of life. Sixteen billion dollars were spent in the final sixty days of a person's life. These statistics would suggest an over-treatment of some people at the expense of others in need.[48]

---

[45] See Gerald A. Arbuckle, *Grieving for Change: A Spirituality for Refounding Gospel Communities* (Westminster: Christian Classics, 1991) 43–58.

[46] Daniel Callahan, *What Kind of Life: The Limits of Medical Progress* (New York: Simon & Schuster, 1990) 23; see also McCormick, "The Catholic Hospital Today," 652.

[47] See Anton Obholzer, "Managing Social Anxieties in Public Sector Organizations," *The Unconscious at Work: Individual and Organizational Stress in the Human Services*, ed. Anton Obholzer and Vega Z. Roberts (London: Routlege, 1996) 171.

[48] See Thomas S. Bodenheimer and Kevin Grumbach, *Understanding Health Policy: A Clinical Approach* (Stamford, Conn.: Appleton & Lange, 1995) 183.

Aging Population

In Western democracies populations are aging.[49] For example, in Australia in 1981, 9.8 percent of the population was over sixty-five years of age, but by 2011 an estimated 13.8 percent will be over that age, increasing to 20.3 percent by 2031. In these countries, where youthfulness is exalted and aging is presented as a social problem, many elderly people are unhappy to be talked about as though they were unable to decide matters for themselves and to have things done for them, rather than with and by them.[50] An attitudinal revolution in thinking and action is necessary. Elderly people are forming political movements, such as the Gray Panthers and the National Council of Senior Citizens in the United States, to pressure governments to be involved in decisions that concern them.[51] Many elderly, however, lack collective support.

In the United States retirees account for about 40 percent of the national health bill, the dependent elderly requiring the most assistance. Governments struggle to cope with the holistic needs of this group with varying degrees of success. Rarely is there a consistently worked out policy, particularly in relation to the elderly poor. It has been claimed that in the United States "in possibly thousands of cases, nursing-home residents are dying from a lack of food and water and the most basic level of hygiene."[52] In Australia and New Zealand, as a result of their governments' economic rationalist planning, the financial burden of caring for the elderly must be carried increasingly by poorer sections of the population. People who most need nursing-home care either have to be cared for at home by families already under financial strain or occupy beds in acute care hospitals because they have nowhere else to go.[53]

---

[49] See William A. Mundell and Jack Friedman, "A Low Price for Better Health Care," *The New York Times* (June 22, 1997) 13.

[50] See Terry Smyth, *Caring for Older People* (London: Macmillan, 1992) 11–45.

[51] See Ken Tout, "The Aging Perspective on Empowerment," *Empowering Older People: An International Approach,* ed. Daniel Thursz and others (London: Cassell, 1995) 11–35; John McCallum and Karin Geiselhart, *Australia's New Aged* (St. Leonard's: Allen & Unwin, 1996) ix, 15–33.

[52] Mark Thompson, "Fatal Neglect," *Time* (October 27, 1997) 22; see also Chris Hackler, "Health Care Reform for an Aging Population," *Health Care for an Aging Population,* ed. Chris Hackler (New York: State University of New York, 1994) 1–13.

[53] See Sue Macri, "Aged Care Reforms: A Provider's Perspective," *Australian Seniors* 1:1 (1998) 15–16. The Australian government permitted private health insurance funds to drop palliative care from their hospital policies. The Catholic Health Association

Although churches have long responded to the needs of the dependent aged, for example through aged-care facilities, with the declining government assistance countries such as Australia find it difficult to maintain these services. However, they can still educate the public so that people do not see the elderly as a social problem, but as a resource to be collaborated with in building a just and healthy society. Father McCormick argues with good reason that in the United States the Catholic Church should increasingly direct their investment away from acute care hospitals to long-term home care and hospice care: "We are an aging population, and health care needs of such a population cry out for a helping hand far more than a cutting scalpel."[54]

Christian Healthcare: Internal Challenges

The philosopher Alfred North Whitehead observed that the major changes "in civilization are processes which all but wreck the society in which they occur."[55] Christian healthcare could be wrecked if the churches do not acknowledge the ministerial implications of the external pressures described above. Internal influences at work in Christian healthcare could also destroy the achievements of the past. I explain what is happening with particular reference to the Catholic Church, and then summarize theological trends in other churches that have implications for healthcare ministries.

Catholic Church in Turmoil: Impact on Healthcare Ministries

Before the Vatican Council II the American Catholic Church was "the best organized and most powerful of the nation's subcultures—a source of both alienation and enrichment for those born within it and an object of bafflement or uneasiness for others."[56] As in the United States, so it was for Catholics in many other parts of the world. While they had certain symbols in common with other citizens, many pivotal symbols and myths

---

condemned this as a "strategy by the funds to reduce their outlays and get members who won't draw on their insurance." See Francis Sullivan as reported in *The Sydney Morning Herald* (April 11, 1997) 6.

[54] McCormick, "Hospitals Will Vanish," 7. See comments by Julia T. de Alvarez, "Hearts and Minds: Elder Empowerment," *Empowering Older People: An International Approach,* ed. Daniel Thursz and others (London: Cassell, 1995) 105–9.

[55] Alfred N. Whitehead as cited by Daryn R. Conner, *Managing at the Speed of Change* (New York: Villard Books, 1993) 3.

[56] John Cogley, *Catholic America* (New York: Image, 1974) 135.

that gave meaning, identity, and security to their lives came from their adherence to the Church subculture.

Catholic hospitals developed in the United States, Canada, Australia, and New Zealand, as did the schools, in response to the needs especially, but not exclusively, of Catholic immigrants. Existing hospitals were seen to be in reality Protestant and, as Professor Charles Rosenberg recounts, "all-too-often proselytizing institutions."[57] By 1885 the Church had opened 154 hospitals in the United States, more than had developed in the country overall in the late 1860s.[58] Catholic hospitals, unlike many Protestant hospitals, had little endowment for support and had to depend on payments by patients and/or on the free services of doctors.[59]

Catholic hospitals, as with facilities of other denominations, were commonly divided into private and public. In private hospitals patients paid for services and their payments supported the charity care given the indigent in the public wards. Doctors would commonly use the private hospitals as their source of revenue and then provide free services to the poor in the public wards.

The average hospital began to resemble a traditional parish, sometimes with its own priest-chaplain and a good-sized chapel for Catholic services and morning and evening prayers. The hospital's main concern was for the health of the individual patient—especially for the soul. There was a strongly visible presence of religious sisters or brothers in the main administrative positions, a rigidly hierarchical model of administration, and a public display of papal photographs and blessings.[60]

There was no mission statement. It was not needed, as the purpose of a Catholic hospital was clear for all to see and experience: to be compassionate to the physically and mentally sick and to make sure the sacraments were readily available to them when needed. The religious providers of healthcare had little or no direct involvement in issues of social justice, because this was not considered integral to the mission of the Church. As for ethical problems, they were reasonably simple and people could find ready-made answers by referring to a moral theologian in a local seminary or in a textbook of moral theology.

---

[57] Charles E. Rosenberg, *The Care of Strangers: The Rise of America's Hospital System* (Baltimore: Johns Hopkins University Press, 1987) 111.

[58] Ibid.

[59] Ibid.

[60] See Christopher J. Kauffman, *Ministry and Meaning: A Religious History of Catholic Health Care in the United States* (New York: Crossroad, 1995) 3.

Fr. Bryan Hehir, professor at Harvard Divinity School, describes the development of this model of healthcare in the United States:

> Catholic healthcare [before Vatican II] . . . was driven by an ecclesial impulse to heal, to teach, and to serve, and by a social impulse to serve specifically the needs of the Catholic community. We feared that this community would not be well instructed in a total vision of life or well cared for if we did not create our own institutions.[61]

This is no longer the model for Catholic healthcare. In a Catholic hospital today one commonly finds places for ecumenical services, an ecumenical pastoral team of male and female chaplains, an ethics committee regularly confronted with moral problems unimaginable in the 1950s, religious rarely—if at all—present, laity at all levels of administration, and an office of mission effectiveness. The trustees may still be members of a religious order, but their major concern will be to maintain the Catholic identity of the facilities when their congregation ceases to exist. Why the dramatic change in so short a time?

Vatican II catalyzed a theological and cultural paradigm shift that has influenced Catholic healthcare ministries ever since. This radical change has helped to "wreck" the pre-Vatican II culture of the Church. For centuries the Church had become an inward-looking culture: anti-world, defensive, personal piety-based, highly stratified, authoritarian, and rule-oriented, but the council articulated a mythology challenging the existing culture to its very roots, with revolutionary implications for all ministries.[62] The council emphasized the need for a ministry of holistic healthcare involving the commitment to social justice, a preferential option for the poor, a servant model of leadership, direct involvement of laity in the apostolate of healing, dialogue with cultures of other healthcare systems, and dialogue and collaboration with other Christian traditions or beliefs.

Cultural Impact of Vatican II: Implications for Healthcare

Sociologist Peter Berger comments that Catholics back in 1961, unlike their Protestant brothers and sisters, "still seemed to be sitting pretty on their Rock of Peter," secure in their numbers and in the allegiance of the

---

[61] J. Bryan Hehir, "Identity and Institutions: Catholic Healthcare Providers Must Refashion Their Identity," *Health Progress* 76:8 (1995) 19.

[62] See Arbuckle, *Earthing the Gospel,* 15–16, and Arbuckle, *Refounding the Church,* 18–20.

faithful. Within one year of the council's end, however, Catholics suffered the same fate as other Christian denominations: they were rushing to find "plausible lifeboats with the rest of us."[63] Theologian Fr. Avery Dulles, S.J., wrote in 1981 that the Roman Catholic Church "seems, for the first time in centuries, to be an uncertain trumpet."[64]

The chaos that resulted from Vatican II was inevitable. The reality is that when the founding myth of a culture is disrupted, even for the best of intentions, cultural chaos is bound to result and the Church is no exception. The council had challenged Catholics to break out of their ghetto culture in order to confront the world with Christ's healing mission of justice and love, but after centuries of isolation they were unprepared for this confrontation. It would have been difficult to relate to the world at any time, but just when the Church was opening its windows the world was in the midst of the intensely disruptive postmodernist revolution. The effects of the combined impact of the council and this revolution were traumatic for many believers; their meaning system, the coherent and well-integrated world-view of a ghetto Church, collapsed with remarkable suddenness.

Out of the chaos have emerged at least four cultural models of Church, each with a different approach to the ministry of healthcare, as the following summaries indicate.[65]

Model 1: The Restorationist Church

In this model people seek the *re*-establishment of a pre-Vatican II, monocultural, Rome-centered Church, and theological orthodoxy rather than pastoral creativity. Jesus is presented as king and judge of a people who "break the rules," not as one who has come to liberate cultures and peoples from oppression. Evangelization is concerned with the conversion of the soul, not with the whole person and a healthy society based on principles of social justice. Catholic identity in this model is sharply defined, as it was in the pre-Council era.

Application to Catholic Healthcare Ministries: Services such as hospitals are to stand alone, with minimal interaction with non-Catholic institutions or personnel. Religious congregations must retain their distinctiveness, so mergers of institutions of different religious orders are to be avoided. Only

---

[63] Peter L. Berger, *Facing up to Modernity: Excursions in Society, Politics and Religion* (Manchester: Penguin, 1979) 228.

[64] Avery Dulles, *The Resilient Church: The Necessity and Limits of Adaptation* (New York: Doubleday, 1981) 11.

[65] See Arbuckle, *Refounding the Church,* 67–97.

lay Catholics would be allowed to assume key administrative roles, provided congregational members are unavailable to do so. Decision-making in institutions is from the top down, consultation being seen as having no theological foundation. Efforts are to be made to turn hospitals into quasi-parish structures, with an emphasis on the conversion of patients to the Catholic faith. Healthcare is about restoring individual patients to good health—especially their souls—not about the struggle for justice in the wider society or the removal of those external/structural forces that cause people to be ill.

Model 2: The Vatican II Church

This way of being a Catholic is a balance between the hierarchical and the collegial values of the council. It assumes that the Holy Spirit is in all members of the Church and in peoples of other beliefs. The decision-making groups in the Church must listen to what the Spirit is saying in all peoples and events. God is Jesus the Incarnate One, the God who has become one with us through the incarnation and yearns to share his vision with humankind, a message of liberation from oppression within ourselves and society.

Catholics are called to critique oppressive structures and together struggle for a just society, the very struggle being itself the sign of the fullness of the kingdom to come. The message of hope is directed especially to the marginalized, those without power to control their own lives. In this sense, health is not synonymous with individual well-being, but with a just society.[66] Leadership is characterized by collaboration, dialogue, and interdependence in decision-making. This way of being Catholic requires a high tolerance of ambiguity as people continue to grapple with the pastoral implications of their faith within a changing world.

Application to Catholic Healthcare Ministries: This model recognizes that Catholic healthcare facilities are no longer Catholic in the pre-Vatican II institutional sense, but rather community hospitals supported by and serving people who are often non-Catholic. Staff members, including senior management, are not necessarily Catholic. Healthcare under Catholic inspiration is inextricably involved in complex relationships in a changing world. There is acceptance of the fact that the Church must minister and evangelize within a pluralistic society; this demands collegial searching to clarify what Catholic

[66] See comments by Richard A. McCormick, "Not What Catholic Hospitals Ordered," *America* (December 11, 1971) 511–3.

identity means in pluralistic organizations. Catholic identity "is a process and, as such, it has no ultimate answers, only questions that each organization must work through according to the dictates of persons, circumstances, mission, and values."[67] It is definitely not an uncritical return to the symbols of the pre-Vatican II Church's role in healthcare.[68]

In this model Catholic healthcare "providers will be part of networks and will often be in a position of influence, but not control."[69] Providers will clarify in a collaborative way what is at the heart of Catholic identity—the vision, mission, and values of the healing Jesus—and expect employees to respect this identity. People who have appropriate gifts of leadership and a living commitment to values fundamental to the healing Jesus, and to the social and ethical teachings of the Church, will be appointed to administrative positions. They need not be Catholic or members of a religious congregation. In order that institutions be called "Catholic," however, the approval of the appropriate ecclesiastical authorities is needed.

Model 3: The Accommodation Church

Catholics, while possibly still being church-goers, uncritically adopt cultural values in conflict with Gospel/tradition imperatives, such as individualism, competitiveness, and authoritarianism. They choose "comfortable" doctrines and practices that do not challenge the secular culture. Such Catholics have no heart or passion for Gospel values; in fact, they can—even while claiming to be Catholic—obstruct those who actively adhere to these values. Sermons and church publications may reinforce this way of being Catholic, for example, by exhorting people to serve others not primarily because of Christ's example but to make them "feel good." New Age alive in the sanctuary!

Application to Catholic Healthcare Ministries: From the early 1970s this type of Catholicism was rapidly on the increase, certainly in the United States,[70] and today it is very popular. One survey in the late 1980s

---

[67] Anonymous, "How to Approach Catholic Identity in Changing Times," *Health Progress* (April 24, 1994) 6.

[68] See Peter Steinfels, "Catholic Identity: Emerging Consensus," *Origins* 25:11 (1995) 176.

[69] Consolidated Catholic Health Care, *Critical Choices: Catholic Health Care in the Midst of Transformation* (Oak Brook: CCHC, 1993) 65.

[70] See William C. McCready and Andrew M. Greeley, "The End of American Catholicism," *America* (October 28, 1972) 334–8.

found that 54 percent of Catholic men and 41 percent of Catholic women believe that one can be a good Catholic without obeying the Church on abortion.[71]

Catholics in this category, especially if they are in positions of authority, like board members and CEOs, are grave obstacles to developing a Vatican II identity in healthcare services. There is a serious split between their public, even boisterous, commitment to the institutional Church (generally understood as the power model of the pre-Vatican II Church), and their behavior. They are individualistic and authoritarian and with little or no concern for social justice. The philosophy of economic rationalism is more acceptable to them than that of the healing mission of Jesus Christ. For them the bottom-line is the dollar, though they may verbally pay respects to the "sacred traditions of the founders" of the healthcare facility. Mission leaders in healthcare facilities are merely tolerated and they are marginalized from significant involvement in decision-making.

Model 4: The Protest Church

This way of being Catholic applies to three groups of people: those who cannot accept restorationism and yearn for a Vatican II Church, those who cannot tolerate restorationism and may have ceased to be actively involved in contemporary Church structures, and those who are not formally Catholic but hold in practice to fundamental Gospel values and the social and ethical requirements of the Catholic Church. The three groups have in common a commitment to several fundamental values of the healing Jesus—justice, compassion, mercy, charity, unity—and their practical implications.

Application to Catholic Healthcare Ministries: This way of being Catholic is common among care-givers in healthcare facilities who have been drawn with a sense of mission to the sick and yearn to share their vision with others. Many are suspicious of, or alienated from, the institutional Church claiming it has lost empathy with the poor and marginalized, such as HIV/AIDS patients. These people respond positively to scriptural reflections, especially to the healing incidents of Jesus, and to the development of base or intentional communities which nourish their apostolic work, but may not have significant contact with the institutional Church.

---

[71] See William D'Antonio and others, *American Catholic Laity in a Changing Church* (New York: Sheed and Ward, 1989) 66.

Religious Congregations in Chaos: Implications for Healthcare

I have explained elsewhere the causes for the chaos in religious congregations and the startling decline in recruits,[72] but the following is a summary of the most significant factors.

Prophetic action is at the very heart of the founding of religious life, that is, the call to live the radical values of the gospel. Over the last few centuries religious congregations had tended to drift away from the prophetic foundations of religious life and by way of substitute had developed a mythology based on three assumptions: the world is evil and to be avoided; religious are the spiritual elite of the Church; their task is to be uncritically supportive of the ecclesiastical and pastoral status quo.

When the council challenged these three assumptions and the culture that had developed out of them, many religious lost their sense of purpose in the subsequent chaos. With the council restating that all, including the laity, are called to holiness, religious could no longer assume that they were the spiritual elite in the Church. When reminded that the world is not evil in itself and that all are called to listen to the Spirit in the hearts and cultures of people, religious could no longer flee the insecurities and tensions of the world around them. Religious congregations have yet to recover. In fact, most existing congregations can now expect to die.

All this is mirrored in the present state of healthcare ministry in the Church. In 1965 13,618 women religious staffed over 800 hospitals in the United States[73] and laity rarely held administrative positions. But by 1992[74] 81 percent of Catholic hospital CEOs and 51 percent of Catholic system CEOs were lay people. In Canada in 1967 there was a total of 61,942 women religious, but by 1990 this had dropped by 47 percent and the decline continues dramatically.[75]

Many religious, as the following case study illustrates, have used the chaos resulting from the council to ask themselves questions about their future ownership and governance of healthcare ministries.

---

[72] See Gerald A. Arbuckle, *Strategies for Growth in Religious Life* (New York: Alba House, 1986) 3–22; Gerald A. Arbuckle, *Out of Chaos: The Refounding of Religious Congregations* (New York: Paulist Press, 1988) 65–86; Gerald A. Arbuckle, *From Chaos to Mission: Refounding Religious Life Formation* (Collegeville: The Liturgical Press, 1996) 27–32.

[73] See Kauffman, *Ministry and Meaning,* 273.

[74] See Semple, "From Ministry to Market," 23.

[75] See President's Task Force on Ownership, *Sponsorship of Catholic Health Institutions in Ontario* (Toronto: Catholic Health Association of Ontario, 1991) 9–15.

CASE STUDY ▮▮▮▮▮▮▮▮▮▮▮▮▮

Healthcare Providers Question Themselves

In the United States in 1990, participants at an assembly of a religious congregation committed to the healthcare ministry recorded their conclusions. Fourteen years later their questions remain relevant to all congregations engaged in healthcare.

We recognize that healthcare has changed dramatically and we could never again, even if we had the numbers, run our hospitals alone. Now we must ask ourselves these questions:

- How will the mission of Christ continue when we cease to exist or are so few that we must confine our ministry to being trustees only, remote from the action of healing?
- Is ownership of our healthcare institutions alone sufficient to guarantee that the mission will continue?
- What will happen to the mission and ministry when there are no religious even to be trustees?
- What formation assists executives to be effective leaders in Christian healthcare ministry?
- What will happen to the Catholic healthcare culture when a significant percentage of the staff are not Catholics or of no religious faith at all?
- What are the essential qualities of Catholic identity in the post-Vatican II Church?
- Is it time for committed and informed laity, not just to be co-ministers with us in healthcare, but to become sponsors of our institutions, with structures in place to guarantee that Catholic identity of these facilities be maintained?

The assembly agreed that it was necessary to understand the meaning of "sponsor" before they could take practical steps to hand their facilities over to laity.

In this case study the participants recognize at least three critical realities that have relevance to all congregations in healthcare:

(1) Today religious in healthcare find themselves "part of a medical-industrial complex where technology, bonds, marketing, government intervention, and third party reimbursement are as much a driving force as Jesus' beatitudes."[76] Even if there were large numbers of recruits to religious life no congregation could ever again have the resources of qualified personnel to cope with the contemporary complexity of healthcare.

(2) Lay people through baptism have the right to be involved in the healing mission of Jesus Christ. If religious do not train and entrust their institutions to them the mission will most likely die with them, if not before, and healthcare facilities will be Catholic in name only. In the United States I once visited a hospital owned by a religious congregation which had become well-known locally for its excellent medical technology. I left sad, because I concluded that the only thing Catholic about the place was its name! The congregation during the period of its withdrawal from the hospital had failed in its duty to form laity for their ministry.

(3) In order to involve lay people appropriately in the healthcare ministry there is need to understand the terms "sponsor" and "sponsorship." The expressions connote something more than the ownership of facilities. Sponsorship means *governance or leadership to protect what is cherished and to maintain its identity intact.* The task of governance is to establish an organization's purpose and to develop policies to promote this end.[77] In Chapters 4 and 6 I explain the kind of leadership required to protect and further Christ's mission of holistic care, and in Chapter 7 I further clarify the meaning of sponsor.

Other Christian Theological Traditions: Impact on Healthcare

There are many other theological traditions influencing healthcare in addition to that of the Roman Catholic Church; it is impossible to do them justice here. However, I think three broad theological views of healthcare can be identified:[78]

---

[76] Margaret M. Modde, *The Search for Identity: Canonical Sponsorship of Catholic Healthcare* (St. Louis: CHA, 1994) vii.

[77] See Mary K. Grant, "Sponsorship Challenge: Influence through Governance," *Health Progress* 57:1 (1986) 38.

[78] See Arbuckle, *Earthing the Gospel,* 21–4.

Healthcare Focus: "Horizontal" Social Justice

Healthcare is concerned only with the struggle for the just restructuring of society so that individuals can exercise their rights to medical care, employment, housing, etc. Its relationship with the transcendent is not important. I call this the "horizontal" approach to healthcare because the "vertical" relationship with God is unimportant.

This view, held in the late 1960s by some theologians such as Gibson Winter and Harvey Cox, eliminates the transcendent aspect of the healing mission entirely and simply makes salvation and or holistic healthcare synonymous with the pursuit of social justice.[79]

Healthcare Focus: Conversion of the Soul

The mission of the healing Jesus is the personal inner conversion of individuals: someone is in good health if he/she relates personally in faith to God. Conversion is primarily about turning the soul to God. Concern for social health, that is, the just society, is secondary. The world in fact is so evil that the possibilities of its redemption are remote.

Many contemporary Evangelicals with strong foundations in biblical reflection and commitment to the person of Christ, such as Billy Graham, accept this view: social justice within cultures is important, but it is not a priority of the mission of Jesus Christ.[80] Back in 1964, an influential Evangelical preacher, Jerry Fallwell, did not want Christians to be involved in social justice/political action, condemning the civil rights activism of liberal preachers: "Preachers are not called to be politicians but to be soul winners. Our only purpose on this earth is to know Christ and to make him known."[81]

In 1979 Jerry Fallwell and other Evangelicals changed, accepting that on certain issues Christians must become involved in direct political action. And so was established the Moral Majority—a movement directly aimed at influencing the holistic health of the nation. However, its focus of concern has tended to be narrow, sticking to anti-abortion and anti-euthanasia campaigns. Historian Leonard Sweet comments that Evangelicals in the United States have proved themselves to be "the least prepared to vote to pay taxes for programs designed to provide better alternatives to

---

[79] See Ronald J. Sider, "Five Conflicting Viewpoints," *International Review of Mission* 64:255 (1975) 255.

[80] See Arbuckle, *Earthing the Gospel,* 21.

[81] Jerry Fallwell, *Strength for the Journey* (New York: Simon & Schuster, 1987) 290.

abortion or to support the needs of children through . . . guaranteed health and educational opportunities."[82]

Under the influence of the Charismatic/Pentecostal revival movement in the 1970s and 1980s, many Evangelicals recognized that there are diverse gifts of the Holy Spirit. It was then seen as wrong to stress the gift of calling souls to salvation without also directly attacking unjust structures. Every congregation will include people with various gifts; some have the talent to call individual souls to salvation and others have the grace to be involved directly in the struggle for a healthy and just society.

Healthcare Focus: Holistic Mission

The mission of Christ is holistic; that is, it is directed at the conversion of the whole person and the just restructuring of society. Good health is not to be confined to the struggle for wholeness in this life only, but includes in faith and hope the vision of justice and charity in the world to come. According to Professor Kenneth Vaux of Chicago University this view is in accordance with the Calvinist or Presbyterian tradition which "fosters a strong commitment to human advocacy and a call for comprehensive and edifying care for persons. . . . [The] spirit is not . . . radical individualism. . . . We are given to mutual care in covenant communities because we are all caught in the tragedy and delight of life together."[83]

Within the Anglican tradition over the last century groups have developed with a strong practical commitment to Christian Socialism, which is the belief that people must work together and not in competition, and that social justice is a Gospel imperative. This conforms to the fundamental thrust of Vatican II. Gillian Paterson, education secretary in the Churches' Commission on Mission of the Council of Churches for Britain, having shown that the traditional medical model of healthcare is no longer credible, writes that holistic health is the "product of a just and loving environment, just as disease can be a symptom of one that is inadequate." She continues:

> The healer is God. The role of the health professional is to alleviate, as far as possible, those factors which cause disease. . . . These may be cancers, viruses and fractures; but they are just as likely to be poverty. . . . Holistic healing . . . is a three-way partnership, involving the one in the patient role,

---

[82] Leonard I. Sweet, *Health and Medicine in the Evangelical Tradition* (Valley Forge, Pa.: Trinity Press International, 1994) 110.

[83] Vaux, *Health and Medicine,* 129.

the one in the healer role, and God. . . . Theologically, such an approach takes seriously the logic of the incarnation.[84]

The more recent official documents of the World Council of Churches (WCC) seem to accept this view of healthcare. The WCC's position has changed over the years; during the 1960s there was a tendency toward the "horizontal" social justice focus described above. The preparatory statement for the WCC's Fourth Assembly at Uppsala in 1968 emphasized the secularized approach to good healthcare: "We have lifted up humanization as the goal of mission."[85] At times, official statements seem to underplay the reality of personal sin, the call to radical conversion, and the final realization of justice and health in the world to come. However, in a 1982 document[86] on mission and evangelism from the WCC, the emphases, for example on sin and conversion and liberation of people from unjust structures, resemble closely some themes of Vatican II and subsequent social documents from the Vatican and episcopal conferences. The Roman Catholic tradition markedly diverges nonetheless from several Christian denominations on certain moral issues of holistic health, such as abortion and euthanasia.[87] Though there are many different views on these topics within the WCC and the Anglican tradition, the Catholic Church finds support in its pro-life stand from many Evangelical groups.

Summary

The Christian healthcare ministry, particularly through hospital services, has become successful beyond the wildest dreams of its founders, but now,

---

[84] Gillian Paterson, *Whose Ministry? A Ministry for Health Care for the Year 2000* (Geneva: WCC, 1993) 46–7. Also see Report of the Archbishop of Canterbury's Commission on Urban Priority Areas, *Faith in the City: A Call for Action by Church and Nation* (London: Church House, 1985) 61–70; and David J. Bosch, *Transforming Mission: Paradigm Shifts in Theology of Mission* (Maryknoll, N.Y.: Orbis Books, 1991) 368–510.

[85] WCC Fourth Assembly as cited by Sider, "Five Conflicting Viewpoints," 255.

[86] See World Council of Churches, "Mission and Evangelism: An Ecumenical Affirmation," *International Review of Mission* 71:284 (1986) 438; also Priscilla Pope-Levison, "Evangelism in the World Council of Churches," *International Review of Mission* 77:344 (1998) 95–107.

[87] See Conference of Bishops of the United States, "Ethical and Religious Directives for Catholic Health Care Services," *Origins* 24:27 (1994) 249–62; and John Paul II, Encyclical *Evangelium Vitae, Origins* 24:42 (1995) 689–727.

like healthcare everywhere, it is in chaos. Problems include ever-increasing costs, the administrative burden of coping with rapid changes in medical technology and funding sources, increasingly complex bioethical challenges, the pastoral implications of the medical model of healthcare and the decline of acute care hospitals, the for-profit motivation in healthcare, the impact on the poor of today's powerful economic rationalism.

For Catholics there are added challenges. Since Vatican II Catholic identity is no longer so clearly defined. Religious congregations, which had become the primary carriers or "sponsors" of the mission of Christ, especially in hospital cultures, are in rapid decline. Now lay people must assume their baptism-based right to be carriers of this mission.

Little wonder that Christians ask the question: Is the world of healthcare now so complex that it is impossible any longer to find ways to witness to the healing message of Christ? Some feel that we must concentrate only on the conversion of the soul and not the physical and social sicknesses.

Others believe that the healing message of Christ is holistic, that no matter how daunting the challenges we can find even radically new ways to minister to the whole person and society. That is, they accept that refounding is an imperative of the Gospel: "For the love of Christ urges us on, because we are convinced that one has died for all" (2 Cor 5:14; NRSV).

This means opting for vitality in ministry over chaos and entropy and for consciously driven change under appropriate leadership, which is at the heart of the creative transformation of Christian healthcare (see Chapter 4). Every existing ministry must be evaluated by the criteria of the healing mission of Christ, available resources, and the priority of people's needs. At times this may mean giving up long-cherished and successful ministries such as acute care hospitals. In refounding we learn to put the future ahead of yesterday.

Part II

Refounding Christian Healthcare

Chapter 4 ▰▰▰▰▰▰▰▰▰▰▰▰▰▰▰▰▰▰

Culture, Chaos, and Leadership in Healthcare

Change [in healthcare] has become so rapid, so complex, so turbulent, and so unpredictable that it is sometimes called simply chaos.[1]

—W. Jack Duncan and others

The true objective is to take the chaos as given and learn to thrive on it. The winners of tomorrow will deal proactively with chaos. . . . Chaos and uncertainty are . . . opportunities for the wise.[2]

—Tom Peters

This chapter explains:

- how the findings of modern physics and applied anthropology can help healthcare workers better understand the type of leadership required in the contemporary industrial turmoil;

- that chaos can lead to dysfunctional behavior in healthcare organizations;

- that chaos can also be the catalyst for radical creativity; provided leadership is exercised appropriately.

---

[1] W. Jack Duncan and others, *Strategic Management of Health Care Organizations* (Oxford: Basil Blackwell, 1995) 9.

[2] Tom Peters, *Thriving on Chaos: Handbook for a Management Revolution* (New York: Alfred A. Knopf, 1987) 176.

- that the tension between "mission" and "business" can be creative;
- that biblically, chaos connotes both danger and opportunity.

At no previous stage of history have healthcare institutions been confronted by a more turbulent, threatening, or chaotic environment—and the situation will not ease. That is the theme of the last two chapters of this book. The healthcare professional must be both a creative strategist and a manager of organizational cultural chaos.

This chapter clarifies the dynamics of organizational cultural chaos in healthcare ministries and the leadership skills required to manage it positively. These issues are approached from the perspectives of two different disciplines—modern physics and applied cultural anthropology. It will be seen that the practical conclusions of these two branches of knowledge are similar in a significant respect; namely, that chaos destroys routine and predictability and forces us to choose and to act. With the right leadership the experience can be the occasion for radical personal and cultural change. The chapter ends with an analysis of chaos as a pivotal biblical symbol.

"Chaos Theory" and Healthcare Leadership

Traditional Physics and Chaos

Traditional explanations of organizations are founded on Newtonian classical physics. Isaac Newton (1642–1727) depicted a clockwork universe governed by a set of immutable laws, a model that continues to the present day to shape perceptions of reality. The philosopher John Locke (1632–1704) believed that there are laws of nature controlling human society similar to the laws described by Newton as directing the physical world. Words that best describe the Lockian ideal society are: stability, predictability, equilibrium, order.

For Newton and Locke, relationships must be seen as linear; that is, each unit can act independently, no matter what other influences are occurring. Many processes follow linear paths, for example, the melody from a flute and its piano accompaniment. In other words, each unit in the system acts separately, even when they intermix. Mathematically, if we add three to five we expect to have eight. In the short term, linear or two-factor relationships can explain a good deal of what happens; for example, the weather forecast for tomorrow is usually accurate, but beyond that weather systems are normally unpredictable. We lack methods to unravel the complex forces that affect long-term weather systems.[3]

A manager's role in a healthcare organization traditionally has been determined by the assumptions of Newton and Locke. The primary task of healthcare managers is to make decisions that foster and maintain orderly relationships, and this requires that managers have the right information available.[4] Excellent managers have above-average skills of prediction and planning and the preferred model of leadership is hierarchical, with every member in the organization knowing exactly what is expected. Information moves upwards; planning decisions are made at the top and communicated downwards in a controlled manner. The organization's structure must mirror the ideal reality—that which is controlled, orderly, and predictable. Whatever is confused, disorderly, or chaotic is "unnatural" and is to be considered dangerous to the survival of the organization.

Contemporary Physics and Chaos

Contemporary physics now assumes, contrary to Newtonian thought, that the universe is not a machine, but one indivisible whole, the parts of which are essentially interrelated in a cosmic process.[5] Most relationships in physics are non-linear, that is, irregular, capricious, messy, unpredictable. Traditional orthodox science simply cannot make sense of such relationships, but through quantum physics all kinds of bizarrely fluctuating things, such as populations of animals, bubbling pots on a stove, or malaria epidemics, can begin to make sense. Systems are inherently unstable.[6] But systemic instabilities are not random, because there is a pattern within them based on ordering principles termed "strange attractors." There is such complexity in these "attractors" and systems themselves that they are not fully understood.

In brief, the struggle by scientists to understand complexity has resulted in what is popularly known now as "chaos theory," which is broadly defined as "the science of process rather than state, of becoming rather than

---

[3] See Bernice Cohen, *The Edge of Chaos: Financial Booms, Bubbles, Crashes and Chaos* (Chichester: Wiley, 1997) 81.

[4] This section draws on the insights of Reuben R. McDaniel, "Strategic Leadership: A View from Quantum and Chaos Theories," *Health Care Management Review* 22:1 (1997) 21–37.

[5] See Cohen, *The Edge of Chaos*, 94.

[6] See "Tilting at Chaos," *The Economist* (August 15, 1992) 705; and "Balancing Broomsticks," *The Economist* (June 25, 1994) 85.

being . . . [resulting in] a science of the global nature of systems."[7] It attempts to understand complexity which arises from nonlinearity, interdependence, motion, and form; complexity that involves the mixing of symmetry with asymmetry, predictable periodicity with unpredictable variation, order with disorder.[8]

Example: Medical Application of Chaos Theory

While physics cannot predict what will happen in nature, it nonetheless can open up ways to control the world. One technical application of chaos theory in medicine is the explanation of heart fibrillation. When the heart begins to flutter as a result of a mechanism that is explicable in chaos terms, a defibrillator gives it a good push with an electric shock to disrupt the chaotic process and set it right again.[9]

Chaos Theory and Management

Though scientists have mainly been concerned about chaos from the perspectives of physics and biology, their approach can be applied to human relationships which are both complex and non-linear. Traditional management assumes the world is knowable provided we get enough facts, but management based on the insights of chaos theory assumes that the world of human relationships can never be fully understood. Corresponding leadership styles will be different. The following is a summary of chaos theory and its implications for leadership in contemporary healthcare. Chaos theorists, drawing on quantum physics, conclude that:

(1) The world is fundamentally unknowable: It is impossible to predict the future behavior of a system, especially in the long term, no matter how well the present state of the system is known.

(2) The world consists of systems: Every organism from the smallest bacterium to a human is an integrated whole and a living system, inter-

---

[7] James Gleick, *Chaos: Making a New Science* (New York: Penguin, 1987) 5.

[8] See Addie Fuhriman and Gary M. Burlingame, "Measuring Small Group Process: A Methodological Application of Chaos Theory," *Small Group Research* 25:4 (1994) 504.

[9] See Padric P. McGuiness, "Out of Chaos Could Come Order," *The Australian* (January 23, 1990) 11; and Mark Buchanan, "Fascinating Rhythm," *New Scientist* 157:215 (1998) 20–5.

dependent and interrelated; relationships between components are more important in the nature of a system than the components themselves.

A system is a set of interrelated elements; that is, a change in one element influences other elements. In fact, very small differences in initial conditions can lead to large differences in the future state of a system.[10]

The movement of change is not smooth, but lurching, and its necessary impetus is stress. At certain points, changes may amplify into disturbances so profound and deep that the system breaks apart, but may reconfigure itself at a higher, more complex level.

Such reconfiguring or self-renewing systems are resilient rather than stable, maintaining themselves not through rigidity but through adaptation. The breakdown or "bifurcation" point is the moment when extraordinary things occur. Instead of deterministically moving down a set path, the system makes a radical shift. At the level of elementary particles, this is called a "random moment"; in people it is a "creative choice." At this bifurcation point, the system recreates itself into a pattern ungoverned by the past. A new future begins. Nobel Prize winner Ilya Prigogine concludes we must let go the Aristotelian insight of past, present, and future being on a straight line: "Time is creation, the future is just not there."[11]

Chaos Theory: Implications for Healthcare Leadership

Possibly the most valuable insight for contemporary strategic leaders in healthcare today is that if organizations are to survive and grow, leaders must abandon any fixation with control and stability; the struggle to know with certainty what is happening in complex systems; and the assumption that one person alone can achieve meaning in chaos. Following are practical guidelines for leaders from this insight.

Guideline 1: Think in Systems. Systems thinking recognizes that all aspects of an organization are interrelated or connected in a thoroughly complex network. Touch one relationship and all are affected to some degree. The weather system is a helpful metaphor. The weather is driven by nonlinear forces: minute changes in air pressure in one part of the world, perhaps started by a butterfly flapping its wings, may reverberate through the system to cause hurricanes in a distant part of the world. Leaders, therefore, will foster within their organizations relationships that are collaborative

[10] See McDaniel, "Strategic Leadership," 25.

[11] Ilya Prigogine as cited by Marjorie Kelly, "Taming the Demons of Change," *Business Ethics* (July–August 1993) 6.

and interdependent in order to ensure that problems are dealt with before they affect the entire system.

The following case study of an incident in a hospital illustrates the impact of the so-called "butterfly effect,"[12] in which tiny changes in a system greatly escalate with ever-widening negative consequences.

CASE STUDY

The "Butterfly Effect" Ignored

A small country hospital where employees were not members of trade unions employed a rural health researcher but had initial difficulties in finding an office for her in the most appropriate position. Eventually the CEO arranged with the pharmacy department for office space, as the pharmacy had several unoccupied rooms available. However, after several months the department's manager demanded for no legitimate reason that the researcher leave her office within three days. When the researcher asked to meet with the manager she was refused, as also was the request to extend occupancy for a few more days to allow for time to find other accommodations. Late that evening, within hours of the decision, the manager broke into the office and removed everything belonging to the researcher, including private and research files, and deposited them at various points in the building.

The CEO, on hearing of the incident, remonstrated with the manager, but took no further action, telling the researcher to forget the incident and find an office elsewhere. The researcher, however, refused to do this, claiming that her human rights of privacy had been violated. The action, she said, had effectively marginalized her as a person and member of the hospital staff. Grudgingly the CEO arranged for the property to be restored to the researcher and another office was found for her.

As the months passed, the "butterfly effect" became obvious as the incident began to impact on the entire hos-

[12] See Gleick, *Chaos*, 22.

pital system and beyond. Out of fear the CEO consistently refused to ask the manager for an apology, and eventually turned the blame for the incident onto the victim herself. Individuals who came to the aid of the researcher were condemned for "interfering in matters that had nothing to do with them." As word spread about the incident, the CEO's credibility among hospital employees began to disintegrate. Every time he spoke in public addresses about the need to respect the core values of the hospital (namely, justice, mercy, compassion, and concern for the marginalized), he was greeted with cynicism and anger. Patients remarked on a drop in morale in the hospital. One patient wrote to the congregational leadership congregation in Rome complaining about "the poor spirit that has crept into the hospital; and that something must be done about it." A small group of employees supported the CEO and refused to cooperate with those who kept requesting that the manager apologize to the researcher. After many months, the board of directors, who also had lost credibility for failing to act earlier, finally asked the CEO and the manager to resign.

These consequences of the violation of the researcher's office would not have occurred if the CEO had understood the requirements of justice and had appreciated the interconnectedness of systems.

Guideline 2: Foster Participative Decision-Making. Leaders who think in terms of systems will understand that they cannot grasp the meaning of what is happening by themselves and will foster as wide a participation in decision-making as is possible. As Margaret Wheatley, a management expert in the application of chaos theory to leadership, says: "Participation, seriously done, is a way out from the uncertainties and ghostly qualities of this nonobjective world we live in. We need a broad distribution of information, viewpoints, and interpretation if we are to make sense of the world."[13] The following case study illustrates what can happen when this advice is not taken.

[13] Margaret J. Wheatley, *Leadership and the New Science: Learning about Organization from an Orderly Universe* (San Francisco: Berret-Koehler, 1992) 64. See also

CASE STUDY ▰▰▰▰▰▰▰▰▰▰▰▰▰▰▰▰▰▰▰▰▰▰▰▰▰▰▰▰▰▰

Participation Neglected

A CEO of a large hospital decided that a new and more efficient method of serving meals to patients should be introduced. Previously, unskilled labor had been employed to approach each patient personally to obtain meal preferences, but this was seen as too costly. The CEO decided that the meals should be prepared with the advice of the dietitians alone, and then distributed with as much speed as possible to patients. The employees were dismissed.

Following the introduction of this cost-saving method patients began to complain. The CEO was puzzled. He could not understand why people were dissatisfied when they were now receiving meals more efficiently prepared and without having to talk to staff. He failed to think in systems terms. If he had asked the patients and the employees, he would have discovered that the latter were appreciated, not primarily for their distribution of meals, but for their willingness to spend time daily chatting with the patients. Nurses were too busy for this human interaction. Patients were prepared to put up with meals imperfectly arranged on trays because they looked forward to the personal interaction with the food distributors. If the CEO had consulted the patients and the staff he would have avoided the problem.

▰▰▰▰▰▰▰▰▰▰▰▰▰▰▰▰▰▰▰▰▰▰▰▰▰▰▰▰▰▰

Guideline 3: Recognize What Is Unknowable. As the unfolding of the world over time cannot be known with certainty, strategic leaders cannot control long-term development of their organizations. Commenting on the

---

Duncan, *Strategic Management,* 14–17; Ralph D. Stacey, *The Chaos Frontier: Creative Strategic Control for Business* (Oxford: Butterworth-Heinemann, 1993) 153–230; Edgar E. Peters, *Chaos and Order in the Capital Markets* (New York: Wiley, 1991); Torsten H. Nilson, *Chaos Marketing: How to Win in a Turbulent World* (Maidenhead: McGraw-Hill, 1995) 19–61; Michael L. Heifetz, *Leading Change, Overcoming Chaos* (Berkeley, Calif.: Ten Speed Press, 1993) 99–132; Susan M. Campbell, *From Chaos to Confidence* (New York: Simon & Schuster, 1995) 197–225.

implications of chaos theory, Reuben McDaniel refers to "gatekeepers" in contemporary health maintenance organizations in the United States:

> [The] emerging roles of primary care providers as gatekeepers in health care are reshaping the patterns of behavior among physicians and between primary care physicians and hospitals. Strategic leaders [in healthcare] cannot control [any longer] the direction of these new patterns of behavior and, therefore, cannot determine the future state of physician-hospital relationships.

McDaniel argues that no matter how successful or unsuccessful former managerial practices were in shaping positive physician-hospital relationships, "the new situation is indeterminate and the strategic leader is not in control."[14]

Guideline 4: Value Diversity and Conflict. Creativity can flourish in an atmosphere of instability because customary ways of thinking and acting are questioned. Strategic leaders will thus welcome chaos in healthcare environments as an opportunity to innovate. Yet in order to make use of chaos, there must be diversity of thinking, and this means cultivating conversations between people of different professional backgrounds within the organization. Then there is hope that the organization will find suitable ways to use the chaos creatively.[15] Strategic leaders see even conflict as potential for creativity, when skills exist to focus not on personalities but on issues.[16]

Guideline 5: Recognize Vision and Values as "Strange Attractors." Charles Handy writes that "chaotic and energetic but uncontrolled organizations can exhibit movement without meaning unless they have found their strange attractor, which gives them point and purpose." He says that some "have called this the 'soul' of the organization." He believes that "the principal task of leadership [is] to find the strange attractor which will give meaning to movement, and around which a field of trust can be built which will allow the organization to devote most of its energies to its product instead of to its own entrails."[17]

The "strange attractors" in healthcare organizations are their vision, mission, and values, which provide the rationale for all decision-making

---

[14] McDaniel, "Strategic Leadership," 25.

[15] Ibid., 30–1.

[16] See Alison Morton-Cooper, "The Politics of Health Care," *Excellence in Health Care Management,* ed. Alison Morton-Cooper and Margaret Bamford (Oxford: Blackwell, 1997) 227–8.

[17] Charles Handy, "Unimagined Futures," *The Organization of the Future,* ed. Francis Hesselbein and others (San Francisco: Jossey-Bass, 1997) 381.

and inspirational energy for change. The task of leaders is to keep people focused on them and the changing healthcare environment.

Culture Shifts and Chaos in Healthcare

This section looks at chaos from the perspective of cultural anthropology. Contemporary healthcare literature calls for radical change. We read of the need for healthcare overall to move from the emphasis on illness in planning to a focus on wellness. To move from an illness to a wellness priority necessitates a massive organizational cultural shift, but other equally challenging cultural transformations are expected to be undertaken at the same time as Figure 4.1 indicates. Likewise profound cultural changes are necessary in hospital organizations themselves if they are to survive and be competitive. This means they must organizationally shift from a mechanistic to an organic culture model of acting (see Figure 4.2).

Thomas Burns and George Stalker explain the dramatic nature of this cultural turnabout.[18]

In *organic* cultures the focus is not primarily on rules and regulations; the emphasis is on innovation, creativity, and evaluative feedback in order that the organization may keep responding adequately to a changing environment. Leaders foster a collaborative atmosphere in which people feel they can create and be supported by others in the group.

Decision-making is primarily proactive rather than reactive to crisis solving. That is, organic administrations consist of "anticipative people"; as they see changes about to happen they plan ways to adapt to them, recognizing the need to create and control change rather than being its passive agent.

In *mechanistic* cultures, on the other hand, the tasks of the organization are considered predictable or unchanging; the leader's role is to ensure that these long-established and neatly set-out rules of operation are being followed. Creativity is unnecessary and is to be discouraged because it threatens a predictable way of acting. Until recent times hospital cultures needed to be fundamentally mechanistic; since their primary task was to care for patients there was little need for creativity. But the mechanistic culture model is totally unsuited for today's healthcare emphasis on curing, efficiency, and competition.

These culture shifts in healthcare in general and in hospitals inevitably cause organizational chaos simply because too much change is expected to occur in short periods of time. Organizations and people suffer change-

---

[18] See Thomas Burns and George M. Stalker, *The Management of Innovation* (Chicago: Quadrangle Books, 1961).

overload, but the cultural and personal implications of this are rarely referred to in the literature on healthcare management. The popular but false assumption is that cultures, like machines, can be changed easily.[19] Consultants who believe this—and there are many—are tantamount to "witch doctors" or "makers of magic"[20] in healthcare, because, like their counterparts in pre-modern cultures, they offer unfounded panaceas to anxious managers trapped in the chaos of change. Their advice fails, and managers turn to other consultants for quick-fix solutions to cultural problems. But they fail and other consultants are hired, and the cycle continues.

Culture Shifts:
Movements in Healthcare Today

from an illness *to* a wellness emphasis

from a bio-medical *to* a holistic model

from a hospital *to* a community focus

from acute care *to* prevention/primary care

from episodic *to* integrated delivery

from fee-for-service *to* capitation

from bureaucratic *to* adaptive systems

from patriarchal *to* gender equality

from welfare philosophy *to* economic rationalism

from clinician centered *to* clinician and managerial centered

from patient passivity *to* mutuality

from unrestricted expenditure *to* control/rationing

from simple *to* complex/costly technologies

from separate units *to* mergers

Figure 4.1: Culture Shifts in Healthcare

[19] See Alan B. Thomas, *Controversies in Management* (London: Routledge, 1993) 176–80; David C. Wilson, *A Strategy of Change: Concepts and Controversies in the Management of Change* (London: Routledge, 1992) 72–91.

[20] See John Micklethwait and Adrian Wooldridge, *The Witch Doctors: What the Management Gurus Are Saying, Why It Matters and How to Make Sense of It* (London: Heinemann, 1996) 374.

Hospital Cultures: Shift		
	From Mechanistic	**To Organic**
Vision	Clearly articulated: inward/status-quo oriented	Clearly articulated: outward/change oriented
Risk	Fearful of ambiguity	Prepared to accept ambiguity as integral to risk-taking
Mission	Status quo has priority	Priority over maintenance of status quo
Structures	For status quo	For growth
Creativity	Vigorously discouraged;	Vigorously encouraged
Evaluation	Reality testing not needed	Emphasis on reality testing to assess effectiveness
Rules	Multiplied to maintain status quo	Constantly assessed lest they obstruct creativity
Leaders	Primarily administrators; priority given to detailed planning/status quo	Not primarily administrators; priority given to creating, articulating a vision, and strategizing for action/evaluation
Conflict resolution	Through suppression/ coercion	Through negotiation/ dialogue

Figure 4.2: Culture Shift Required in Hospitals

CASE STUDY

Magic and Re-engineering

A magical word in healthcare reform is "re-engineering," often associated with downsizing. The promised economic efficiency rarely happens.[21] Re-engineering means the "radical redesign of business processes to achieve dramatic improvements in critical . . . measures of perfor-. mance, such as cost, quality, service, and speed."[22] The texts that explain the term seldom refer to culture and the turmoil evoked by culture change. For example, the book by Michael Hammer and James Champy that launched re-engineering as the solution to many business problems does not discuss culture at any stage.[23]

Some disillusionment is occurring. Downsizing in healthcare services when the cultural implications are ignored has proved to be a disruptive management fad with a devastating impact on innovation, as skills and contacts developed over years are destroyed.[24] The staff who remain give more time to discussing their new workload and who will be dismissed next than to creativity. Often middle managers are the first to be dismissed, this places more administrative burdens on senior managers, who then have less time for creative leadership.[25]

Culture: Further Thoughts

As explained in Chapter 1, our culture with its symbols, myths, and ritual provides us with what we so desperately need in human life, namely, protection through networks of meaning against chaos.[26] These networks define what is good and bad, right and wrong, and what are the appropriate ways for members of a group to feel, think, and behave. Once we sense

[21] See Thomas, *Controversies in Management,* 75–86.

[22] See Mike Oram and Richard S. Wellins, *Re-Engineering's Missing Ingredient: The Human Factor* (London: Institute of Personnel and Development, 1995) 4.

[23] See Michael Hammer and James Champy, *Reengineering the Corporation: A Manifesto for Business Revolution* (New York: HarperBusiness, 1993) 32.

[24] A 244-page manual for re-engineering by Daniel C. Morris and Joel S. Brandon, *Re-Engineering Your Business* (New York: McGraw-Hill, 1994), contains only two pages about culture.

[25] See Ross Gittins, "The Down Side to Downsizing," *The Sydney Morning Herald* (April 23, 1997) 15.

[26] See Peter L. Berger, *The Social Reality of Religion* (Harmondsworth: Penguin, 1973) 31–2.

the meaning and significance of things, we are able to develop that comfortable feeling of "being at home" in one small section of the world.

Guideline 6: Recall that Culture Is Resistant to Change. People resist change for at least two reasons (see Chapter 1): concern about the cost of the change to themselves, and fear of falling into a world without familiar meanings.[27] Change is a threat to their investment in the status quo, and the more they have given the more they tend to hold back from accepting change. There is the anxiety that status, power, friends, finance, will be lost. Older people, because of their long investment in the status quo, often resist more tenaciously than younger people.

The following case study illustrates the professional resistance by physicians to attempts to change their cultural dominance.

CASE STUDY

Professions in Conflict

Nurses and medical staffs in hospitals both work to serve the needs of patients, but they form two different subcultures. Traditionally, nurses in hospital cultures were seen by doctors as their female servants, people with far less knowledge than doctors, who were unable to make medical decisions without express permission. Doctors gave the orders and nurses were submissive. In Britain in the early 1970s, with the new departments of nursing in universities and polytechnics, nurses began to press for a change in their relationships with the medical staffs in hospitals. Nurses asked doctors to change their subcultural assumptions of superiority, recognize the professional skills of nurses, and develop a more collaborative approach to patient care. There is strong resistance to this in medical subcultures.[28]

---

[27] See Richard H. Hall, *Organizations: Structures, Processes, and Outcomes* (Englewood Cliffs: Prentice-Hall, 1996) 191.

[28] See helpful insights of Helle Samuelson, "Nurses between Disease and Illness," *Anthropology and Nursing,* ed. Pat Holden and Jenny Littewood (London: Routledge, 1991) 190–201; Margaret Bamford, "Health Careers in the Twenty-First Century," *Excellence in Health Care,* ed. Morton-Cooper and Bamford, 20–44.

In the next two case studies planners failed to take into account the resistant power of culture in implementing their deliberations.

Changing a Parking Space

A hospital had undergone radical and much-needed upgrading, requiring considerable staff re-adjustment. People found the changes at times too demanding. For example, physicians had been allocated modernized suites and all seemed to adapt positively to the changes until their parking spaces were shifted a few yards. To the surprise of the CEO and planners this created strong negative reactions. One doctor summarized the general feeling:

> The change to our parking lots is the last straw! Why all these changes? Why can't things be left the way they were? Now even our parking spaces are changed! When will this all stop and things return to normal? Moreover, we were never involved in planning these changes.

These physicians were suffering from grief or change overload; that is, they were expected to adjust to so many changes in a short space of time that they could take no more. If they had been involved in planning the changes their adjustment would have been faster. The issues of change and grief are more fully explained in Chapter 9.

Scenery—No Substitute for Jobs

A hospital administration had long been concerned about the state of its central food preparation department housed in a restricted and windowless building. Having decided to upgrade the buildings the administration was surprised to find considerable resistance among the department's employees, especially the less skilled. Various protest meetings were held. The CEO attempted in vain to assure the employees that the reconstruction would not mean loss of jobs. The primary aim, he said, was "to improve the service for the patients, but especially for you, the employees, who will now be able to look out over parkland surrounding the hospital." A researcher discovered that people resisted the changes simply because they feared they were part of a secret downsizing plan.

Guideline 7: Recognize that Culture Is a Defense against Anxiety. Resistance to change can be overt or hidden. When people publicly protest over the closure of a hospital this is overt resistance to the decision, but the most potent resistance is generally hidden in the unconscious, where fears about the unknown lurk. For this reason culture is sometimes defined as a "defense against anxieties."[29] Gareth Morgan compares a culture to a "psychic prison"[30] to illustrate the power a culture has to hold people back from reflecting objectively on new ways of acting. I would use the metaphor "cultural seductiveness" to illustrate the same dynamic. A culture may *seduce* people into directing their energy to maintain the status quo and not consider the possibility or desirability of change.

The following is a psychoanalytical explanation of the way in which hospital cultures can become "containers of anxieties."

Hospitals as "Containers of Anxieties": Psychoanalytical Explanation

Psychoanalyst Wilfred Bion has developed a way to look at the inner dynamics of the cultures of healthcare facilities.[31] Healthcare (along with schooling and other significant institutions), in addition to providing for specific health needs, controls basic anxieties around life, death, and annihilation.

[29] See Isabel Menzies Lyth, *The Dynamics of the Social: Selected Essays* (London: Free Association Books, 1989) viii.

[30] See Gareth Morgan, *Images of Organization* (Beverly Hills: Sage Publications, 1986) 199–231.

[31] See Wilfred Bion, *Second Thoughts* (London: Heinemann, 1967); Isabel Menzies Lyth, ed., *Containing Anxiety in Institutions: Selected Essays* (London: Free Association Press, 1988) 1–99.

Anton Obholzer,[32] explaining Bion's thinking, says that in the unconscious part of our being we have no sense of health, but we have a concept
of death. In order to control our anxieties over death we repress them, that
is, we "push down" these unwanted impulses into the unconscious. Various
defenses are used, including the formation of various institutions and rituals, as part of this defensive approach. All cultures deal with the anxieties
evoked by death.[33] In Christianity, death is seen as a transition to a higher
life in Christ (1 Cor 15:54-55). With the growth of secularism, however,
this understanding of death no longer gives meaning to many people. Now
the fear of death is allayed by such institutions as hospitals and medical
staffs, the postmodern substitutes for the churches and their ministers.

Healthcare institutions and professions do not provide a transition to a
new life beyond death, but in the collective unconscious they hold our anxieties about death. For this reason, as Obholzer notes, "our health service
might more accurately be called a 'keep-death-at-bay' service."[34] There is
a popular fantasy that hospitals and their staffs (and by extension the national healthcare services themselves) will shield us from death. They will
find the right medical solution to mortal illnesses and aging. If they do not,
then they have failed in their task. Patients and medical personnel collude
in this fantasy "to protect the former from facing their fear of death and the
latter from facing their fallibility."[35]

Today when hospitals close, even when the reasons are sound, there are
often vociferous protests from people; sometimes politicians are so surprised and threatened by these reactions that they rescind the decisions.
No amount of logical argumentation will convince people that the closures
are in their best interests. I believe one significant factor behind these out-
cries is the hidden function of a hospital: it exists to contain people's fears
of death. The closure reminds people that this fantasy is not a reality.

The next case study illustrates that the resistant power of culture can seduce people away from the task of engaging with reality.

[32] This analysis comes from Anton Obholzer, "Managing Social Anxieties in Public
Sector Organizations," *The Unconscious at Work: Individual and Organizational Stress
in the Human Services,* ed. Anton Obholzer and Vega Z. Roberts (London: Routledge,
1996) 170–1.

[33] See Gerald A. Arbuckle, *Change, Grief and Renewal in the Church* (Westminster:
Christian Classics, 1991) 25–58.

[34] Obholzer, "Managing Social Anxieties," 171.

[35] Ibid.

CASE STUDY ▰▰▰▰▰▰▰▰▰▰▰▰▰▰▰▰▰

A Healthcare Consultant is "Seduced"

The administrations of four small neighboring hospitals agreed to unite to rationalize resources and provide better services to the community. The decision was made with considerable enthusiasm. Two process consultants were invited to work over a four-day period with the four administrations so that they could become one executive. At the beginning, the consultants checked to see if all administrations were willing to proceed with the merger. They were.

However, after two days, a usually dynamic consultant found himself unusually weary, which became obvious in the style of his processing. The second consultant noticed this and drew the other's attention to his lack of clarity and forcefulness in keeping the group on task. The first consultant rather dramatically then perceived what was happening:

> They have seduced me from my task of leading them into a merger! These four staffs at the conscious level are committed to the merging, but deep down in their unconscious they do not want to surrender their cultural identities. The tension between the conscious and unconscious is so strong that it wearies them and I have caught their tiredness in my own body.

When the participants were able to recognize the tension in themselves with the help of the facilitators, they were able to turn their energy toward resolving it. The merger was then able to take place successfully.

▰▰▰▰▰▰▰▰▰▰▰▰▰▰▰▰▰

Culture: Chaos and Change

So far I have particularly referred to culture as an entity, something static. However, it can very usefully be described in terms of a process whereby people seek to articulate meaning or significance as they struggle to adjust to a changing world. I now explain culture as a process through the use of two axioms:

Axiom 1: Chaos: Potential for Creativity[36]

An experience of chaos—that is, the radical breakdown of the personally or culturally predictable—contains potential for immense creativity. One has the chance to rediscover, and be re-energized by, one's roots.

Chaos is a freeing or subversive experience, for it breaks the crust of custom or habit, allowing the imagination to dream of alternative or radically different ways of doing things. When people own their own chaos, admitting to their powerlessness, they return to the sacred time of the founding of the group. There they can ask fundamental questions about the group's origins, about what is essential to the founding vision and should be kept, and what is accidental and should be allowed to go.

An example from the experience of the giant corporate cultures of IBM and AT&T in the United States illustrates this basic axiom. Through government anti-trust action, AT&T had to be broken apart, but not IBM. The latter rejoiced. AT&T's organizational culture went into chaos, IBM's did not; yet it is AT&T that has triumphed. It used chaos to radically rethink its purpose and moved dramatically to rebuild itself. Its stock rose 222 percent, at the same time winning awards for quality, but IBM lost two-thirds of its market share.[37]

CASE STUDY

Personal Journey In and Out of Chaos

Several years ago, on my first visit to Japan, I took the subway to a Tokyo hotel to visit a friend. All went well until I alighted from the train at the wrong station. Crisis! I was stunned. The signs were in Japanese, and I could not read them. I was utterly lost, angry because I was lost, and panic-stricken. My own culture had ceased to give me comforting points of reference and belonging.

But then I noticed in a shop window woolen blankets made in my home country, New Zealand, at the bottom of each blanket a symbol of the nation—a small, stylized kiwi bird. Supportive memories of my family, friends, and magnificent scenery came flooding back to

---

[36] See Gerald A. Arbuckle, *From Chaos to Mission: Refounding Religious Life Formation* (Collegeville: The Liturgical Press, 1996) 87–90.

[37] See Kelly, "Taming the Demons of Change," 7.

me, evoking feelings of belonging, self-worth, and the security I had lost in my panic. "How would other New Zealanders react in my situation?" "How did my forebears react to chaos?" I asked myself. Not with self-pity, but with resourcefulness, initiative, and courage. Energized by this rediscovery of our nation's founding story, I too became creative. Holding high a piece of paper on which I had written the word "help," I was quickly aided by an English-speaking Japanese.

This simple incident explains that when a culture fails to give meaning, the resulting chaos can be the catalyst for a burst of creative energy. Notice what happened when I saw the kiwi on the blanket: I quickly experienced the power of the three elements found in all cultures: symbol, myth, and ritual. Recall from Chapter 1 that symbols are experienced meanings; myths as narrative symbols inspire people and tell them who they are, what is good and bad, and how they should organize themselves and maintain their feeling of unique identity in the world. As explained in Chapter 1, the most powerful myth in every culture is its creation story. In New Zealand the founding myth of the European population is that no matter how hopeless a situation may be, New Zealanders will find creative ways through. Rituals express myths in practice. My holding up the sign "help" was such a ritual, illustrating that I had indeed re-owned the founding story.[38]

CASE STUDY

A Hospital Moves into Chaos

A North American hospital sponsored by a religious congregation was forced to close for financial reasons. The staff and public were first stunned by the decision, then intensely angry, turning their rage against the sisters as sponsors one minute, and the management board the next.

In the midst of this chaos the sponsors themselves felt despondent, helpless, and uncertain about the wisdom of

[38] See Gerald A. Arbuckle, *Earthing the Gospel: An Inculturation Handbook for the Pastoral Worker* (Maryknoll, N.Y.: Orbis Books, 1990) 26–8.

their decision. They began to ask themselves questions such as: "What is at the heart of the founding story of the congregation?" "Did the founder explicitly call them to establish a hospital or to respond to the healthcare needs of people in whatever way was appropriate?" To their surprise they discovered the founder said nothing about building hospitals, but much about caring for the sick. It just happened that last century the only way they could do so was to build a hospital. Having been re-energized by the founding story, the sisters decided to establish community clinics and mobile healthcare services in the poor sections of the city. They were re-assured that the decision to close the hospital was the right one.

Axiom 2: Change: A Three-Stage Process through Chaos

Significant cultural and personal change involves three dynamically related, cyclically repeated stages: the separation stage, the liminal or chaos-evoking stage, and the re-entry stage. Progress through these stages is generally extremely slow, filled with uncertainties and dangers; we are constantly tempted to escape from the learning experience (see Figure 4.3).

The first stage of change is initial unease or malaise. In my Tokyo example, at the beginning of my journey from the security of the English-speaking community into the subway system I was apprehensive, fearful that I might become lost. In the account of the hospital's closure people were initially uneasy on hearing the news. They could not fully comprehend what was about to happen, some describing how they felt in these ways: "shocked," "stunned," "It can't be true," "What's going to happen to me?"

The second stage, the liminal or chaos phase, is sometimes called the *reflection* stage. It is a phase of profound ambiguity that must be accepted with respect, awe, and patience. For me in the Tokyo subway, it was knowing I was utterly lost. It is a very dangerous stage, because in the emotional experience of chaos it is difficult to be reflective about issues of identity and purpose. Many kinds of dysfunctional behavior can occur: anger, denial, scapegoating, dreams of instant solutions, nostalgia for the past, bullying, dreams of a messiah, a sense of drifting without goals, breakdown of trust, feuding, forming alliances to hold on to power, marginalization of innovators, addictive behavior, inability of leadership to lead, emphasis on structural changes alone, envy of creative people, weariness or cynicism about more and more planning meetings to get out of the mess, dependency on fads/gimmicks.

If people succumb to these reactions, they either become paralyzed or struggle to return to the assumed golden age of the past. If, however, they own the enormity of the trauma and the psychic pain of loneliness and fear, and get in touch reflectively with what is essential in their personal or cultural founding myths, then it becomes possible to move forward with creativity and hope. This is the time for re-visioning and re-strategizing.

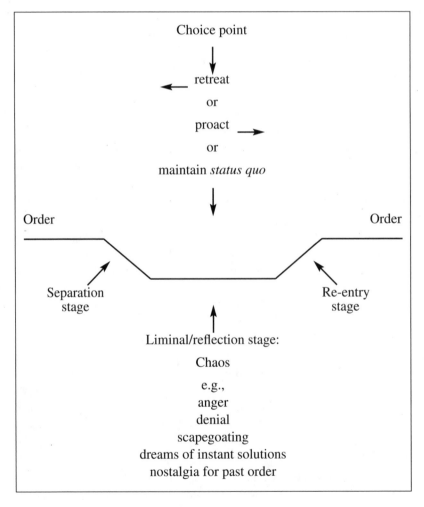

Figure 4.3: Culture as a Process

In brief, there is a point of choice in the chaos of the liminal stage: to re-treat nostalgically to past securities; to stand still, paralyzed by the chaos; or to move with risk and hope into an uncertain future. If the vision is not clear, if the individual or the group is not in touch with the vision of the founding experience (that is, the "strange attractor" in chaos theory), the struggle to move forward into the unknown can easily be given up. In the Tokyo incident having re-identified with the founding story of my people I responded creatively. So did the sponsors of the hospital when confronted with the chaos of its closure.

The third stage, in many ways the most difficult, is the re-entry or re-aggregation stage, that is, the ongoing movement out of chaos to a new personal or organizational cultural integration. It is still easy in this stage to give up the struggle, to fall back into self-pity, nostalgia, denial, cyni-cism, to give way to fantasies of unreal quick-fix solutions to the chaos, or to be overwhelmed by the fear of the unknown. If one is not aware of and committed to the vision of the founding experience of one's group, then one may cease struggling in the darkness.

This analysis of how significant cultural change occurs is based on the writings of two anthropologists: Arnold Van Gennep[39] and Victor Turner.[40] However, contemporary management writers also use a three-stage model to illustrate how significant organizational change occurs. For example, Edgar Schein refers to the first stage as one of "unfreezing" old attitudes and behaviors; stage two occurs through a process of "cognitive restruc-turing" in which new behaviors, values, and meanings are acquired; stage three is the "refreezing" phase in which the new world-view becomes safe and unquestioned.[41] I find this approach inadequate, for it conveys the impression that the process is culturally an easy one, when, on the contrary, it is fraught with all kinds of dangers, uncertainties, and human/cultural pain.

---

[39] See Arnold Van Gennep, *The Rites of Passage* (Chicago: University of Chicago Press, 1960).

[40] See Victor Turner, *The Ritual Process: Structure and Anti-Structure* (New York: Al-dine, 1969). For commentaries on Turner's insights see Ronald L. Grimes, *Beginnings in Ritual Studies* (Washington, D.C.: University Press of America, 1982); Kathleen M. Ash-ley, ed. *Victor Turner and the Construction of Cultural Criticism* (Bloomington: Indiana University Press, 1990); Arbuckle, *From Chaos to Mission*, 115–23.

[41] See Edgar H. Schein, *Organizational Culture and Leadership* (San Francisco: Jossey-Bass, 1992) 298–300.

Symptoms of Chaos: A Commentary on an Example

I now analyze in more depth symptoms of chaos when a decision was made to close a long-established hospital.

CASE STUDY

A Hospital Culture in Chaos

As part of its rationalizing policies a provincial government in Canada decided to close a public hospital which had been managed by a religious congregation for many years. The news came as a great shock to staff, patients, and the wider community. Up to this point, staff morale had been high; the hospital had a good name for excellent service and concern for the community, including the poor in the area. Following the announcement of closure various symptoms of dysfunctionality appeared within the hospital culture. The government became an immediate target of scapegoating. No matter what explanations were given they were not heard. The sisters, who had not been involved in the decision, were themselves also blamed for the closure. Comments such as the following were made:

> "We have worked for these sisters for years, and they betray us!"
>
> "This would not have happened if Sister X were still alive. She would have told the government to rescind the decision; she would have known what to do. We need a strong leader like her again. The present sisters have nothing like the strength of Sister X. She had the vision, today's sisters don't."
>
> "The government is anti-Catholic. It is out to get us."
>
> "The chairman and CEO are weak. They should have stood up to the government."
>
> "What we really need right now is a strong leader, one we can look up to and follow to be protected in all this mess."
>
> "Let's wait, because I have hope that the right person will emerge to solve the chaos and then we can get back to the work of this hospital."

"We must trust the new management and their consultants. The sisters have never been good managers. Now is the time to put our trust in some sound management. The vision of the sisters is too up-in-the-air."

"It is fine to have the 'good' sisters around the hospital. They are no good at management, but at their job of keeping the vision alive they are fine. The real work rests with the new management group. They know what they are doing."

"The trustees and the CEO keep speaking of the need for departmental heads to lead with the vision of the founding sisters. Frankly, it is not a question of leadership. What we need are solid managerial structures and techniques in place. Leadership and vision are too 'wishy-washy.'"

Before the decision to close people of the various subcultures within the hospital had been cooperating and communicating reasonably well, but now they viewed each other with distrust. Some doctors reverted to authoritarian behavior, even bullying the nursing staff. The CEO, who had been known for his openness and affability, became difficult to approach.

Wilfred Bion's insights[42] can explain the symptoms of chaos evident in this case study. Groups and individuals, he says, can negatively react to chaos in a dependency manner, by pairing, or by fight-or-flight. I now explain these expressions and their relevance. Two further reactions evident in the case study are also described, namely, bullying and the process of splitting as a social defense against anxiety.

Dependency

Dependency reactions are evident in the above case study, for example, in the comment "What we really need right now is a strong leader, one we

---

[42] See Wilfred R. Bion, *Experiences in Groups* (London: Tavistock/Routledge, 1989); and Malcolm Pines, *Bion and Group Psychotherapy* (London: Routledge and Kegan Paul, 1985). For a summary of Bion's insights see Morgan, *Images of Organization,* 216–20; and Margaret J. Rioch, "The Work of Wilfred Bion on Groups," *Psychiatry* 33:1 (1970) 36–66.

can look up to and follow to be protected in all this mess." When dependency occurs people want to be helped by a "revered, omnipotent leader, a person who is dependable."[43] They desire to share in the strength of, and be protected by, the idealized all-powerful leader. However, at the same time, people feel depressed that they must depend on someone else, for this exposes their own inability to cope.

There is also envy of the idealized leader who, unlike those around them, is adjusting positively to the chaos. Envy is a feeling of sadness/resentment aroused by the desire to have what another possesses. An envious person or group experiences an emptiness and a consciousness of inferiority to the person or group envied; envy lessens the ability of people to hope and be hopeful. Because envy is an emotion that is essentially both selfish and malevolent, it has destructive results when uncontrolled. Since no leader will measure up to the aspirations of the group, commonly the one in charge will be overthrown by the envy of the group. Another will be selected, but the same dynamic will occur. This dynamic of envy is well illustrated biblically, for example, by the killing of Abel by Cain, the abandonment of Joseph by his brothers, and it was "out of envy that the chief priests had handed Jesus over" (Mark 15:10) to Pilate to be crucified.[44]

Fight-or-Flight

In this reaction a group simplistically feels that certain people have caused the chaos; the group expresses this through scapegoating or witch-hunting. The assumption is that "there is someone or some group out there trying to destroy us." Witch-hunting or scapegoating in modern or traditional cultures has several functions: to escape having to face unpleasant issues, to explain what cannot be understood, to control the uncontrollable, and to account for the problem of evil in individuals and in society. Down through the centuries people have blamed and punished others for misfortunes that were in fact usually a result of complex causes. By passing the blame for our afflictions onto others, we conveniently distract ourselves from the real causes and the efforts we must make to remove them.[45]

While scapegoating may unite a group, it nonetheless distorts reality and the group is unable to deal with the chaos in a positive manner. In the

---

[43] Manfred F. R. Kets de Vries and Danny Miller, *The Neurotic Organization* (San Francisco: Jossey-Bass, 1985) 51.

[44] See Arbuckle, *Refounding the Church,* 139.

[45] See ibid., 68–94.

case study several comments fit this reaction: "We have worked for these sisters for years, and they betray us!" "The government is anti-Catholic. It is out to get us." "The chairman and CEO are weak. They should have stood up to the government."

Pairing and Cargoism

In pairing the group dreams of a future messiah to lead them out of the troubling times; someone will emerge to resolve all problems and peace will again reign. Of course, no one can ever fulfill these utopian aspirations. As long as the savior does not appear, the group maintains considerable energy and optimism, but once the messiah is found and "anointed," reality hits and the way is open for despair and disillusionment. In the case study one comment directly refers to a pairing reaction: "Let's wait, because I have hope that the right person will emerge to solve the chaos and then we can get back to the work of this hospital."

Historically, millenarian movements are examples of pairing. People yearn in the midst of their cultural and personal confusion for the imminent and miraculous transformation of their world by superhuman means. Most are messianic, that is, salvation is to be directed by a human agent of charismatic qualities, and the sect's adherents must commit themselves totally to this person. "Cargo cults" or "cargoism" is the name given to such millenarian movements in Melanesia in the South Pacific.[46] Like witch-hunting they thrive in periods of social, political, and economic disruption. It is claimed that adherence to specified ritual actions and bizarre practices will suddenly bring followers material goods and a better, even paradisaical, life. They are led by messianic leaders, who demand that their followers destroy cherished possessions as a sign of their loyalty to the vision.

In the case study of the hospital culture in chaos cargoism is at work. Managerialism is to be the magical ritual to bring the hospital into a new era, even if this means ignoring or destroying the vision of the founding sisters. This is also an example of "splitting," as will be explained below. Sometimes consultants to healthcare facilities are expected to be messianic leaders equipped with magical solutions to problems. However, the moment they uncover the real issues they are dismissed and new ones appointed.

---

[46] See Arbuckle, *Earthing the Gospel,* 116–7; for a classic study of a movement see Kenelm O. L. Burridge, *Mambu: A Melanesian Millennium* (London: Methuen, 1960).

Bullying

In the case study nurses complained of being bullied by some doctors. I have seen it happening at other levels of healthcare cultures, for example, in the way CEOs and managers relate to staff members, board members to colleagues, trustees to trustees. Bullying can be a significant problem in any chaos situation, and healthcare facilities are no exception. Sometimes people with bullying tendencies are actually selected by trustees as "hatchet people" to make sure "things are put right."

Bullying is "repeated aggression, verbal, psychological or physical, conducted consciously or unconsciously by an individual or group against others."[47] Heinz Legman describes it as a form of "psychological terrorisation."[48] Bullies wish to force people to do what they want them to do, and will try all kinds of intimidation to achieve this. The victim feels helpless, especially when, as is commonly the case, the bully has seniority over the victim. The behavior of bullies takes many forms. Some examples of bullying are: the use of abusive language, public or private humiliation of employees, taking credit for the achievements of others, refusing to take blame for failures, constantly criticizing and being sarcastic to others, withholding information to maintain power over people, expecting unreasonable results from people, flattering superiors and gossiping to them about other employees, having difficulties delegating authority, and being destructive of team work.

Bullies are inadequate people, fearful of losing face, overly sensitive to criticism, deeply lonely within themselves. They evade dealing with their deficiencies, and divert people's attention from them by bullying the less powerful. They have an uncanny ability to sense the vulnerabilities of others and capitalize on their weaknesses. Bullies are often skilled in hiding their actions from others; sometimes they flatter people who might challenge them or make them unduly dependent on them through gifts or acts of assumed generosity.

A bully methodically undermines the self-confidence and self-esteem of their victims. Commonly people who are bullied lack the power to defend

[47] See Brendan Byrne, *Bullying: A Community Approach* (Dublin: Columba Press, 1994) 21.

[48] Heinz Legman as cited by Byrne, *Bullying,* 28; see also Lesley Wright and Marti Smye, *Corporate Abuse* (London: Simon & Schuster, 1997) 50–4, 179–80. See also Kaye Healey, ed., *Bullying and Peer Pressure* (Balmain: Spinney Press, 1998) 1–36; Paul McCarthy and others, eds., *Bullying: From Backyard to Boardroom* (Brisbane: Millennium Books, 1996) 1–25.

themselves and they experience fear, self-doubt, impotence, rage, and shock that they are the object of attack. If the bullied try to defend themselves the bully will react with further abuse; when a victim complains they are commonly branded as trouble-makers. Often the victim becomes ostracized by others who fear that they themselves will become victims. The onlookers then collude in the terrorization. Andrea Adams describes what happens when bullies are not confronted with their destructive behavior:

> In adulthood it is common for people to try to pacify an aggressor rather than tackle them. The wish to placate can stem from a deep-rooted need to be loved, and a misguided belief that if one appeases an aggressor they will cease their attack. In fact, this response increases the likelihood of attack.[49]

Pilate colluded with the bullying crowd who cried for the death of Jesus, but he sought to dissociate himself by ritually washing his hands in public (Matt 27:24).

Over time the bullying behavior of one person, if left unchecked, can infect an entire organizational culture, so that systemic abuse becomes an acceptable way of life.[50] Then we can speak of a culture of bullying. However, when the abuse is confronted people feel liberated and their dignity respected. On one occasion a nurse complained to a CEO about the bullying behavior of a doctor. The CEO called a meeting of her administrative staff and said to them: "This behavior is not acceptable. It is contrary to the values of this healthcare institution. I will immediately deal with the matter." She did and morale in the facility at once improved.

CASE STUDY

Systemic Bullying in a Hospital

The mission statement of a Catholic hospital stated that employees would be treated with respect due to them "as sons and daughters of a loving God," that "subsidiarity and consultation would be among the esteemed core values of the hospital culture." However, employees, including senior management, rarely experienced these qualities, because the CEO fostered a

---

[49] Andrea Adams, *Bullying at Work* (London: Virago, 1992) 102.
[50] See Wright and Smye, *Corporate Abuse,* 71–166.

culture of abuse. One manager described what was happening:

> The CEO on assuming his position said that his door was always open to people with complaints or good ideas. But he listened only to certain individuals and downgraded the normal structures of delegation and consultation. Gossip flourished, because he would tell one person something about policy, but never communicate it to the system. He developed a patronage procedure: if you were subservient to him, flattered him, then there was a chance you could get what you wanted. If he did not like you, then you lived in fear lest suddenly you would be told to leave or ignored for promotion. There developed a demoralizing atmosphere in which no one could trust anyone in the system. To the board members and trustees he was most charming, so that we were unable to complain to them.
>
> We could not trust them to be confidential, because cases had occurred when they informed the CEO that certain people were "dangerous agitators" or "disloyal managers."

Systemic bullying flourishes in some circles where one would not expect to find it, such as in religious communities and in the institutional Church in the post-Vatican II cultural breakdown.[51] We should not be surprised to find it in Christian healthcare facilities. Jesus himself experienced systemic bullying throughout his ministry, in fact from its very beginning: " 'In truth I tell you, no prophet is ever accepted in his own country. . . .' When they heard this everyone in the synagogue was enraged. They sprang to their feet and hustled him out of the town" (Luke 4:24, 28-29). Throughout his ministry Jesus was subjected to bullying tactics, particularly from the Pharisees who came to feel increasingly insecure as the influence of Jesus grew (Matt 22:15-22).

In Britain, one in three people leave their employment because of bullying. Carey Cooper, an expert on stress in the workplace and factors that cause it, estimates that in Western societies one-third to one-half of all stress-related illnesses are due to bullying.[52] It is impossible to estimate the financial cost of

---

[51] See Arbuckle, *Refounding the Church,* 73–8.
[52] Carey Cooper as cited by Byrne, *Bullying,* 28; Healey, *Bullying and Peer Pressure,* 30.

this bullying, but in the United States the Bureau of National Affairs states that annually businesses are losing five to six billion dollars in decreased productivity alone, due to real or perceived abuse of employees.[53]

Splitting

A basic assumption throughout this book is that "one can neither work nor play nor theorize with chaos. Pure chaos is pure terror. One must find forms and frames within which to contain it."[54] The process of splitting is a common method of containing the chaos, but in a way that is not life-giving. In the case study there are several examples of splitting: the "good sisters" are seen to be weak but the "new management and consultants" are the liberators; "leadership and vision" are "wishy-washy" but not the "solid management structures and techniques."

Splitting Explained. Splitting is "a cultural and psychodynamic process whereby individuals and groups, in an effort to cope with the doubts, anxieties and conflicting feelings caused by difficult work, isolate different elements of experience, often to protect the perceived good from the bad."[55] This division then forms a social defense,[56] that is, a system of relationships that people feel protects them from cultural disintegration or loss of meaning.[57] The contemporary rise of extreme nationalism in Western democracies, with its anti-immigrant dynamic, is an example of splitting. In the midst of rapid social changes people feel threatened. They want to feel good again, so the more immigrants are marked as "bad" the more the locals feel good.

A helpful way to understand the dynamics of splitting is to appreciate the inner structuring of myths (see Chapter 1). Every myth contains polar opposites; for example, the rights of the individual and the common good in the founding story of democracy. If these polar opposites are allowed to

[53] U.S.A. Bureau of National Affairs as cited by Adams, *Bullying at Work,* 14.

[54] C. Fred Alford, "The Group as a Whole or Acting Out the Missing Leader," *International Journal of Group Psychotherapy* 45:1 (1995) 133.

[55] See Gareth Morgan, *Images of Organization,* 206.

[56] The term "social defense" was first used by Isabel M. Lyth in 1961. See her paper "The Functioning of Social Systems as a Defense against Anxiety," *Containing Anxiety,* ed. Lyth, 63–4.

[57] See Larry Hirschhorn and Donald R. Young, "Dealing with Anxiety of Working: Social Defenses as Coping Strategy," *Organizations on the Couch,* ed. Manfred F. R. Kets de Vries and others (San Francisco: Jossey-Bass, 1991) 223.

interact the tension between them will be creative. In practice, because of the ambiguities or uncertainties inherent in this tension, the common tendency is for people to move toward one pole rather than the other; one is seen to be "good" and the other "bad." In other words, splitting takes place. By way of illustration, in the documents of Vatican II there are many paradoxical statements: "Priesthood is a sacrament and ministry established by Christ, *but* all who are baptized are priests"; "Heaven is our final destiny, *but* for our salvation we must struggle for justice in the workplace and the world at large." Nowhere in the documents does it say how these polar opposites are to be balanced. The polar opposites in both statements are true, but without clear guidelines (and no one could give them) chaos results and today there are people holding tenaciously to one view or the other, considering their opponents heretics.[58]

In contemporary management literature, distinctions are made between management and leadership, though different words may be used of them: "transactional" and "transformational,"[59] "implementors" and "pathfinders."[60] I myself distinguish between "people in authority positions" and "refounding" persons.[61] As I explained earlier both management and leadership are needed; leadership is about vision, management about administration. An organization can neither function nor survive unless both roles are kept in a creative tension. However, in practice, a split often develops between the two roles and one role is exalted over the other. For example, leadership is depicted as charismatic and management is seen as an evil destroyer of leadership, or vice versa.

The insight of splitting refines the anthropological explanation of scapegoating by introducing the notion of *projection.* When people feel threatened or inadequate they can attribute these feelings and impulses to others as individuals or as groups. For example, when men cannot acknowledge their sense of vulnerability they can imagine women are the vulnerable ones; poor whites refusing to admit their own feelings of inferiority may conclude that blacks are the inferior ones.

Application to Healthcare: Examples. In the face of ongoing uncertainty in healthcare today there is potentially dangerous splitting. Figure 4.1 above lists some possible splits, such as acute and community care, ill-

[58] See Arbuckle, *Refounding the Church,* 37–41.
[59] See James McGregor Burns, *Leadership* (New York: Harper & Row, 1978) 3.
[60] See Harold Leavitt, *Corporate Pathfinders* (New York: Penguin, 1987) 1–24.
[61] See Arbuckle, *Refounding the Church,* 98–127, 146–9.

ness and wellness. The list could be extended at all levels of healthcare: federal and state government control, management and leadership, public and private healthcare facilities, trustees and the management board, the CEO and the management board, doctors and nurses, male and female.

The following are several case studies that help to illustrate the process of splitting in healthcare facilities.

Illness versus Patients. Isabel Menzies Lyth pioneered a study of nursing staff in hospitals in Britain, and illustrated how the process of splitting can also defend nurses against the anxieties caused by the emotionally distressing nature of much of their work. In sickness there are two poles of reference: the illness, and a living person whose suffering can evoke in nurses painful empathies and repulsions. In her research Lyth found that division of nurse-patient care into discrete tasks delegated to different nurses, in addition to rotation and charting practices, lessened nurses' awareness of or responsibility for patients as whole persons. Sick people became the "cancer cases in room three" (the "good" pole in the tension) instead of suffering patients with personal names (the "bad" pole). While the splitting strategies protected nurses from the anxiety-creating issues of life, sickness, and death, they did so at great cost to the healing of the patients.[62]

CASE STUDY

Accounts Department Versus Senior Management

While working in a hospital deeply affected by chaos a researcher frequently heard derogatory comments about the accounts department from members of other sections of the organizational culture. The accounts department had for many years been poorly managed and slack in requesting budgets and financial reports, allowing other departments to over-spend without good reasons. Senior management hired a new departmental head with excellent credentials to reform the entire accounting system. She did, but the hostility toward her and her colleagues was intense. The following types of comments were made: "The senior management is fine. They are human, but not the accounts department and

[62] See Lyth, *Containing Anxiety,* 43–85.

especially not its head. After all, we are in touch with
the patients. Money is not the issue. We must be more
human." "In the past this hospital trusted in providence,
and look how the sisters survived, but today the accounts department has lost the spirit of the place. They
are out to get us at all costs!"

Over time several departmental heads privately approached members of the management board to complain about the reform in the accounts section. Without
checking, these board members expressed sympathy and
requested that the board chairman use his influence with
the CEO to slow-down reform. The chairman refused.

This is an example of splitting. In order to survive the hospital culture is
called to face reality by budgeting, cost-cutting, and accountability. The
majority of departmental heads do not want this, so the accounts department is split-off from the "good" culture and is labeled as "bad." Even the
sisters are invoked in support of the case. The board chairman refuses to be
trapped in the destructive dynamic of splitting.

CASE STUDY

CEO Versus Management Board

Tensions had developed between a CEO and the management board of a major acute care hospital. The board
had appointed the CEO with the mandate to develop
strategies for the survival and growth of the hospital, but
after several months members began to complain amongst
themselves and to the trustees about the CEO and his
proactive plans. Most board members had been selected
at a time when healthcare in the region was relatively
stable; they had been chosen to maintain the status quo,
not to develop policies for a time of turbulence. Eventually the CEO was dismissed and his successor chosen to
return things to a state of "normality."

In this example the first CEO was branded as "bad" and the board, in the estimation of its members, as "good." The researcher found that most board members were personally frightened of change in their own lives; they projected their fears on to the CEO who was perceived as "a dangerous disturber of the status quo." In theory they wanted change, but in practice they were so fearful of it that they could not implement their own decisions. The hospital eventually had to sell out to a rival because these board members could not cope with their fears of change and the new CEO was inadequate for the task.

Laity versus Religious. Frequently I still hear a process of splitting involving lay people and religious (the original sponsors of a healthcare facility). For example, comments are made like: "If only we had the sisters back, things would again be normal." "We religious have nothing left to offer. Our numbers are down. The lay people are far more skilled than we are to take over." The first statement (by a lay person) idealizes religious; the second (by a religious) over-exalts the laity in contrast to the role of religious.

CASE STUDY

Mission Versus Business

A management board of a Catholic hospital decided to appoint a new CEO because, as she said in her interview, "I believe that only if we get the margin right can we think of the mission." The board, confronted with grave financial problems, agreed with this assumption. The trustees accepted the appointment but the decision was not unanimous. In their minority report the dissenters stated:

> We are unable to accept the logic behind the decision to appoint the CEO simply because the profit motive runs contrary to our Christian values. We need to make a profit, but in ways that conform to our mission. If we are mission-driven and use business methods in accordance with this mission we will find a way. If we cannot do so, then we should withdraw from this ministry.

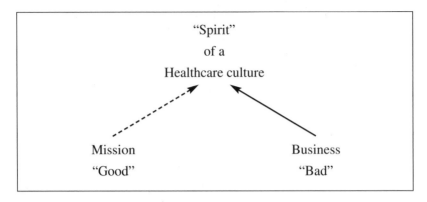

Figure 4.4: Business Ethos Predominates

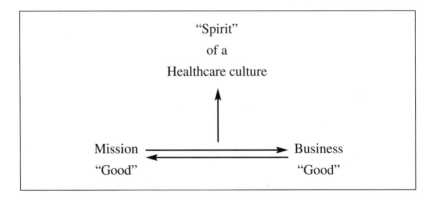

Figure 4.5: Mission Is the Dominant Partner

The minority report is correct. The Christian spirit of a healthcare facility is dependent on achieving a creative balance between the mission
and business methods. It is not one or the other. Figure 4.4 illustrates
what happens when splitting takes place. Economic rationalism triumphs.
People, however, can use the mission of healing as an escape from facing
the realities of life. It becomes the "good" and business an "evil" of the
profane world. One should not "dirty one's hands" with business efficiency, but instead place one's trust in Providence. This is as destructive
as the over-emphasis on business management. Figure 4.5 represents the
ideal. There is an ongoing creative interaction between the mission and
business, but the mission is the senior partner in the dialogue. The board,
CEO, and managers must know the mission and make all decisions in
light of it.

Psychoanalyst Melanie Klein discovered that the unconscious dynamic of splitting begins very early in life; in early infancy a child separates good and bad experiences of the same object (breast) or person (mother).[63] Klein points out that it is a sign of maturity for a person to accept the emotions of hate and love for the same person, without escaping into the false comfort of splitting as explained here.

It is also an indication of growth when a culture or a group of people recognizes why they are tempted to scapegoat others individually and collectively. To be aware of this deeply-rooted dynamic in the midst of cultural turmoil is the beginning of a creative solution. It is neither one pole nor the other, neither mission *nor* business. It is *both*. If organizational leaders are able to maintain a balance between these opposites by encouraging an atmosphere of dialogue and mutuality, then ruinous splitting can be avoided and creative action will occur for the common good. Methods of avoiding splitting are further explained in the following chapter.

Biblical Reflections on Chaos

In the Hebrew Scriptures, and later in the Christian Scriptures, chaos is not once and for all dead matter or sterile nothingness. It is described in terms of confusion, darkness, emptiness, nothingness, but carries with it the notion of indeterminacy and potentiality (e.g., see Gen 1:1 and Psalm 88). The primary motif or symbolic use of chaos is that through God's creative power and mercy radically new and vigorous life can spring up, but this cannot happen without human cooperation. To be creative, therefore, the experience of darkness must be openly acknowledged and personally/corporately owned; we cannot learn from this ordeal if we deny it is happening to us.

Creation in its entirety is pictured as being constantly in danger of falling back into destructive chaos; only God as Creator can ultimately control chaos and order. As YHWH explains to Job, in life's journey as God's face turns away from us and we encounter the fear-evoking force of darkness and uncertainty, we come into contact with the chaos out of which we were made and the lessons it symbolizes (Job 41). That is, we can encounter afresh—if we choose to do so—the mythical roots of our

---

[63] See Melanie Klein, *New Directions in Psychoanalysis* (London: Tavistock, 1955); Paul Avis, *Authority, Leadership and Conflict in the Church* (London: Mowbray, 192) 108–12.

being, namely our own powerlessness, and at the same time the saving, recreative, and energizing power of God.

The message given to the prophet Jeremiah depicts the same dynamic. The destruction of the three pivotal symbols of Jewish culture—the monarchy, the Temple, and Jerusalem—is foretold:

> I looked to the earth—
>   it was a formless waste . . . .
> I looked—the fruitful land was a desert,
> all its towns in ruins
> before Yahweh (Jer 4:23, 26).

For Jeremiah the chaos remains merely potentiality, because the people fail to admit it and enter into individual and group conversion (Jer 4:26). Jeremiah begs the Israelites to admit to the chaos and their dependence on God. If they do so, then the seemingly impossible will happen: there will be creativity beyond all human imagination. YHWH speaks:

> Look, today I have set you
> over the nations and kingdoms,
> . . . .
> to build and to plant (Jer 1:10).[64]

The biblical understanding of chaos will be further elucidated in the following chapter.

Summary

Ongoing technological changes, escalating costs, rising expectations of people, and an aging population are some factors certain to force continuing chaotic change in healthcare. Chaos, however, has immense potential for creativity. We can use the breakdown of old predictabilities to ask ourselves questions of fundamental importance: What is the founding myth of holistic health? How can it be revitalized in contemporary conditions? How can hospital and community care best be coordinated? If chaos is ignored or mishandled it will destroy people and cultures.

---

[64] See Walter Brueggmann, *Texts Under Negotiation: The Bible and Postmodern Imagination* (Minneapolis: Fortress Press, 1993) 83–5, 89–91; Bernhard W. Anderson, *Creation Versus Chaos: The Reinterpretation of Mythical Symbolism in the Bible* (New York: Association Books, 1967) 11–42.

The extent to which groups use chaos effectively and avoid being over-whelmed by it depends largely on leaders exercising their authority in a collaborative way. In the stressful atmosphere of chaos, leaders can be trapped into dysfunctional styles of leadership. At least unconsciously they can mirror the negative behavioral symptoms of chaos.[65]

Leaders can avoid these traps and maintain objectivity if they have them-selves learned to manage their own encounters with inner and external chaos. When Job suffers afflictions he returns to the God-allowed chaos and there experiences the timely lesson of the powerlessness of humankind and God's creative love (Job 40:15).

So also with contemporary leaders in healthcare. Faith in the healing presence of Jesus Christ in the midst of turmoil one is experience can pro-vide balance and energy to maintain the struggle (see Chapter 5). The ad-vice of the fourteenth-century author of *The Cloud of Unknowing* remains relevant: "So set yourself to rest in this darkness as long as you can, al-ways crying out after him whom you love. For if you are to experience him or to see him at all, as it is possible here, it must always be in this cloud."[66]

To live in this darkness in the hope that newness in healthcare ministries will emerge requires a spirit of detachment, as St. John of the Cross re-minds us:

> In order to arrive at possessing everything,
> Desire to possess nothing. . . .
> In order to arrive at that which thou knowest not,
> Thou must go by a way thou knowest not.[67]

If Christian healthcare ministers are to reach "at possessing everything" then they can only venture "by a way [they] knowest not." This means let-ting go familiar but irrelevant ministries, and together being open to the new that will result from the present turmoil (see Chapter 9).

---

[65] See Manfred F. R. Kets de Vries and Danny Miller, "Leadership Styles and Organi-zational Cultures: The Shaping of Neurotic Organizations," *The Neurotic Organization* ed. Kets de Vries and Miller, 243–63.

[66] Anonymous, *The Cloud of Unknowing,* ed. John Walsh (New York: Paulist Press, 1981) 121.

[67] St. John of the Cross, *The Complete Works of St. John of the Cross,* vol. 1, trans. Edgar A. Peers (London: Burns, Oates and Washbourne, 1953) 62.

Chapter 5

Vision and Mission in Christian Healthcare

Where there is no vision the people get out of hand.

—Prov 29:18

If we do not have a religiously grounded, theologically articulated under-standing of who we are and what we are, we will lose our way in this complex context [of healthcare].[1]

—J. Bryan Hehir

This chapter explains:

- the meaning of the terms "vision," "mission," and "values";
- the nature of vision, mission, and values in Christian healthcare;
- the vision, mission, and values of Christian healthcare as contained in its founding myth;
- the Christian meaning of holistic healing;
- the actions of Jesus in his healing ministry;
- the biblical understanding of evil and sickness;

---

[1] J. Bryan Hehir, "Identity and Institutions: Catholic Healthcare Providers Must Refashion Their Identity as Actors and Advocates in the World," *Health Progress* 76:8 (1995) 18.

■ the need for healthcare ministers to be involved in holistic liberation and inculturation.

Recall from Chapter 1 that contrary to popular understanding a myth (or cultural story) is an effort to reveal or articulate, and so make comprehensible, some truth about the world and our life in it. That is, a myth is a large, controlling image that provides philosophical meaning to the cultural realities of everyday life.[2] The most important myth for a group is its founding or creation story, which contains the group's vision, mission, and values in life. This myth should bind the group together at the deepest level of its collective being, providing it with its unique reason to exist and operate in the world. Since myths can die or become distorted it is essential for a group, especially in times of chaos, frequently to re-identify its founding story and re-own it.

After clarifying terms this chapter explains the complex founding myth of Christian healthcare, followed by a description of the biblical roots of its founding myth. Without a clear understanding and appreciation of this myth, which is grounded in the Scriptures and theology, our ministries in the present chaos will either cease or continue to be Christian only in name. In Chapters 6 and 7, I concentrate on *how* this myth, with its vision, mission, and values, can permeate with appropriate leadership every decision within healthcare cultures and ministries.

Clarifying Terms

Mission, vision, and values are the building blocks of organizational culture. If people are to be expected to creatively adapt to change, they must understand [them] (W. J. Duncan and others).[3]

Vision, Mission, and Values

By *vision* we articulate our hopes for the future. Being part of a founding myth a vision is not just a rational statement, for anything that is directed only to the intellect will move no one; nor can it be vague. Rather, it is a gripping story about what we yearn for, inspirationally speaking to minds and hearts. When we retell the story we get, as it were, itchy feet.

---

[2] See Henry A. Murray, *Myth and Mythmaking* (Boston: Beacon Press, 1968) 355.

[3] W. Jack Duncan and others, *Strategic Management of Health Care Organizations* (Oxford: Blackwell, 1995) 465.

We want to do something immediately. For example, whenever Moses re-articulates YHWH's vision of the Promised Land, "a country flowing with milk and honey" (Exod 3:17), to the people caught in the desolation of the desert, one senses even thousands of years later the urge of the people to act once they make the story their own. That should be the power of a vision. A statement of *mission* sets out the primary task people must undertake to realize the vision.

Values flow from a people's vision of life. They are action-oriented priorities, determining, for example, what people believe is evil or good, clean or unclean, ugly or beautiful, healthy or unhealthy. Values are basic convictions that one specific way of acting or end-state of existence is personally or socially preferable to another.[4] Brian Hall defines values as "units of information that mediate our inner reality into full expression in our everyday lives."[5]

Vision, Mission, and Ministry in Christian Healthcare

This is a working definition of healthcare ministry, founded on the vision, mission, and values of Jesus Christ:

- The vision of Christian healthcare ministry is the fullness of the reign of God (Rev 21:1-4).

- The mission is that of the healing Jesus Christ: to call people to holistic health; that is, to heal all dimensions of life, namely the physical, psychological, social, environmental, and spiritual, according to the requirements of biblical faith-justice, as interpreted by the Church's traditions. This mission is to all peoples and cultures, but there is a preferential option for the poor.

- Therefore the ministry, the mission in action, is twofold: (1) to society as a whole, through the work for holistic health nationally and internationally, for example by legal and political advocacy programs; (2) to individuals who experience physical/mental/spiritual illness.

The meaning and implications of this definition will be clarified in this and remaining chapters.

---

[4] See Stephen P. Robbins, *Organizational Behavior: Concepts, Controversies, and Applications* (Englewood Cliffs, N.J.: Prentice-Hall, 1989) 117–21.

[5] Brian Hall, *The Genesis Effect* (New York: Paulist Press, 1986) 23.

Health, Healthcare, and Biblical Tradition

Summary

Recall that there is no simple, generally accepted way of defining health
and disease (see Chapter 1). The medical view of health is negative and restricted, namely, the absence of disease and infirmity.

However, health can be defined positively and more broadly as "a complete state of physical, mental and social well-being not merely the absence
of disease and infirmity."[6] A society is in good health when it is struggling
to liberate people from economic, social, political, and religious structures
that diminish them as human persons and cause medical ill-health.

In the Bible health is defined primarily in this second or holistic sense;
that is, as a complete state of physical, mental, and social well-being.

It is used, especially in the Hebrew Scriptures, to refer first to the body
corporate—Israel as a people—and only secondarily to the individual. We
find the idea of healing applied in YHWH's response to the pain of Israel's
Exile: "I shall restore you to health and heal your wounds" (Jer 30:17).
When relationships based on justice are restored through YHWH's initiative and the willing response of the people as a whole, there will be true
peace *(shalom)*.

Therefore, healthcare founded on biblical assumptions is a process whereby
humanity (i.e., society and individuals) is gradually restored to the divine
image in which it was created. St. Paul grasps the yearning of all creation for
holistic health when he writes with passionate feeling and hope:

> We are well aware that the whole creation, until this time, has been groaning
> in labour pains. . . . Even we are groaning inside ourselves, waiting with
> eagerness for our bodies to be set free. . . . But having this hope for what
> we cannot yet see, we are able to wait for it with persevering confidence
> (Rom 8:22-25).

The Christian, while doing everything possible to foster wholeness in
body and relationships, realizes that perfect health for society and individuals is attainable only at the end of time in the fullness of God's reign.

Cardinal Joseph Bernardin summarizes this quality of Christian healthcare when he writes on physical illness. Ultimately, suffering has meaning
in the mystery of Christ's death and resurrection:

---

[6] Definition of the World Health Organization 1948, as cited by David Locker, "Prevention and Health Promotion," *Sociology as Applied to Medicine,* ed. Graham Scambler (London: W. B. Saunders, 1997) 244.

Although [physical] illness brings chaos and undermines hope in life, we seek to comfort those who are ill, whether or not they can be physically cured. . . . Our distinctive vocation in Christian healthcare is not so much to heal better or more efficiently than anyone else; it is to bring comfort to people by giving them an experience that will strengthen their confidence in life. The ultimate goal of our care is to give to those who are ill . . . a reason to hope. . . . In this we find the Christian vocation that makes our healthcare truly distinctive.[7]

Vision and Mission: Old Testament Roots

It is to Genesis and related books that we turn to discover the meaning of good health for the Israelites. Jesus Christ later built his own teachings on these foundations. The definitive version of the book of Genesis dates from the sixth century B.C.E. and is addressed to exiles in Babylon.[8] In that dreadful period of Exile the Israelites were wanderers lost in despair, depression, benumbed and burdened with guilt. Their entire world order had disintegrated into chaos. Sense the pain of the exiles in this psalm: "The enemy have sacked everything in the sanctuary; / . . . / Their axes deep in the wood, hacking at the panels" (Ps 74:3, 5).

The nation sick at heart yearned for meaning in the midst of this chaos. The writers of Genesis restore this meaning to the people. To despairing exiles, the God of Israel is pronounced as the Lord of all life. Just as God at the beginning of time decided to breathe, and with that, chaos began to give way to cosmos, order, meaning, and hope, so God's recreative action is to be repeated in the chaos of the Exile.[9]

The vision YHWH had of a healthy society was a group of people living in harmony with one another and with him; this is what is called the covenant. In order to realize this vision of good health the Israelites had to act in certain ways and YHWH would respond in a supportive and loving manner. These ways can be summarized in six action-oriented truths[10] which are at the heart of the founding myth of the Israelites (see Figure 5.1). The truths contain core values and are today found in mission statements of many secular and religious healthcare facilities.

---

[7] Cardinal Joseph Bernardin, *A Sign of Hope: A Pastoral Letter on Healthcare* (October 18, 1995) 7, 5.

[8] See Walter Brueggemann, *Genesis* (Atlanta: John Knox Press, 1982) 25.

[9] See John L. McKenzie, *A Theology of the Old Testament* (New York: Doubleday, 1974) 173–202.

[10] The first three truths are helpfully explained by Fred Kammer, *Doing Faith-Justice: An Introduction to Catholic Social Thought* (New York: Paulist Press, 1991) 18–22.

1. Gift of creation

Core values:
- respect for life
- justice
- humility
- hospitality

2. Commitment to stewardship

Core values:
- excellence
- compassion
- mercy
- empathy
- simplicity

**Healthcare:
Founding Truths**

3. Commitment to community

Core values:
- unity
- collaboration
- dialogue

4. Chaos integral to living

Core values:
- identity
- detachment
- hope

5. Preferential option for the poor

Core values:
- justice
- compassion
- detachment

6. YHWH/prophets are healers

Core values:
- love
- memory
- lamentation
- forgiveness
- worship

Figure 5.1: Old Testament: Founding Truths and Values of Healthcare

Six Truths: Foundations of a Healthy Society

First Truth: The Gift and Goodness of Creation

God freely created the world from nothing and because it is of God's making it is good: "God saw all he had made, and indeed it was very good" (Gen 1:31). At the heart of this creation is humankind, formed in mind and heart in the image of God: "God created man in the image of himself, . . . male and female he created them" (Gen 1:27). This truth gives dignity to all creation, especially to humankind. It contains several core values: respect for the sacredness of life—especially human life—justice, hospitality.

All life must be respected as coming from God. Human persons particularly mirror God's power, in the sense that they can think and act freely. However, freedom must be exercised in ways that respect the purpose of the creator. Abortion and euthanasia have no regard for sacredness of life and are therefore wrong. Respect for human dignity is a value from which other values flow. Every person should expect from society equitable access to what is necessary to live with dignity, in ways that respect the rights of others. This is what is meant by justice.

Hospitality primarily means welcoming strangers as guests:[11] "If you have resident aliens in your country, you will not molest them. You will treat resident aliens as though they were native-born and love them as yourself" (Lev 19:33-34). The reasoning is that all goods ultimately belong to God, and when we receive a stranger we are but sharing what rightly belongs to all.

Second Truth: The Commitment to Stewardship

Humankind is called to co-create with God, that is, to continue God's creation in this world in ways that reflect the dignity of God. This truth contains the core values of justice, mercy, compassion, empathy, excellence, simplicity.

The two texts which are the primary sources of these values are: "Yahweh God took the man and settled him in the garden of Eden to cultivate and take care of it" (Gen 2:15); and "God blessed them, saying to them 'Be fruitful, multiply, fill the earth and subdue it. Be masters of . . . all the living

---

[11] See John J. Pilch and Bruce J. Malina, eds., *Biblical Social Values and Their Meaning: A Handbook* (Peabody: Hendrickson, 1993) 104–7; Victor H. Matthews, "Hospitality and Hostility in Genesis 19 and Judges 19," *Biblical Theology Bulletin* 22:1 (1992) 3–11.

creatures that move on earth'" (Gen 1:28). These texts have wrongly been used as an excuse to exploit or abuse the environment. Scripture scholar Walter Brueggemann, explaining the meaning of stewardship, says that the "subjugation" or "domination" mandated by them refers to animals. The domination is that of a shepherd who tends and feeds the animals. When the mandate is transferred to political action, the image is that of a shepherd king (Ezekiel 34). "Thus," Brueggemann writes, "the task of 'dominion' does not have to do with exploitation and abuse. It has to do with securing the well-being of every other creature and bringing the promise of each to full fruition."[12] This is an expression of *justice.* To speak of justice is to concentrate on restoring and maintaining relationships with God, one another, and the universe according to the Creator's design.

One Hebrew word for "mercy" *(rahamim),* as applied to God, is derived from the word for uterus or womb, and is remarkable for its maternal nuance. The nuance becomes explicit in Isa 49:15:

> Can a woman forget her baby at the breast,
> feel no pity for the child she has borne?
> Even if these were to forget,
> I shall not forget you.[13]

The measure of what mercy should be—that is, loving clemency or forgiveness for the guilty—is the example of YHWH, who maintains good relations even when people attempt to destroy them: "Yahweh, God of tenderness and compassion, slow to anger, rich in faithful love and constancy, maintaining his faithful love to thousands, forgiving fault, crime and sin" (Exod 34:6).

Compassion as a value resembles mercy, but there is a difference. Compassion is a value founded in kinship obligations, whether natural or contrived. The Hebrew word is also derived from the word for womb, implying the need to feel for others because they are born of the same mother. YHWH is that mother, and we are all children of that womb and must accordingly feel with, and care for, each other as brothers and sisters. In Western societies compassion—contrary to its biblical roots—has often come to imply a mildly contemptuous sorrow for someone who is suffering due to their own fault or inferiority.[14]

---

[12] Walter Brueggemann, *Genesis,* 32.

[13] See Bruce M. Metzger and Michael D. Coogan, *The Oxford Companion to the Bible* (New York: Oxford University Press, 1993) 512.

[14] See Pilch and Malina, *Biblical Social Values,* 28–30.

Empathy is the ability to put oneself in another person's shoes and comprehend their needs and feelings. YHWH exemplifies this gift and we are called as stewards of God's gifts to model our behavior accordingly. This quality of YHWH is movingly expressed in his relations with Israelites in the Exile. Their grief is YHWH's: "Let them lose no time / in raising the lament over us!" (Jer 9:17).

The core value of *excellence* flows from the fact that one's gifts come from God and are to be used in God's service. Excellence in this sense covers all human endeavor, including research, that is at the service of God and humankind, not for self-aggrandizement. It allows for no selfishness, mediocrity, or laziness in the use of one's talents. The more one in fact struggles to excel in justice and all that it involves, the more one knows God, because God is justice. Theologian Gustavo Gutiérrez summarizes the insight: "To know Yahweh, which in Biblical language is equivalent to saying to love Yahweh, is to establish just relationships among men. . . . When justice does not exist, God is not known; he is absent."[15]

Simplicity is not synonymous with ignorance that causes people to act imprudently (Prov 22:3). On the contrary, people with true simplicity will struggle to act with only the will of God in mind. Out of love God has given creation to humankind to be used as God wishes; namely, with the single-minded commitment to justice and love. There will be no holding-back, fuss, pretense or double-dealing in the simple-hearted as stewards of God's gifts: "Knowing, my God, how you examine our motives and how you delight in integrity, with integrity of motive I have willingly given all this" (1 Chr 29:17).

Third Truth: Commitment to Community

YHWH desired to build an intentional community with the Israelites;[16] that is, the Israelites were invited to join YHWH in developing a way of living in justice and peace that would be radically different from the lifestyle of surrounding peoples. He decided to build a covenant relationship with them: "I shall fix my home among you. . . . I shall live among you; I shall be your God and you will be my people" (Lev 26:11-12). It was to be such an intimate and loving community that it was expressed in metaphors

---

[15] Gustavo Gutiérrez, *A Theology of Liberation* (Maryknoll, N.Y.: Orbis Books, 1973) 195.

[16] See Walter Brueggemann, *A Social Reading of the Old Testament* (Minneapolis: Fortress Press, 1994) 17.

of father to son (Exod 4:22-23; Deut 14:1; 32:6; Jer 31:20) or husband to wife (Hosea 1–3; Jer 2:2). The foundation of this interaction was freely-given divine love (Deut 7:7-8; Jer 31:2-3). In addition to the core values of previous truths this community would be noted for its unity, collaboration, dialogue, and mutuality.

These values must be understood in light of their radical biblical roots. Surely one of the most beautiful texts in the Hebrew Scriptures describes the intimacy that YHWH wishes for his people. God places himself on our level to dialogue, or more simply to speak with friends about their waywardness: "'Come, let us talk this over,' says Yahweh, / 'Though your sins are like scarlet, / they shall be white as snow'" (Isa 1:18).

Fourth Truth: Chaos Is Integral to Living

After Genesis onwards, the Bible does not depict God overcoming or doing away with chaos. On the contrary, throughout the Bible God is pictured as allowing chaos to develop as a prelude to a creative faith response from his chosen people; the Israelites experience plague, famine, flood, exile, war, political upheaval, and treachery. Yahweh had high hopes for Israel: "I thought: You will call me Father / and will never cease to follow me" (Jer 3:19), yet Israel repeatedly rejected the invitation: "But like a woman betraying her lover / . . . you have betrayed me" (Jer 3:20).[17] Repeated chaos offers the Israelites the chance to reflect on their betrayal and to embrace again in hope YHWH's loving invitation.

The period in the wilderness after leaving Egypt and becoming a people (Exodus 16–18) is the archetypal experience of what chaos means: the Israelites are travelers without a sense of direction, bickering with one another, angry at YHWH and Moses his spokesman, hungry, a prey to all kinds of diseases and attacks from enemies, without a tribal homeland to give them an abiding sense of belonging. They yearned for land they could call their own, and for the chance to grow their own good food. They were in such misery that even the oppression of Egypt seemed desirable, as they complained to Moses: "Why did we not die at Yahweh's hand in Egypt, where we used to sit round the flesh pots and could eat to our heart's content! As it is, you have led us to this desert to starve this entire assembly to death" (Exod 16:3).[18]

---

[17] See Brueggemann, *Genesis*, 74.

[18] See Walter Brueggemann, *The Land: Places as Gift, Promise, and Challenge in Biblical Faith* (Philadelphia: Fortress Press, 1977) 28–44.

For the Israelites the Exodus is an initiation ritual, and chaos is an essential stage in its process. In all initiation rites for groups or individuals there are two oppositional processes of detachment/engagement at work. First, there is the process of letting go of the status of a former life; second, there is the process of engaging or taking up a new status. These two processes occur within the span of the three stages described in the previous chapter: separation, chaos or liminality, and re-entry. In the liminality stage, people are symbolically stripped of whatever binds them to a former way of life. In this betwixt-and-between stage they suffer the uncertainty and insecurity of chaos, but in so doing unprotected by the security of their former status, they are disposed to be initiated into a new way of life (see Chapter 9 for further explanation).[19]

The Exodus was such an initiation ritual for the Israelites. In the chaos prior to entering the Promised Land, they discovered that YHWH, despite their many faults, remained creatively faithful and protective even though he seemed at times distant and uninterested in them: "You, out of all peoples, shall be my personal possession, for the whole world is mine" (Exod 19:5). The choice of the Israelites by Yahweh is unique: "You alone have I intimately known / of all the families of earth" (Amos 3:2). The memory of the chaos of the Exodus and the abiding and loving creative presence of Yahweh would be for the Israelites in all subsequent chaos experiences a dramatic source of identity, hope, and consolation: life could emerge out of the most traumatic experience of chaos as it had done in the past.

Brueggemann explains that for the Israelites the experience of chaos, the antithesis of rest, is often described as "weariness." They are weary when they want to live a settled and comfortable life which takes no account of YHWH's plans for them. They are condemned to remain weary because "they would not listen to" (Isa 28:12) YHWH. In the Lamentations "weariness" is being slave to a false master, while "rest" connotes service to the one true God: "The yoke is on our necks; we are persecuted; / exhausted we are, allowed no rest" (Lam 5:5). Brueggemann, after examining many other texts, comments that "it is clear that weariness refers to a time of misery and trouble of drastic proportions and rest means a context of security and well-being." Only YHWH's powerful intervention, and the cooperation of the people themselves, can remove the state of chaotic

---

[19] See Gerald A. Arbuckle, *From Chaos to Mission: Refounding Religious Life Formation* (London: Geoffrey Chapman, 1996) 113–23.

weariness: "These texts play upon an old mythological pattern of chaos and creation."[20]

In brief, "chaos," in its various biblical expressions, carries with it the notion of indeterminacy and potentiality. YHWH can create a new, vitally alive people out of the chaos into which they have fallen, but the Israelites, as a pre-condition of this new life, must acknowledge before God their own inner powerlessness, weariness, lostness, or affliction. They must let go the past and risk walking with Yahweh into a new way of living. The same message runs through the New Testament.

Application to Christian Healthcare

The biblical truth that chaos is integral to living has profound significance for people in contemporary healthcare institutions—a powerful faith dynamic reinforcing the conclusions of the previous chapter. We live in a culture that does not want to acknowledge dying,[21] yet the facts are: creation comes out of chaos, and even what has been created and is now orderly needs to revert to chaos so that it can be recreated in a more dynamic and relevant form; healthcare ministers may be the cause of their own weariness or depression when they resist God's invitation to let go of the old and be open to new ways of expressing the healing mission of Jesus Christ.

Fifth Truth: A Preferential Option for the Poor

In the Bible poverty is sometimes the result of sheer laziness or frivolity, as we read, "Pleasure-lovers stay poor" (Prov 21:17). However, more commonly "the poor" mean "the little ones" (the *anawim*), that is, those who are powerless in society through no fault of their own. Structures of oppression condemn them to poverty.

There are four categories of such marginalized people: widows, orphans, strangers, and the poor.[22] The common factor is that they all experi-

---

[20] Walter Brueggemann, "Weariness, Exile and Chaos: A Motif in Royal Theology," *The Catholic Biblical Quarterly* 34:1 (1972) 38.

[21] See Gerald A. Arbuckle, *Change, Grief and Renewal in the Church: A Spirituality for a New Era* (Westminster: Christian Classics, 1991) 43–58.

[22] See Kammer, *Doing Faith-Justice,* 26.

ence oppression that excludes them from community and power. For example, a woman in the patrilineal (i.e., descent and property rights are traced through the male line), kin-oriented Israelite society depended upon her husband or father for support and protection, but she could not inherit from her husband. Hence, a widow could fall into poverty, especially if distant from her father's people, as would customarily be the case. A widow who failed to obtain legal protection from her in-laws was at the mercy of dishonest judges (Isa 10:2).

The same was true for orphans who did not have close kin to care for them. Strangers such as sojourners, refugees, migrants, and immigrants, who did not have rights to land and its accompanying legal support and power, were also liable to be oppressed. "The poor," to which of course the other groups could also belong, referred to people who were economically deprived. Without economic security they were defenseless, marginalized from political power.

Cause of Poverty

The cause of the poverty was mainly structural—the rich got richer at the expense of the poor:

> Lying on ivory beds
> and sprawling on their divans
> . . . .
> they drink wine by the bowlful (Amos 6:4, 6).

The system had become sick and no amount of almsgiving would alter the structures of greed or oppression, so YHWH threatened the rich with devastation:

> For trampling on the poor man
> . . . .
> although you have built houses of dressed stone,
> you will not live in them (Amos 5:11).

YHWH waits in vain for the rich to reform:

> We are hoping for peace—
>   no good came of it!
> For the time of healing—
>   nothing but terror! (Jer 8:15).

The plight of the *anawim* pointed to the breakdown of the covenant or the holistic health of the community; people by right were to share equitably in the goods of the world and that was not happening. In the early periods of Israelite life there was legal recognition that the nation had an obligation to care for the poor; the poor were to have a fair hearing in judicial issues, food from the harvest, and loans without interest (Exod 22:25). Hence, the scathing language that the prophets used against the rich, condemning them for "extortion and banditry" (Ezek 22:29), land grabbing (Mic 2:2; Isa 5:8), oppression and enslavement of "the little ones" (Jer 34:8-22), the abuse of power, and the corruption of justice itself (Amos 5:7). To ignore the poor was to ignore God. That is why oppression was such a serious crime: "I shall certainly hear their [the poor's] appeal, my anger will be roused and I shall put you to the sword; then your own wives will be widows and your own children orphans" (Exod 22:22-23).

Changing the Understanding of Poverty

Over time "the poor" and "poverty" take on further meanings. YHWH is not against wealth or power as such, but condemns their misuse. When people become attached to wealth and power for selfish interests, and refuse to use them in the service of the community, then that is evil. The dangers of attachment are so great that the ownership of material goods is problematic. Those who have little are more disposed to place their entire trust in God. So to be poor in this sense means that one is humble and trusting in YHWH's presence: "Listen to me, Yahweh, answer me, / for I am poor and needy" (Ps 86:1); "A pauper calls out and Yahweh hears" (Ps 34:6).

There was danger, however, in this development in the interpretation of poverty. The rich and powerful could wrongly think that, provided they were "humble in heart," they could forget to destroy the structures that caused marginalization and poverty.

YHWH does not promise that the poor will be appreciated for their detachment from material goods. On the contrary they can expect persecution because the rich and powerful do not want to be criticized by people who demand social justice or holistic health:

> As for the upright man who is poor, let us oppress him;
> let us not spare the widow,
> nor respect old age. . . .
> Let our might be the yardstick of right,
> since weakness argues its own futility.
> Let us lay traps for the upright man, since he annoys us
> and opposes our way of life.
> . . . .
> Let us test him with cruelty (Wis 2:10-11, 19).

Sixth Truth: YHWH and the Prophets are Healers

After his deliverance of Israel from slavery in Egypt by means of plagues and the crossing of the Red Sea, YHWH promised that if Israel obeyed the Commandments, the nation would escape all the diseases which harassed the Egyptians: "I am Yahweh your Healer" (Exod 15:26). Sometimes healing was associated with forgiveness (Ps 103:3), with deliverance from destruction (Ps 107:19-20), and with renewal of wounded human spirits (Ps 147:30).

The image of YHWH as healer in a more specific sense was most fully represented by the prophets. YHWH speaks through Ezekiel of his condemnation of Israel for its failure to care for the sick and the lame: "'You [Israel] have failed . . . to care for the sick ones, or bandage the injured ones" (Ezek 34:4)—a task that YHWH promised to do himself: "I shall . . . bandage the injured and make the sick strong" (Ezek 34:16). God was so moved by the plight of the oppressed that he foretold the coming of the suffering Servant who would be one with the poor:

> He was despised, the lowest of men,
> a man of sorrows, familiar with suffering,
> one from whom, as it were,
>> we averted our gaze.
> . . . .
> Yet ours were the sufferings
>> he was bearing (Isa 53:3-5).

The prophets were Israel's creative, dynamic, and questioning memory. While listening to YHWH and to the people's waywardness they repeatedly returned to the creation myth of the nation: YHWH loved his people and they had to respond with sincerity of heart, worship, justice, and love. The special objects of their concern had to be the poor and defenseless ones. Feel the penetrating power of memory and condemnation of the rich in these stinging words of Amos

> Listen, Israelites, to this prophecy which Yahweh pronounces against you, against the whole family which I brought up from Egypt:
> . . . .
> I sent plague on you like Egypt's plague,
> . . . .
> I filled your nostrils
>> with the stench of your camps
> and still you would not come back to me (Amos 3:1; 4:10).

Year of Jubilee: Land and Identity

The Year of Jubilee is significant to our reflections because it sets out in summary form the truths listed in this chapter. It is found in the book of Leviticus (Lev 25:8-17, 29-31) and prescribes that every forty-nine or fifty years the people should restore everything to its original wholeness: property to be returned to the original owners, slaves freed, all marginalized peoples to be restored to full membership of the community. The moral imperative that justice, mercy, and kindness should be shown to slaves was founded on God's deliverance of Israel from slavery in Egypt: "Remember that you were once a slave in Egypt and that Yahweh your God redeemed you; that is why I am giving you this order today" (Deut 15:15).

No reference exists that the Year of Jubilee and its requirements were ever practiced; it was an ideal: all land belonged to YHWH and all Israelites were his tenants. Hence, the text: "Land will not be sold absolutely, for the land belongs to me, and you are only strangers and guests of mine" (Lev 25:23). Land monopoly was seen as contrary to YHWH's will. Hence, prophets saw it as a source of oppression of the poor (Isa 5:8-10).

For people of a folk or pre-modern culture, as Israel was, land is not just an economic resource but the fundamental symbol of identity. For example, the Maori people in New Zealand have a strong affection for their ancestral soil; it is there that the ancestors lived, fought, and were buried, and their spirits remain there today. From this relationship the Maori obtained and maintained their identity, so much so that they could say, "Mine is the land, the land of my ancestors."[23] Little wonder that many oppressed people, such as aboriginal peoples in Australia, Maoris in New Zealand, and Indian tribes in Canada, struggle for the return of their ancestral land as an integral step in their return to holistic health!

Likewise for the Israelite the land is owned by God (*the* ancestor) and is a gift to the chosen people. It was land YHWH promised in the Exodus, the symbol of his relationship to the people and they to him in the covenant. It connoted grave moral and practical obligations, for example, the rights of the poor to share equitably in the resources of the land. When they forgot these duties the people failed to honor their identity. Prophets warned the people that their failure to respect the theological and human significance of land in their behavior would mean expulsion from the land and loss of their identity. Feel the pathos of the Israelites in the Exile without their land. All energy is lost:

[23] Cited by Raymond Firth, *Economics of the New Zealand Maori* (Wellington, N.Z.: R. E. Owen, 1959) 368.

By the waters of Babylon
we sat and wept
at the memory of Zion.
. . . .
How could we sing a song of Yahweh
on alien soil? (Ps 137:1, 4).

Return to the land would mean that YHWH has truly forgiven them and that holistic health has returned to them.[24]

Core Values: Avoiding Splitting

Several times in working with hospital staffs, I have heard comments like this:

> The core values of this facility are justice, mercy, compassion, and excellence. Yet in the downsizing that has been happening I see no reference to these values except for justice. The CEO speaks about the need for justice to our patients, and without reducing staff we cannot continue to provide proper services. But what about mercy for us employees? Compassion?

The Bible offers neither a simple answer to this complaint nor ways to resolve the tension between polar opposites such as mercy and justice (see Chapter 4). In fact, the tension between divine mercy and justice is one of the most profound dilemmas of our belief in God. YHWH is the "God of tenderness and compassion, . . . forgiving fault, . . . yet letting nothing go unchecked, and punishing the parent's fault in the children" (Exod 34:6). The paradox of a God believed to be merciful and forgiving on the one hand and ultimately just on the other remains unresolved. Biblical writers return to the dilemma many times, especially in prayer: "If you kept a record of our sins, / Lord, who could stand their ground? / But with you is forgiveness" (Ps 130:3-4).[25]

The story of Job confronts the paradox in the form of a dialogue. This is where the answer is to be found—in honest and unthreatening dialogue. Job comes to grips with the mystery of suffering because there is an interaction between God and Job in which each aims to give himself as he is and seeks also to know the other as he is (Job 40:15). In the New Testament

---

[24] See Christopher J. H. Wright, "Year of Jubilee," *The Anchor Bible Dictionary*, vol. 3, ed. David N. Freeman and others (New York: Doubleday, 1993) 1025–30; John L. McKenzie, *Dictionary of the Bible* (London: Geoffrey Chapman, 1965) 460.

[25] See Metzger and Coogan, *The Oxford Companion*, 513.

the same dynamic is operative. When faced with the humanity of Jesus and signs of his divine gifts, Mary seeks creative refuge in prayer: "She treasured all these things and pondered them in her heart" (Luke 2:19). Christ, overwhelmed with the mystery of his own death and resurrection, resolves the tension creatively in prayer: "'Father!' he said, 'For you everything is possible. Take this cup away from me. But let it be as you, not I, would have it'" (Mark 14:36). So also in healthcare. People need space to ponder the polar tensions in their ministry, for example between core values; that means there must be excellent communication. I am convinced from experience that when people feel they are being listened to something begins to happen. They compassionately feel the tension that managers face, and are able to express empathy both with them and with employees who have lost their jobs.

Vision and Mission: New Testament Roots

Summary

The God whom Jesus reveals desires health for the individual and for society. The reaffirmation of God's will for human and social wholeness stands at the very center of our understanding of health and healing in the New Testament.[26]

In his vision Jesus goes beyond the dreams of the Israelite prophets and declares that the fullness of the reign of God means the end of all suffering and injustice, the coming of a new community of perfect justice and love, "*a new heaven and a new earth; . . .* there will be no more death, and no more mourning or sadness or pain" (Rev 21:1, 4).

His mission from the Father is to proclaim in speech and action what must be done to realize this vision. His ministry of healing is the visible, compassionate sign of what his followers must do and a momentary experience of the reign of God in the here and now.[27]

Jesus wants the poor to be recognized as the heirs of God; he is the Messiah of the poor (Luke 4:18). In Hebrew times YHWH was one with those who suffered, and in Christ there is total identification. Now Jesus is himself the poor one, born in a stable (Luke 2:7), the one who is killed for the people (Luke 27:35).

---

[26] See John T. Carroll, "Sickness and Healing in the New Testament Gospels," *Interpretation* 49:2 (1995) 130–42.

[27] See Robert A. Lambourne, *Community, Church and Healing* (London: Arthur James, 1987) 35–9.

Physical healing is intimately related to spiritual health. Often healing of the body follows public forgiveness of sins, in answer to an act of faith of the sick person (Mark 2:1-2). In fact, in the accounts of healing, faith is essential for healing to take place; it may be the faith of the sufferer or of a relative or friend. Jairus' faith in Jesus leads to the healing of his daughter (Mark 5:23), just as the faith of the woman "who had suffered from a haemorrhage for twelve years" (Mark 5:25) heals her when she touches Jesus.

Holistic Healing: Ministry through Proclamation

> God . . . chose those who by human standards are weak to shame the strong, . . . those who count for nothing—to reduce to nothing all those that do count for something (1 Cor 1:27-28.)

Mary's Magnificat is the bridge between the Old and New Testaments. She states without ambiguity that Jesus has come especially for the healing of *anawim.* Her hymn is one of the most subversive statements in all literature. For the faithful trapped in oppression it expresses a deep and dangerous hope of a better world.[28] The song proclaims three revolutions: a moral revolution ("He has used the power of his arm, / he has routed the arrogant of heart" [Luke 1:51]), a social revolution (*"He has pulled down princes / from their thrones / and raised high the lowly"* [Luke 1:52]), and an economic revolution (*"He has filled the starving with good things, /* sent the rich away empty" [Luke 1:53]).[29] Jesus explains the meaning of this threefold revolution, the message of holistic health, in three significant speeches.

The Nazareth Declaration[30] (Luke 4:16-21).

In publicly proclaiming his mission, Jesus asserts he is the one promised in Isaiah (Isa 58:6; 61:12); he is the one to bring good news to the poor, release the captives and the oppressed, and give sight to the blind. This is revolutionary; people see it as such and do not want to hear any more because his words go against their ideals of human perfection. For them the "beautiful people" are the socially and politically powerful and the ritually clean, that is, those who

---

[28] See Walter Brueggemann, *First and Second Samuel* (Atlanta: John Knox Press, 1990) 21.

[29] See Hermann Hendrickx, *Bible on Justice* (Quezon City: JMC Press, 1978) 50; William F. Maestri, *Mary: Model of Justice* (New York: Alba House, 1987).

[30] See Kammer, *Doing Faith-Justice,* 43–55; Juliana Casey, *Food for the Journey: Theological Foundations of Catholic Healthcare Ministry* (St. Louis: Catholic Health Association of the United States, 1991) 17–29.

do all external things correctly. The sick and poor are polluted or unclean, outside the boundaries of the community. To speak to them or touch them renders others unclean and unloved by God, but Jesus claims that God especially loves them.

In the public announcement of his mission to the Year of Jubilee, Jesus chooses these significant words: *"The spirit of the Lord is on me, / . . . / to proclaim a year of favour / from the Lord"* (Luke 4:18). Through his words and actions a world of justice, peace, forgiveness, compassion, and mercy for the poor ordered for the Year of Jubilee is to be a reality. The fullness of God's reign is now operative in the midst of the people. The rich and powerful in his audience immediately understand the implications for themselves of what Jesus is saying and are so frightened that they want to destroy him there and then (Luke 4:28-30).

Proclaiming the Beatitudes (Luke 6:20-26; Matt 5:3-12). In Matthew's text of the Beatitudes Jesus speaks of two groups of people especially loved. First, the *anawim.* Their attitudes and lifestyles are contrary to the culture around them. For them wealth, power, and selfishness have nothing to do with one's true happiness, which is to be found only in the reign of God and in his righteousness. The second are those advocates who stand up to protect the rights of the powerless and, suppressing self-love and ambition, show mercy. They struggle to develop peace in an unjust society, and are prepared to suffer for the defense of justice: "the kingdom of Heaven is theirs" (Matt 5:3).

In contrast to Matthew's version, in which the "poor" are referred to metaphorically, in Luke's text Jesus speaks of the materially poor: "How blessed are you who are poor" (Luke 6:20) and "But alas for you who are rich" (Luke 6:24). These verses do not praise the lack of money or condemn people having it. The expressions "rich" and "poor" are correlative; what the Beatitudes address is the gap between the two. Jesus is simply saying more bluntly than in Matthew's text that this chasm cannot be justified, and in the reign of God there will be an economic reversal.[31]

The Judgment Discourse (Matt 25:31-46). In Jesus' last speech prior to his passion he says unambiguously that the ultimate indication of good health is whether or not one is committed to justice, especially justice to the powerless, the hungry, the oppressed and deprived in society. One's

---

[31] See John P. Miranda, *Marx and the Bible* (Maryknoll, N.Y.: Orbis Books, 1974) 16–17.

sentence on the day of judgment will be decided by one's attitudes and behavior in this life. Jesus so identifies with the poor that when people refuse them justice they are refusing *him,* even if they are unconscious of this fact (Matt 25:40, 45).

In summary, Jesus sought to describe signs of the reign of God which were culturally unacceptable to the people of his time. There are six parables in Luke's Gospel which are stories of social, economic, and political reversal: the Samaritan is good, not the status-proud priests and Levites (Luke 10:30-37); Lazarus is good, not the wealthy rich man (Luke 16:19-31); the tax-collector is good, not the Pharisee (Luke 18:10-14); the last-seated at the wedding are good, not the first-seated (Luke 14:1-24); the uninvited guests at the banquet are good, not the rich invited ones (Luke 14:15-24); and the prodigal son is good, not his envious and self-righteous brother (Luke 15:11-32). His words, as we will see, are given flesh by his actions.

Holistic Healing: Ministry through Action

The Jewish people in Christ's time had their own vision of a healthy society and the rules to maintain correct social relationships. The cultural laws of the time defined what was clean and unclean. For example, various foods, menstruation, prostitutes, tax collectors, leprosy, and blindness were all considered dangerous. The Jewish concern about leprosy was not that it was contagious, but that it was ritually polluting or "soiling."[32] By associating with or touching lepers one risked suffering all kinds of misfortune.

The Pharisees had come to interpret these laws with such rigidity that they evoked some of Jesus' strongest condemnation. He proclaimed all foods equally clean (Matt 15:11-20) and denounced the Pharisees for their hypocrisy in tolerating injustice provided they remained ritually clean (Matt 23:13-36). Jesus instructed his disciples to ignore the rules of ritual uncleanness (Matt 15:1-20) and himself broke the laws of the Sabbath because healing was more important (Mark 3:1-6). Thus, in both word and action Jesus made powerful political statements about the thoroughly unhealthy nature of the culture in which he lived, where ritual laws of purity/impurity oppressed people, causing or exacerbating physical and psychological sickness and affliction.

---

[32] See John J. Pilch, "Understanding Healing in the Social World of Early Christianity," *Biblical Theology Bulletin* 22:1 (1992) 31; and John J. Pilch, "Understanding Biblical Healing: Selecting the Appropriate Model," *Biblical Theology Bulletin* 18:2 (1988) 60–6; Mary Douglas, *Purity and Danger* (Harmondsworth: Penguin, 1966) 54–72.

These two points are well illustrated in the examples of Jesus healing lepers and blind people. In the Bible leprosy is an abhorrent skin condition viewed culturally as an illness, that is, an unclean condition that excluded a person from the community. The inner affliction this caused can only be imagined—a sense of psychological and spiritual lostness. Jesus, by his contact with lepers such as Simon (Matt 26:6), ignored their ritual exclusion from the community, treating them with respect.[33] When Jesus healed one leper and sternly told him to "tell no one anything" (Mark 1:44), the relieved man could not contain his joy and "started freely proclaiming and telling the story everywhere" (Mark 1:45).

CASE STUDY ▐▬▬▬▬▬▬▬▬▬▬▬▬▬▬▬▬▬▬▬

The Holistic Healing of Bartimaeus

Healing the blind is one of the characteristic activities of Jesus (Matt 9:27-30; Mark 8:22-25; John 9:1-7). It was interpreted as a sign of a messiah: "Then the eyes of the blind will be opened" (Isa 35:5; see also Matt 11:4; Luke 4:18-21).

I think the curing of the blind Bartimaeus summarizes the healing aims and sensitive style of Jesus (Mark 10:46-52). Bartimaeus, a blind beggar sitting by the roadside, heard that Jesus was passing and persistently requested to be healed, but the bystanders were worried that he might cause a disturbance: "And many of them scolded him and told him to keep quiet, but he only shouted all the louder" (Mark 10:48).

Then something remarkable occurred. Bartimaeus, in response to the call of Jesus, threw off his cloak, "jumped up and went to Jesus" (Mark 10:50). A cloak was the official license to beg in Jewish culture, so by throwing it aside and running to Jesus while still blind Bartimaeus illustrates his profound faith in Jesus. He is prepared to become a total outcast by leaving behind his only official sign of identity. Despite this dramatic witness of

---

[33] See Pilch, "Understanding Healing," 31; Stephen Barton, "Jesus and Health," *Theology* 87:718 (1984) 266–71.

faith Jesus, out of respect for the freedom of Bartimaeus, asked him what he wished: "The blind man said to him, 'Rabbuni, let me see again'" (Mark 10:51). Jesus first acknowledged that there had been an inner healing through faith and then Bartimaeus received his sight: "'Go; your faith has saved you.' And at once his sight returned . . ." (Mark 10:52).

Significantly, Mark adds: ". . . and he followed him along the road" (Mark 10:52). Bartimaeus is now fully restored to the community from which he had been exiled through blindness. Through this healing, the fullness of the reign of God is anticipated: Bartimaeus is physically, interiorily, and socially healed and the bystanders were confronted with a challenge to the cultural exclusion of the sick from community.

As healing the sick is no less a part of his ministry than preaching (Mark 4:23), Jesus commands his disciples to also heal the sick and demon-possessed. The command itself, received in faith, gives them the power (Matt 10:1); the risen Savior repeats the commission, and in Jesus' name the apostles heal (Acts 3:1-10; 5:16; 28:8-9). Healing is prevented, however, by a faulty attitude: skepticism in Nazareth (Luke 4:23; Mark 6:5), and the weak faith of the disciples in the case of the epileptic boy (Matt 17:14-21).

Jesus, like the prophets before him, recognized the intimate relationship that can exist between sickness (a perceived human abnormality), illness, the inner affliction that a sick person experiences, and injustice. People who are racially or culturally discriminated against also experience the inner affliction of loneliness and the loss of self-worth. Not only does Jesus verbally condemn the socially-imposed diseases like racism and sexism, but in line with his vision of holistic health he personally breaks down racial, gender, and cultural barriers. He does so in the following ways:

Jesus Heals across Racial Barriers. Jews looked on Samaritans in a racist manner. They perceived them as stupid, lazy, and heretical, and the Samaritans had similar views of their Jewish neighbors. Scripture commentator Fr. John McKenzie, S.J., notes that there was "no deeper break of human relations in the contemporary world than the feud of

Jews and Samaritans, and the breadth and depth of Jesus' doctrine of love could demand no greater act of a Jew than to accept a Samaritan as a brother."[34]

Hence, when Jesus told the story of the good Samaritan, his listeners would have had no doubt about its meaning (Luke 10:29-37). A Jewish man is left to die on the roadside, and some very important people in the Jewish social hierarchy system see him dying, but excuse themselves from any obligation to help because they are too busy. A Samaritan, considered by the Jewish people to be stupid and uncouth, sees the dying Jew and immediately goes to his aid. Jesus' listeners would have been shocked to hear him say: "Go, and do the same yourself" (Luke 10:37). The Samaritan's actions reveal his commitment to core messianic values: he recognizes that the injured man has a right in justice to help; he exercises hospitality in giving of his goods; he acts with compassion and empathy because the Jew is not only physically injured, but interiorily afflicted as he has been abandoned as ritually impure by his own countrymen. The Samaritan also shows immense courage because the incident is in bandit territory and in dismounting from his horse he becomes more vulnerable to a surprise attack on his own life. The story has a delayed ending: Jesus himself dramatically becomes a good Samaritan when he dies on the cross so that others may live.

Today also there are people such as HIV/AIDS patients, homeless people, the unemployed, the culturally deprived, the elderly, various ethnic groups, who fall outside the established order and are not served by it. The good Samaritan story condemns society when it marginalizes these people, blames them for causing their conditions, claiming God is punishing them for "what they have done." Some people believe that for these reasons they have no right to justice, compassion, and hospitality!

Jesus Restores the Equality of Women. In the time of Christ women had become second-class Jews, excluded from the worship and teachings of God, with status hardly above slaves.[35] Throughout his life Jesus opposed this cultural assumption. Although his teaching on this issue is not revolutionary, his behavior was.[36] Often in his daily life Jesus expressed concern for the welfare of women in ways that were not condescending or prejudiced. He performed miracles for them, just as he did for men; for

---

[34] McKenzie, *Dictionary of the Bible,* 766.

[35] See Metzger and Coogan, *The Oxford Companion,* 806–16.

[36] See McKenzie, *Dictionary of the Bible,* 937.

example, the miracles he performed for Peter's mother-in-law (Matt 8:14-15), the daughter of Jairus, and the woman with a hemorrhage (Matt 9:18-26; Mark 5:21-43; Luke 8:40-56). He spoke with a Samaritan woman at Jacob's well, thus simultaneously breaking both gender and race barriers (John 4:6-26). His disciples, reflecting the racial and sexist prejudices of their time, "were surprised to find him speaking to a woman" (John 4:27).[37]

Prejudice against women still exists in healthcare (see Chapter 2), and the example of Jesus remains relevant.

Jesus Ignores Social Distinctions. Unlike the Pharisees, Jesus associated with "sinners," that is, publicly known violators of the Jewish moral and ritual code. Tax-collectors and publicans were despised for two reasons: they were thought to be morally depraved and they worked for an oppressive foreign imperial power. In the Gospels they are commonly linked with "sinners" (Matt 9:9-13; Mark 2:13-17). The Pharisees were enraged by Jesus' actions: "The tax collectors and the sinners, however, were all crowding round to listen to him, and the Pharisees and the scribes complained saying, 'This man welcomes sinners and eats with them'" (Luke 15:1-2).

It is easy for administrators and staffs of healthcare facilities to become like the Pharisees, looking on the government departments responsible for financing services, or even the accounts section of their own facilities, as modern-day biblical tax-collectors who may be scapegoated as "unfeeling," "irresponsible." Perhaps at times there are insensitive people in finance departments, but to assume that all of them are insensitive is prejudice, a sickness to be healed.

Jesus Tolerates Ideological Differences. While disagreeing theologically with the scribes and Pharisees, Jesus nonetheless remained friendly and unprejudiced toward them. He is even pictured as dining with a Pharisee, overlooking at first the fact that his host had given him no welcome. Jesus used the occasion to point out gently what true conversion means by reflecting on the repentance and love of the woman—one assumed to be culturally inferior—who washed his feet with her tears and "wiped them away with her hair" (Luke 7:44).

---

[37] See George Soares-Prabhu, "The Unprejudiced Jesus and the Prejudiced Church," *The Way* (January 1987) 4–13.

Evil, Sickness, and Liberation: The Inculturation Imperative

> *He has sent me*
> *to proclaim liberty to captives* (Luke 4:18).

Summary

A basic assumption of this chapter, and of the book itself, is that action that deprives others of their humanity to any degree, from small assaults on dignity and basic rights, to outright spiritual, psychological, social, or physical murder, is evil. In this sense, disease or illness is an evil.[38] Healthcare is a process whereby people are liberated from whatever restrains them from obtaining a sense of control over their lives.[39]

In the Bible evil results from personal and cultural forces. In his ministry of holistic healthcare Jesus confronts by his words, actions, and healing miracles not just physical evils, but personal and cultural deprivation. For example, sexism is challenged by Jesus not only as an injury to an individual, but as a socially sanctioned behavior pattern. Sexism is culturally supported and Jesus demands not just personal but cultural conversion.

Contrary to the teaching and example of Jesus, the contemporary biomedical model of disease ignores such cultural realities and their impact on the health of individuals and society. Institutions or systems, including Christian-sponsored hospitals, though they may have started with the right motives, can become evil by becoming culturally oppressive of human dignity.[40] For example, a hospital built originally for the poor can develop a culture where the poor feel unwelcome because either they cannot pay or the medical staff are unable to speak their language and nothing is done to provide translation services.

Christian healthcare ministers need a theology that helps them to focus on the connection between individual health and the cultural environment and to critique the life of their institutions: are they in conformity with the teaching of Jesus Christ or are they not? Two theologies based on the holistic health principles of the Gospels have developed since the mid-1960s and help to answer these needs: the theologies of liberation and inculturation.

---

[38] See Fred E. Katz, *Ordinary People and Extraordinary Evil* (New York: State University Press, 1993) 5.

[39] See Alastair V. Campbell, *Health as Liberation: Medicine, Theology and the Quest for Justice* (Cleveland: Pilgrim Press, 1995) 11.

[40] See Walter Wink, *Engaging the Powers: Discernment and Resistance in a World of Domination* (Minneapolis: Fortress Press, 1992) 8–9; Lawrence Osborn, *Restoring the Vision: The Gospel and Modern Culture* (London: Geoffrey Chapman, 1995) 171–84.

Liberation Theology and Healthcare

> I shall free you from the forced labour of the Egyptians; I shall rescue you from their slavery (Exod 6:7).

History

Over the last hundred years Western societies have grown enormously rich on capitalism, and many wealthy Christians have come to assume that the biblical references to the poor are to be taken metaphorically only; that is, as referring to the "poor in spirit," those who place their total trust in God. In this sense the rich can say to themselves that they also are poor and feel no obligation to assist the marginalized.[41]

A theological critique of this state of affairs has two sources. First, the World Council of Churches meeting in 1968 acknowledged the reality of widespread economic and political poverty: "We heard the cry of those who long for peace; of the hungry and exploited . . . ; of the victims of discrimination who claim human justice."[42] From then on, the poor became the dominant theme in the council's reflections and documents; words such as "liberation" and "solidarity" were substituted for less threatening terms such as "salvation" and "fellowship."

Second, there was the discovery of "the poor" in the Roman Catholic tradition. In 1968 Latin American bishops met at Bogota and Medellin and laid the foundations for the first major contemporary local theology, which became known as "liberation theology." Earlier, at Vatican II the Church hierarchy had acknowledged the extensive social problems of humankind and had committed itself to search for solutions. At Medellin, the bishops described poverty in the South American continent as "a collective fact, [expressing] itself as injustice which cries to the heavens."[43] They called for "a total change of Latin American structures," saying "political reform [is] its pre-requisite."[44] Liberation theologian Gustavo Gutiérrez speaks of our days bearing "the mark of a vast historical event: the irruption of the poor" who, he says, have been absent in our society and in the Roman Catholic Church,

---

[41] See David J. Bosch, *Transforming Mission: Paradigm Shifts in Theology of Mission* (Maryknoll, N.Y.: Orbis Books, 1991) 435.

[42] World Council of Churches, *The Uppsala Report 1968,* as cited by Bosch, *Transforming Mission,* 435.

[43] See "Medellin Documents: Justice, Peace, Family and Demography: Poverty of the Church," *The Gospel of Peace and Justice: Catholic Social Teaching since Pope John,* ed. Joseph Gremillion (Maryknoll, N.Y.: Orbis Books, 1975) 445.

[44] Ibid., 452.

and seen as "of little or no significance, as well as being without the opportunity to manifest their sufferings, solidarities, projects, and hopes."[45]

Significant Characteristics

No Splitting of Faith and Culture. At the heart of liberation theology is the theological assumption that the reign of God means "the comprehensive politics of God, to be implemented in the history of the cosmos, of nations, of the chosen people, and in the depths of each human heart."[46] There can be no split between our faith and our human response in the secular social order.

Jesus Christ as Liberator. Jesus Christ as liberator from personal and social sin is at the center of this theology; in his time he worked to liberate the people on the margins of society. The very struggle for justice is itself the anticipation of the definitive reign of God.[47]

While this theology is concerned with the liberation of peoples and societies in this world, it includes, as Paul VI writes, "the prophetic proclamation of a hereafter, our profound and definitive calling." Hence, the Catholic Church's contribution to "liberation is incomplete, if she neglects to proclaim salvation in Jesus Christ";[48] salvation is not only the struggle for, and achievement of, political justice.

Action-Oriented Theology. While other theologies seek understanding of revelation, this theology seeks to bring about holistic health within society. It is a theology elaborated in dialogue with *non-persons,* that is, with people denied their rights by oppressive structures. It requires that evangelizers immerse themselves in the culture of the poor; otherwise dialogue and action are impossible. Since the Church belongs to the culture of the elite, or oppressing class, the first act of liberation must be to liberate the Church itself from its own diseases.[49]

[45] Gustavo Gutiérrez, "Option for the Poor," *Mysterium Liberationis: Fundamental Concepts of Liberation Theology,* ed. Ignacio Ellacuria, and Jon Sobrino (Maryknoll, N.Y.: Orbis Books, 1993) 235.

[46] Leonardo Boff, *New Evangelization: Good News to the Poor* (Maryknoll, N.Y.: Orbis Books, 1991) 32.

[47] See Jon Sobrino, "Central Position of the Reign of God in Liberation Theology," *Mysterium Liberationis,* ed. Ellacuria and Sobrino, 350–88.

[48] Paul VI, *Evangelii Nuntiandi* (Vatican: Sacred Congregation for Evangelization, 1975) par. 34.

[49] "Justice in the World," Synod of Bishops, 1971, *The Gospel of Peace and Justice,* ed. Gremillion, 522–3.

A Grassroots Theology. It is a theology from the grass-roots which means that the chief and conscious agents of liberation are the poor themselves; others must cooperate but in ways that foster this movement of the poor in their own growth. It aims to empower laity, especially the poor, to discover their own baptismal authority to challenge injustices.

It proposes that the poor learn the art of reflecting on reality in the light of gospel truths of liberation. This requires an emphasis on social analysis, which is an action-oriented educational process helping people to become aware of both the ways they themselves are oppressed and the ways they themselves are oppressors of others.[50]

Recognition of "Sinful Structures." It is a theology that recognizes that power is used consciously or unconsciously to exploit and manipulate the poor. The most common form of oppression is structural; hence theologians speak of "evil structures" or "sinful structures."

A sinful structure is a social habit, an institutionalized way of life, a political or economic arrangement or structure, which of its nature causes injustice to people or leads them knowingly or unknowingly into sinful ways of acting.[51] Examples are educational systems that do not take into account the special needs of ethnic groups in society, government health programs that ignore cultural causes of poverty, and healthcare systems that make profit the overriding purpose of their decision-making. Liberation theology highlights the sinful structures that Jesus confronted even in his day. As Jesus identified and judged these structures as sinful, so today the same judgment must be made.[52]

CASE STUDY

Credit Union Liberates

My first introduction to the theology of liberation, even before the name was given to it, occurred in Fiji in 1966

[50] See Joseph Holland and Peter Henriot, *Social Analysis: Linking Faith and Justice* (Maryknoll, N.Y.: Orbis Books, 1984) 1–44.

[51] See Latin American Bishops, "Puebla Document 1979," *Puebla and Beyond,* ed. John Eagleson and Philip Scharper (Maryknoll, N.Y.: Orbis Books, 1979) 183–4; Francisco Moreno, *Moral Theology from the Poor: Moral Challenges of the Theology of Liberation* (Quezon City: Claretian Publications, 1988) 107–22.

[52] See George V. Pixley, "Divine Judgment in History," *The Idols of Death and the God of Life,* ed. Pablo Richard and others (Maryknoll, N.Y.: Orbis Books, 1983) 46–65.

while I was researching the impact of credit unions on village life. A credit union is a group of people bound by some intangible bond of association, perhaps the bond of the same employer, the same religion, the same profession or trade, the same village. The people who are bound by this invisible bond pledge themselves to save money together, and lend their savings to one another at the lowest possible rates.

Fijians under paternalistic British colonial rule were subjected to governmental structures that assumed they were incapable of saving money. Fr. Marion Ganey, S.J., disagreed, and successfully established credit unions supported by an educational program that helped people to identify structures oppressing them and to foster economic self-help.[53] One villager, in reply to my question asking what his credit union had taught him, stated: "I found Jesus Christ is a liberator. My credit union is Jesus Christ, because I saved a little money which I had never before done. One day I woke up and said to myself: 'Because I can save money, I am truly a man. I can stand on my own feet and do things myself—just like other people. And people trust me and I trust them in the credit union. Before I did not. Jesus liberated me from a bad image of myself and of others! Christianity meant nothing to me before. It seemed always to be about the life to come. Not now. I and my friends today live in a healthy community. We trust each other!'"

Liberation theology draws attention to what Hannah Arendt calls the *banality of evil;* that is, sinful structures can develop and be supported by the actions of ordinary persons. Through compromising with evil in small ways people contribute to wider and wider structural evil; finally, structural sin becomes something "taken for granted."[54]

[53] See Gerald A. Arbuckle, "Economic and Social Development in the Fiji Islands through Credit Union," *Credit Unions in the South Pacific,* ed. Neil Runcie (London: University of London Press, 1969) 90–108.

[54] See Hannah Arendt, *Eichmann in Jerusalem: A Report on the Banality of Evil* (New York: Penguin, 1964).

Focuses on Oppression. Liberation theology is a local theology in South America, but it has inspired people to adapt it to other parts of the world, including Western society. The common factor is the need for the poor to be liberated from oppression through their own power.[55]

The following case studies illustrate the positive results that can occur when people take the initiative to challenge unjust structures in the light of Gospel values.

CASE STUDY

A Town Reclaims Its Hospital

Without any local consultation a provincial government in Canada announced that the only hospital in a small, remote milling town in Canada with high unemployment would close within three months. People would be expected to go to a hospital a hundred miles south. Townsfolk were stunned and depressed, even fatalistic, about the decision, as they saw themselves as politically and nationally so unimportant no one would listen to them. The chaplain to the hospital, a religious sister, thought otherwise, and she invited workers, in particular the unskilled, to a series of meetings.

Participants were encouraged to reflect on the closure in the light of biblical texts on social justice. Sister repeatedly explained that the hospital had been founded last century by religious women with minimal resources but "an enormous faith in Christ, lover of the poor." There emerged from these gatherings a small group of highly committed people who recognized that together they could find a way to impel the government to rethink its decision, and they succeeded. Enthused by their achievement, they successfully encouraged local mill workers to reflect on their own poor working conditions.

---

[55] For applications of liberation theology to Western societies see Stephen Pattison, *Alive and Kicking: Towards a Practical Theology of Illness and Healing* (London: SCM Press, 1989); and Stephen Pattison, *Pastoral Care and Liberation Theology* (Cambridge: Cambridge University Press, 1994).

CASE STUDY

Nurses Unite Against Bullying

A director of mission in a Catholic hospital had been encouraging small faith-centered groups to develop. She invited them to concentrate on identifying sinful structures in their workplace. All felt bullied by some of the medical staff. What did Scripture say to them about this? People felt paralyzed when they read the text: "Offer no resistance to the wicked. On the contrary, if anyone hits you on the right cheek, offer him the other as well" (Matt 5:39). Does this mean Christians should remain passive in oppression? One group checked the meaning of the text and found it connoted something quite different. It means rather that the oppressed are to resist their persecutors in annoying ways. Thus to turn the other cheek symbolizes that the attempts to shame the victim into further servility have failed. The action tells the persecutor that the initiative—however small—still remains with the persecuted.[56]

The insight was a turning point in the growth of the groups, so that they worked out a way together to let the offending doctors know non-verbally that "enough is enough." They agreed whenever bullying took place they would just stop what they were doing and simply look at the perpetrator "with accusing eyes." It worked.

Theology of Inculturation and Healthcare

The Word became flesh,
he lived among us (John 1:14).

History

In 1977 the term "inculturation" was first used in an ecclesial document coming from the Fifth World Synod of Catholic Bishops.[57] Vatican II laid the foundation for the re-emergence of a more interactive relationship be-

---

[56] See Wink, *Engaging the Powers,* 184–9.

[57] See Gerald A. Arbuckle, *Earthing the Gospel: An Inculturation Handbook for the Pastoral Worker* (London: Geoffrey Chapman, 1990) 9–25; Aylward Shorter, *Toward a*

tween the Gospel and cultures (e.g., hospital, business cultures), the type of openness that had characterized the missionary life of the early Church. The theological term "inculturation" describes this relationship. It is a way of "doing theology" at the grassroots or of evangelizing anywhere in the world. Liberation theology is a form of inculturation.

Significant Characteristics

Focus on Culture(s). Inculturation spells out two primary aspects of evangelization: the object (culture) and the actual method or process. Culture is here understood to embrace all aspects of life—economic, educational, political, religious (see Chapter 1). Paul VI succinctly comments: "What matters is to evangelize humankind's culture and cultures (not in a purely decorative way as it were by applying a thin veneer, but in a vital way, in depth and right to their very roots) . . . always coming back to the relationship of people among themselves and with God."[58]

This quotation defining inculturation is historically remarkable. For centuries in the Roman Catholic Church, following the Protestant Reformation, evangelization had become spiritualized—something directed to individual souls; the body and material culture being considered something evil and to be discarded at death. In consequence of Vatican II the Church rejected this false dichotomy, returning to the theology of early centuries: culture and individual behavior are intimately linked, influencing each other. All creation—humankind, cultures, the universe—is from God and is to be redeemed in Christ. Paul VI comments: "The split between the Gospel and culture is . . . the drama of our time. . . . Therefore every effort must be made to ensure a full evangelization of . . . cultures. They have to be regenerated by an encounter with the Gospel."[59]

A Process of Cultural Transformation. Inculturation is a *process* whereby the Christian life and message become incarnated in "a particular culture . . . [so that it] animates, directs and unifies the culture, transforming and remaking it so as to bring about a 'new creation.'"[60]

Theology of Inculturation (London: Geoffrey Chapman, 1988) 10–13; and Aylward Shorter, *Evangelization and Culture* (London: Geoffrey Chapman, 1994) 32.

[58] Paul VI, *Evangelii Nuntiandi,* par. 20.

[59] Ibid.

[60] Pedro Arrupe, as cited by Michael Amaladoss, "Inculturation and Internationality," *East Asian Pastoral Institute* 29:3 (1992) 239.

This definition highlights the faith-founded nature of inculturation. It is a movement of conversion for the culture and people at the invitation of God through evangelizers. Fr. Michael Amaladoss, S.J., notes that four mysteries of faith are especially involved in the process of inculturation: the reliving of the incarnation; the dying of cultures to what is not of God; the elevation of attitudes, values, and customs that are in conformity with Christ's message; and the creative Pentecostal energizing of people and cultures to share their love of Jesus with others.[61]

Experience of Reciprocity/Dialogue. Inculturation connotes a dynamic faith interaction "between the Christian message and culture or cultures; an insertion of the Christian life into a culture; an ongoing process of reciprocal and critical interaction and assimilation between them."[62] The words "reciprocal" and "interaction" are significant for two reasons. First, inculturation is a process of *exchange,* that is, new insights can be achieved into the message of Christ as evangelizers listen to, and are questioned by, the people being evangelized. For example, by working with the poor we are able to grasp more deeply what the Gospels mean by oppression, so not only is there a giving to a culture, but there is also a receiving in return.

CASE STUDY ▉▉▉▉▉▉▉▉▉▉▉▉▉▉▉▉▉▉

Volunteers Learn

Several medical, administrative, and nursing staff in a Catholic hospital in the United States had been meeting for several months to reflect together on Bible readings. Recognizing that the gospel was calling them to develop a medical outreach to the poor in a nearby slum, they moved rapidly to organize the finance and personnel. They were surprised, however, that so few people came to them for help. On enquiry a local leader told them:

> You came into our suburb. You did not ask us if it was a good idea, or how the building should be arranged. When

---

[61] See ibid.

[62] Marcello de C. Azevedo, *Inculturation and the Challenge of Modernity* (Rome: Gregorian University, 1982) 11.

we come for help you do not listen to our stories. You
just tell us we are sick and what medicine we must take.
You all talk down to us. We are not dumb. We have survived here in the midst of poverty and we have kept our
dignity. This you do not understand.

The volunteers accepted the truth of these comments.
On reflection they became aware that they had not been
not listening adequately to patients in the hospital.

This case study illustrates that inculturation involves exchange. The
volunteers as professionals assumed their task was just to give and not to
receive, to change others and not to be changed themselves—especially
when relating to a lower socioeconomic group. The poor taught the volunteers that paternalism demeans people and that no matter how materially
deprived individuals may be they still have something to teach others
about human dignity. The volunteers were deeply affected by the experience. They recognized that they themselves had to change their attitudes
of superiority, and from then on this affected their approach to patients
also in the hospital.

Second, inculturation is not a simple encounter between the Gospel and
a culture, because the Gospel comes to our times as already embedded in a
particular culture of the time of the evangelists. There must be ongoing
discernment to discover what is at the heart of Christ's message, and what
belongs to the Hebrew/Greek cultures of his time and of the time of the
evangelists.

Ongoing Process. This process of faith-interaction must never cease,
because cultures are not static entities, thus the term "inculturated" can
never be used as though the process reaches a point of perfection when
further inculturation is unnecessary.

Furthermore, the purpose of inculturation is to make a culture open to
other peoples and their needs. That is, inculturation is not synonymous with
a false nationalism or the cultivation of cultural superiority. Sometimes the
word "interculturation" is used to emphasize this essential openness.[63]

---

[63] See Bosch, *Transforming Mission,* 455–7.

CASE STUDY ▐███████████████████████████████

A Hospital Refuses Interculturation

One Catholic hospital (St. X) in a rural part of United States recognized the importance of merging with another Catholic facility (St. Y) in order to provide better services for people. St. Y was not interested. Its trustees and board combined to write a reply (though it was much modified when sent to St. X):

> We do not believe it is in our best interests to merge. Our hospital has a particular charism and a culture respected by patients through the years; if we merge these will be destroyed. We provide the very best services here and we have no need of others to survive and grow.

The decision of St. Y was not based on the healing mission of Christ at any point. They felt themselves culturally superior and had neither the need to learn from, nor the wish to give of their experience to others.

███

Faith Experience. The primary agents of inculturation are the Holy Spirit and the local community. As in the case of liberation theology a cleric or religious does not act alone, but with the community in a dialogue.[64] Inculturation is an interaction between believing people and culture(s), resulting in action.

CASE STUDY ▐███████████████████████████████

A Mission Leader Surprised

A mission leader had fostered the development of a faith community of nurses which met regularly to reflect on the Scriptures and their practical application in their hospital culture. It was customary for the leader to set the times for the meetings without consulting anyone,

[64] See Louis J. Luzbetak, *The Church and Cultures* (Maryknoll, N.Y.: Orbis Books, 1988) 66.

because this is how other leaders in the organization made decisions. At one meeting a member spoke up:

> Sister, by our reflections we have discovered that we to-gether are church. This means we must act collaboratively and in dialogue, but you are telling us when we are to meet and what we are to reflect on. This is not dialogue. You need to consult us about the most convenient times for meeting. We also can choose the texts from the Bible!

Others agreed with her and the leader, surprised by the admonition, apologized. She now understood that incul-turation demands collaboration, not authoritarian action.

Slow Hesitant Process. Inculturation is slow simply because culture by definition is resistant to change, *a fortiori* to conversion. John Paul II comments: inculturation "presupposes a long and courageous process . . . in order that the Gospel may penetrate the soul of living cultures."[65] In the following case study people discover that inculturation is a slow journey.

CASE STUDY

A Community Opts for the Poor

The leadership team of a religious congregation of sisters, which sponsored several prestigious private acute care hospitals, decided several years ago to evaluate their commitment to healthcare ministry according to the principles of inculturation and refounding (for explanation see Chapter 6). They first commissioned a professional study of the historical origins of the congregation. To the surprise of the sisters, it was shown that the foundress was primarily concerned with socioeconomically and culturally deprived immigrants; at the time the construction of hospitals had been the most effective ways to respond to their needs. The second and most difficult step

---

[65] John Paul II, *The Church as a Creator of Culture: Address to the Pontifical Council for Culture* (Melbourne: ACTS, 1983) 6.

was to take this information and evaluate the cultures of their twelve hospitals, asking themselves the following questions: "Are our patients mainly the socially and economically marginalized?" "If not, can we be true to our founding story?"

They pondered these two questions over several months and finally recognized with embarrassment that: (1) their hospitals were primarily devoted to the needs of the rich and powerful; (2) that while the hospitals funded outreach programs to the poor, the administration of the hospitals was absorbing the entire energy of a declining number of sisters; (3) that there was a significant gap between mission statements committing the sisters to the poor and the reality; (4) that the apostolic impact of the small number of sisters on the healthcare cultures was extremely limited or non-existent, contrary to the fine words of publicity documents.

Despite considerable resistance from both the congregation and the lay staff, the leadership team decided to transfer the sponsorship to the laity over a two-year period. Appropriate legal structures were arranged to guarantee that the founding vision and mission could be revitalized and continue. During the interim period they concentrated their resources on establishing educational processes to encourage the founding story to continue, but this was more complex and slower than they had expected.

The legal structures to facilitate the transfer of ownership were easy to form. However, both the sisters and lay people were slow to accept the cultural changes that the new form of sponsorship required. Many lay people refused to believe the sisters were withdrawing and several sisters found it difficult to accept that they were no longer in control of the facilities. The congregational leadership persisted with their plans of dialogue with their sisters and laity. Several years later, after the community healthcare centers had been established in the midst of local slums and in developing countries, it was widely recognized that the decision to transfer the sponsorship was a wise one.

Differences between "Enculturation" and "Acculturation." Inculturation is a theological term; "enculturation" and "acculturation"[66] are purely
sociological expressions. Enculturation is the process, usually informal
learning, that enables one to become an integrated part of one's culture.
Acculturation is the acquiring by one society or organization of the cultural qualities of another society.

Both terms have a significant feature in common: the processes of learning are very deep and condition us to feel, think, and act unconsciously in
certain ways. Cultural characteristics may be accepted without Gospel
critique; to evaluate them is the task of inculturation. The following case
studies show what happens when the challenge of inculturation is not
accepted.

CASE STUDY

Sponsors Trapped in Enculturation

A religious congregation in the United States had
been administering an acute care hospital for over a hundred years, but in recent years it had experienced dramatically reduced utilization and pressure from managed
care operators and local competitors. The sponsors, the
congregational leadership team, believed that their charism required they remain in acute care ministry. With
considerable cost, they extended their facilities but eventually their efforts were financially unsuccessful and
the hospital closed. Later research revealed that the sponsors had become so enculturated into an acute hospital
culture that they could think of no better way of ministering to the sick. They also misinterpreted the intention
of the foundress; her primary motivation had been the
healing mission of Jesus Christ and an acute care hospital was then the right ministry to express this. Finally,
they failed to recognize that people's needs had changed;
the suburb now urgently needed community nursing services, not an acute care hospital.

---

[66] See Arbuckle, *Earthing the Gospel,* 17–18.

CASE STUDY   ▮▬▬▬▬▬▬▬▬▬▬▬▬▬▬

Acculturation to Economic Rationalism

When a Catholic hospital system in the United States was experiencing deep-seated financial problems, a group of consultants recommended to its trustees that they obtain a new managerial team committed to sound business practices. The trustees acting on this advice asked the consultants to "head-hunt" for the right CEO and supportive staff. On the advice of the consultants alone, a new team was approved by the trustees who felt that they themselves lacked the skills to assess the applicants.

Within a year, the system's finances showed definite signs of improvement, but the trustees began to receive complaints that the culture of the system was changing in negative ways under a non-consultative accounts department. Nurses deplored the fact that to cut costs they could no longer have coffee with those going off duty; the cleaning staff could not continue to recommend kinsfolk for employment as janitors; welfare agencies could not expect the systems' medical services for the poor to be as liberal as before, and staff had to be firm in refusing assistance, as "the hospital does not exist for charity!"; the mission leader had increasing difficulties in arranging reflection days for the staff.

Overall morale continued to drop, and the trustees became increasingly alarmed and surprised. Acting on the advice of the new finance personnel they let it be known that "people just have to be patient. There can be no viable mission without a very sound profit margin." This statement was greeted with cynicism and resignations from long-employed and dependable staff.

I believe the situation in this second case study is far from unique. An analysis of this incident showed the following:

(1) The trustees allowed themselves to be bullied into believing that they had no competency in business matters because they were told by the consultants that "religious are only concerned about 'holy' things." By abdicating their authority to safeguard the values of Catholic healthcare the

trustees allowed the system to become acculturated to a for-profit philosophy. The trustees should have insisted that applicants for management posts were committed to the vision, mission, and values of the healing Jesus. They wrongly assumed that the system's mission had nothing to do with financial management.

(2) The new CEO and staff acted according to their own values, believing in change no matter what the human cost. On being questioned they replied that the hospital's mission statement was "far too fuzzy and in the clouds" to be of help in business efficiency.

(3) It took several years, following the withdrawal of the economic rationalists and the employment of new staff who were financially efficient and respectful of the system's mission, before morale improved and the poor were again served with compassion.

(4) The economic rationalists were ill-advised to condemn the practice of allowing the cleaning staff to recommend their kinsfolk for available jobs. Most of the housekeeping staff came from Mexico or other third world countries, and they were happier working with people they knew and trusted. The happier the atmosphere, the better they worked. In addition, this provided informal cultural ways to make sure jobs were well done and absenteeism kept to a minimum. As a consequence of the decision not to continue kin-based work groups, the cleaners' morale and efficiency dropped and absenteeism rose.

In the following case study a reflection on the Beatitudes leads people to significant changes in their hospital culture.

CASE STUDY

A Community Welcomes a Minority Culture

A lay mission leader and her support group of hospital employees from different departments set themselves to critique the hospital culture after they had spent several sessions reflecting on the Beatitudes (Matt 5:1-12). They asked themselves: "Is the hospital culture open to receiving minority cultures?" "How can we find the answer to this question?" They moved out into the local district contacting various Hispanic welfare and recreational centers to find out how people would answer the first question.

Once trust had developed, the questioners were surprised to receive the answers:

"The foyer of the hospital is too rich . . . it puts us off!"

"We would like something simpler and some welcoming symbols of Hispanic origin—but let *us* choose them!"

"We want interpreters at the emergency desk and in the wards."

"We feel our relatives are not welcome when we are sick. We like to come in family groups to see the sick, but the hospital seems not to want this."

"We need clear signs in our language—and what about signs for other minorities?"

The mission support group successfully pressured the hospital administration to act, and developed ongoing communication links with the groups that had responded to their questions in order to evaluate the hospital's new minority-oriented policies.

Summary

A myth is an effort to reveal some truth about the world and our life in it. It attempts to give the meaning behind ever-changing experiences that influence human life, "to pin down an Absolute in which the human mind can rest with some feeling of security."[67] It is through myths that we are raised "above the captivity in the ordinary,"[68] articulating "how chaos [becomes] cosmos."[69]

When a people are threatened with chaos they feel the urge to rediscover their founding myth in order to recapture their identity, self-worth, and energy.[70] The Israelites in the chaos of the Exile would retell their founding story and new hope would emerge: "Remember the people you took to yourself long ago. / . . . You . . . turned primordial rivers into dry land" (Ps 74:2, 15).

---

[67] Roderick A. MacKenzie, *Faith and History in the Old Testament* (Minneapolis: University of Minnesota Press, 1963) 63–4.

[68] Peter L. Berger, *Pyramids of Sacrifice: Political Ethics and Social Change* (Harmondsworth: Pelican, 1977) 32.

[69] Victor Turner, "Myth and Symbol," *International Encyclopedia of Social Science,* vol. 10 (Assen: Van Gorcum, 1977) 579.

[70] See Gerald A. Arbuckle, "Mythology, Revitalization and Refounding Religious Life," *Review for Religious* 46:1 (1987) 14–43.

Christian healthcare is in chaos. This is the time for its creation myth with its particular vision, mission, and values to be rearticulated and re-owned. The vision of Christian healthcare is "the new heavens and new earth, where uprightness will be at home" (2 Pet 3:13) and where there will be "no more death, and no more mourning or sadness or pain" (Rev 21:4).

The mission of Christian healthcare is that of the healing Jesus Christ who calls us to struggle together for holistic health, concentrating particularly on the needs of the marginalized. Christian healthcare is a process whereby people are liberated from whatever constrains them from being fully human (e.g., political, physical, psychological, or spiritual oppression) and being responsibly in control of their lives.

The task of the good leader, when an organization is in chaos, is to encourage people to retell the founding story. Margaret Wheatley (winner of the 1994 United States Management Book Prize), speaking to the National Assembly of the Catholic Health Association of the United States, said:

> I want everyone . . . in Catholic Health to answer: Who are we? Where are we going? Who is Jesus Christ to us? What is the meaning of our ministry? And I do not want just leaders to go through that wilderness of spiritual desolation leading to a great peacefulness. . . . We need visionary organizations [as well].[71]

The Scriptures provide no ready-made answer to polar tensions in the vision of healthcare, for example between mercy and justice. Biblical writers often return to the problem, especially in prayer where ultimately resolution occurs. When faced with the humanity of Jesus and the signs of his redemptive gifts, Mary seeks creative refuge in prayer (Luke 1:19). Christ, overwhelmed with the mystery of his own death and resurrection in Gethsemane, ponders and resolves the tension creatively in prayer (Mark 14:36).

So also in healthcare. People need to be given regular space, such as workshops and retreats, to grapple and resolve together the polar tensions they experience. The Scriptures provide the focus for these reflections.

The next chapter concentrates on what leaders must do to re-own the founding story of Christian healthcare and apply it to contemporary needs.

[71] Margaret J. Wheatley, extract from joint video by Gerald A. Arbuckle and Margaret J. Wheatley on theme of *Chaos and Leadership in Healthcare Services* (St. Louis: Catholic Health Association of the United States, 1995).

Chapter 6

Refounding Christian Healthcare: Responsibilities of Trustees, Boards, and CEOs

[There needs do be a] relentless focus on pursuit of the organization's mission.[1]
—David H. Smith

While some have concluded that this is the beginning of the end of Catholic healthcare as we have known it, it can be a time of refounding.[2]
—Cardinal Joseph Bernardin

This chapter explains:

- the necessity of refounding healthcare;

- the meaning of refounding as a collaborative process not synonymous with renewal or restorationism;

- the nature of and need for refounding persons in Christian healthcare;

- the role of formal position persons (FPPs), for example, trustees, board members, and CEOs, in refounding;

- application of the axiom "the new belongs elsewhere" to healthcare;

---

[1] David H. Smith, *Entrusted: The Moral Responsibilities of Trusteeship* (Bloomington: Indiana University Press, 1995) 113.

[2] Cardinal Joseph Bernardin, *A Sign of Hope: A Pastoral Letter on Healthcare* (October 18, 1995) 16.

■ the importance of Christian non-profit healthcare ministries, including acute care hospitals.

This chapter clarifies the meaning of refounding and the leadership it requires. Refounding is not about incremental change, but the fundamental reorientation of attitudes and structures. It is not about changing what is, which is renewal, but of bringing about what does not yet exist.

For example, the current chaos in healthcare calls Christian "healthcare organizations toward a refounding of the Church's healing ministry and the values that have framed that mission."[3] Without refounding, the healing mission of Jesus Christ will not survive into the twenty-first century. With the rapid decline of religious sisters and brothers in Catholic healthcare facilities as the primary carriers of the healing mission of Jesus Christ, there is no way that organizations will remain based on Christian values simply through minor organizational and educational processes. Radical pastoral rethinking and action are required. This is what refounding means.

At the same time as the Christian healing ministry is to be refounding, healthcare services throughout the Western world must also enter into a refounding stage. Traditional methods and structures are unable to cope with the demands being made of them in these turbulent times. Thus, to shift from acute hospital to community care, from isolated services/providers to coordinated care, demands a quantum-leap in cultural and human creativity, which is at the heart of refounding.

Understanding Refounding

In Chapters 2 and 3 I have explained why refounding is necessary in healthcare. Before I define more precisely the nature of refounding, however, the following example highlights this urgency.

"Community Care"—Need for Refounding

It is increasingly expected that people need to be looked after "in the community," but in the case of the elderly, sick, and mentally handicapped few realize, as the following analyses show, that the shift from institutional

---

[3] Catholic Health Association of the United States, *A Workbook for Understanding Capitation* (St. Louis: CHA, 1994) 7.

to community care is a refounding task demanding radical rethinking and action.

Care of Elderly and Sick People

The need for elderly and sick people to be cared for in their community is commonly justified by the following:

Technological Advances. These advances have enabled the rapid rise of day surgery resulting in a dramatic drop in the use of hospitals as places for post-operative recuperation (in 1950 in Australia the average stay was six weeks, but in 1994 it had fallen to three to ten days). Post-operative care has now primarily shifted to the community.

Aging Populations: "Demographic Timebomb." Of all the people who have ever turned sixty-five in the history of the world, more than half are alive today. It is predicted that the number of Americans aged sixty-five and older will increase from thirty-one million in 1990 to forty million by the year 2010, a 20 percent increase in twenty years.

Home, hospice, respite, adult day-care, and assisted living services will be needed to serve an ever-growing number of aging people,[4] yet resources are still trapped in the traditional hospital sector.[5] Meanwhile, the burden of non-institutional care is carried largely by women care-givers.[6]

Psychological factor. People needing long-term care prefer to remain at home as long as possible.

Cost efficiency. Institutional care is a more expensive option than community care.

Despite the unprecedented challenges resulting from technological changes and aging, legislators are reluctant to grapple with questions such as: What is community care for? Who are the care-givers in the community? How are they financially supported? In societies that are fragmented

[4] See Catholic Health Association of the United States, *A Workbook for Long Term Care in Integrated Delivery* (St. Louis: CHA, 1995) 24.

[5] See Margaret Bamford, "Health Careers in the Twenty-First Century," *Excellence in Health Care Management,* ed. Alison Morton-Cooper and Margaret Bamford (Oxford: Blackwell, 1997) 25.

[6] See Debra Jopson, "Dr Mum: Unfair Burden Women Carry," *The Sydney Morning Herald* (February 4, 1998) 6; Sarah Nettleton, *The Sociology of Health and Illness* (Oxford: Polity Press, 1995) 181–4.

and individualistic can we speak of community at all? Should taxes be increased to provide for new forms of home or neighborhood care?

Governments frequently speak of the need for "care in the community," but the implications of the major shift from institutional to community care remain unaddressed. Roy Griffiths, author of the British report *Community Care: An Agenda for Action,* wrote in 1988: "Community care has been talked of for thirty years and in few areas can the gap between the political rhetoric and policy on the one hand, and between policy and reality in the field on the other, have been so great."[7] Seven years later Judith Allsop could report no change: "The gap between rhetoric and reality is far from being closed and community care has entered a period of greater uncertainty and instability than hitherto."[8]

John McKnight concludes Americans are also confused about the meaning of community care: "At the very least, community usually means not in a hospital, clinic, or doctor's office. Community is the great 'out-thereness' beyond the doors of professional offices and facilities."[9] Some believe that governments maintain the rhetoric about the human benefits of caring for the sick in "the community" simply because it costs less financially than institutional care.[10]

Governments still consider hospitals to be the primary focus of healthcare and believe that they require only minor adjustments to allow for "care in the community." However, the move from institutional to community focus demands a radical alteration in healthcare thinking and action. It requires creating what does not yet exist, which is an act of refounding.

The Mentally Ill and Community Care

The failure on the part of governments to rethink in a refounding way what community care means is poignantly evident in what has happened to mentally ill people over the last two decades.

---

[7] Department of Health and Social Security, *Community Care: Agenda for Action* (Griffiths Report) (London: HMSO, 1988) iv.

[8] Judith Allsop, *Health Policy and the NHS: Towards 2000* (London: Longman, 1995) 108.

[9] John L. McKnight, "Two Tools for Well-Being: Health Systems and Communities," *Community Organization and Community Building for Health,* ed. Meredith Minkler (New Brunswick, N.J.: Rutgers University Press, 1997) 20.

[10] See Ruth Levitt and others, *The Reorganized National Health Service* (London: Chapman and Hall, 1995) 137.

Since the early 1980s British social policy has included a planned shift from institutional to community-based care for the mentally ill, the assumption being that this would be "a more humane and cheaper alternative to care in a mental hospital."[11] Christine McCourt Perring argues that too little thought was given to the nature of community-based care, and the decision to close psychiatric hospitals was taken with little consultation or involvement by hospital staffs and insufficient sensitivity to the human effects of such radical change. People who had been living in institutions for years found it difficult, if not impossible, to change to a more flexible and unstructured environment.[12] The effectiveness of drugs was also overestimated.

It became evident that resources did not exist in the community to care for the mentally ill. A 1992 report from the British Medical Association commented that "there is concern . . . that most authorities lack the skills and expertise to take on the responsibility for supporting mentally ill people in the community."[13] It is now recognized that the "pressure for change and the expectation for change have thus grown, often outstripping the economic, political, or managerial capacity for change."[14]

Reflecting on the American experience, Eli Ginzberg believes that the rapid de-institutionalization of state mental hospital patients proved to be a seriously flawed policy, with often tragic consequences. In most major urban centers there are large numbers of homeless people, about one in three of whom has a prior history of institutionalization in a mental hospital.[15] Ginzberg claims that "it was an unjustified leap of faith to equate ineffective hospital treatment with the superiority of community care in the absence of postdischarge treatment facilities, to say nothing of the adequate protective living facilities."[16]

---

[11] Allsop, *Health Policy and the NHS,* 52.

[12] See Christine M. Perring, "Community Care as De-Institutionalization?" *Anthropology of Organizations,* ed. Susan Wright (London: Routledge, 1994) 168–80.

[13] British Medical Association, *Priorities for Community Care* (London: BMA, 1992) 20; see also Robin Means and Randall Smith, *Community Care: Policy and Practice* (London: Macmillan, 1994) 1–46, 154–65.

[14] Andrew Pettigrew and others, *Shaping Strategic Change: The Case of the National Health Service* (London: SAGE, 1992) 149; also see pp. 145–85 for a review of the changes in psychiatric services.

[15] See Eli Ginzberg, *The Road to Reform: The Future of Health Care in America* (New York: Free Press, 1994) 57.

[16] Ibid., 56–7. See comments by Lillian Gelberg, "Homeless People," *Changing the U.S. Health Care System,* ed. Ronald M. Anderson and others (San Francisco: Jossey-Bass, 1996) 280–92.

The pattern in New Zealand is the same. Social observer Mike Moore comments:

> Contracting out and so-called "community care" have come together in New Zealand and conspired to create a disaster. . . . Too often, desperately sick people are released without backup . . . only to go into psychotic episodes that have resulted in murder, rape and suicide. . . . Care in the community is not working for many, and it is getting worse.[17]

Clarifying Terms

Contemporary writers on management invent new terms or recycle old ones to articulate how leaders of businesses can achieve productivity improvements in a competitive environment. Some such terms are re-engineering, restructuring, reframing, downsizing, relayering, reconfiguring. Now we introduce the term "refounding." By clarifying some of the above expressions it is possible to sharpen understanding of the unique nature of refounding.

Reframing connotes changing the way people and organizations think about themselves; *restructuring* refers not to the mind of an organization, but to altering the parts of the organizational body that hamper growth. *Renewal* in corporate language implies the process whereby people are moved to develop new skills that will lead to the regeneration of the group, but does not connote any need to radically restructure the organization.[18] *Re-engineering,* however, means "the fundamental rethinking and radical redesign of business processes to achieve dramatic improvements in critical . . . measures of performance, such as cost, quality, service, and speed."[19]

The texts explaining these popular terms improve the financial profitability of companies; the reality of culture and the complexity of culture change are rarely referred to. It is assumed that organizations are akin to machines, made up of parts that can be changed with little or no injury to the people involved.[20] But culture is first about people, not mechanical processes that can be changed at will for the sake of profit (see Chapter 1).

---

[17] Mike Moore, *Children of the Poor* (Christchurch: Canterbury University Press, 1996) 51.

[18] See Francis J. Gouillart and John N. Kelly, *Transforming the Organization* (New York: McGraw-Hill, 1995) 7.

[19] Michael Hammer and James Champy, *Reengineering the Corporation: A Manifesto for Business Revolution* (New York: HarperBusiness, 1993) 32.

[20] Hammer and Champy never refer to organizational culture at any point in their book. Likewise Peter Senge in his best-selling management book, *The Fifth Discipline:*

Some management writers criticize colleagues who ignore the human aspects of organizational cultures. For example, Peter Drucker warns against the cult of downsizing, a form of re-engineering in which an organization's middle management may be removed. He believes that the first reaction to chaos is to patch, then to downsize, but in most cases this leads to what "surgeons for centuries have warned against: 'amputation before diagnosis.' The result is always a casualty."[21] According to Drucker, organizations must rethink themselves, not downsize; that is, they should confront questions such as: "What is our mission?" "Is it still the right mission?" "Is it still worth doing?" He points to Beth Israel hospital in Boston as an example of an organization that turned itself around, not by downsizing, but by struggling to answer these questions and their practical implications.[22]

Of the above terms it is "re-engineering" that comes closest to "refounding." It speaks of radical redesign; that is, creatively getting to the roots of issues, not making superficial changes. It is about dramatic change, not "about making marginal or incremental improvements but about achieving quantum-leaps in performances."[23] The term "refounding" certainly shares this sense of going to the roots of problems, of radically rethinking the way we do things, and of quantum-leap creativity, but there are fundamental differences, as is now explained.

Defining Refounding

Refounding is a collaborative process whereby people return to the original founding story (i.e., myth) of their group. They (1) identify the vision of the founding experience and (2) are so pained/annoyed by the gap between the vision and reality around them that they (3) are prepared to struggle to bridge that gap by creating radical responses aimed at the heart

---

The Art and Practice of the Learning Organization (New York: Doubleday, 1990). Alceste T. Pappas attempts to humanize the definition of re-engineering for use by non-profit groups in *Reeningering Your Nonprofit Organization: A Guide to Strategic Transformation* (New York: John Wiley, 1996) 57–8; Stephen L. Watson, "Reengineering Hospitals: Evidence from the Field," *Hospital and Health Services Administration* 42:2 (1997) 143–63.

[21] Peter Drucker, "Really Reinventing Government," *The Atlantic Monthly* (February 1995) 54; see comments by John Micklethwait and Adrian Wooldridge, *The Witch Doctors: What the Management Gurus Are Saying, Why It Matters and How to Make Sense of It* (London: Heinemann, 1996) 41.

[22] See Drucker, "Really Reinventing Government," 54.

[23] Hammer and Champy, *Reengineering the Corporation*, 33.

of contemporary issues, while being sensitive to the human and cultural factors involved.

As has been explained, every culture has a founding myth that binds its people together at the deepest level of their being (see Chapters 1 and 5). People often emerge from a chaos experience by retelling and re-owning that story. For example, during the worst periods of World War II Winston Churchill would draw the English people back to the founding story of the nation in order to restore their energies; he reminded them that they were an island people stubbornly resourceful, patient, and gifted with dry humor in the presence of apparently overwhelming difficulties, with heroes like Lord Nelson of Battle of Trafalgar fame to inspire them. The founding myth retold becomes a regenerative myth.

Refounding is not renewal. Renewal projects aim to improve existing methods, say, of poverty relief, by speeding up food supplies to the poor through more efficient transportation systems. Refounding, however, begins with the rediscovery of the myth of human dignity. Having re-owned this foundational insight we are inspired with the energy to invent, through quantum-leap innovative actions, entirely new structures and programs that attack the fundamental causes of poverty, such as the corruption of officials and the paucity of educational facilities.

Refounding is not synonymous with "restorationism"; that is, the uncritical return to the structures and attitudes of an assumed golden past. Restorationism is a predictable reaction to chaos (see Chapter 4); people lost in the turmoil of change yearn for the past securities and certitudes.[24] What is refound in refounding is the original pain or anxiety that founders experienced when they looked at the gap between their vision and the reality around them, and the thrill they felt as they moved in uncertainty to bridge that gap creatively. What is historically accidental to this founding vision is left behind. That is truly creative fidelity.

Refounding is not the same as re-engineering because refounding acknowledges the human and cultural aspects of change. In summary, refounding is about a paradigm shift in thinking, attitudes, structures, and action, not the incremental improvements of renewal.[25] This shift can occur if people are prepared to retell and re-own the founding experience of the

---

[24] See Gerald A. Arbuckle, *Refounding the Church: Dissent for Leadership* (Maryknoll, N.Y.: Orbis Books, 1993) 2–3.

[25] For an example of how incrementalism can interfere with innovation see Dennis L. Nowlin, "Creating a Culture of Innovation and Quality at 3M," *Quality Management in Health Care* 2:3 (1994) 36–43.

group. From this comes the energy to make radical adjustments to contemporary circumstances.

A Secular Example of Refounding: One-Day Cricket Games[*]

Major cricket games, such as those between national teams which traditionally lasted for several days, were invented at a time when life was slower and less demanding. Under the rules, if a team desires to win it must give the other side a chance also, so the game was built on a moral standard of fairness.

Then in recent times "instant" cricket (i.e., one-day games) became popular (in England in the 1960s and internationally in 1972), and its followers claim it is rescuing the sport from the lingering death of the old, long, drawn-out game, in which it was common for neither side to win. The leisurely middle- and upper-class game suited a stable British Empire, but the pace of life and the breakdown of class barriers in the contemporary age required a refounding of the game. Australian entrepreneur Kerry Packer responded. Healthy competition, not fairness, and excitement for all groups in society, not a sleepy atmosphere for people with ample leisure time, power, and money, are the up-to-date values.[26] The refounding has proved immensely popular with spectators and has revived the game of cricket.

Mission and Refounding

Since the mission of an organization is the task that must be done for the vision to be realized, it can change—and sometimes must change—while the vision remains the same. For example, founders of many religious congregations last century inspired their followers with the vision of serving the sick and the poor. Their mission was to build hospitals, since historically that was often the only way to respond to the needs.

But today there are other, sometimes better ways for the vision to be realized. To refound communities devoted to the sick poor, people need to return to the original vision and see whether radically new ways are necessary to implement it. This may mean changing the mission quite dramatically, such as moving from acute care hospitals to community ministry.

---

[26] See "It's Not Just a Game, Good Grief," *The Economist* (October 31, 1987) 44.

CASE STUDY

Refounding Veterans' Hospitals

The Veterans' Administration in the United States controls 171 hospitals and 130 nursing homes. The hospitals were first established in the 1930s as a practical response to the vision that veterans should receive good medical services, particularly in rural areas and small towns where many veterans resided and adequate hospitals were lacking. Today, quality hospitals are readily available to veterans in most places. However, veterans' hospitals are generally of mediocre quality and financially expensive for the government to run. Worse, they are not neighborhood facilities, so veterans sometimes must travel long distances from their families and communities at a time when they most require family and community assistance.

The vision remains unchanged: veterans are to receive adequate medical services. However, the mission, that is, the running of hospitals and nursing homes just for veterans, must change. Peter Drucker claims that these facilities should be closed and their job contracted out to local hospitals and HMOs.[27] This radical change would be an example of refounding.

Refounding Is a Collaborative Process

The collaboration of three kinds of people is required for refounding: formal position persons, refounding persons, and renewal persons. Formal position persons, such as trustees, boards of management, CEOs, and managers, are an organization's official gatekeepers to change; that is, by their position they can prevent or foster change. Renewal people with "nuts and bolts" skills and a willing commitment to a group's mission are indispensable collaborators in the refounding process.

Refounding persons have gifts of imagination, intuition, creativity, innovation, collaborative skills, courage, and hope. They are dreamers who do, contemplatives who act; that is, they are able to relive at depth the

---

[27] See Drucker, "Really Reinventing Government," 56.

founding experience of the group and in a collaborative way take innovative, quantum-leaps into the present world, seeking to put aside what is historically accidental to the vision. While going back to the founding story, they not only become myth revitalizers but also myth-makers because they adapt its message to contemporary issues.

Passionately committed to the refounding vision, they are not lightly dissuaded from action or moving to the edge of chaos where creative ideas occur. Such persons challenge a group's or an individual's comfortable acceptance of the cultural status quo. An organization that domesticates them achieves peace, but loses its future.[28]

Refounders need other people to sharpen their insights and help bring these insights to fruition. They need high ego, emotional stability, little need for the affirmation of other people, and a considerable tolerance of cognitive ambiguity. Their self-esteem needs to be independent of organizational measures such as reward and punishment, and they must be able to resist undue group pressures toward conformity in thinking.

In summary, refounding is neither a cult of individualism nor the exaltation of a hierarchical, self-centered status system. Rather, its priority is the collaboration of people with skills and commitment for the sake of a common vision and mission.

Examples of Refounding Persons

Henry Ford introduced the Model T in 1908 and for years the car dominated the market because it was of unquestionable value and relatively inexpensive. During the 1920s, however, the automobile market changed; people wanted different designs and colors, but Ford failed to respond to changing tastes and demands for higher engineering standards; the company developed organizational calcification. It was finally saved from collapse through the refounding initiatives of Henry Ford II who, on taking over the operation, quickly developed modern methods of organization favorable to creativity and quality control.

In the midst of the chaos of the Great Depression and against considerable opposition, President Franklin Roosevelt developed the New Deal, based on the rediscovery of the dignity of the human person inherent in the founding story of the nation. To be true to this founding story, Roosevelt

[28] See Gerald A. Arbuckle, *Out of Chaos: Refounding Religious Congregations* (New York: Paulist Press, 1988) 88–111.

argued, the nation had to let go of excessive individualism and embrace a collaborative approach to solving problems of unemployment and poverty. Followers of Roosevelt would see him as a refounder of the nation; that is, as one who, with the collaborative help of many people, went to the heart of the founding story and adapted it, at considerable political risk, to the most urgent needs of his day.

Likewise in Canada, Tommy Douglas as a political leader created Medicare in response to the poverty of Saskatchewan. Convinced of the right of a person to healthcare and protection against the catastrophic cost of illness, Douglas led the crusade that resulted in the birth of Canada's system of universal health insurance. For this reason he is a refounding person of the Canadian way of life.

In the economic chaos of the 1930s in New Zealand, Prime Minister Michael Savage explicitly returned to the social justice vision of the nation's founding experience as a European settlement in the nineteenth century, and established the first comprehensive and integrated system of social security in the Western world. "Social justice," he said, "must be the guiding principle, and economic organization must adapt itself to social needs."[29]

As Western medicine focused on the medical model it lost its caring touch. This was particularly evident in the approach to the dying who increasingly found themselves to be unwelcome anomalies in the system of high technology medicine which had developed in search of cures. In England Dame Cicely Saunders recognized this and refounded care of the dying through the creation of the contemporary hospice or palliative care movement. She created a medical speciality which uses skills based on the most up-to-date scientific knowledge, while at the same time recognizing the importance of a truly caring attitude and approach. At the heart of the hospice movement is a philosophy that embraces a network of values and attitudes that tries to lessen the indignities of dying so as to maximize the human life potential of the dying and their families.[30]

---

[29] Michael J. Savage as cited by Keith Sinclair, *A History of New Zealand* (Harmondsworth: Penguin, 1959) 255; see comments by Derek A. Dow, *Safeguarding the Public Health: A History of the New Zealand Department of Health* (Wellington: Victoria University Press, 1995) 122–4.

[30] See Michael Kearney, "Palliative Medicine: Just Another Specialty?" *Palliative Medicine* 6 (1992) 40; Cicely Saunders, "Hospices Worldwide: A Mission Statement," *Hospice Care on the International Scene,* ed. Cicely Saunders and Robert Kastenbaum (New York: Springer, 1997) 3–12; David W. Moller, *Confronting Death: Values, Institutions and Human Mortality* (New York: Oxford University Press, 1996) 42–3.

The question is often asked: can groups of people, not just individuals, be refounders? I believe this is possible, though rare. There must be considerable mutuality and interdependence between the people involved, leading to synergy, so that ideas can be freely tossed around, pondered over, and a group-mind can emerge. When this happens it is difficult to isolate any particular individual as a refounding person. In a patriarchal culture, which is still dominant in the Western world, it is taken for granted that individuals lead others along the path of creative action. However, I believe that as gender equality develops the gifts of intuition and cooperativeness particularly associated with women may more readily foster the development of the "group refounder."

CASE STUDY ▰▰▰▰▰▰▰▰▰▰▰▰▰▰▰▰▰▰

The Prophets as Refounders: Pained by the "GAP"

The major initiative for refounding the Israelite culture in line with the three fundamental values—total dependence on God, justice, and love—did not come from the people. It came from YHWH, who acted through personally selected prophets: "Prepare yourself for action. / Stand up and tell them / all I command you" (Jer 1:17). They were the ones whose hearts and lives were totally committed to YHWH and the refounding of the Israelite way of life according to the values of the covenant. With pain they saw the gap between YHWH's vision on the one hand and the reality of idolatry and injustice on the other. They knew there was another way of living designed by YHWH, and they insistently called others to this way of thinking, seeing, and acting.[31] Their mission and ministry is the creation of a community with the courage and the freedom to act with a different vision of what the world should be.[32]

---

[31] See Arbuckle, *Out of Chaos,* 57–62; Walter Brueggemann, *The Prophetic Imagination* (Philadelphia: Fortress Press, 1978) 62–79.

[32] Walter Brueggemann, *Hopeful Imagination: Prophetic Voices in Exile* (Philadelphia: Fortress Press, 1986) 99.

Like other refounding people the prophets had periods of doubts about their own ability and fears about proclaiming the message. In fact sometimes they yearned to escape the challenge: "I said, 'Ah, Lord Yahweh; you see, I do not know how to speak: I am only a child!'" (Jer 1:6). The people tempted them to gloss over or deny their sinful ways:

> To the prophets, "Do not prophesy
>   the truth to us;
> tell us flattering things;
>   have illusory visions;
> turn aside from the way, leave the path,
> rid us of the Holy One of Israel" (Isa 30:10-11).

Yet they did not fail the Lord, even though they were persecuted for the truth, because they themselves were radically converted to YHWH and the founding experience of the nation in the Exodus. Whether people listen or not, the prophet must speak of this experience and its urgent relevance for the world in which they live.

Refounding Christian Healthcare

Insanity is doing the same thing again and again but expecting different results (Rita M. Brown).[33]

The explanation so far has concentrated on the role of the refounding person in general, but now I turn to healthcare. What qualities should we expect to find, in addition to those already listed, in a refounding person (or group) in Christian healthcare? I define a refounding person in healthcare ministry in this way: A refounding person, in response to the inspiration of the Holy Spirit, is one who acutely sees the contemporary chasm between Gospel values and the healing needs of people in a postmodern world by imitating the "faith shock" and reaction of the founding person, who also perceived the gap between the healing message of the Gospel and the world

---

[33] Rita M. Brown as cited by Tracy Goss and others, "The Reinvention Roller Coaster," *Harvard Business Review on Change* (Boston: Harvard Business Review, 1996) 91.

of their time. Through creative strategies the refounding person moves to bridge the chasm. At the same time he or she restlessly summons others—especially people committed to healthcare reform—to faith/justice conversion and to go out into the unknown to implement the Gospel call for holistic healing. The following case study earths the definition.

CASE STUDY

Maria Will Not Give Up

Maria, a poor Italian immigrant to the United States, lived in a central city slum with her family and traveled daily to work as a housekeeper in a Catholic hospital. Each morning, as she entered the foyer, she would notice the mission statement elegantly framed under a spotlight. It began: "This hospital, in accordance with the founder's vision, is primarily committed to the health needs of the poor. . . ." Maria did not believe this. In fact, over the hundred years since its founding the hospital's primary ministry had moved to the care of middle- and upper-income patients, with less and less commitment to the poor.

If Maria was early enough, and no one was looking, she would vent her anger on the statement by shifting it off-balance, all the time praying to St. Anthony that things at the hospital would be different. The saint had to tell her what to do! After all, Anthony was a good friend of St. Francis, and St. Francis of Jesus, so St. Francis must know what to do. She was particularly happy if someone had gotten there before her and had removed the mission statement and placed it on the floor.

After several months Maria could not remain silent any longer, so she called a meeting of the housekeeping staff—mostly poor immigrants—and asked them what they thought of the gap between the mission statement and reality. They all felt enormous pain and agreed that they must do something. Months went by, but nothing happened. Finally, Maria could not take the pain any longer, so she called another meeting: "Where is the power in this hospital?" she asked. "In the board room on the thirty-first floor!" one employee answered. "But you cannot get in there!" Maria found a way. She exchanged jobs with Giovanni, the coffee waiter.

After several months on the job, despite her stumbling English, Maria set out to personally get to know the trustees (congregational owners) and lay board members, particularly by asking the latter about their families and their health. Finally, having prayed to St. Anthony for courage with the other cleaning women, she felt confident enough to speak directly to the board chairman. The interaction went this way: "Mr. Chairman, why are you here?" The chairman was surprised by the question, but answered: "I am here to serve the hospital and through it the patients!" "But," responded the nervous Maria, "the mission statement is a lie!" The chairman, stunned by the accusing language, listened to Maria explaining her pain and that of the other housekeepers and the poor in the suburb.

The chairman pondered what he had heard and he in turn eventually challenged the trustees and board, but not without resistance. He called on Maria to speak to them more formally. Some board members kept saying: "Let's be realistic! No margin, no mission! We cannot look after the needs of poor and cut back on our wealthy patients." But the chairman and other converts to the mission refused to be dissuaded from their task of refounding the hospital. Over a period of time they succeeded, despite the major adjustments needed in financing the hospital, and the poor again became the primary focus of the hospital. Several members of the board resigned in protest when the decision to refound was made.

The simple story has profound lessons, because Maria illustrates the definition of a refounding person. As a refounding person she experienced a "faith-shock"; that is, deep pain as she recognized the wide gap between the Gospel values of healing, as set out in the mission statement, and the reality. Unknowingly she relived the original faith-shock of the founder of the congregation last century. Maria was not a formal theologian, but a "theologian at the grassroots." She reflected in faith on reality, in light of the fundamental healing values of Jesus Christ; she had a faith-stubbornness and a humility that comes from an awareness of her weakness and her utter dependence on God. Maria was prepared, following her faith-shock and discovery that the hospital had drifted away from its founding myth, to do something by moving into the risky world of the unknown, even though this might have cost her her job. In addition, Maria recognized that she could not act alone; she summoned others to join her in refounding the hospital's culture—her friends and coworkers, and finally the chairman and board members and trustees. She also understood the need to use imagination to strategize at each stage of the project. Finally, Maria acted in faith as a prophet challenging people with an alternative and liberating way to view reality.

Formal Position Persons (FPPs): Refounding Task

> Management in [healthcare], important as it is, is not leadership. Leadership involves setting direction or creating a vision, enfranchising people in decision making, building coalitions that get things done, and inspiring and motivating others (W. Jack Duncan and others).[34]

Refounding persons are not just visionaries. They are visionaries who are stimulated and supported to act effectively by formal position persons exercising their leadership role appropriately. In the case study Maria was able to influence the hospital culture only because the chairman, as a formal position person, correctly acted as an official gate-keeper to the change.

FPPs and Transforming Leadership

Leadership, as explained briefly in Chapter 4, is a complex topic. Its nature varies in any given situation with the qualities of the leader, the group, the goals and tasks that have to be done, and finally the environment itself. Therefore, leadership that succeeds depends on the group choosing a leader able to take on the style of leading suited to the overall purpose of the group at a particular time. This is generally termed "situational leadership"; that is, the capacity of the leader to delegate, persuade, provide directives, or foster collaboration according to the occasion.[35]

---

[34] W. Jack Duncan and others, *Strategic Management in Health Care Organizations* (Oxford: Blackwell, 1995) 465.

[35] See Paul Hersey and Ken Blanchard, *Management of Organizational Behavior: Utilizing Human Resources* (Englewood Cliffs, N.J.: Prentice-Hall, 1982) 149–92;

Transformation leadership based on trust, mutuality of learning, and participation is necessary when that which has to be done is uncertain or ill-focused, as will be the case in times of rapid change or chaos. A transforming leader is one who molds and communicates a task-oriented vision for founding and refounding, providing transforming focus for the actions of others so that they are able to foster within themselves their own potential for creative change.[36] Maria could not have succeeded in her mission if the chairman had not himself encouraged an atmosphere of trust and openness to develop in his relationship with Maria.

Another way of describing transforming leadership is in terms of four functions which must be balanced: to conserve, to nurture or empower, to manage or renew, and to pro-act or refound. Maria exercised a conserving function by identifying with the heart of the founding experience; she managed by utilizing and transforming through her conversational style the simple process of providing coffee for the board room; she empowered her fellow workers to use their skills to support the project. Above all, she was pro-active because she used the coffee service as a means to challenge the trustees and board to be true to the mission statement. In doing this she became a refounder of the hospital ministry to the poor, bringing it back, with the empowering assistance of the chairman of the board, to its founding myth.

Given the difficulties of being pro-active, leaders may escape the challenge by over-stressing one or more other functions. For example, leaders can emphasize their nurturing role to the detriment of the pro-active or managerial functions. Or the managerial role can become an end in itself, human factors and the need to be pro-active being ignored. More commonly today the management function dominates.[37] The reforms of the National Health Service in Britain since the 1970s have been criticized precisely for failing to balance the four leadership functions by overstressing the management role. Sometimes sound management methods have also been neglected when the caring function has been given too much emphasis.

Managers are necessary, but their role differs from that of the transforming leader (see Chapter 3). As leadership adviser Warren Bennis comments: "The manager maintains; the leader develops. . . . The manager

Jonathan S. Rakich and others, *Managing Health Care Organizations* (Philadelphia: W. B. Saunders, 1977) 281–97.

[36] See James M. Burns, *Leadership* (New York: Harper Torch, 1978).

[37] See Allsop, *Health Policy and the NHS,* 42–59.

relies on control; the leader inspires trust. . . . The manager has his eye on the bottom line; the leader has his eye on the horizon."[38]

FPPs: "Gate-Keepers" to Change

The formal position person/group (e.g., trustees, boards, CEOs) has a fourfold task in order to be pro-active:

To Call People to Be Accountable to the Founding Myth. The vision is a mental passage from the known to the unknown, creating the future from a mass of existing facts, hopes, dreams, dangers, and opportunities (see Chapter 5). If it is to be owned as a statement, the FPP will involve as many people in the organization as possible in clarifying it; there is no more powerful force in driving a healthcare facility toward excellence than an inspiring and achievable vision, extensively shared. The mission statement sets out what must be done if the vision is to be realized, but if people are not committed to its implementation or challenged to accept it, it is a useless piece of paper. Maria recognized this and rightly became angry.

A study of mission statements of hospitals in the United States revealed that almost 85 percent of respondents with mission statements felt there was little commitment by employees to them.[39] This means that the appropriate FPPs in these hospitals were not calling their staffs to be accountable.

To Foster a Pro-active Healthcare Culture. The ultimate aim of an FFP is to establish an environment that guarantees the survival of the organization into the future, in a way that fits its founding vision. However, every FFP needs to be sensitive to four potential traps when confronted with organizational chaos:

(1) An FFP must be sufficiently aware of how difficult it is for a culture to change, even if it is in the state of chaos. A review of the New Zealand government's reform of healthcare and other departments concluded that "culture is what persists even when a department has been reorganized, new techniques introduced, its leaders and managers replaced."[40]

(2) An FFP cannot be seduced into the emotional or fantasy life of the group culture; unless FFPs are careful they will themselves unconsciously mirror the dysfunctionality of the culture in chaos.

[38] Warren Bennis, *On Becoming a Leader* (Reading, Mass.: Addison-Wesley, 1989) 45.
[39] See Charles K. Gibson and others, "An Empirical Investigation of the Nature of Hospital Mission Statements," *Health Management Review* 15:3 (1990) 35–46.
[40] Allen Schick, *The Spirit of Reform: Managing the New Zealand State Sector in a Time of Change* (Wellington: State Services Commission, 1996) 51.

(3) An FFP cannot attempt to energize a group when in fact at the time it is unable to be energized. Like an alcoholic, the group may need to be left alone to allow chaos to reach a point when some people can no longer deny it and express a need for change.

(4) Finally, an FFP must avoid developing a "savior complex," acting as an amateur therapist to the entire group, seeing failure as an insult to one's ability; better to use the skilled talents of the human resource or counseling departments.

Creative people, such as refounding persons, will make change happen, and can even overcome resistance, provided the FFP is prepared in practical ways to find innovative and committed persons; to place them in situations where they can act creatively and to support them; and to recognize the need for organizations/cultures to grieve over losses as a pre-condition for the acceptance of innovative people. I will now explain the first two steps, but the third will be considered in Chapter 9.

To Find Innovative People. Old Testament prophets were covenant-refounding persons, loving YHWH dearly, praying and yearning above everything else to build a community of believers committed to worship, mutual love, and justice. Yet in their lifetime there were others who claimed to be prophetic but were in fact dangerous agitators; in their hearts they were enemies of the people and their welfare.

Likewise in any human organization, including healthcare facilities. People may use the language of refounding, but if they lack authenticity they are dangerous to themselves and to others. Therefore, let FFPs exercise appropriate discernment and avoid concluding too quickly that this or that person is a refounder. In fact, it is inadvisable to apply the term to anyone until the person has truly proved worthy of it by actions over a lengthy period. The blunt and worldly-wise advice of Warren Bennis is relevant here:

> Guard against the crazies. Innovation is seductive. It attracts interesting people. It also attracts people who will distort your ideas into something monstrous. . . . A change-oriented administrator should be damned sure that the people he or she recruits are change agents but not agitators. . . . Eccentricities and idiosyncracies in change agents are often useful and valuable. Neurosis isn't.[41]

---

[41] Warren Bennis, *Why Leaders Can't Lead: The Unconscious Conspiracy Continues* (San Francisco: Jossey-Bass, 1990) 148.

To Position Creative Persons Strategically: "New Belongs Elsewhere."
Readers are reminded of an essential truth: if there is to be an innovation-producing healthcare facility, open to radical change, FPPs must work to effect an environment in which this kind of growth can occur. It means a climate in which members can view one another as resources rather than competitors or judges; a climate of openness and mutual support in which differences are confronted and worked through, and in which feedback on performance is a mutual responsibility among members so that all can learn to contribute more. This is a most challenging task.[42] Not only may it demand radical change in existing organizational culture, but it runs counter to the wider secular postmodern culture of individualism and competition, and to prevailing management theory.

As has been explained, resistance to change in organizational cultures is to some degree natural and inevitable. For example, people can hold back from change because they do not see the need for it, or because they fear losing their job, status, or identity (see Chapter 4). Not surprisingly, innovative people are feared because they challenge the accepted order of things. They are often referred to in pejorative terms as "dissenters," "deviants," "traitors to tradition," and "corporate heretics,"[43] and efforts are made to stop their "dangerous" ideas from infecting the culture. Harold Leavitt and Homa Bahrami speak of group pressure against a "deviant" moving through several stages: from rational argument through emotional seduction to attack and, finally, amputation.[44]

I have seen this pattern acted out on many occasions; the following case study illustrates the dynamic.

CASE STUDY

An Innovator Is "Amputated"

George, manager of the orthopedic department of a non-profit hospital in the United States, explained to me

---

[42] See Raymond A. Bauer, "The Obstinate Audience," *The Planning of Change,* ed. Warren Bennis and others (London: Holt, Rinehart and Winston, 1970) 507–25.

[43] See Art Kleiner, *The Age of Heretics: Heroes, Outlaws, and the Forerunners of Corporate Change* (London: Nicholas Brealey, 1996) ix–xii.

[44] See Harold J. Leavitt and Homa Bahrami, *Managerial Psychology: Managing Behavior in Organizations* (Chicago: University of Chicago Press, 1988) 190–8.

his experience of marginalization. The stages are indicated in the text.

I had researched for several months into how our department could best extend its services into a poor area of the city. The report was sent to other members of the executive board, but the moment I formally presented it to the group I felt a coldness and an impatience. Without my knowledge, the CEO and other executives had an alternative plan. The CEO said: "Your plan is good, but it is not as good as ours." He and others tried to argue with me about the value of their plan *[rational approach]*. But it became obvious that the group had not studied my plan. After the CEO called for a coffee break several executives came to me and said: "Look, George, you are a good friend *[emotional seduction]*. Why can't you see our way like you have always done?" I stood my ground asking that my plan be seriously considered, but this evoked the response: "You are stubborn! It is impossible to work with you!" *[attack* or *bullying]*. Back at the conference table the meeting resumed and I felt very strange, because it was as though I no longer existed. No eyes turned to me. No questions on other matters *[amputation* or *ostracism]*.

George finally left the hospital for a similar facility in the same city where his plan was accepted and implemented. The previous hospital failed to act even on the CEO's plan.

Others have shared the ways in which their reports on the necessity of change within their healthcare facilities have been rejected in subtle and not-so-subtle ways. There is the "pass-the-buck method" ("We are submitting your report to a subcommittee."); the "minoritis" response ("There are minor inaccuracies, so we feel they raise serious questions about your entire argument."); the "bottom-drawer method" ("Thank you for the fine report. Expect to hear from us in due course." Then nothing is done.)[45] Others have confided in me that so much energy has gone into

[45] See Gerald A. Arbuckle, "The Marginalization of Social Scientists within the Church," *Human Development* 10:2 (1989) 16–21.

defending themselves that they are too weary to give of their best to the institutions.

Creative people are rare and precious resources. The organization needs them to be heard, productively challenged, and encouraged. The manager's task is to facilitate this and preempt unnecessary de-energization from group pressure.

This does not mean that creative people are to be shielded from all conflict, because creativity and adaptation are born of tension, passion, and conflict. It is a question of protecting creative people from negative conflict, conflict that simply does not serve the mission. Dispute does more than make us more creative; it makes us whole, challenging us to move along the way of development. Psychologist Robert Johnson notes: "No aspect of the human psyche can live in a healthy state unless it is in tension with its opposite. Power without love becomes brutal; feeling without strength becomes sentimental."[46]

Example: Jesus Provides the Solution

Using colorful imagery Jesus warns of the danger of being depowered by the forces of the status quo: "No one puts a piece of unshrunken cloth onto an old cloak, because the patch pulls away from the cloak and the tear gets worse. Nor do people put new wine into old wineskins; otherwise, the skins burst, the wine runs out, and the skins are lost" (Matt 9:16-17).

Then Jesus gives the solution: "No; they put new wine in fresh skins and both are preserved" (Matt 9:17). Each innovative project in a refounding process is the new wine, requiring some degree of protection lest it be smothered by existing structures and attitudes of the surrounding organization or culture in chaos.

Recall also the instruction of Jesus to the apostles: "And if anyone does not welcome you or listen to what you have to say, as you walk out of the house or town shake the dust from your feet" (Matt 10:14). That is, if people are not interested in refounding, and especially if they seek to subvert it deliberately or otherwise, following Jesus' admonition our energies must be unequivocally directed elsewhere. Go wherever there is life, not death:

---

[46] Robert A. Johnson, *We: Understanding the Psychology of Romantic Love* (New York: Harper and Row, 1983) 23.

"Leave the dead to bury their dead; your duty is to go and spread the news of the kingdom of God" (Luke 9:60).

The word of wisdom is this: build structures and lines of accountability that protect creative persons from undue interference from other people and systems. I call this advice the axiom of "the new belongs elsewhere." The following two case studies illustrate in practical ways the meaning of this axiom.

Examples of the Axiom: "The New Belongs Elsewhere"

Example 1: Japanese Firms Learn a Lesson

With few exceptions, Japanese firms venturing abroad now prefer to build their own organizations, for fear that taking over an existing firm will involve a de-energizing culture clash. In buying existing firms the Japanese often found they were taking over pre-existing negative cultures with, for example, a history of labor disputes, outdated working practices, and adversarial management. They find it is far safer to build a new firm from scratch, thus developing a new culture that is open to change.[47]

Example 2: A Board Protects a Heart Specialist

The board of management of a hospital, supported by the trustees, accepted the plans of a heart surgeon to establish a research unit. However, the surgeon felt the unit could be attached to an existing vascular research department, but the board disagreed. Being concerned that unnecessary time and energy of a specialist would be lost in obtaining the department's approval and support to begin and continue the venture, the board decided to establish the unit as a separate entity directly responsible to itself. This was done and the unit is flourishing today.

I have seen cases where the axiom has been applied successfully, but also numerous projects where it has not been that have ended in failure. In the heart research project above the board formulated clear lines of authority, which made for regular accountability; outsiders knew that they could not interfere. This was a recipe for success. The project was ex-

---

[47] See "When the Bridge Caught Fire," *The Economist* (September 7, 1991) 83.

plained to other departments, and any significant interaction with the heart unit had to go through the board's representative for five years. The heart surgeon was instructed to keep the board regularly informed of the progress of the unit and the board agreed that for five years it would have the responsibility of informing and educating the hospital and community about the unit. In this way the heart surgeon and fellow researchers were free to use their talents directly for the project.

FPPs and Servant Leadership

Patriarchal management with its roots in modern culture (see Chapter 1) is a one-way process; namely, the managers, backed by the authority of their status, tell people what to do, call them to be accountable at set times, but do not expect and are not willing to receive honest feedback on their own performance. It is "top-down" management.

Servant-leadership is a new paradigm characteristic of a paramodern culture. It is built on a two-way process that is to be ongoing: the servant-leader expects to receive honest feedback as well as to offer it to those served. This evokes trust and people grow and become creative in such an atmosphere.[48] Sr. Joyce DeShano of the Sisters of St. Joseph Health System in the United States comments: "Servant-leadership is the power to influence rather than the power to control. We realize that when we choose to influence people rather than control them, it at first might seem like weakness, but it really calls forth an inner strength."[49]

Peter Block uses the word "governance" instead of leadership in order to avoid any connotations of the old patriarchal control model. Governance is the way we define the purpose of our organization and use power and resources,[50] and "stewardship" is at the heart of governance. By stewardship Block means "accountability without control or compliance."[51] This is exactly what servant-leadership is about. Servant-leadership, like stewardship, assumes a commitment to serving others' needs and stresses the use of openness and persuasion, not control or coercion.

---

[48] See Ann McGree-Cooper, "Accountability as Covenant: The Taproot of Servant-Leadership," *Insights on Leadership,* ed. Larry C. Spears (New York: John Wiley, 1998) 78–9.

[49] Joyce DeShano as cited by John S. Lore, "Servant Leadership in a Christian Organization," *Insights on Leadership,* ed. Spears, 307.

[50] Peter Block, *Stewardship: Choosing Service over Self-Interest* (San Francisco: Berrett-Koehler, 1993) 5.

[51] Ibid., xx.

CASE STUDY

British National Service Fails the Test

Anton Obholzer[52] claims that the Thatcherite style of management in Britain's healthcare systems gave managers more power not to have consultation with healthcare staffs because it was thought to be a waste of time and therefore inefficient. This top-down approach views dialogue and cooperation between the different sectors of health care as out-of-date. Managers (95 percent of whom are not doctors) are kept away from clinicians and the patients.

Obholzer examines the effects of organizational splitting whereby doctors are not involved in the detail of budgets or financial management of the healthcare system. It encourages doctors to share with the public and media the fantasy that if only they had unlimited health funds there would be nothing they could not do. Obholzer concludes: "It makes for the creation of a system . . . that fosters individual and professional omnipotence, a system in which weakness, doubt and distress are seen as undesirable qualities and where failure can be attributed to uncaring managers and insufficient resources."[53]

The implications of this case study are serious. The future of healthcare in the Western world depends not on managers and clinicians going their separate ways, but on partnership in which dialogue is the accepted way of acting. So fundamental is the split between the parties that this partnership will not develop without the aid of people of refounding qualities.

Jesus Christ: Servant-Leadership—Attitudinal and Action Change

Jesus Christ made it quite clear by word and action that refounding or transformative leadership means servant-leadership. This requires cultural

---

[52] Anton Obholzer, "Managing Social Anxieties in Public Sector Organizations," *The Unconscious at Work,* ed. Anton Obholzer and Vega Z. Roberts (London: Routledge: 1996) 169–78.

[53] Ibid., 173.

and personal attitudinal changes in the leader as well as followers: "You know that among the gentiles those they call their rulers lord it over them, and their great men make their authority felt. Among you this is not to happen" (Mark 10:42-43). That is, leadership is to be exercised in a collaborative not a patriarchal way. This is possible, Jesus insists, provided there is an inner conversion to this way of leading. Only then is one prepared to listen to others and to be changed by them as well as lead them.

When the sons of Zebedee sought the first places in the kingdom, Jesus responded by asking them a very awkward question: "Can you drink the cup that I shall drink, or be baptised with the baptism with which I shall be baptised?" (Mark 10:38). They did not grasp this startling new form of leadership and the personal demands it would place on them. In contrast to the use of one-way coercive authority commonly practiced by leaders in Palestine and much desired by the sons of Zebedee, Jesus proposed this paradox: "Anyone who wants to become great among you must be your servant, and anyone who wants to be first among you must be slave to all" (Mark 10:43-44). During the Last Supper he reiterated that authority among his followers must be at the service of building community: "For who is the greater: the one at table or the one who serves? The one at table, surely? Yet here am I among you as one who serves!" (Luke 22:27).

So accustomed were the apostles to authority being synonymous with coercive power over others, with status and privileges attached, that they could not grasp the meaning of Jesus' instructions. So he did what he preached, hoping that they would understand his message. He personally exemplified kindness, listening, service, humility, and love for others:

> I have come
> so that they may have life
> and have it to the full.
> I am the good shepherd:
> the good shepherd lays down his life for his sheep (John 10:10-11).

The apostles finally understood, and in their own teaching they repeated that authority was synonymous with service—the service of listening and persuasion, not exploitation and the use of fear to obtain compliance: "Do not lord it over the group which is in your charge, but be an example for the flock" (1 Pet 5:3). St. Paul insists that only through love can we begin to understand the depth of the demands that servant-leadership commits us to; the measure of love is the sacrifice of Christ for us (1 Cor 13:4-7).

Thus servant-leadership begins in the heart of a leader. Hospital staffs know intuitively when their CEOs and managers are truly committed to dialogue. While in Fiji researching the impact of credit unions on village life, a study initiated by Jesuit missionary Fr. Marion Ganey, I wondered why they were successful when similar projects established by government were failures. I believe Father Ganey was effective because of his deep inner conversion. He was able to give to others because he was first willing to learn from them, as he said:

> One thing I have learned. . . . I was never able to do anything for the people . . . until I fully realized through my whole heart and soul that I was not doing them a favor by coming, but that they were doing me a favor and a great one, by permitting me to come into their lives. . . . We are not the people's boss; we are their servant.

One villager described the missionary's leadership style: "When Father Ganey comes into our village, we all immediately feel ten years younger and ten feet tall!" In refounding or transformative leadership all grow tall.

Trustees, Boards, and CEOs: Roles and Relationships

Stewardship is maintaining something in trust for others. In healthcare, trustees, governing boards, CEOs, and staffs are called into a cooperative venture to maintain their facilities in trust for the good of the community. However, there is confusion about the meaning of the terms "trustees" and "governing boards." For example "trustees" sometimes means "members of the governing boards"; at other times that is not the case.

In this text I mean "trustees" to be those people who own or legally represent the owners of an organization. The trustees of a healthcare facility have the primary responsibility for ensuring that the mission continues; this means reaffirming the vision, mission, and values of the organization. David Smith reinforces the need for trustees of healthcare facilities to acknowledge the importance of their task:

> [The] optimal trustee is someone willing and able to discuss and assess the identity of an organization, someone with moral insight . . . and the ability to consider options reasonably. . . .[54] Medical expertise cannot determine the relative importance of a well-baby clinic or a cardiac catheterization unit. . . . [They] are not simply the territory of medical or administrative experts but must be taken up by the group [trustees] responsible for determining the hospital's identity.[55]

[54] Smith, *Entrusted,* 109.
[55] Ibid., 29.

Governing Boards

> Effective governance by the board of a non-profit organization is a rare and unnatural act (Barbara E. Taylor and others).[56]

According to Cyril Houle, a governing board is "an organized group of people with the authority collectively to control and foster an institution that is usually administered by a qualified executive and staff."[57] This means that boards exist to formulate policies in light of the vision, mission, and values set out by the trustees. They are to shape the organization according to the founding myth as interpreted by the trustees. If they fail to keep to their task in today's healthcare turmoil refounding will be very difficult, if not impossible. The board will be blocking creativity at key levels of the system, not fostering it.

The history of boards is not encouraging. Peter Drucker comments bluntly: "There is one thing all boards have in common . . . they do not function."[58] Given this sobering comment on the ineffectiveness of governing boards it is especially important to further clarify their roles and those of the trustees of healthcare facilities.

Governing Boards: Failures and Need for Refounding

When healthcare facilities existed in the relatively orderly environment of the pre-1960s there was little need for a board of governance. Today, however, in the world of healthcare chaos, a board consisting of skilled people is essential if appropriate policies are to be made and executives are to be accountable to them. It demands a profound, refounding shift in thinking and action.

Healthcare boards of non-profit organizations may fail for the following reasons:

- the trustees are confused about their own task, which evokes a malaise in their board of management;

---

[56] Barbara E. Taylor and others, "The New Work of the Nonprofit Board," *Harvard Business Review* (September–October 1996) 36.

[57] Cyril O. Houle, *Governing Boards: Their Nature and Nurture* (San Francisco: Jossey-Bass, 1997) 6.

[58] Peter Drucker as cited by James E. Orlikoff and Mary K. Totten, "Board Job Descriptions," *Trustee* (January 1997) 1. See also Dennis D. Pointer and Charles M. Ewell, *Really Governing: How Health System and Hospital Boards Can Make More of a Difference* (Albany: Delmar, 1994) xv–xvi.

- there is no knowledge and ownership of the founding myth as articulated by the trustees;

- their job description is unclear; therefore, boundaries are confused, energy lost;

- the CEO is unsure of the board's primary task;

- members lack appropriate expertise, so the CEO's time is taken up educating the board;[59]

- board members lack skills for team action;

- the chairperson is unable to lead appropriately;

- the board spends too little time planning for the future; it just reacts to problems[60] (James Orlikoff recommends that boards spend at least 80 percent of their time planning for the future);[61]

- the principles of delegation and subsidiarity are not understood or adhered to; trivial items or matters that should be left to subcommittees clutter the board's agenda;

- the CEO and the board are in competition; for example, the CEO holds back information until the last moment in an attempt to force a favorable decision;

- the board does not regularly evaluate itself in the light of clear goals;

- the sources of the board's information for decision-making are too narrow;

- members are chosen not on the basis of their skills and acceptance of the sponsors' values, but for their leadership of representative groups in the wider community; hence, the board is ill-equipped for the complex world of healthcare turmoil and decision-making.[62]

There are two types of boards in non-profit organizations: the "philanthropic" and the "task." Traditionally boards have been primarily philanthropic; that is, their purpose has been to link the hospital to its surrounding community so they have been made up of representatives of the commu-

[59] See Taylor, "The New Work," 36; and Orlikoff and Totten, "Board Job Descriptions," 1.

[60] See Pointer and Ewell, *Really Governing,* 52–4.

[61] James E. Orlikoff as cited in *Health Progress* 78:4 (1997) 26.

[62] See Terese Hudson, "Bye, Bye Big Boards," *Hospitals and Health Networks* (June 5, 1997) 33–4.

nity, such as business people, doctors, and local politicians. Philanthropic boards are unlikely to respond pro-actively in times of chaos simply because their members are not chosen for their expertise.[63]

By contrast, task governing boards are composed of members chosen on the basis of ability to aid the organization to achieve its primary goals. Consequently they have more chance of successfully leading healthcare facilities through tumultuous times. To move from a philanthropic to a task board is a process of refounding.

Trustees: Responsibilities

In order to facilitate refounding through the establishment of a task board trustees must:[64]

- be convinced that a task governing board, as opposed to a philanthropic governing board, is essential.

- clarify the purpose and job description of the board in the light of the conditions of chaos: "The most fundamental characteristic of excellent governance is that board members have a shared understanding of their job."[65] A shared understanding on the part of board members cannot be achieved suddenly, so trustees will need to provide initial and ongoing orientation. This orientation will provide members with a clear understanding of the vision, mission, and values of their healthcare facility, as well as what is expected of board members.

- clarify what powers are to be retained by the trustees and explain them clearly to the board.

- choose board members on the basis of their skills for the task and their willingness to make decisions in light of the vision, mission, and values of the trustees.

- alert the board to the fact that it may have to assume prophetic or advocacy roles in the facility and/or in the wider community in defense of its vision, mission, and values.

- insist that the board allows adequate time for members to develop skills necessary for teamwork.

[63] See Duncan and others, *Strategic Management,* 477.
[64] See Pappas, *Reengineering Your Nonprofit Organization,* 101–22.
[65] Orlikoff and Totten, "Board Job Descriptions," 1.

- work with the board to clarify the task and role of the CEO. In choosing the CEO trustees need to be aware that the person will be responsible for the maintenance of the vision, mission, and values in the healthcare facility, so this means being sure that the person accepts them.

- check that the board makes the CEO's task "doable" and that the person is seen as a colleague in policy development.[66]

- appoint a chairperson with proven skills of delegation and the ability to call board members, subsidiary committees, and CEOs to account for tasks set.

CASE STUDY ▬▬▬▬▬▬▬▬▬▬▬▬▬▬▬▬▬▬▬▬▬▬

A Board Refuses to Clarify/Own its Task

The trustees of a large non-profit Catholic healthcare facility had established a task governing board, but had not provided its members with an adequate explanation of their Gospel-based vision. They assumed, after interviewing each member personally, that lengthy orientation was unnecessary as the members were practicing Christians.

Within a short time problems began to emerge within the board. First, the board spent an inordinate amount of time criticizing the CEO and other members of the executive board, failing to formulate adequate pro-active policies for the ongoing development of the hospital complex and outreach ministries. Second, board members began to treat the trustees in a patronizing manner, making comments like: "The sisters are too removed from the real world of business, so they have nothing to give to our deliberations." The trustees were kept informed of the board's decisions, but were not in a position to contribute to its deliberations. Third, the board made some policies on the basis of economic rationalist principles in direct opposition to the healing mission of

---

[66] See Karen M. Sandrick, "How to Support Your CEO," *Trustee* 50:2 (1997) 14–18.

Jesus Christ. Fourth, the CEO, highly committed to the mission, found herself increasingly excluded from the board's deliberations. After complaining several times she resigned. Finally, after a year several board members also resigned due to the fact that they frequently felt bullied and marginalized by two members.

The trustees, realizing the board was dysfunctional, invited the chairperson to choose a consultant to evaluate its performance. It was found that:

- board members, though highly qualified, had remained from the beginning a group of individuals, never becoming a team committed to a common vision and mission; they frequently referred to themselves as a team, though their behavior contradicted this. Several board members were strong personalities brought in from the secular corporate arena "to get things done," and they were unwilling to work in a team.

- the chairperson had a strong desire to control everything, subtly bullying board members, especially female members, while being deferential and ingratiating to the trustees.

- the board was split, the majority submitting to the chairperson and the minority eventually resigning.

- the board was unable to address the real internal and external issues.

In this case study the trustees had made several serious mistakes: they had neglected to provide a solid orientation to the vision, mission, and values of the hospital complex, which meant that the board was never clear about its primary task; they had not ensured the board's commitment to operating according to principles of servant-leadership, with the role and accountability of each member being clarified; and they had waited too long to call the chairperson and the board to be accountable for their actions.

The trustees had also accepted the board's negative and incorrect view that, as sisters, the trustees knew nothing about the world of business and lacked expertise to evaluate the board's actions. Lacking self-confidence, the trustees had hesitated to challenge the board's decisions. It was recommended that the trustees seek ongoing expert assistance to develop their own sense of self-worth as a team and their ability to act on their authority as trustees. The advice was accepted.

After months the board was refounded by the trustees. In their interviews with prospective board members the trustees spelled out their expectations. For example, board members must seek to embody the vision, mission, and values of the healing Jesus in their policy-making; members were expected to develop team or partnership skills according to the philosophy of servant-leadership. They were told that the trustees viewed a team as "a small number of people with complementary skills who are committed to a common purpose, performance goals, and approach for which they hold themselves mutually accountable,"[67] and places its primary emphasis on the achievement of a common purpose, not the satisfaction of the needs of individual members.

CEOs: Called to Be Refounders

The success of a healthcare facility depends more on the CEOs creative ability, competence, and drive than on any other individual.[68] In today's healthcare turmoil they need the qualities of a refounding person. Andre Delbercq describes why this must be so: "With the hyperturbulence of industry readjustment . . . CEOs have less personal and organizational control. They have to create organizations that can respond to change, which means they are [to be] constantly readjusting, redesigning, reconceptualizing."[69]

The CEO must believe in the philosophy of Christian healthcare. If the CEO (together with the board) believes passionately in it as the guiding principle of the facility, it will be at the heart of all decision-making. Barry Eisenberg comments on the importance of this point in healthcare organizations: "Nothing is more critical to the achievement of customer service . . . than the personal beliefs of the senior executive and board. It's really that simple."[70]

The CEO in particular must fulfill six functions, all of which demand quantum-leap resourcefulness:

[67] Jon R. Katzenbach and Douglas K. Smith, *The Wisdom of Teams* (New York: Harper-Business, 1994) 45.

[68] See Pointer and Ewell, *Really Governing*, 63.

[69] Andre Delbecq as cited by Sandrick, "How to Support Your CEO," 16.

[70] Barry Eisenberg, "Customer Service in Healthcare: A New Era," *Hospital and Health Services Administration* 42:1 (1997) 25.

(1) Articulate a Christian vision of healthcare services, which will holistically and financially best serve patients and the community. The vision will involve *inter alia* an emphasis on managed care/integrated delivery services,[71] wellness programs, and a preferential option for the poor.

(2) Implement all policies in ways that conform to the vision, mission, and values of the healing Jesus.

(3) Call all within the organization to be accountable to the founding philosophy.

(4) With the support of the board and others, develop a courageous strategic plan that will guide the healthcare system into the future based on the changing needs of people.[72]

(5) Educate all concerned, including board members, to prepare them for the inevitable and radical changes that refounding demands.

(6) Become adept at linking trustees/boards, managers, and physicians, which requires significant analytic and interpersonal skills to overcome an often long and contentious history. The relationship between these three subcultures has been likened to "a three-legged wobbly stool—each pursuing somewhat different goals and having a different view of the organization's mission."[73]

A healthcare CEO can be subject to considerable stress. For actual stress to occur there must be uncertainty about the outcome and the outcome must be important; stress is greatest for people who sense that they are uncertain as to whether they will succeed or fail.[74] In today's healthcare industry there is considerable uncertainty about the consequences of any significant planning, and CEOs are the first to experience the accompanying stress. They can feel pulled in many directions at the same time, because different clients often have conflicting expectations. Since CEOs are also often the bearers of bad news, for example, laying off employees

---

[71] See Andrea Y. Coleman, "Managing Managed Care," *Health Progress* 78:1 (1997) 36.

[72] See Edward S. Schneller, "Accountability for Health Care: A White Paper on Leadership and Management for the U.S. Health Care System," *Health Care Management* 22:1 (1997) 47.

[73] Ibid., 42.

[74] See Stephen P. Robbins, *Organizational Behavior: Concepts, Controversies and Applications* (Englewood Cliffs, N.J.: Prentice-Hall, 1989) 501.

or closing services, they are also apt to be the targets of people's anger. It can be a very lonely job indeed. No one who cannot cope with considerable ambiguity should apply!

The pressures on contemporary CEOs will increase. I do not see any person surviving for long in the job if they and their boards do not adopt a servant-leadership style of partnership and mutual accountability.[75] Significant changes can take place in a board's structure and function when the CEO engages with the board in critical analysis of issues.[76]

It is true that the relationship between a board and the CEO is a sensitive one. The CEO is simultaneously an equal, as normally CEOs in healthcare systems are board members, and a subordinate whose performance needs to be evaluated by the board.[77] If the board and CEO are not prepared to develop a partnership then neither party will function adequately in today's healthcare environment. This in itself is a refounding challenge, because traditionally healthcare boards have seen CEOs more as employees than as peers in a common project. Healthcare consultant Keith Pryor warns that boards should be "as demanding of themselves as they are of their CEOs."[78] This necessitates that a board: participate in strategic planning with the CEO, prioritizing issues according to the objectives of the healthcare system; keep as informed as the CEO about the healthcare environment; codify the criteria for evaluating the CEO's performance; provide clear and unbiased feedback on the CEO's performance; and be open to critical self-analysis.[79]

Non-profit Healthcare: Can It Be Justified?

[The] fate of Catholic health care will depend upon our ability to communicate the positive theological vision undergirding the corporal works of mercy (M. Cathleen Kaveny and James E. Keenan, S.J.).[80]

---

[75] See Manfred F. R. Kets de Vries, "On Becoming a CEO: Transference and the Addictiveness of Power," *Organizations on the Couch,* ed. Manfred F. R. Kets de Vries and others (San Francisco: Jossey-Bass, 1991) 120–39.

[76] See Anthony R. Kovner and others, "Board Development in Two Hospitals: Lessons from a Demonstration," *Hospital and Health Services Administration* 42:1 (1977) 98.

[77] See Pointer and Ewell, *Really Governing,* 63.

[78] Keith Pryor as cited by Sandrick, "How to Support Your CEO," 16.

[79] See ibid.

[80] M. Cathleen Kaveny and James F. Keenan, "Ethical Issues in Health-Care Restructuring," *Theological Studies* 56:1 (1995) 150.

Criticisms of Non-Profit Healthcare

The move in recent decades from philanthropic to task hospital boards; the waiting lists for operations in countries such as Australia, New Zealand, and Britain; and the millions of uninsured in the United States have eroded the good regard once enjoyed by hospitals. In addition, public cynicism has intensified over the excess profits that non-profit hospitals are perceived as experiencing.[81]

For-profit organizations are claiming that the voluntary hospitals have an unfair financial advantage. Notwithstanding the fundamental legal distinctions, non-profit hospitals are looking increasingly like investor-owned hospitals from several perspectives. For example, in the United States by the 1980s 95 percent of the income of non-profits was being obtained from the sale of services to patients, compared with about 98 percent for for-profit hospitals. Like the for-profit hospitals the non-profits cannot attract capital investment unless they are being financially successful, which means competing for patients in the marketplace.[82] And like for-profits, non-profit facilities must in today's world of great uncertainties have adequate financial reserves.

The fact is that Christian-based non-profit healthcare is big business. Secular critics, while praising sponsors for their business acumen, wonder if the mission of the healing Jesus has been lost sight of as institutions strategize to survive financially in a highly competitive and uncertain market. In a front-page article *The Wall Street Journal* recently reported with obvious amazement that the Daughters of Charity National (U.S.A.) Health System had reserves of $2 billion in cash and investments, "believed to be one of the largest reserves of any non-profit hospital system in the country."[83] Staff reporter Monica Langley comments: "The health system's financial success demonstrates just how profitable many of the nation's so-called 'non-profits' have become."[84] The article failed to point out the

---

[81] See Marc D. Smith, "Missions, Margins, and the Multitudes," *The Anatomy of a Merger: BJC Health System,* ed. Wayne M. Lerner (Chicago: Health Administration Press, 1997) 53.

[82] See Bradford H. Gray, *The Profit Motive and Patient Care: The Changing Accountability of Doctors and Hospitals* (Cambridge, Mass.: Harvard University Press, 1991) 65–6.

[83] Monica Langley, "Nuns' Zeal for Profits Shapes Hospital Chain, Wins Wall Street Fans: But as Daughters of Charity Builds $2 Billion Reserve, Some Question Its Goals," *The Wall Street Journal* (January 7, 1998) 1A.

[84] Ibid.

considerable assistance being given by this system to the poor. The National Catholic Reporter, commenting on this report, felt that "in many cases, distinctiveness [of Catholic healthcare] is blurred. Even if gospel values . . . are driving institutions from within, those values are obscured by the public face of megasystems that rival the largest U.S. for-profit corporations in financial scale."[85]

Other critics complain that, in order to survive as costs continue to escalate, non-profit healthcare is serving the rich even more than in the past. Not surprisingly, some sponsors wonder if, in view of their mission, they can continue to justify holding on to their healthcare institutions. Have these institutions, they ask, become obstacles to preaching the Good News? Is the financial efficiency demanded by the risks of managed care inimical to good stewardship? In other words, can the realities of big business and the healing mission of Jesus Christ ever be related positively?[86] Are institutions barriers to the proclamation of the Gospel? Does the preferential option for the poor exclude concern for the wealthy in society?

The following guidelines may help readers to respond to questions of this kind. People expect Christian hospitals to be different from other healthcare facilities. Provision of healthcare for the poor is not only at the core of the Christian mission, but is also the foundation of their tax-exempt status. Christian healthcare must not only say that the poor are a high priority; they must be seen to be fulfilling this commitment.[87] Actions must mirror rhetoric of mission statements!

Responding to Criticism: Guidelines

Guideline 1:
Recognize the Potential Split between "Mission" and "Business"

The potential split between mission and margin has already been explained (see Chapter 4). Note here that the tension is not resolved by downplaying either mission or business. The fact is that Gospel stewardship demands that we use resources efficiently. This may mean that health-

[85] Editorial, "Catholic Health Care Poised between Mission and Money," *National Catholic Reporter* (January 23, 1998) 36.

[86] See Richard McCormick, "The End of Catholic Hospitals," *America* 179:1 (1998) 5–11.

[87] See Kaveny and Keenan, "Ethical Issues," 142.

care systems need significant reserves and investments to protect them from the negative effects of an uncertain economy.

However, the mission is to be the senior partner. Trustees should not be embarrassed to request that at every board meeting time be set aside for a brief reflection on the founding story. Margaret Wheatley believes that the future of Catholic healthcare is ultimately dependent on owning the mission of the healing Christ, and economic decisions must respect these foundations:

> I know [people will say] . . . we have this bottom line responsibility now. My observation is that the way one gets to these new accountabilities in health-care is still through the heart. . . . We've separated out economic well-being from spiritual practice . . . and this is just a travesty and it's time to realize that what you're describing [i.e., mission] is the source of all prosperity.[88]

CASE STUDY

Christian Values Become Part of Every Decision

A management board of a Catholic hospital on an annual retreat weekend acknowledged that it was minimally conscious of the role of mission in its decision-making. After decisions had already been made members occasionally felt embarrassed that the mission leader had not been approached for her comments. When she did comment, however, board members listened condescendingly, impatient to move on to "more practical things."

It was decided that:

• all board members are to be responsible for the mission of the hospital; therefore, they had to know the mission, with its biblical and historical roots;

• no one person could decide if a particular project was in conformity with the mission; it had to be a decision in which all had the chance to publicly evaluate the project according to the criteria set by the mission;

---

[88] Margaret Wheatley, in joint video interview with Gerald A. Arbuckle, Catholic Health Association of the United States (March 15, 1995).

- to achieve a common sense of the mission, each meeting would begin with a twenty-minute faith sharing around an appropriate biblical reading;

- the trustees would not appoint future board members unless they were prepared to accept this mission-based process of decision-making;

- the board would have two weekends annually to learn more about the biblical and theological foundations of the mission of the hospital.

One year later the board members evaluated their progress. They concluded that:

- the more they accepted the process the more trust, energy, and openness to one another they experienced for their task;

- most commonly a consensus emerged and decisions were grounded in both the values of the hospital and the advice of business experts; people felt "comfortable" with these decisions;

- the mission leader no longer felt defensive or marginalized, but a valued member of a team;

- all agreed that they needed a sharper definition of Catholic identity; most recognized that they were "working out of a pre-Vatican II model" of identity.

One board member commented: "At the beginning the process was difficult. I was itching to get on to practical issues, but gradually my impatience lessened and has now disappeared. I now wonder how we were ever able to make correct decisions in the past." All agreed with this view.

No commentary on this case study is necessary except to conclude that a non-profit healthcare facility cannot preserve its special character unless there is a "relentless focus on pursuit of the organization's mission."[89]

[89] Smith, *Entrusted,* 113.

Guideline 2:
A Significant Institutional Presence Is Required to Protect Mission

> Catholic institutions [e.g., healthcare] must survive. . . . The stakes are too high and potentially too great: to make a difference for sacredness, stewardship, and the social fabric of this country (Fr. J. Bryan Hehir).[90]

Postmodernist ideology is not kind to institutions (see Chapter 1). During the cultural revolution of the 1960s there was a massive erosion of the legitimacy of traditional institutions: business, government, education, the churches, family. Overall, the revolution was an attempt to make uncertainty not a passing feature of life, but a total way of living. Since institutions are about certainties, boundaries, secure identities, they became objects of suspicion, and this feeling still lingers in the collective mind today.[91]

It is naive to assume life can proceed without institutions. People cannot govern themselves without political institutions, earn an income without economic institutions.[92] Institutions are simply stable, orderly patterns of behavior which persist and crystallize in the course of time, and to which people become attached as a result of their role in the formation of identity, or through investments of energy and social interest.[93] Loosely patterned activities can become institutions, as when a coffee break becomes both a right and a ritual. A story (myth) will develop that legitimizes this right and ritual. Once an institution is formed it shapes collective and individual experience, providing a sense of identity to the people who adhere to it.

Morally good institutions, however, can become corrupt when the founding story is lost and nothing matters but that the institution continues no matter what the human cost. Instead of being a means to help their members they become ends in themselves, a process often termed "institutionalization." For example, wealth and power that has accumulated for service to the poor become instead the primary purpose of an institution.[94]

---

[90] J. Bryan Hehir, "Identity and Institutions," *Health Progress* 76:8 (1995) 7.

[91] See Arbuckle, *Earthing the Gospel*, 119–20.

[92] See Robert Wuthnow, *Christianity in the Twenty-first Century* (New York: Oxford University Press, 1993) 5–6.

[93] See Roy Wallis, "Institutions," *The Social Science Encyclopedia,* ed. Adam Kuper and J. Kuper (London: Routledge and Kegan Paul, 1985) 400.

[94] See Robert Bellah and others, *The Good Society* (New York: Alfred A. Knopf, 1991) 3–18.

Very often institutionalization develops without people being aware of what is happening.

Fr. J. Bryan Hehir, in his commentary on Catholic healthcare institutions, identifies two fundamental practical reasons why they must continue. Healthcare institutions allow us to influence people at the most critical, vulnerable points in life's journey; in a world where the sanctity of life is no longer taken for granted, people's right to wholeness is recognized. Second, without these institutions there is no political power base from which to credibly challenge and influence healthcare policies of governments.[95]

Catholic healthcare institutions, argues Father Hehir, "must survive, but with a distinctive posture and presence in society";[96] that is, on condition they remain true to their founding story. There must be no corruption of power and wealth or institutionalization as it is defined above: "an institution that loses its moral compass and its sense of identity is a . . . threat to society."[97]

Guideline 3: The Option for the Poor Must Be Respected

The phrase "a preferential option for the poor," as explained in Chapter 5, is not an exclusion of the affluent and powerful. Moreover, there are different degrees of affluence. For example, there are many people on private insurance in Australia and the United States who could be categorized financially as "lower middle class."[98] In a spirit of stewardship they save from limited incomes to provide healthcare protection for themselves and their families. However, the obligation to assist the poor remains for every institution and ways need to be found to respond.

Fr. Donal Dorr observes that "there is no reason to believe that the rich and powerful should be entirely neglected or ignored; however, the crucial question is, what should committed Church people be saying to the rich, by their words and actions?"[99] In order to be true to the Gospel message, trustees of healthcare institutions that cater significantly to the affluent have an obligation to:

---

[95] See Hehir, "Identity and Institutions," 2–7.

[96] Ibid., 7.

[97] Ibid.

[98] More than 700,000 Australians earning less than $20,000 a year have private health coverage. See Lauren Martin, "Health-Care Rebate," *The Sydney Morning Herald* (November 25, 1998) 4.

[99] Donal Dorr, *Option for the Poor: A Hundred Years of Vatican Social Teaching* (Dublin: Gill and Macmillan, 1983) 243.

- display mission statements committing their organizations to serve the poor;

- ensure that the option for the poor is kept to the fore in policy-making and management groups;

- publish regularly and widely the nature and financial extent of the contributions of their institutions in the service of the poor;

- use their finances and political power publicly (networking with similar institutions where possible) to challenge structures that beget poverty and oppression of the weak in society;

- use the financial and human resources of their facilities to develop outreaches to the marginalized, for example, through healthcare facilities in poor areas, legal and court services;

- educate their staff about the biblical origins of the option for the poor, encouraging them to use their talents individually and collectively for the poor.

By demonstrating commitment to a just and compassionate society even as they serve the affluent, institutions can bear witness to the Christian vision.

Guideline 4: The Mission Is at the Service of Patients and Employees

As explained in Chapter 5, the central aim of Christian healthcare is the formation of a community based on Gospel values such as justice and compassion. Staff, as well as patients, are to be part of this community. This means *inter alia* that employees have a right to belong to trade unions. Moral theologian Charles Curran, however, notes that "it is a grave understatement to say that Catholic hospitals [in the United States] have not supported and encouraged unions."[100]

Guideline 5: Trustees Must Discern whether or not Existing Resources Should Be Directed to More Urgent Healthcare Community Needs

David Smith writes of three principles that must guide trustees in healthcare. The first is the fiduciary principle; that is, trustees must be loyal to the founding myth of their institutions. The second is the common good

---

[100] Charles Curran, "The Catholic Identity of Catholic Institutions," *Theological Studies* 58:1 (1997) 95; Editorial, "Nuns' Resistance to Unions Belies Legacy," *National Catholic Reporter* (September 4, 1998) 36.

principle; that is, trustees must ask themselves if their institutions conform to the needs of people today.

The third principle is that the trustees must become a community of interpretation; that is, they must develop "the habit of and procedures for talking together about issues of institutional mission and purpose."[101] Their task is to interpret the founding story in light of contemporary needs. If they are open to dialogue with one another and in contact with their external environment, then they will be prepared to make the right and difficult decisions. This could mean, for example, a drastic shift of resources from acute care hospitals to community-care projects.

Summary

The speed of change in contemporary healthcare calls for a refounding of Christian healing ministry. Modifications of ministries that were successful a few years ago cannot guarantee that the healing mission of Jesus Christ will continue into the future. Refounding is not about incremental change, but is a fundamental reorientation of attitudes and structures.

Refounding is a collaborative process whereby people return to the founding myth of Christian healthcare; energized by this experience, they seek to create radical responses that relate to the causes of contemporary healthcare problems.

Three groups of people are involved in a collaborative way in refounding: formal position people (trustees, management boards, CEOs), refounding persons, and renewal persons. Formal position persons are to foster a culture in which creativity for mission has priority. Refounding persons are to be radically creative in today's ministry in a collaborative way. Renewal persons place their less innovative talents at the service of refounding.

Refounding people are uncomfortable to be with as they relentlessly question conventional wisdom for the sake of the mission. Unless formal position persons act correctly refounding people will be relegated to backwaters or pressured to resign; then the organization would wither and die. An organization that domesticates its rebels has acquired its peace, but it has lost its future.

Refounding necessitates a servant-type of leadership, as modeled by Jesus Christ, which is collaborative and transformative: both the led and

[101] Smith, *Entrusted,* 21.

leaders are attitudinally changed through the experience. To listen to Christ's mission demands both receiving and giving: "If you love listening, you will learn, / if you pay attention, you will become wise" (Sir 6:33).

The task of management boards is to shape the organization according to the philosophy established by the trustees. This cannot be achieved without a spirit of collaboration between board members, trustees, and the CEO. The CEO is responsible for the implementation of a board's decisions. This person must be ardently committed to the healing mission of Christ and insist that the actions of staff members conform to this.

Trustees are to evaluate the use of resources according to the founding story and the contemporary healthcare needs of people. This may demand, for example, a radical shift from acute care hospital ministry to home-care services.

Chapter 7

Refounding through Intentional Faith Communities

Coupled with the emerging need to pursue alternatives to more traditional forms of sponsorship, operations, and control, the ultimate challenge is the changing nature of ministry leadership itself.[1]

—John E. Curley

Attending to the theological and spiritual formation needs of the [healthcare] system will enable many of the structural issues to find satisfactory resolutions.[2]

—Francis Sullivan

This chapter explains:

- the urgency to develop in the transition to lay leadership appropriate structural and formation processes;

- "sponsorship" as a way of viewing the respective roles and responsibilities of religious congregations and lay people;

- the reasons why traditional mission leaders find their task difficult, if not impossible;

- intentional faith communities as vehicles of refounding.

[1] John E. Curley, president of Catholic Health Association of the United States, "Catholic Health Ministry Will Succeed," *Health Progress* 78:4 (1997) 37.
[2] Francis Sullivan, "Dreaming the Impossible Dream," *The Australasian Catholic Record* 73:2 (1996) 132.

Prior to Vatican II, Catholic healthcare in the Western world was almost totally under the control of religious sisters or brothers. They owned the institutions, held the key administrative positions, and were very visibly present through their religious attire. They were the professional carriers and guardians of the Catholic healthcare story by right of their vows; they were present in such large numbers, few thought to challenge the status quo theologically or culturally (see Chapter 3).

From the mid-1960s, change began to occur for two reasons: the Vatican II Council declared that all—not just religious—are called to the ministry of healing by the gift of baptism, and the numbers of religious started to decline rapidly, necessitating the employment of more and more lay people. The move toward involvement of lay people will accelerate. For example, within the next three years at least 90 percent of Catholic health systems in the United States will be directed by lay CEOs; an estimated 95 percent of all Catholic hospitals will probably be managed by lay administrators, and more than 50 percent of these executives will not be Catholic.[3]

However, if lay people are to bear witness to the healing mission of Christ in ways that are compatible with a lay vocation, refounding people are required to develop appropriate structures and formation processes. Congregations have responded to this challenge with varying degrees of success. It is true that lay advisory boards have been transformed into full boards of management while remaining accountable to the trustees (congregational leaders); lay directors of mission have been appointed, and the legal ownership of facilities has sometimes been handed over to lay people. Too often, however, emphasis is given to structural changes and the formation of lay people to lead the changes is neglected.

I argue in this chapter that, in addition to the appointment of appropriately selected and trained lay people to key positions, throughout healthcare cultures there must be communities of people who become the primary carriers of the founding myth. These communities are a method of forming lay people for mission and "power houses" for refounding Christian healthcare. The groups may be referred to as "intentional communities for mission," "basic Christian communities" (BCCs), or "basic ecclesial communities" (BECs); the terminology is unimportant. Not so their purpose and urgency. Without such groups I believe Christian healthcare has little future.

---

[3] See Alan M. Zuckerman and Russell C. Coile, "Catholic Healthcare's Future," *Heath Progress* 78:6 (1997) 24.

Clarifying Sponsorship

The use of the term "sponsorship" in recent years in Catholic healthcare is an effort to grapple with questions relating to the rights and responsibilities of religious congregations in governance in view of the rapid decline of religious congregations in healthcare ministry. Sponsorship of an institution, as explained in Chapter 3, means leadership or governance to protect what is cherished and to maintain its identity intact. In other words, sponsorship commits people to continue retelling the founding story of an organization in an authentic way. Archbishop Rembert Weakland, O.S.B., comments:

> [When] we speak of those who "own" a Catholic health care institution, we prefer to use the word sponsor and sponsorship so as to convey that deep sense of responsibility, that bond or promise which unites sponsor to operation. It demands on the part of the sponsor the best Christian stewardship.[4]

Clarification of sponsorship has mainly been the domain of ecclesiastical lawyers who have tended to concentrate on the legal rights and obligations of the owners of healthcare institutions. It is time to extend the meaning of the term to embrace the rights and duties of others in healthcare as carriers of the mission and ministry of Christ. I do this by distinguishing two categories of sponsorship: "potential sponsorship" and "actual sponsorship" (see Figure 7.1).

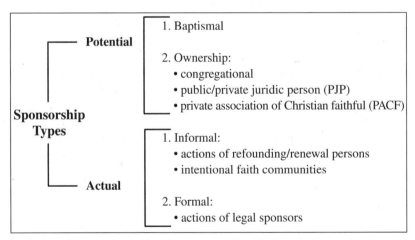

Figure 7.1: Sponsorship Types

[4] Melanie Di Pietro, foreword to *Congregational Sponsorship: Practical Issues in a Community Dialog,* by Rembert Weakland (Milwaukee: CHA-Wisconsin, 1985) 8.

There are two types of potential sponsorship: "baptismal" and "owner-ship." Baptism gives legitimacy to all to be sponsors of the healing mission of Jesus Christ. Legal ownership of institutions gives a secondary legiti-macy to the people or congregations concerned. "Ownership sponsorship" offers sponsors, on the basis of their legal possession of assets, "a potential means of influence both in the institution and in the political-economic sys-tem."[5] It has been helpfully clarified by Sr. Agnes Henkel, S.S.S.P., as "the religious community's ministry to its service institution(s)."[6]

Through ownership sponsorship, sponsors can exercise their authority through the use of at least five "reserve powers": (1) by articulating the philosophy of Catholic identity; (2) by establishing and amending corpo-rate charter and bylaws; (3) by appointing or approving trustees; (4) by buying, selling, or encumbering real estate; and (5) by merging or dissolv-ing the corporation.[7]

Forms of sponsorship other than congregational sponsorship are begin-ning to emerge that are led by lay people, such as "private associations of the Christian faithful" (PACF), and "private" or "public juridic persons" (PJP). A congregation can transfer its ownership sponsorship to such bod-ies rather than to public commercial companies in order to safeguard the original founding purpose. These bodies take the place of a congregation in that they assume the responsibility of maintaining their Catholic iden-tity of the facilities. Church lawyer Fr. Francis Morrisey, O.M.I., describes a juridic person in this way: "Although the comparison is not entirely cor-rect, a juridic person in canon law could be compared to a corporation in civil law."[8]

A PACF's property is not Church property, so a bishop's authority re-lates not to the management of it but to matters of faith and morals; he can withdraw the right to use the word "Catholic" if abuses develop. In the case of a PJP, however,

> the emphasis is on an organization or an institution rather than on persons (as with the PACF). Once the bishop approves its statutes, the particular prop-

[5] Ibid., 8.

[6] Agnes M. Henkel as cited by Ken Tremblay and others, *Sponsorship of Catholic Health Institutions in Ontario* (Toronto: Catholic Health Association in Ontario, 1991) 35.

[7] See John R. Amos and others, *The Search for Identity: Canonical Sponsorship of Catholic Healthcare* (St. Louis: Catholic Health Association of the United States, 1993) 81.

[8] Francis Morrisey as cited by Tremblay and others, *Sponsorship,* 27.

erty (a hospital, for instance) becomes a PJP with perpetual existence under canon law. . . . The bishop must ensure that the PJP is administered in accordance with the statutes.[9]

"Actual Sponsorship" Necessitates Major Cultural Changes

"Actual sponsorship" is the exercise or implementation of sponsorship obligations deriving from baptism ("informal sponsorship") and/or ownership ("formal sponsorship"). Trustees have formal authority to be sponsors, but they become so in practice only when they *act* accordingly: "actual sponsorship" is doing everything possible as owners to guarantee that the healing mission of Jesus continues.

This distinction between potential and actual sponsorship is a pivotal one because there is a temptation to assume that once legal structures are in place on paper all is well, whereas it requires leadership of a refounding kind to implement their requirements. Anyone who acts according to the mission of the healing Jesus is an "informal sponsor." As will be explained below, I believe that insufficient consideration is given to this form of sponsorship, that is, to new forms of sponsorship in action, because lay ministry in healthcare necessitates significant cultural change. Without the necessary change I do not see that the healing mission of Jesus Christ will continue with the visibility and strength needed in today's postmodern society.

From "Family" to "Franchise" Models of Sponsorship

The distinction common in the world of business between "family" and "franchise" models of ownership can help explain the challenge religious congregations face in healthcare. According to the family business model, family members are the owners and the primary carriers of the organization's culture and mission.[10] They are fully in charge of the business. In the franchise model, however, an organization legally authorizes others to be carriers of the original story. The name of the parent group cannot be used unless conditions are met, such as set standards of quality. The parent group will establish evaluative procedures to guarantee these conditions are kept.

[9] Barbara McMullen, "A Closer Look at Lay Sponsorship," *Health Progress* 77:1 (1996) 28–9. See also Peter Campbell, "Evolving Sponsorship and Corporate Structures," *Health Progress* 76:6 (1995) 35–44.

[10] See Consolidated Catholic Health Care, *Critical Choices: Catholic Health Care in the Midst of Transformation* (Oak Brook: CCHC, 1993) 8–10.

So also with healthcare.[11] In the past a congregation was like a family. Its members owned the "business" and were primarily responsible for transmitting the culture and its mission. As explained, today this is not possible for two reasons: congregations are numerically in decline and lay people have the right to be ministers of the healing message of Jesus Christ. Religious congregations, therefore, establish franchises (for example, through public juridic persons) in which lay people continue the mission but the congregations have the right and obligation to insist on standards and appropriate formation processes. Some may object to the use of business terminology; nonetheless, the distinction is a useful one because it highlights in contemporary language the nature of the change in sponsorship.

CASE STUDY

The "Family" Leadership Style Continues

Several years ago a religious congregation decided to withdraw all its members from leadership positions in a hospital and appoint lay people. The sisters had governed the hospital in a "top-down" manner, but the trustees requested that the lay executives adopt a servant-style of leadership at all levels of administration. This did not happen for two reasons. First, the religious trustees themselves did not understand the servant-style of leadership and selected lay administrators according to the non-consultative model that they were familiar with. Second, the hospital's culture resisted efforts by the CEO to introduce a listening form of administration, simply because the staff had become so accustomed to being told what to do. As one employee said: "We like to know exactly what we are to do. We like a strong leader!" Those who did not like this moved elsewhere.

[11] See Francis Morrisey, "What Makes an Institution 'Catholic'?" *The Jurist* 2 (1987) 536.

Lay Sponsorship: Effectiveness

The experience of actual lay sponsorship has been varied.

In 1988 the Commission on Catholic Healthcare Ministry in the United States was not optimistic about the success of lay sponsorship. The commission felt that if nothing was done to change current practices, then by the end of the century

> [there] will be . . . the loss of Catholic identity for most of the current facilities; . . . the laity who occupy virtually all positions of leadership in Catholic health ministry will have the requisite professional capabilities, but will lack understanding of their role as leaders in ministry or any opportunity to develop such an understanding. Further they will not experience any support from the larger church community.[12]

In 1995 the Catholic Health Association of the United States surveyed seven member organizations that use either PACF or the PJP as sponsorship models and concluded that "leadership development appeared somewhat weak." For some there was "a lack of clarity in the reporting mechanisms between the organization and the diocese." There was a general and disturbing feeling that though respondents believed that lay leadership must develop, these models "are not promising steps in that direction."[13]

CASE STUDY

A Successful PJP Described

In October 1996 the St. Joseph's Province of the Sisters of Charity of Montreal (Grey Nuns) in the United States established a public juridic person and transferred ownership of its healthcare institutions to it (namely, Covenant Health Systems or CHS).[14] The major change in this new model was that most decisions once taken by the Grey Nuns went to the lay-led CHS board of directors. The board has the final say, except for a limited

---

[12] Commission on Catholic Health Ministry, *Catholic Health Ministry: A New Vision for a New Century* (St. Louis: Catholic Health Association of the United States, 1988) 11.

[13] McMullen, "A Closer Look," 28–30.

[14] See Nancy Mulvihill, "Public Juridic Person Ensures Catholic Presence," *Health Progress* 77:1 (1996) 26.

number of matters referred to Rome. The Grey Nuns maintain control in certain areas, including appointment of CHS board members.[15] CHS is a "pontifical" juridic person in that it is answerable to the Holy See in its internal government, instead of to the Grey Nuns' provincial administration or to local bishops.

I was briefly involved in assisting the process of transition and I was impressed by the way in which all parties concerned were prepared for the changes. For example:

• the congregational and CHS leaders clearly and systematically explained to their membership and the nine thousand employees, board members, and volunteers what the changes would involve;

• grieving rituals were arranged;

• every effort was made to establish processes and guarantees for the ongoing education of lay people in the Christian and ethical values of the Roman Catholic tradition;

• there was awareness throughout that, because other institutes, systems, and healthcare facilities could eventually join the PJP, the ultimate binding philosophy would not be the particular charism of the congregation but the healing Good News of Christ.

Mission Leaders

In this section I argue that the ministry of mission leaders needs to be re-defined because they are commonly expected to do the impossible.

Mission Leaders: Role Expectations and Problems

As the numbers of religious decline it has become common for each healthcare facility to have a "mission leader" (sometimes referred to as a "director of mission"). This person (a religious in most case until recent years) is expected to:

[15] See ibid., 26–7.

- help re-articulate the vision, mission, and values;
- influence decision making within the board and/or executive committee;
- represent a Catholic ethical perspective;
- promote a spirituality of healing and wholeness;
- highlight needs and be an advocate for the poor and marginalized;
- develop relevant symbols, rituals, and celebrations to deal with change or highlight Catholic mission;
- be a visible symbol of commitment to the healing ministry of Jesus;
- develop guidelines for an ongoing evaluation of mission effectiveness.[16]

Sr. Teresa Stanley, C.C.V.I., lists wide-ranging talents that a mission leader needs to be effective in ministry: the ability to work as a team member, understanding of the Catholic healthcare ministry, knowledge of Scripture and spiritual issues, knowledge of sponsor's charism, organizational development gifts, etc. She emphasizes four special qualities needed for this time of transition in healthcare: "willingness to live in ambiguity; creativity; ease with risk taking; energy to forge new relationships with different traditions."[17]

An accurate assessment of the effectiveness of this role is difficult, though two surveys provide some insights.

In 1993 the Catholic Health Association of the United States attempted to obtain a "snapshot" of mission leaders' roles and functions by surveying eighty-five full-time mission leaders. The results were generally positive; for example, most showed that, overall, the mission leaders believed the CEO greatly valued the mission role. Significantly, only "7 percent [of mission leaders] reported that they do not participate in making decisions such as budgeting, planning, staff reduction, and joint ventures."[18]

In 1997 the same association's Mission Services surveyed 105 system-level mission leaders. The findings that have been published are also generally positive, as Julie Jones, mission associate for Catholic Health Association of the United States, concludes. However, she notes that some mission leaders "have experienced a sense of being 'dismissed,' indicating

[16] See Teresa Stanley, "Mission in a Time of Transition," *Health Progress* 74:2 (1994) 29.

[17] Ibid., 31.

[18] Ibid., 28–9.

that the mission is not seen as related to other items on the agenda and is not used to evaluate them."[19]

Mission Leaders: Doubts about Their Effectiveness

In my own work I have found that mission leaders are less positive about the effectiveness of their ministry in fostering informal actual lay sponsorship than the results of the above surveys indicate. When healthcare facilities are publicly funded, as is common in Canada and Australia, the work of mission leaders is especially difficult. In several workshops for groups of mission leaders I found their experience generally negative. I list representative comments, and conclude with some personal observations.

Comments of Mission Leaders

1. "I am at a loss to know what more to do, but I get very little sympathy from the board or trustees."

2. "I am marginalized by the CEO and executives."

3. "We mission leaders are not taken seriously because management do not see that the mission has any role in decision-making. Significant executive decisions have been made without any reference to us. Staff then blame us for these decisions which affect their lives."

4. "In some ways we laity are coping well. But just when we think we can take over the role of mission leaders fully, we lose energy. The sisters will not let go. We feel that unconsciously they want to hold on to their positions."

5. "Our CEO has no feeling for mission at all. He keeps saying that is 'our business,' but he does everything to undermine what we are trying to do. In fact, he was appointed by the trustees deliberately to get the finances right, but the cost to the culture is enormous, as he is an economic rationalist."

6. "We sisters as mission leaders feel just tolerated by the executives and management. We are told that sisters know nothing about the real world of business."

[19] Julie M. Jones, "New Opportunities for Mission Leaders," *Health Progress* 78:6 (1997) 46–7.

7. "My role is confined to arranging celebrations for anniversaries for long-service personnel."

8. "I feel overwhelmed by the task. I am the only visible presence of my congregation and everyone expects me to do what dozens of sisters did several years ago. It is an impossible situation and no one has the answers!"

9. "The board and/or the executives say: 'We must wait before we worry about mission. The important thing is to get the margin right, then we can look to the mission!'"

10. "This is quite an impossible situation. This is a public hospital in which staff generally are unchurched. The executive board and staff accept there is a place for pastoral care, but they see no relevance for mission leaders."

11. "We have yet to arrange some sound procedure for succession. I am the last religious who can hold this posting, but no procedure is in place for a lay person of the right qualities to take over and be guaranteed an income commensurate to their qualifications."

12. "The sisters are constantly speaking about their particular charism from their foundress, but rarely do they speak about the story of Jesus as a healer. It is less threatening to keep referring to the foundress; we can talk about 'nice things,' but is that really mission? We are selling ourselves short."

13. "In our public hospital the CEO, without reference to the board and the trustees, removed the crucifixes from the rooms because, he said, they would offend the patients. Both the board and trustees refused to discuss the issue as they claimed the CEO could make such a decision."

14. "We sense that our model is out-of-date, but we cannot find out why or what to do."

15. "Each year we run orientation courses (one hour) for new staff members; the managers are not ready to allow more time. This is education, minimal though it be, but no formation."

16. "Our trustees and board of management in their annual reports repeatedly write of the effectiveness of our mission programs. In fact, we mission leaders know that these grandiose statements are untrue (for example, our commitment to the marginalized is minimal) but when we complain, we are told to be 'more positive,' because

'our mission statement is so pro-active.' At board meetings where we try to speak of reality, sometimes the CEO complains: 'People like you are disloyal to the organization and the sisters.'"

17. "My CEO and other senior executives do not believe a mission leader is now necessary. They argue: 'Everyone in the system is to be responsible for mission. By having a mission leader we are giving the impression to people that they are not responsible for mission.' I do not accept this. I am no longer even on the board and mission is not taken seriously in decision-making."

18. "I have a support group in my role, but I still feel the burden rests too much on me."

There are several identifiable patterns in these comments.

Comments two, three, five, and nine fit the category of "splitting" (see Chapter 4). The difficulties of resolving the tensions between "business" and "mission" are too great, so CEOs and management see themselves as the "goodies," and those concerned with mission, the "baddies," are to be avoided. The board and trustees collude in this splitting. In fact, in all the comments the authority position persons (board and trustees) are depicted as failing to assume their rightful leadership.

There is pain and frustration in many of the comments; the mission leaders frequently feel marginalized because "mission" is seen as irrelevant. Trustees and boards either avoid or deny the reality that healthcare cultures in Catholic institutions are being influenced by the postmodern world and the breakup of pre-Vatican II traditional culture (see comments one, seven, eight, and ten to fifteen inclusively). The chaos is intolerable, so people ignore it.

One symptom of chaos is grandiosity, that is, pretending that an organization is more, or something other, than it is. Comment sixteen is an example of grandiosity. Anne Schaef and Diane Fassel observe that an organization "becomes an addictive substance when its actions are excused because it has a lofty mission. The grandiosity of the mission is a fix. It can reassure us that we . . . do an important work."[20] To illustrate their insight, the authors described a mission statement which committed its healthcare facility to the marginalized: when it was pointed out that in

---

[20] Anne W. Schaef and Diane Fassel, *The Addictive Organization* (San Francisco: Harper & Row, 1990) 123.

practice the system's concern for the poor was gravely deficient, the management rationalized that their mission was to the spiritually poor, not the materially deprived. Schaef and Fassel claim this is fast thinking, a self-deluded conclusion: "Addicts are consummate cons. Initially their con looks good to others. . . . (But) they come to believe their own lie."[21] When grandiosity is pointed out, people may react with feelings of rage and anger, and act vindictively.[22] All this is evident in comment sixteen. The CEO, board, and trustees have unconsciously bonded together in an addictive group. They believe that what is written in their mission statement is happening.

In comment four, unconscious forces are operating to prevent lay sponsorship from developing because, despite protestations to the contrary, the sisters are blocking the process of handing over to lay mission leaders. The board and trustees should intervene to remove undue obstacles to the transition to lay people; this is not something lay mission leaders can achieve on their own.

In comment twelve a mission leader is worried that there is such emphasis on the life of the founder that the mission of Jesus Christ is neglected. She correctly sees that this can be a way of avoiding the radical imperatives of Jesus' teaching.

In comment seventeen the CEO and others do not appreciate the importance of the mission leader's role; they are prepared to suppress it. The axiom "everyone's responsibility becomes no one's duty" is applicable here. Appointing a mission leader to the management board, particularly when there is so much emphasis on the business side of healthcare, reminds healthcare workers that mission is important.

Mission Leaders: Models of Ministry

I believe that mission leaders are commonly hampered in their task of developing "formal" and "informal" actual lay sponsorship for the following reasons: too much is personally expected of them with the withdrawal of religious congregations from healthcare; there is little understanding and support of their role by trustees, boards, and CEOs; there is insufficient

[21] Ibid., 124.
[22] See Manfred F. R. Kets de Vries and Danny Miller, "Leadership Styles and Organizational Cultures: The Shaping of Neurotic Organizations," *Organizations on the Couch: Clinical Perspectives on Organizational Behavior and Change*, ed. Manfred F. R. Kets de Vries (San Francisco: Jossey-Bass, 1991) 253.

appreciation of the cultural obstacles to their ministry and the difficulties of inculturation in healthcare facilities in postmodern societies; and contemporary thinking is confined to the renewal of existing methods, although there needs to be refounding of the role.

These conclusions are best explained through the use of models. A model is a fundamental sketch, a guiding instrument, which simplifies the complex real world. Three models of mission leaders can be identified, but only the third fits the conditions required for refounding the role of mission leader today.

Model 1: "Family" Type: The Culture Carries the Myth

Anthropologically the "family" type is a culture model in which identity and boundaries are sharply defined. People are expected to fit into a tradition-based, bureaucratic, hierarchical, and patriarchal system which is presumed to have the monopoly of knowledge; dependency and conformity are the esteemed qualities. To maintain conformity there are detailed, rigid, morally sanctioned rules, and those in authority have significant coercive power over individuals/groups within the culture.[23] This model describes the pre-Vatican II Catholic Church[24] and Catholic healthcare facilities staffed almost entirely by religious congregations. In such a tightly ordered culture there was no need for mission leaders. The culture was itself the mission leader.

Model 2: "Transition" Type: Mission Leader Carries the Myth

The culture of the "transition" model is distinguished by symptoms of chaos such as the breakdown of identity, individualism, loss of clear vision, drifting without goals, organizational paralysis, nostalgia for former predictability, moves to uncritically restore the identities and boundaries of the past, grandiosity of leaders, bullying, quick-fix solutions, and denial. As explained in Chapter 4, this phase of culture change is potentially creative but equally can lead to the destruction of groups or organizations.

This model helps to describe Catholic healthcare since the 1970s (see Chapter 3). Catholic identity itself is no longer clear. Religious are rarely to be seen. Hospitals have ceased to be quasi-parishes; now there are pas-

---

[23] See Gerald A. Arbuckle, *Refounding the Church: Dissent for Leadership* (Maryknoll, N.Y.: Orbis Books, 1993) 81.
[24] See ibid., 82–4.

toral teams at the service of different faiths and denominations. Nostalgia for the former culture remains: "If only the sisters were in charge again, all would be well." "It is not like it was when the sisters were around!"

In this situation trustees are vulnerable to quick-fix solutions such as appointing economic rationalists to boards and key administrative offices, allowing Catholic restorationists with anti-Vatican II values to dominate boards because they are thought to be "strong Catholics" who will maintain the congregational identity, or indiscriminately selling facilities to for-profit systems.

The observations of the mission leaders earlier in this chapter reflect the breakup of the traditional Catholic healthcare culture and the subsequent chaos. The mission leaders are expected to be the primary carriers of the mission; they are often alone in their ministry, though large hospitals encourage support systems or teams. Their task is an impossible one. They cannot be substitutes for religious communities as carriers of the mission. Nor will they be effective if they continue to offer only orientation programs for new staff members and an occasional educational program for existing staff. While membership of the board and/or executives is necessary, this can also be a barrier to communication to staff members. The mission leader can be seen as one of the "bosses," especially when difficult decisions have to be made.

Refounders recognize these problems. They search for more appropriate methods of continuing the healing ministry where the emphasis will not primarily be on imparting information, but on people motivating themselves and others to be involved in ministry. The next model illustrates what can be done when priority is given to forming and motivating communities to be the cultural carriers of the founding myth of Christian healthcare.

Model 3: "Community" Type: Faith Communities Carry the Myth

> Carrying on the mission and ministry in the future will require a core group of persons committed, most likely not vowed, to be stewards of . . . health ministry (Consolidated Catholic Health Care).[25]

This quotation defines where and how the mission of Christian healthcare could continue, but it requires one significant modification. The challenge is too great for a single core group to be the primary cultural carrier of the founding myth of healthcare. Rather, the story will continue only if

---

[25] Consolidated Catholic Health Care, *Critical Choices,* 76.

there are many groups (that is, small, intentional faith communities) committed to this task at different levels of a healthcare culture. This is not to downplay the refounding roles of trustees, boards, CEOs, or the various tasks of mission leaders, but their influence will remain remote without the motivational presence of intentional faith communities (IFCs).

Refounding through Intentional Faith Communities

IFCs, which are sometimes referred to as basic Christian communities, basic ecclesial communities, house churches, grassroots churches, and churches from below, are "gatherings of three to twelve people who meet regularly with the common aim of growing in the fullness of life in Christ the healer in order to extend this life of faith/justice individually and together into the local culture and beyond."[26]

The word "intentional" means "deliberate" or "consciously chosen"; that is, people deliberately choose to come together to live more abundantly the life of Christ (John 10:10) in order to share that life with others. An IFC is more than a support group where people congregate to sustain one another because of some common problem or interest, such as a bereavement group, a recreational club serving the individual needs of its members, or a bible study group. Rather, it is oriented to a ministry outside the group, and people support each other for this purpose. For example, they pray together, study together, and nourish each other so that they may be more effective ministers of the Good News to others. IFCs are faith-based, that is, their members believe in the healing mission of Christ and wish it to continue through their collaborative efforts.

Theologians Fr. Bernard Lee, S.M., and Michael Cowan write from their own considerable experience of such groups. For them, an intentional Christian community "is a relatively small group of persons committed to ongoing conversation and shared action along four distinguishable but interrelated dimensions."[27] The four dimensions are: (1) a high level of mutuality in relationships; (2) critique of the world from a standpoint of gospel values and effort to transform the cultures in which they live ac-

---

[26] See comments by Roberta Hestenes, *Building Christian Community through Small Groups* (Pasadena, Calif.: Fuller Theological College, 1985) 25–30.

[27] Bernard J. Lee and Michael A. Cowan, *Dangerous Memories: House Churches and Our American Story* (Kansas City, Mo.: Sheed and Ward, 1986) 91. See also Michael A. Cowan and Bernard J. Lee, *Conversation, Risk and Conversion: The Inner and Public Life of Small Christian Communities* (Maryknoll, N.Y.: Orbis Books, 1997) 65–6.

cording to these values; (3) sustained, inclusive, and "lively connections with other persons, communities and movements of similar purpose";[28] and (4) members "attend faithfully to the Christian character of their community's life."[29]

I would add a fifth dimension to this list: the culture of intentional communities needs to be strongly egalitarian in social and gender relationships. Rigid rules of conduct based on tradition are irrelevant; far more important is the interior conversion and effective commitment of members to the group's vision, mission, and values. There is government by direct democracy or consensus. Consensus is not synonymous with unanimous agreement; rather, it is a decision that appears at a particular moment to be most acceptable to the group as a whole. It results from authentic dialogue, and for this four conditions must be met: (1) people feel that they have understood the position of others; (2) they feel that others understand their points of view; (3) responsible dissent is encouraged in order to surface alternative ways of acting in, or influencing, cultures; (4) there is a readiness on the part of all to accept what is decided.

Historical Development of IFCs

Third World Experience

CASE STUDY

An IFC Emerges in the Philippines

In 1986 I came to know of Arturo, a poor sugar plantation worker on the island of Negros in the Philippines who lived with his wife and four young children in a small hovel. One day, after receiving a copy of the New Testament from his local pastor, he opened it and by chance noticed the text "Blessed are those who hunger and thirst for uprightness: / they shall have their fill" (Matt 5:6). Though he had heard this beatitude many times, it had an impact as never before, so he called his fellow-workers together and asked them what they thought it meant. One said, "Let's pray about it!" and they did in silence, until one friend said: "It means that to follow

[28] Cowan and Lee, *Dangerous Memories,* 92.

[29] Ibid., 91.

Jesus we must struggle for justice here on earth." Arturo and others agreed. Arturo then said: "We are poor and oppressed by injustice, and this text means we must ourselves struggle for just wages from the rich plantation owners. What should we do?" They prayed, and his friends said to Arturo: "You go to the manager and we pray for you!" Arturo did, but was angrily chased off the property by the manager, and a second time dogs were set on him.

The community continued to pray and reflect on the problem, even going as a group to confront the manager peacefully, but with no success. One day a rock was thrown into Arturo's hovel with a note: "Stop the agitation or we kill you!" The community prayed about this together for several weeks, but Arturo could only say: "We must continue to struggle for justice together, that is the message of Christ." And so they did, but one day masked men in a jeep rushed past Arturo's poor dwelling and sprayed it with machine-gun fire, killing him and four of his family members.

Arturo and his friends had formed an intentional community which is commonly termed a "basic Christian community" (BCC) in the Philippines and South America. The radical newness of BCCs within the Catholic Church is stressed by theologian Leonardo Boff: "theologically they represent a new, ecclesiological experience, a renaissance of the very church itself, and hence an action of the Spirit on the horizon of the matters urgent for our time."[30] They evolved for the four following reasons: (1) the inadequacies of the traditional, impersonal hierarchical parish model (BCCs are ways to be Church other than through territorially-based parish structures); (2) the Gospel calls people to worship together, even when priests are unavailable; (3) awareness by people at the grassroots that oppression is contrary to Gospel values and that by praying and acting together change is possible; and (4) recognition that small-scale, natural communities already exist and can be used as foundations for inculturation.

[30] Leonardo Boff, *Ecclesiogenesis: The Base Communities Reinvent the Church* (Maryknoll, N.Y.: Orbis Books; London: Collins, 1986) 1.

These reasons are evident in the story of Arturo and his friends. The tragic incident demonstrates the stages in the development of BCCs:

Stage 1: People meet to reflect prayerfully on their lives in light of the Gospel message.

Stage 2: Communities of mutual aid emerge—localized expressions of the wider Church—as people discover the Gospel imperative of charity and justice.

Stage 3: Social/economic/political movements develop as people discover, on the one hand, their Gospel-based social justice rights, and, on the other, that they have the power within themselves, if united, to seek/demand structural changes for justice.

Arturo and his friends became involved in an act of refounding the Church: from a communitarian Gospel base they confronted sinful economic structures and were prepared to die for doing so. The initiative to set up BCCs often comes from bishops, priests, or religious. However, once the lay communities become self-motivating, they inevitably, usually at stage three above, begin to critique traditional ecclesiastical structures in light of Gospel values. In some cases, this "new birth" of the Church may involve the bishop and priest in an identity crisis: the leaders are called to become followers of their own disciples.

First World Experience

CASE STUDY

Families Become Church

Four years ago RENEW (a parish revitalization process established in the United States in 1978) was initiated in a parish with three goals: to foster Gospel witness, to form vibrant faith communities, and to promote responsibility for social justice. Three families in one street decided to form an IFC inspired by these goals, but enthusiasm waned quickly until one member called them together and challenged them in this way:

> We agreed to the goals and we planned times to meet, but in fact we did not center our gatherings in Gospel prayer. We thought we could give prayer a brief space, recreate together, and plan social justice action in our

> neighbourhood. This did not work. Let's begin with
> prayer and Gospel reflection, then move to action.
>
> The members pondered this, recognized the truth of
> the insight, and acted accordingly. Three years later, the
> IFC continues. Recently, one member led the faith reflec-
> tion on Yhwh's call to justice for the poor (Isa 1:13-20)
> and, after much dialogue, all three families agreed to cut
> back on the number of their cars, giving them to a volun-
> tary agency for battered women. One lawyer joined an
> anti-abortion pressure group.

In the First World, IFCs have been slow to emerge, as conditions that
fostered their emergence in the Third World are rarely present:

- people have yet to become fully aware of the rapid decline of the
  number of clergy and religious and its pastoral implications;
- natural small communities rarely exist in Western urban societies
  characterized by a high level of mobility;
- people experiencing poverty commonly turn to existing agencies,
  such as trade unions and government services;
- people expect things to happen quickly and since the development
  of IFCs requires time and patience, people are tempted to withdraw
  from membership;
- Western cultures, unlike many Third World societies, emphasize individualism and self-fulfillment rather than concern for other people's
  needs. People commonly prefer to foster loose support groups,
  which allow them to withdraw easily from cooperative ventures that
  interfere with their freedom. In his analysis of small-group movements in the United States Robert Wuthnow comments: "We want
  community, but nothing very binding. We want spirituality, but we
  prefer the sacred to serve us instead of requiring our service."[31]

---

[31] Robert Wuthnow, *Sharing the Journey: Support Groups and America's New Quest
for Community* (New York: Free Press, 1994) 365; see also Robert Bellah and others,
Habits of the Heart: Individualism and Commitment in American Life (New York:
Harper & Row, 1985) 142–63; Arbuckle, *Refounding the Church,* 90–3.

Intentional Faith Communities: Their Necessity and Foundations

Despite these difficulties, however, IFCs are as necessary in cultures of the First World as in the Third.

Ecclesially

As explained in Chapter 5, we are called in both Old and New Testaments to be community, with lives bonded together in imitation of the Trinity itself: "May they all be one, just as, Father, you are in me and I am in you, so that they also may be in us, so that the world may believe it was you who sent me" (John 17:21). St. Paul uses the analogy of the body: "Now Christ's body is yourselves, each of you with a part to play in the whole" (1 Cor 12:27).

Historically

Historical examples of IFCs are the early Christian community in Jerusalem (Acts 1:12-14) and religious congregations, particularly in their first stage of founding (e.g., St. Francis and his early followers). Scripture scholar Gerd Theissen, in writing on the early Palestinian Christian communities, pinpoints their counter-cultural witness:

> [A] small group of outsiders experimented with a vision of love and reconciliation in a society . . . to renew this society from within. . . . A good deal of aggression could be transformed into criticism of riches and possessions, Pharisees and priests, temple and tabus, and thus be made to serve the new vision.[32]

Refounding movements in the Church begin through IFCs,[33] and history shows that they customarily meet considerable resistance. They are able to maintain their reforming energy in the face of such opposition only to the degree that they remain internally bonded in faith and prayer. Today, IFCs are seen as the way to refound the Church itself, as Leonardo Boff comments: "We are not dealing with the expansion of an existing ecclesiastical system, rotating on a sacramental, clerical axis, but with the emergence of another form of being church, rotating on the axis of the word and laity."[34]

---

[32] Gerd Theissen, *Sociology of Early Palestinian Christianity* (Philadelphia: Fortress Press, 1978) 110.

[33] See Raymond Hostie, *Vie et mort des ordres religieux* (Paris: Desclee de Brouweer, 1972) 316.

[34] Boff, *Ecclesiogenesis,* 2.

Pastorally/Prophetically

The purpose of all ministry is ultimately not the evangelization of individuals, but the building of faith communities in and through which individuals are supported and encouraged to grow in faith, and cultures are critiqued according to Gospel values. Jesus himself set the example by spending much of his time fostering faith communities to be agents of evangelization in his day: "And he appointed twelve; they were to be his companions" (Mark 3:14). He then commanded intentional communities to be the primary carriers of his story down through the ages (Matt 28:19-20).

Scripture scholar Walter Brueggemann describes the biblical imperative to form communities of memory: "The central task of ministry is the formation of a community with an alternative, liberated imagination that has the courage and the freedom to act in a different vision and a different perception of reality."[35] The faith community—with its commitment to faith, justice, love, and hope—witnesses to the Gospel's message and power. It signifies an anticipation of, and preparation for, the time when people will be gathered with God in perfect love and justice. Grassroots ecclesial communities are this people now journeying to this end-time.[36] Their public exercise of the values of servant-leadership, mutuality, and moderation in the use of this world's goods challenges peoples and institutions whose way of life is in conflict with the Gospel.

Sometimes a complaint is made that to foster IFCs is to encourage elites within society, parishes, or healthcare facilities, and this is contrary to the Gospel. The word "elite" has come to have a pejorative connotation of self-ascribed superiority, as in the term "elitist." It can connote a selfish, manipulative, conspiratorial use of power. However, "elite" originally referred to people who had the greatest access to and control of values.[37] Members of IFCs claim access to core values of the Christian message and cherish them so much that they wish to interiorize them more deeply and share them with others. When an IFC is not open to others, the charge of elitist in its pejorative sense may be correct. The IFC then becomes a sect and ceases to be an authentic IFC.

---

[35] Walter Brueggemann, *Hopeful Imagination* (Philadelphia: Fortress Press, 1986) 99.

[36] See Leonardo Boff, "Theological Characteristics of a Grassroots Church," *The Challenge of Basic Christian Communities,* ed. Sergio Torres and John Eagleson (Maryknoll, N.Y.: Orbis Books, 1982) 134–5.

[37] See Harold D. Lasswell and others, *The Comparative Study of Elites* (Stanford, Calif.: Standford University Press, 1952) 6.

Existentially

Postmodernity, with its emphasis on individualism and loss of meaning, can generate yearning for a community in which people can experience self-worth and significance. IFCs can respond to this disquiet, but usually the inner turbulence of individuals is insufficient to sustain the levels of intimacy that authentic community demands. Ongoing formation of IFC members is essential; otherwise these faith gatherings will be a passing fad, only temporarily assuaging individuals' desire for community.

There is a growing revulsion, particularly at society's grassroots, against the coercive power of contemporary managerialism. Coercive power may produce outward conformity, but not real, inner changes in an individual's feelings or beliefs. In IFCs, however, members are called to an inner conversion, so that their behavior will change on the basis of solid conviction that the Gospel values are right. Arturo and his friends underwent this conversion and were prepared to resist unjust coercion even if it meant death. IFCs recognize that this kind of conversion is slow and each person's journey is different in speed and kind.

IFCs acknowledge the reality of evil and sin. The tendency to sin within each person and in the group itself can lead, unless constantly checked, to arrogance, oppression, and self-destruction. "Test the spirits," warns St. John, "to see whether they are from God" (1 John 4:1). Vigilance and prayer are the ultimate foundations for community growth. There is no simple, fast track to the development of IFCs, just as there is no magical formula for personal conversion.

Organizationally

Since IFCs are self-nourishing, self-governing, and self-supporting, the role of the pastor/pastoral staff, for example in a parish, is changed. Their task is to coordinate the activities of the heads of IFCs, namely the pastoral facilitators. The pastor is left free to relate directly to the pastoral facilitators and to respond to their particular needs, for example, the organizing of leadership training sessions for facilitators.

The pastoral facilitator's role is twofold. First, as facilitator he/she is to be of service to others in the group, to help them connect with each other, and to keep the group true to its task. Though decision-making is democratic or by consensus, there needs to be an official facilitator to ensure that all members have an opportunity to contribute and are not oppressed in any way by others or the group.

Second, the word "pastoral" in a parish context refers mainly to the task of tying the small church to the larger parish and maintaining Catholic

identity.[38] Each level of the Catholic Church is connected to the next level
by a pastoral person; for example, the pastor is the bridge between a parish
and the local diocesan church. The pastoral facilitator is the link between
the base church (IFC) and the pastor/pastoral staff of a particular parish.
As Fr. Arthur Baranowski notes: "Without this pastoral connection, even
though all the very same sharing and activity goes on, the group is not a
base church. . . . We are Catholic—and not congregational—because of
the way we are linked pastorally to every level of church."[39]

Culturally

For cultural change to occur we need a radical shift in the way we think
about and practice leadership (see Chapters 4 and 6). The contemporary
world is far too complex for one person alone to initiate and sustain positive cultural change. The exercise of leadership should be a cooperative or
collective effort extended throughout the organizational network or system. Refounding people must empower others to act in a collaborative
manner. IFCs are based on this servant-leadership model.

Liturgically

Theology in IFCs is a "theology from below," the result of people reflecting on their experience of life in the light of the Gospel. Liturgies are
simple, often biblically based, and mirror the faith experience of members
as pilgrims in the world. Pilgrims have little room for the baggage of titles
or social status. On the basis of baptism every member has a ministerial
role in the group; so do clerics and religious, who are not singled out for
special status or influence beyond what their sacramental duties may require of them.[40]

Intentional Faith Communities in Healthcare

The job description of the mission leader and the skills required in that
person, as described earlier in this chapter, cannot possibly be fulfilled by
one individual, even with support staff. This calls for a refounding of the
role of the mission leader. While they may still be involved in the forma-

[38] See Arthur R. Baranowski, *Creating Small Faith Communities: A Plan for Restructuring the Parish and Renewing Catholic Life* (Cincinnati: St. Anthony Messenger
Press, 1988) 53–63.
[39] Ibid., 17.
[40] See Arbuckle, *Refounding the Church,* 93.

tion of key individuals, such as board members, CEOs, and senior management, their primary duty will be to foster IFCs, chiefly through animating and training pastoral facilitators.

The focus shifts from the mission leader as chief carrier of the mission to intentional communities. It is primarily through faith communities, whose influence can reach into all parts of a culture, that inculturation will occur in a healthcare facility (see Chapter 5).[41] Pastoral facilitators will be accountable to the mission leader for maintaining Catholic identity, and the latter is ultimately accountable to the CEO. To be effective in the role, however, the mission leader must be a member of the board of management.

Maria, as described in the case study in Chapter 6, encouraged her fellow workers to form an intentional faith community from which she drew support to challenge the board to act according to the founding values of the hospital. The following case study illustrates in more detail how one mission leader was encouraged to develop IFCs in her hospital.

CASE STUDY

A Mission Leader Establishes IFCS

A mission leader describes her experience in a large Catholic hospital.

When I became the mission leader of the hospital I felt overwhelmed. I spent a lot of time arranging hospital celebrations such as farewells to retiring staff members. I would conduct orientation programs for new employees, but they had to be brief because the CEO was not supportive and participants rarely seemed interested.

An IFC Develops

One day I met with two senior nurses for coffee and shared with them the problems of my role. The nurses (one a Catholic and the other with no formal religion) were deeply committed to the core values of the hospital and asked if they could invite five other staff members to a meeting to discuss my problems. We began the meeting with the reading of the lamentation Psalm 74; we

[41] See comments by Thomas A. Droege, "Congregations as Communities of Health and Healing," *Interpretation* 49:2 (1995) 117–29.

then shared with one another the feelings of sadness as
we looked at the weakening commitment in the hospital
culture to the core values of compassion, justice, mercy,
and hospitality. We all agreed to meet the following week
during a lunch break, one member planning to lead the
reflection on the story of the good Samaritan. Thus began
our first intentional faith community, which has acted as
the guide for others to develop.

Lessons of Experience

It has been four years since these events, and my role
as mission leader has changed dramatically. There are
ten IFCs throughout the hospital. The communities that
have the most vibrant life are those which meet regularly (for example, every two weeks), focus on the mission to others, and emphasize mutuality and action. The
communities are mostly work-place based; that is, participants already know one another because they work
or recreate together. People are invited to join if they
believe in the core values of the hospital and respect the
requirements of Catholic identity [see Chapter 8]; no
pressure is ever placed on people to become Catholics.
The Scriptures have the power to draw people of goodwill together in healthcare because our core values are
biblical. It was important for me to explain to the CEO
and managers of units the reasons for the communities,
and to reassure them that participants would hold meetings in free time. IFCs develop slowly, because it is a
conversion process; I had to learn this because other participants and I expected mutuality and evangelizing
action to emerge speedily. There is need for regular for-
mational programs for pastoral facilitators, especially in
scriptural studies, ethics, Catholic identity, and leadership skills. Catholic identity, not congregational charism, becomes the common point of reference in these
communities.

Impact of IFCs

The IFCs have positively affected the hospital. Acting
without fuss, the members model how core values can

influence their lives and work. They are the vehicles through which the story of Christ's healing comes alive. Two years ago, after learning about these communities, the trustees began their own meetings in the same reflective manner. They then convinced the board to do the same, and requested that I become a member of the board. The board was slow to act as a faith community. Members said they were too busy. I did not press them, but waited for the right moment. It came when the board was forced to reduce the number of employees. They knew that people would blame them for not being compassionate, yet they felt that justice to the wider community demanded the difficult decision be made. However, they felt saddened by the decision.

It was then that the chairman asked me for help. I invited them to reflect on Psalm 130 where the psalmist articulates and grapples with the tension between God's need to insist on justice yet be forgiving at the same time (vv. 3-4). The psalmist discovers inner peace only by pondering this tension in faith. I said that in Psalm 85 the writer recognizes that the tensions in implementing values cease only at the end of time, when the reign of God is perfectly achieved (vv. 10-11).

I invited board members to think over in silence what I had said and then to share their responses if they wished. Most were comforted to discover that their own tensions in decision-making were not unique. I was asked to lead them in a biblical reflection at every board meeting, and members no longer feel self-conscious about participating. The atmosphere of meetings has changed for the better. Certainly the mission and values of the hospital are now seen to be integral to all significant decisions.

The insights provided by this case study and similar experiences can be summarized in practical guidelines.

Guideline 1: A Core Group Is Required to Begin IFCs;
They Do So by First Becoming a Faith Community Themselves

The first task of the mission leader is to develop a core group,[42] the purpose of which is fourfold: (1) to form an IFC themselves, (2) to model to others what a community for mission means in healthcare, (3) to foster the development of other IFCs in the healthcare facilities, and (4) to support the leadership of these IFCs. The members of the core group will need to have qualities of refounding (prophetic) people (see Chapter 6); that is, they must be gifted with the following:[43]

Commitment to the Need for IFCs. They are prepared to make sacrifices of time and energy because they believe that these communities are essential for their own and other people's apostolic development.

Commitment to Working with Others. Prophets or refounding persons are not loners (see Chapter 6). The prophets of old, even when banished by an ungrateful people to the margins of the Israelite society, earnestly called the Israelites into a deep communion with one another and with God.

Memories of Hope. Prophets are living and vital memories of Christ's abiding love and what he demands from them: justice and love. Through this memory they can energize others in healthcare cultures with hope.

Faith, Courage, Patience, and Prayer. Prophets are tempted to escape from their burdensome task, but they do not fail Christ because they are converted to him and to his service in faith and love. Prayer sustains prophets in their commitment to their mission of healing, for in prayer they repeatedly discover their own frailties before the Lord and the immensity of his mercy toward them.

Creative Imagination. Imagination is the creative, intuitive ability to see connections between things and events that others do not see. Prophets are gifted with creative imagination because they are able to discover ways of challenging cultures with Gospel values. Likewise members of the core group will have the ability to find ways to foster other IFCs throughout their healthcare facilities.

[42] See Thomas A. Kleissler and others, *Small Christian Communities: A Vision of Hope for the Twenty-first Century* (New York: Paulist Press, 1997) 132–45.
[43] See Gerald A. Arbuckle, *Earthing the Gospel: An Inculturation Handbook for the Pastoral Worker* (Maryknoll, N.Y.: Orbis Books, 1990) 214–9.

Sense of Humor. Humor is that sense within us that sets up a kindly contemplation of the incongruities of life. The most authentic humor is when people recognize that, despite their own sinfulness, Christ the healer still loves them. Prophets have this gift. They see their own lack of gifts and human reluctance to serve Christ on the one hand; on the other hand, God loves them and still wants them to be his messengers. A highly incongruous situation!

Guideline 2: The Mission Leader Needs to Be Able to Explain to the CEO (and Managers) the Purpose of IFCs in the Healthcare Culture

The mission leader is delegated by CEO with the task to be the official guardian of the organization's vision and mission. It is the duty of the mission leader, therefore, to explain the purpose of an IFC to the CEO and to obtain the appropriate support for the project.

Guideline 3: Membership of IFCs Is Open to Anyone Committed to the Mission and Values of Christian Healthcare

The primary task of an IFC is to provide a structure to allow people to focus their energy on furthering the holistic mission of Jesus Christ. Members are not required to belong to the Catholic Church, but must be committed to the mission/values of Christian healthcare; accept that it is founded on the life and teachings of Christ; accept the social and ethical requirements of the Catholic Church; accept the requirements of an IFC, for example, the need to center their prayer on the life of Christ.

Guideline 4: The Core Community, of which the Mission Leader Is a Member, Will Concentrate on the Pastoral Development and Care of Other IFCs, Particularly Their Pastoral Facilitators

The pastoral leader or facilitator of an IFC "feeds, guides, and shows the way"[44] to its members. The task of the core group is to train and support pastoral leaders.

Guideline 5: Membership of an IFC Is a Faith Journey Demanding Ongoing Conversion

Refounding healthcare through IFCs is a faith experience and a gift of God, necessitating members' prayerful journeying into a world of Gospel

---

[44] Kleissler and others, *Small Christian Communities,* 167.

faith, ongoing conversion, and discernment in the midst of agonizing darkness and chaos at times. No amount of human effort or experimentation on our part will bring about refounding.

Summary

Sponsors are people with the responsibility of guarding and developing an important gift. With the rapid decrease in numbers the role of religious as sponsors in Catholic healthcare has weakened dramatically. Lay people have been asked to assume the responsibility where once religious led. Sponsors in healthcare of other denominations have had to face the issue of lay leadership earlier than their Catholic colleagues.

For both religious and lay people of the Catholic tradition the challenge is to refound: to make quantum change in healthcare theologically, culturally, and practically from religious to lay-led ministry.

Throughout the Catholic Church since Vatican II the movement toward lay-led ministries has been hesitant, however, often lacking the boldness mandated by the council. In healthcare also there have been many fine statements about the need for lay people to be ministers of the healing Christ, but too often formation for this task has been inadequate.

As religious congregations withdraw it is customary to appoint mission leaders in an endeavor to guarantee that the mission continues, but this is an impossible task for one person. The role needs to be radically rethought according to refounding principles. IFCs offer a way to do this. They can provide formation and support for lay people to focus on furthering the mission at all levels of healthcare. In brief, the following five qualities identify an IFC: (1) prayer focused on the Scriptures, (2) commitment to challenge culture(s) with Gospel values, (3) high level of mutuality in relationships, (4) governance through dialogue, and (5) gender equality.

The mission leader's task is to develop a core group as an IFC which then acts as the catalyst and founder of other communities.

Chapter 8 ▮▮▮▮▮▮▮▮▮▮▮▮▮▮▮▮▮

Merging Healthcare Facilities

> *Problems in mergers and acquisitions typically stem from . . . a misalignment of two cultures and are compounded by a lack of skill for cultural management on both sides. When cultures are misaligned and poorly managed, change inevitably fails.*[1]
>
> —Daryl R. Conner

This chapter explains:

- the various meanings of "merger";
- reasons for the failure of mergers;
- guidelines for refounding healthcare ministries through successful mergers;
- the elements of Catholic identity in the post-Vatican II Church;
- the incompatibility of non-profit and for-profit healthcare facilities.

Mergers in healthcare are rapidly increasing, prompted in large part by demands for greater efficiency from health maintenance organizations, the growing movement from acute hospital to community care, and the need for non-profit organizations to consolidate in order to resist the aggressive

---

[1] Daryl R. Conner, *Managing at the Speed of Change* (New York: Villard Books, 1993) 174.

competitiveness of investor-owned hospital chains.[2] In a recent national survey of a cross-section of hospitals/systems in the United States, 52 percent of 224 were still independent hospitals in 1995, but just 12 percent expected to be solo by the year 2000.[3]

Christian hospitals mirror this trend. For example, Alan Zuckerman and Russell Coile estimate that "in the next five years, every Catholic hospital and religious sponsor must establish an integration strategy and select partners for the next century . . . [as a result of] the long-term trends of managed care, competition, and capitation."[4] They foresee that within a short space of time "national Catholic systems could consolidate from 63 small and mid-sized organizations to 15 to 20 megasystems, each owning or managing 10 to 100 or more hospitals."[5] The newly established Catholic Health Initiatives of Denver could involve, it is claimed, as many as three hundred hospitals, "thus becoming the largest U.S. Catholic healthcare organization and rivaling all but the largest investor-owned hospital chains."[6]

The merging of healthcare facilities can be a way of refounding the mission of the healing Christ but, given the poor history of mergers, it is necessary first to summarize why mergers commonly fail. I then concentrate on the merging of Christian healthcare facilities, explaining the conditions required for their success.

Mergers: General Comments

Clarifying Terms

Confusing technical terms such as "acquisition," "integration," and "alliance" abound in the literature on mergers of businesses, and they are indiscriminately transferred to healthcare. Non-profits need to be clear about the meaning of these terms and able to judge whether or not the cultural and human costs involved conflict with their Christian values.

---

[2] See Elisabeth Rosenthal, "Mount Sinai and N.Y.U. Seek a Medical Merger," *The New York Times* (June 13, 1996) 3B.

[3] See Barry S. Bader, "Look Before You Leap: Boards Need to Ask 'Why?' Before Merging or Affiliating," *Trustee* 50:3 (1977) 18–19.

[4] Alan M. Zuckerman and Russell C. Coile, "Catholic Healthcare's Future," *Healthcare Progress* 78:6 (1997) 23.

[5] Ibid., 24.

[6] Ibid.

Acquisition is a term that refers to a method of entering rapidly into a particular market through the purchase of an existing organization, unit of an organization, or a product/service. The acquisition of a direct competitor is referred to as *horizontal integration;* much of the development of the for-profit hospital systems has been through this type of integration. *Vertical acquisition* is particularly characteristic of organizations wishing to foster integrated delivery service, such as when a hospital acquires community physician group practices.[7] In horizontal integration the acquiring organization may be interested only in the physical and financial assets of the target company, in which case it will probably destroy the organization's culture, for example, through dismissing most of its staff. The human cost can be severe.[8]

Strategic alliances/networks (or *organizational co-existence*) occur when organizations loosely amalgamate while maintaining significant autonomy. The aim is to obtain some long-term strategic advantage for each unit that is impossible for any single organization.[9] However, though the alignment of cultures is said to be minimal in networks and may be confined to the corporate level of business, for success there needs to be some significant cooperation rather than competition. For this to occur there must be a degree of cultural change in the respective organizational cultures, that is, each facility must be prepared to give up some independence to allow an over-arching organization to emerge with its own appropriate culture and clearly defined decision-making authority.

In Australia there is a movement to develop regional alliances among Catholic healthcare facilities. This is also happening in the United States; for example, seven Catholic hospitals in St. Louis have formed a network to compete with the local giant BJC Health System, and on the west coast a multi-state Catholic network from Seattle to San Diego is developing. Networks have also developed across denominational and secular boundaries: in Columbus, South Carolina, four hospitals (one Baptist, one Catholic, and two public hospitals) have decided to form a network.[10]

---

[7] See W. Jack Duncan and others, *Strategic Management of Health Care Organizations* (Oxford: Basil Blackwell, 1995) 236–7.

[8] See Brian J. Miller, *Mergers and Acquisitions: Back-to-Basics Techniques for the '90s* (New York: John Wiley & Sons, 1994) 236–7.

[9] See Duncan and others, *Strategic Management,* 239–41.

[10] See Zuckerman and Coile, "Catholic Healthcare's Future," 25–6; and Duncan, *Strategic Management,* 241.

A *joint venture* "is the combination of the resources of two or more separate organizations to accomplish a designated task,"[11] allowing some advantages of mergers without the forfeiture of control. In the mid-1990s in the United States the most popular form of joint venture was between hospitals and physicians. Hospitals wanted to control their medical care costs and the physicians wished to increase their market security and profits. Zuckerman and Coile warn that "only large-scale ventures that develop substantial healthcare businesses will be equipped to respond to marketplace pressures favoring larger organizations."[12]

However, even though joint ventures allow partners to retain considerable control over decision-making, potential conflicts are nonetheless considerable, unless the partners are compatible. Before joint ventures are entered into, the prospective partners must be as aware as is possible of each other's cultural values and organization. Second, they must each let go of sufficient control to make the venture efficient. This will necessitate developing a level of cultural oneness sufficient to allow appropriate decision-making.

The term *merger* is loosely used to cover any of the above strategies. Strictly, however, it refers to the process whereby organizations dialogue as equals, with the intention of producing a single new, more powerful organization with its own culture, not infrequently with a new name. A merger requires substantial change in existing cultures; it means identifying the strengths of each organizational culture and using them to form a synergistic combination.[13] The greater the gap or dissimilarity between the cultures committing themselves to a merger, the more radical will be the cultural changes demanded.[14] Successful mergers require that all parties share a common vision/mission and are prepared to preserve aspects of one another's cultures that conform to it.

History of Mergers

Despite the popularity of mergers and acquisitions over the last twenty years, the literature on business is filled with dreary warnings about their negative effects. Tom Peters concludes that "most studies suggest that, in

---

[11] Duncan, *Strategic Management*, 241.

[12] Zuckerman and Coile, "Catholic Healthcare's Future," 27.

[13] See Conner, *Managing at the Speed of Change*, 175.

[14] See Sue Cartwright and Cary L. Cooper, "The Role of Culture Compatibility in Successful Organizational Marriage," *Academy of Management Executive* 7:2 (1993) 68.

general, [business] mergers do not pan out."[15] Mergers have come to be associated with lowered morale, job dissatisfaction, unproductive behavior, sabotage, petty theft, absenteeism, and increased labor-turnover, strikes, and accident rates, rather than with increased profitability.[16] Reflecting on the fate of business mergers in 1994, *The Economist* commented:

> Unlike the hostile takeovers of the 1980s, most of this year's mergers have been friendly. Entailing true romance rather than shotgun weddings . . . no rash of mergers has ever seemed more benign, or better calculated to boost corporate profits. . . . Troubles come later. . . . [The] overall record is decidedly unimpressive. . . . [On] average, they do not result in higher profits or greater efficiency.[17]

Brian Miller, national director of Ernst & Young Corporate Finance, concludes his study of mergers and acquisitions: "Statistics indicate that up to one-third of all mergers fail within five years, and that as many as 80 percent never live up to full expectations."[18]

The statistics for failures in healthcare mergers are no better, as Jill Sherer points out: "Studies show that as many as 75 percent of hospital-hospital mergers are unsuccessful when issues surrounding corporate culture are ignored."[19] Walter A. Zelman of the Harvard Medical School concludes that many hospitals were finding that choosing partners was "the easiest part of the merger process. Finalizing the merger was far more difficult. . . . [Most] partners find conceptualization easier than implementation. What is planned may never happen; and if it does, it may not do or mean all that it intended."[20]

Reasons for Failures

Research shows that the main reasons for the collapse of mergers, or their inability to realize their original expectations, are as follows.

[15] Tom Peters, *Thriving on Chaos* (New York: Alfred A. Knopf, 1987) 7.

[16] See George Meeks, *Disappointing Marriage: A Study of the Gains from Mergers* (Cambridge: Cambridge University Press, 1977); Sue Cartwright and Cary L. Cooper, "The Psychological Impact of Merger and Acquisition on the Individual," *Human Relations* 46:3 (1993) 327–9.

[17] "The Trouble with Mergers," *The Economist* (September 10, 1994) 13.

[18] Miller, *Mergers and Acquisitions*, 230.

[19] Jill L. Sherer, "Corporate Cultures," *Hospitals & Health Networks* (May 5, 1994) 20.

[20] Walter A. Zelman, *The Changing Health Care Marketplace: Private Ventures, Public Interests* (San Francisco: Jossey-Bass, 1996) 91. See comments by Montague Brown,

Failure to Ask the Question "Why?"

Management writer James O'Toole describes the contemporary trend to form business amalgamations as "merger-mania," saying that the "desire of large industrial bodies to merge is insatiable" and that the purpose and strategies for such actions are rarely thought through.[21] Barry Bader summarizes his research into healthcare mergers in the United States:

> Too often the board's decision-making process could be characterized as "aim, fire, ready or not." Boards frequently . . . miss a vital first step: probing indepth their core values and their needs for a strategic partner. . . . Why do we need a merger or affiliation partner to live out our values and vision for the future?[22]

CASE STUDY

Being Clear About the Purpose

The board of the Denver Lutheran Medical Center spent several years investigating the need for a collaborative venture and found it required a partner to assist it in expanding its ambulatory care services, physical network, and geographic presence, but the partner had to have a compatible culture. Consequently, it joined with a similar faith-based organization, St. Joseph Hospital in Denver, which brought to the relationship a much-needed wide experience in managed care.

The venture was successful because both parties gave considerable time to clarifying the need for partnership and its implementation.[23]

"Mergers, Networking, and Vertical Integration: Managed Care and Investor-Owned Hospitals," *Readings in Managed Health Care,* ed. Peter R. Kongstvedt (Gaithersburg, Md.: Aspen Publishers, 1997) 59–67.

[21] James O'Toole, *Vanguard Management* (New York: Berkley Books, 1987) 250, 258.

[22] Bader, "Look Before You Leap," 20.

[23] Case study provided by Bader, "Look Before You Leap," 20.

Ignoring Cultural Factors

Most commentators conclude that mergers fail primarily because leaders do not appreciate the power of culture and consequently are unable to manage the cultural dimensions of change before, during, and after.[24] Stuart Slatter writes that the merger of firms "rarely brings increased efficiencies, unless accompanied by sound post-merger management. In fact, inefficiencies may actually increase as . . . [divisive] splits develop within the new top-management team as each manager retains loyalties to his former business."[25] Other writers are blunter in their conclusions. Daryl Conner says that "lack of cultural management has been catastrophic"[26] for groups seeking to merge.

Culture is sometimes thought to be "irrational," of little importance, or even unbecoming to people concerned with the hard, measurable realities of finance and profits. Yet this admission by Eric Crowell, president and CEO of Trinity Regional Health System, Rock Island, U.S.A., the product of a 1992 merger, is a sobering reminder that cultural issues cannot be ignored:

> I probably spent more time on the economic and legal aspects of the merger and not enough on the issue of corporate culture. Had I been able to do it over again, I would have addressed corporate culture issues as early as in the strategic planning stages of the merger. I know now more than ever that it is a strong force that must be managed.[27]

There must be a cultural compatibility (or what is termed "culture fit") between organizations that seek to merge. If there is insufficient culture fit, then cultural collisions will destroy efforts to merge the organizations.[28] Edgar H. Schein concludes from his own research that "[If] culture determines and limits strategy, a cultural mismatch in an acquisition or merger is as great a risk as a financial, product, or market mismatch."[29] A well-known

[24] See "The Trouble with Mergers," 13, 93–4.

[25] Stuart Slatter, *Corporate Recovery* (London: Penguin Books, 1984) 245.

[26] Conner, *Managing at the Speed of Change,* 173.

[27] Eric T. Crowell as cited by Sherer, "Corporate Cultures," 21.

[28] See Cartwright and Cooper, "The Role of Culture Compatibility," 57–70; Anthony F. Buono and James Bowditch, *The Human Side of Mergers and Acquisitions: Managing Collisions between People, Cultures, and Organizations* (San Francisco: Jossey-Bass, 1989) 163.

[29] Edgar H. Schein, *Organizational Culture and Leadership* (San Francisco: Jossey-Bass, 1987) 34.

case of the lack of culture fit is the attempt by the oil company Exxon to acquire the electronic firm Vydec. Because Exxon's culture was based on oil it was possible for its organization to plan several years in advance as the supply of oil is predictable. Vydec's culture, however, was based on a far more volatile market; its management had to be prepared to change its strategies at a moment's notice and its culture was structured with this in mind.[30]

CASE STUDY ▆▆▆▆▆▆▆▆▆▆▆▆▆▆▆▆▆▆▆

Lack of "Culture Fit" in Healthcare Facilities

St. Joseph's Hospital, St. Paul, Minnesota, entered into a joint venture with St. Mary's Hospital and Rehabilitation Center in Minneapolis, but it ended after a few years: "Cultural differences had overshadowed similarities, and the two decided it was in both communities' best interests to discontinue the agreement."[31]

Inability to Lead in Chaos

Mergers, no matter how well prepared, inevitably add to existing levels of organizational chaos. Unless leaders have the qualities to cope pro-actively with chaos their efforts will fail.

Failure to Communicate

Many companies, even under the best circumstances, have faulty communication systems and styles. During the stress of a merger even the "brightest managers are often ill-equipped to handle what comes up from employee groups."[32] Throughout the merger process it is virtually impossible to over-communicate; people are able to adjust to change more easily if they face the known rather than the unknown.

---

[30] See Miller, *Mergers and Acquisitions,* 229.

[31] Marian Louwagie and Milt Hertel, "Give-and-Take in an Ecumenical System," *Health Progress* 78:2 (1997) 39–40.

[32] Marsha Sinetar, "Mergers, Morale and Productivity," *Personnel Journal* (November 13, 1981) 863.

CASE STUDIES

The Importance of Communication

Case Study 1

Two CEOs of separate hospitals correctly recognized the need for a strategic partnership that would guarantee the ongoing development of their facilities. They discussed their insight informally with various managers but, in their haste, they did not at first include their separate boards and medical staffs in their dialogue. When board members heard they immediately rejected the proposal. Later the CEOs recognized that they should have first involved the board and clinicians in an open and educational process to help them realize the need for a partnership.

Case Study 2

The BJC Health System was formed in 1993 in St. Louis, Missouri, from five strong hospital partners and their subsidiaries and an affiliation with a well-established school of medicine. One review of its development highlights frequent failures to communicate adequately with people. It was admitted at the pre-merger stage that "the time was not taken to build collaborative relationships—individuals conducted their work as they were used to doing in the past."[33] "Unfortunately," comments Donald Wojtkowski, "so many 'things' needed to be done that management's focus was upon 'doing things' rather than managing people."[34] A major lesson of the review is summarized in this way: "Communicate, communicate, communicate. . . . Constant, honest communication about what, why, and how changes affect 'me' is critical."[35]

---

[33] William M. Behrendt and Walter F. Klein, "Organizational Culture and Decision Making," *Anatomy of a Merger: BJC Health System,* ed. Wayne M. Lerner (Chicago: Health Administration Press, 1997) 83.

[34] Donald E. Wojtkowski, "Facilities," *Anatomy of a Merger,* ed. Lerner, 197.

[35] Behrendt and Klein, "Organizational Culture and Decision Making," 89.

Brian Miller concludes from his investigations that "successful mergers happen only when high-level managers make themselves visible and accessible to all employees affected by the merger and when they promote the benefits at all levels. . . . Rumors and speculation, which can have a paralyzing effect on an organization,"[36] can be minimized through frequent and accurate information.

Patriarchal Authoritarianism

Some speculate that the drive to build mergers comes at times from authoritarian, patriarchal values dominant in Western society and further reinforced by the Thatcherite managerial revolution. Patriarchalism, they claim, blinds organizations to the feminine values of creativity and openness to ways of cooperation other than formal mergers.[37]

In brief, mergers break down because leaders fail to acknowledge the following:

- No merger will succeed unless it is clear to the parties involved why it should take place.

- Every organization has a culture. Significant cultural change, such as the integration of different cultures, evokes chaos and is financially expensive, time-consuming, and emotionally demanding, especially if it involves integrating quite different cultures.

- If the cultural issues are not addressed at every stage of a merging process, then collaboration will either fail or fall short of expectations.

- Employees normally view prospective mergers as a major life change, negatively affecting their lives—even their identity. The culture chaos evoked by even the possibility of merging cultures can result in considerable dysfunctional behavior, including widespread worker resistance to any form of integration (see Chapter 4).

Guidelines for Successful Healthcare Mergers

Cultural compatibility is essential for successful mergers, but Edgar Schein writes that "the tools for assessing cultural differences are still rela-

---

[36] Miller, *Mergers and Acquisitions,* 241–3.

[37] See Gareth Morgan, *Images of Organization* (London: Sage Publications, 1986) 210–2.

tively crude."[38] The following guidelines are an attempt to rectify this problem and to provide advice about how to manage the merging of organizational cultures with particular reference to healthcare facilities.

Guideline 1

Evaluate the mission and values of the organizations to be merged, but it is first necessary that would-be partners know their own mission and values. For example, Catholics need to be clear about what constitutes Catholic identity.

When healthcare organizations seek a partnership it is in the interest of both parties that they identify their respective philosophies and ethical directives. Sr. Jean de Blois, S.S.J., Catholic Health Association of the United States, rightly asserts that a major inhibiting factor for Catholic institutions wishing to merge with non-Catholic groups is that they can cripple themselves with a too narrow view of Catholic identity.[39] They concentrate on what Catholic hospitals cannot do. While Catholics must adhere to the ethical and religious directives of the Church,[40] such as the need to avoid all formal cooperation in such issues as abortion, direct sterilization, and euthanasia, they must also be aware of and promote the rich biblical and human foundations of holistic healthcare (see Chapter 5) that encourage collaboration with people of goodwill outside the Church. In addition, false beliefs in the community need to be dispelled, for example, that daily Mass is required for all employees or that profits go to the Vatican.

The Catholic Health Association of the United States has listed five fundamental and positive tenets of Catholic healthcare practice; policies and practice of potential partners can be examined in relation to them. (1) Healthcare is a service and never merely a commodity exchanged for profit. (2) Every person is the subject of human dignity with intrinsic spiritual worth at every stage of human development. (3) People are inherently social; their

---

[38] Schein, *Organizational Culture and Leadership,* 36.

[39] See Patricia Lefevere, "Catholic Hospitals Face Myths, Mergers," *National Catholic Reporter* (November 20, 1998) 10–11.

[40] See National Conference of Catholic Bishops, *Ethical and Religious Directives for Catholic Health Services* (Washington, D.C.: USCC, 1995); Richard P. McBrien writes on Catholic distinctiveness: "There is no one characteristic, apart from the Petrine doctrine, which sets the Catholic Church apart from *all other* churches. On the other hand, a case can be made that nowhere else except in the Catholic Church are *all* of Catholicism's characteristics present in the precise *configuration* in which they are found within Catholicism." *Catholicism* 2 (San Francisco: Harper and Row, 1980) 1172.

dignity is fully realized only in association with others. All must serve the common good; the self-interest of a few must not compromise the well-being of all. (4) A preferential option for the poor calls for commitment to the care of the poor and the disenfranchised. (5) Stewardship requires that we use natural and social resources prudently and in the service of all.[41] Implicit in these principles is the need for the rights of employees to be respected (e.g., their right to join trade unions) not only when employed, but also when circumstances require that their services must cease.[42]

Guideline 2

Recognize that there is a fundamental philosophical difference between for-profit and non-profit healthcare organizations.

These two forms of healthcare were briefly referred to in Chapter 5. However, since there is growing pressure for Christian non-profit facilities to merge with or sell to for-profit organizations, the differences between them need to be more precisely clarified.

The statements from Catholic agencies in the United States are unequivocal. The National Coalition on Catholic Health Care Ministry strongly resists any move by Catholic institutions to be part of "publicly traded, investor-owned hospital chains."[43] The Catholic Health Association of the United States has refused membership to investor-owned providers. It is not surprising, therefore, that controversy erupts each time a Catholic facility reveals it is considering selling to or merging with a for-profit organization.[44]

Following are the reasons Catholic facilities should not merge with or sell to for-profit healthcare organizations.

---

[41] Catholic Health Association, "How to Approach Catholic Identity in Changing Times," *Health Progress* 74:2 (1994) 23–9.

[42] See ibid., 24–8.

[43] Statement of National Coalition on Catholic Health Care Ministry as cited by Charles E. Curran, "The Catholic Identity of Catholic Institutions," *Theological Studies* 58:1 (1997) 99.

[44] For example see "Religious Health Care: Catholic Leaders Vow to Stay the Course," *The New York Times* (June 17, 1996) 6; "Can For-Profit Hospitals Be Catholic?" *National Catholic Reporter* (December 5, 1997) 20–1; Della de Lafuente, "Catholic Health Care Dilemma," *Chicago Sun Times* (April 8, 1996) 43; Michael Place, "Planned Sale of St. Louis University Hospital to For-Profit Chain," *Origins* 27:30 (1998) 497–502; Lawrence Biondi, "A Context of Wrenching Changes in Health Care," *Origins* 27:30 (1998) 502–5.

Conflict of Philosophies

The philosophy and values of for-profit organizations fundamentally conflict with the Christian story of healthcare. John Curley, president of the Catholic Health Association of the United States, states: "Simply put, the investor-owned model is not compatible with the Church's mission in health care—one can't serve both God and money."[45] Curley vividly contrasts the two irreconcilable visions:

> First and foremost, our Church ministry sees itself as a sacrament, an unconditional sign of God's compassionate presence; investor-owned chains see themselves as commercial enterprises like ball bearing manufacturers. Our Church ministry sees health care as an essential human service; investor-owned chains see health care as a commodity to be exchanged for a profit.[46]

A for-profit, when faced with an unproductive service, will focus primarily on the bottom-line. An authentic non-profit, on the other hand, will evaluate the service in light of its mission, and, if it is seen to be important, every creative effort will be made to find ways to pay for it.[47]

CASE STUDY

A Chaplaincy Staff Reduced

Columbia/HCA, a for-profit healthcare organization, took over a Catholic hospital which had a full-time chaplaincy staff of seven led by a Lutheran pastor and a Catholic priest. At its first budget the organization allowed for only one part-time chaplain working twenty hours per week.[48]

---

[45] John Curley, "For-Profit Chains Seeking to Buy Catholic Hospitals," *Origins* 25:5 (1995) 79.

[46] Ibid.

[47] See Amata Miller, "Merging with For-Profits: Flawed Strategies," *Health Progress* 77:4 (1996) 16.

[48] See Gary MacEoin, "Another Catholic Hospital Goes For-Profit," *National Catholic Reporter* (September 18, 1998) 5.

Cardinal Joseph Bernardin cites Peter Drucker in his defense of non-profit facilities. Drucker explains that the distinguishing feature of non-profits is not that they are *non*-profit, but that they do something quite different from either business or government. Business has "discharged its task when the customer buys the product, pays for it, and is satisfied with it," and government has done so when its "policies are effective." But for a non-profit institution "its product is a changed person . . . a cured patient, a child that learns . . . a changed human life altogether";[49] that is, its purpose is to advance important non-economic functions that cannot be as well served by businesses or government.

Education and healthcare, argues Sister de Blois,[50] are essential human needs and must not be left to the vagaries of market forces, as is the case in the United States, for the poor suffer in consequence. Ethicists John W. Glasser and Ronald P. Hamel explain this conclusion by clarifying three realms of ethics: societal, institutional, and individual. *Societal ethics* is about the overall and long-term good of a society, the well-being of a nation. *Institutional ethics* deals with the overall and long-term good of institutions. *Individual ethics* is concerned with the good of the individual. The ways in which a nation values life, education, and health will influence all institutions within its boundaries. Thus when a national government believes that healthcare is a market commodity, not a basic human right, "the connection between health care *service* and *wealth* will be strengthened, and the connection between health care *service* and *need* will be weakened." They conclude that "societal systems and structures will punish those who serve the poor because of a prior societal determination that health care will be treated as market commodity."[51] If Christian healthcare facilities join with investor-oriented organizations, they are publicly condoning a nationwide value-system that oppresses the poor. This is contrary to the requirements of societal ethics.

Amata Miller agrees with this conclusion and adds that the non-profit sector has become the popular scapegoat for the chaos in American healthcare. The very successful partnership between the public and non-profit sectors

---

[49] Peter Drucker, *Managing the Non-profit Organization* (New York: HarperCollins, 1990) xiv. See also Cardinal Joseph Bernardin, "The Case for Not-for-Profit Healthcare," *Origins* 32:32 (1995) 540–1.

[50] Jean de Blois, "Health Care Is a Basic Human Right," *National Catholic Reporter* (September 18, 1998) 20.

[51] John W. Glaser and Ronald P. Hamel, eds., *Three Realms of Managed Care: Societal, Institutional, Individual* (Kansas City, Mo.: Sheed and Ward, 1997) xi.

through Medicare and Medicaid that has long benefited the poor is now blamed for the current healthcare turmoil: "The very effectiveness of this kind of partnership has attracted the ire of the right wing."[52] Under pressure from economic rationalists, federal funding for the poor channeled through non-profit healthcare services is being cut back by $263 billion between 1995 and 2002. This is causing immense suffering for the poor. To join with for-profits is to support this oppressive economic rationalist philosophy.

I think, however, that the common good of a particular *region* of a country may require that a merger with, or sale to, an investor-owned facility take place. But there must be guaranteed safeguards. The following case study provides an example.

CASE STUDY

A Catholic Hospital Struggles to Maintain Its Presence

A Catholic hospital in an isolated and socio-economically depressed town in the United States was no longer financially viable. No other Christian hospital existed in the region. The trustees, with the permission of the local bishop, accepted an offer to become partners with an investor-owned hospital in the same town.

The latter wanted the partnership for two reasons: the Catholic hospital had some facilities that the investor-owned hospital did not have; it also had a culture that local people admired. Legal safeguards to guarantee maintenance of the Catholic identity were approved by both parties. The Catholic hospital's trustees publicly explained to the people that though the two philosophies were in conflict, it was possible to develop a merger that would protect the Catholic identity; for example, the poor would have continued access to the hospital and the hospital would have respect for Catholic ethical values. Since the merger occurred five years ago the purchaser has honored the agreement.

[52] Miller, "Merging with For-Profits," 24.

In this case study the appropriate ecclesiastical authority had to approve this merger, because any facility that takes the name "Catholic" must have accountability to Church authorities, such as the diocesan bishop, the bishops' conference, or the Holy See. Approval is essential for a partnership of this type. Church law states: "no undertaking shall assume the name Catholic unless the consent of competent ecclesiastical authority is given" (Canon 216).[53] The ecclesiastical authority will insist that ethical guarantees are in place before any approval is given. In this example the bishop approved the partnership because the Catholic identity would be legally protected and a regional Christian presence in healthcare would be maintained in an economically depressed area.

In Britain, Australia, New Zealand, and Canada the right of people to healthcare is nationally accepted. Hence, from the perspective of societal ethics there is less risk than in the United States that partnering with or selling to a for-profit organization by a non-profit will negatively affect national values. But as economic rationalist forces are making inroads in these countries this could quickly change. However, even if there is no risk from the standpoint of societal ethics, the requirements of institutional or individual ethics may forbid any form of significant collaboration by non-profit facilities with for-profits, unless safeguards are in place to protect the Christian identity. The following case study illustrates what can happen when safeguards have not been negotiated.

CASE STUDY

Bottom-Line Values Win

A Christian non-profit hospital in Britain had been managing an outreach program for abused women for several years, relying on its own financial resources and government grants. The government withdrew its support and the sponsoring facility itself experienced financial problems. In desperation, the non-profit agency accepted an offer to become a junior partner in a for-

[53] See Germain Kopaczynski, "Catholic Identity in Health Care," *Linacre Quarterly* 64:2 (1997) 26–35; M. Cathleen Kaveny and James F. Keenan, "Ethical Issues in Health Care Restructuring," *Theological Studies* 56:1 (1995) 136–50; Francis G. Morrisey, "What Makes an Institution Catholic?" *The Jurist* 2 (1987) 531–44; Richard A. McCormick, "The Gospel of Life," *America* 172:15 (1995) 10–17.

profit system in the hope it would be able to survive and continue to support the outreach program more effectively. After three years, however, the for-profit facility ceased to subsidize the shelter because the investors were complaining about their declining incomes.

In this example from the perspective of institutional ethics the trustees should not have accepted collaboration until legal protection for the shelter had been obtained. Only in exceptional cases, and with legally binding protective structures in place, should a non-profit collaborate with investor-owned healthcare organizations.

Non-profit Facilities Are Mediating Institutions

Cardinal Bernardin argues that non-profit healthcare institutions stand protectively between the individual and state because "they mediate against the rougher edges of capitalism's inclination toward excessive individualism."[54] If non-profit organizations are closer to people than investor-owned institutions, they are better able to defend the people's rights to healthcare, especially those of the poor. When a non-profit collaborates with for-profit it loses its freedom to critique capitalism in healthcare.

Non-profits Provide Opportunity for Volunteerism

Non-profit organizations traditionally offer good opportunities for volunteerism, expressions of good citizenship, and philanthropy; their cultures are capable of generating a counter-force to the contemporary breakdown of families and the loss of community values.[55] If non-profit and for-profit healthcare organizations merge, this opportunity for expressing people's beliefs in social responsibility will be jeopardized at grave cost to a nation's soul.

Guideline 3

Identify the significant symbols and founding myths of the organizational cultures, including one's own, that are to be changed through merging.

Through its symbols and myths a culture conceals far more than it reveals, and, writes anthropologist Edward T. Hall, "It hides most effectively

[54] Bernardin, "The Case for Non-Profit Healthcare," 542.
[55] See ibid., 541–2; and Drucker, *Managing the Non-profit Organization,* 181–2.

from its own participants." To learn one's own culture "is an achievement of gargantuan proportions for anyone."[56] Like our personalities, organizational cultures are often more obviously visible to others than to ourselves. They are too much part of us for us to grasp them very clearly. Hence, an important skill in cultural analysis is the ability for cultural self-reflection. This means learning to identify one's own cultural myths and the myths of others.

Example: Difficulties in Interpreting Organizational Symbols/Myths

A CEO of a non-profit hospital in the United States decided for financial reasons to close the kitchen services and instead contract with an external catering company. He arranged for existing staff to be employed in several other hospitals and at higher wages. To his surprise, the kitchen workers strongly objected to this decision complaining he had "completely destroyed our way of life."

The CEO had judged that the employees—all immigrants from southern Italy—worked in the kitchen primarily for an income. If he had first sat down and listened to them, he would have discovered that these migrants in a strange land first wanted a sense of belonging. They were used to an extended family system in rural Italy, and they saw the kitchen group as a substitute family-like support system. The maintenance of this myth, the foundation of the kitchen subculture, was more important to them than an increase in wages. The transfer to other hospitals would effectively destroy the much-appreciated family-like bonding.

As explained in Chapter 1, the most important myth in any culture is its creation myth, since it provides the culture with the primary source of their identity as a distinct group. The above case study illustrates this. Various kinds of creation myths affect people in different ways and times; three such myths are public, operative, and residual.

The *public* myth is a set of stated ideals that people openly claim binds them together, such as those formulated in a mission statement. In practice these ideals may have little, if any, cohesive force.

[56] Edward T. Hall, *The Silent Language* (New York: Anchor Press, 1973) 30.

The *operative* myth, however, is what actually in time gives people their felt cohesive identity; it can and often does differ dramatically from the public myth. In the story of Maria in Chapter 6, the trustees and board of management believed the public and operative myths were the same. They thought that they were being faithful to the mission statement and its commitment to the poor. It was difficult for the board's chairman and Maria to convince others that this was not true.

The *residual* myth normally has little or no daily impact on a group's life, but at times can become a powerful operative myth. For example, people of a formerly oppressed nation may be relating amicably with the descendants of their former masters, but bitter memories can suddenly emerge to create a climate of suspicion and antagonism. These memories are residual myths; like all myths, they are difficult to identify. However, if they are not acknowledged from the beginning of merger negotiations they will erupt to destroy or cripple relationships between groups.

CASE STUDIES

The Importance of Identifying the Type of Myths

Case Study 1: Operative Myths Differ

Two hospitals in different parts of a city, sponsored by the same religious congregation but belonging to different provinces (administrative units), decided to unite, claiming that their mission statements were identical because, said their administrators, "we share a common founding story from last century." Within three years of the merger, the agreement collapsed and each hospital sought other partners.

Though a substantial amount of expense and time had been given to organizational re-adjustments of services in both hospitals, the administrators had not recognized that operationally the hospitals had different cultures. The fact that both mission statements (public myths) were the same was of no practical consequence.

Case Study 2: Residual Myths Threaten Merger

Three non-profit hospitals in the same city, longtime competitors, agreed to merge in order to achieve the benefits of integrated delivery services and to successfully compete with a newly established for-profit hospital. Common vision and mission statements were written and ample time given to developing strategies for the merger to be realized. Shortly after the formal merging, however, unforeseen tensions surfaced, sparked off by a small misunderstanding between the managers of the pathology departments. One manager complained to the system CEO: "It is evident to myself and my team that the other pathology departments are not willing to collaborate because they have not kept us informed of times for meetings. We have never trusted them in the past and do not do so now."

The CEO investigated and found that information about one meeting had accidentally not been circulated. So deep had been the competitiveness between the hospitals in the past that this oversight was the catalyst for the residual rivalries and bitterness to emerge. The identities of each hospital had been formed over time by this competitiveness: "We are different. We are not like the other hospitals!" The merger was saved only because the CEO arranged for regular gatherings between representatives of departments of all three hospitals in which people were able to identify the residual myths.

Case Study 3: New Founding Myth Develops

In 1987 St. Joseph's Hospital in St. Paul, Minnesota, joined the ecumenical HealthEast healthcare system. The merger was a success because the denominational differences (i.e., myths) were acknowledged from the beginning. The negotiators then fostered a new founding story by concentrating on and strengthening common healthcare values. Marian Louwagie and Milt Hertel reported that:

> Our common denominational differences were not our downfall—in fact, our common Judeo-Christian heritage has been our strength . . . the glue that held the system together through difficult times. . . . In the end, the devotion to the mission and effective communication with the staff resulted in a merger that successfully blended denomi-

national identity and traditions at each member hospital while
establishing a corporate identity.[57]

Excellent communication has fostered a sharing of values: "The HealthEast system has adopted some of St.
Joseph's policies and practices, particularly in the areas
of mission, ethics, and spiritual care." St. Joseph's has
gained "a more diverse staff respectful of each others'
beliefs, expanded spiritual care, and the means to continue serving its community."[58]

Guideline 4

*Evaluate the cultures to be merged, including one's own, from perspective
of their openness to creativity in the service of Christ's healing mission.*

From the perspective of openness to creativity, it is possible to identify
four models of organizational culture: power; role or mechanistic; person;
and task or organic.[59]

In *power* cultures, such as the Catholic Church and religious congregations in pre-Vatican II times, creativity is encouraged only at the top;
but even that is limited by the rigorous constraints of tradition. Decision-
making is centralized in one person. Employees are motivated by a
sense of personal loyalty to the leader or by fear of retribution. Dissent
is suppressed.

A *role* or *mechanistic* culture (see Figure 4.2) is a bureaucracy which
aims to maintain the status quo and discourage all dissent. As roles are seen
as more important than persons, people feel themselves to be dispensable.

In a *person* culture the individual is central and all is directed to individual welfare no matter the cost to the common good. This type of culture is not conducive to teamwork or collaboration for the common
good.

Where a *task* or *organic* culture exists (see Figure 4.2), however, there is
an atmosphere favorable to the emergence of creativity through responsible

[57] Louwagie and Hertel, "Give-and-Take in an Ecumenical System," 39–40.

[58] Ibid., 39.

[59] See Roger Harrison, "How to Describe Your Organization," *Harvard Business Review* 5:1 (1972) 119–28. I draw on the explanations by Cartwright and Cooper, "The
Role of Culture Compatibility," 62–7.

dissent. In this culture the primary aim is to respond to needs of people beyond the group. Organizational or decision-making structures are determined by this primary purpose; people collaborate together, share talents,
deliberately foster creative dissent—all in view of the urgency to react in-
novatively for the sake of the task. There is gender equality and a willingness of members to be accountable for their work.[60] This is the culture that
is most open to refounding persons.

CASE STUDY

A Conflict of Cultures is Resolved

The administrators of two hospitals—one Catholic
and the other Methodist—began to discuss a full merger.
At first, because their mission statements were substantially the same, the managers felt their two cultures were
compatible. However, on further investigation they discovered that the mission statements hid fundamental
cultural differences: the Catholic was power oriented,
the Methodist task/achievement oriented. In consequence of this discovery it was decided to put the
merger on hold for a year until the administrators of the
Catholic hospital could begin difficult, extensive structural changes and educational programs to help their
staff to be more open to the Methodist mission-oriented
culture.

After the formal merger the tensions between the two
cultures remained; however, since their origins were
understood, appropriate actions could be taken. Over a
period of six years a task culture was firmly established.
Awareness of the cultural differences and the consequent appropriate action facilitated the success of the
merger.

[60] See Charles Handy, *Understanding Organizations* (Harmondsworth: Penguin Books,
1986) 195.

CASE STUDY ▰▰▰▰▰▰▰▰▰▰▰▰▰▰▰▰▰

Insufficient Research Holds Back a Merger

After an initial investigation the administrators of two hospitals found that their cultures were both task oriented and therefore compatible. They proceeded immediately to organize a merger, beginning with their two pathology departments, hoping that success at this level would be a model to other departments. However, within a short period major disagreements developed between the two subcultures, threatening to stop all further collaborative action.

The staff of the two administrations had concentrated their research on the top level of their hospital managements, which were certainly task oriented. However, in one hospital the founder of the pathology department was still in charge and its staff had developed such an intense loyalty to him that they saw the amalgamation as an insult to his authority (and he agreed with this assessment!). Passive aggression on their part made serious collaboration impossible. As the pathology department's head refused to change his authoritarian style, it became necessary for the hospital CEO to ask for his early retirement and that of several of his more vocal supporters.

In this case study a thorough analysis of the pathology department subculture would have warned the leadership to choose another department as the first stage of the merging process, and a great deal of energy could have been saved.

CASE STUDY ▰▰▰▰▰▰▰▰▰▰▰▰▰▰▰▰▰

Medical Practitioners Are Neglected

Three long-established, self-contained hospitals agreed to merge in order to develop integrated delivery services. The trustees entrusted the planning of the merger to a group of lay managers, but from the beginning the latter were constantly frustrated by the refusal of the medical practitioners, especially those who had been serving the hospitals for a long period, to cooperate. The doctors, who had never ever been united in the past, together threatened to withdraw their services if the merger went ahead.

This case study illustrates the conflict between two cultures: the task culture of the leadership team versus the personal culture of the doctors. The medical practitioners were loyal to the hospitals primarily as a source of individual clients; as long as the hospitals responded to this need the doctors remained amenable to changes. However, the plans for integrated delivery service and the involvement of an HMO required that the doctors submit to a degree of control and accountability outside their own profession. They would need to develop a task culture in conjunction with non-medical staff and be prepared to sacrifice at times significant independence in the service of patients. The leaders made a serious mistake from the beginning by not involving the medical practitioners in the planning and execution of the plans for merging the hospitals.

Guideline 5

Recognize that in-depth organizational cultural change is slow; culture has in-built resistances to change.

A culture commonly provides people with their primary sense of belonging. In Western society personal identity is so related to one's work that organizational cultures are especially hard to change. Charles Handy is correct: organizational cultures contemplating merger are "stuck with their past . . . their traditions. These things take years if not decades to change."[61] Whenever there is inconsistency between a particular culture and one's objectives for change, the culture always triumphs.

Guideline 6

Symptoms of culture shock are to be expected when cultures interact during merging; if these symptoms are not dealt with they will obstruct the merger.

[61] Charles Handy, *Understanding Voluntary Organizations* (London: Penguin Books, 1988) 95.

The expression "culture shock" is a general label for a wide variety of different possible responses to culture-contact stress, which may include symptoms of cultural chaos such as disorientation, depression, or apathy. More specifically, it is "a reaction that is blind and unreasoned, a reaction that is but a subconscious flight or escape from a culturally disagreeable environment."[62] Culture shock, which can be experienced by groups as well as individuals, can be expressed *either* through arrogant ethnocentric reactions, like assuming that one's culture is superior in all ways and other cultures are inferior (see Chapter 1), *or* through culturally romantic attitudes/actions, like assuming that another organizational culture is so perfect that it has nothing to learn from one's own.

Unless the feelings evoked by culture shock can be surfaced and sensitively confronted, they will linger on and frustrate intercultural communication, as the following case study illustrates.

CASE STUDY

Group Culture Shock
Endangers a Proposed Merger

For financial reasons a religious congregation decided to merge the senior administrations of two of its hospitals under one CEO. Hospital X was situated in an upper-middle-class suburb and hospital Y in a low socio-economic section of the city. At meetings with their counterparts in hospital X, administrators of hospital Y felt that their views were not being taken seriously. At times members of hospital X would make patronizing comments about the lack of high grade technology in hospital Y. Eventually planning discussions stalled for no reason obvious to the administrators of hospital X, but among themselves they blamed hospital Y for sending insufficiently qualified negotiators to the meetings.

At the request of hospital Y a facilitator was invited to the planning sessions to help participants identify the obstacles blocking communication. They uncovered two

[62] Louis Luzbetak, *The Church and Cultures* (Techny, Ill.: Divine Word Publications, 1970) 97.

dynamics operating unconsciously. First, negotiators from hospital X were able to acknowledge that they had assumed, as theirs was the richer facility, that they had nothing to learn from hospital Y. Second, negotiators from the latter were able to identify feelings of inferiority on visiting hospital X and that at times they felt overwhelmed by what they saw. The attitudes and comments of the administrators of hospital X exacerbated their feelings of inferiority.

Once these culture shock feelings had been identified by both parties, they were able to move forward by recognizing that both cultures had much to contribute to the administrative merger from their widely differing experiences.

Guideline 7

There must be appropriate communication at each stage of the merging process. This guideline becomes more focused through the following four directives.

(1) After undertaking a cultural compatibility study, the trustees and boards of management of the organizations to be merged must formulate, interiorize, and publicize common vision and mission statements based on the vision, mission, and values of the healing Jesus. This necessitates building a task culture founded on servant-leadership.

(2) The trustees and boards of management will ensure that a team of representatives of the cultures to be merged is chosen to lead the transition to a new culture; team members will need to have qualities of a refounding nature. The process of merging different cultures requires quantum-leap thinking and action on the part of leaders; a complex new culture is to be built, but it must do so in ways that respect the values of holistic health.

CASE STUDY

Lessons From a Successful Merger

It was decided that the Leicester Royal Infirmary National Health Service Trust, a large, complex teaching hospital in Britain helping around 500,000 patients annually, needed to undergo radical structural changes to improve the quality and efficiency of its services. Since this necessitated merging many of its internal processes, substantial cultural re-adjustments were necessary. The following lessons can be learned from this successful venture:[63]

- Those responsible for leading the merger must themselves be united as a team and committed to building a task culture; they are to model what the entire system is to be.

- It is necessary to spend considerable time and energy training managers at all levels for their new roles; the involvement of "clinical colleagues in the development of managerial and supervisory roles cannot be underestimated. . . . Senior managers have a critical role [as they] must protect the organisation as it reinvents itself."[64]

- Creative cultural change agents are to be identified and supported; demonstrating positive results is the best way to achieve support from the majority of people.[65]

- Continue to communicate to the whole system clearly and widely, relating information always to the vision and mission of the merger.

(3) Resistance needs to be anticipated, minimized, and overcome through on-going communication based on the values of holistic health.

In the next chapter I detail the communication processes needed in order to respond to people's anxieties in organizational change. At this point, however, it is helpful to summarize the three types of communication that Marsha Sinetar considers necessary during mergers:[66]

[63] See Mike Oram and Richard S. Wellins, *Re-Engineering's Missing Ingredient: The Human Factor* (London: Institute of Personnel and Development, 1995).

[64] Ibid., 129, 170.

[65] See ibid., 111. See article "Communication Eases Pains of Acquisition," *Health Progress* 76:2 (1995) 30–3.

[66] See Sinetar, "Mergers, Morale and Productivity," 866–7.

Communications that steady are required in the pre-merger phase prior to and just after the formal merger announcement. This is the initial stage of shock. People need to know if they will keep their jobs or, if not, that the organization will provide severance pay and assist them in obtaining other employment. At the same time in order to foster stability in the transition, leaders should insist that it is "business as usual" and that standards are to be maintained.

Communications that organize are needed in phase two (the liminality stage), that is, the time between the formal announcement of a merger and the forming of the new organizational culture. The vision and mission of the merger must be widely publicized, time-lines formulated for stages in the merging, and the new roles and training programs for managers are to be set in place.[67]

In this period "the little people" can be forgotten, especially as departments campaign and manoeuvre to hold on to power and to make small issues into major confrontations. The listening and pro-active moves of phase one must be maintained throughout, so that politically powerless groups are treated with justice and compassion. If people have to be laid-off in a merger, leaders must fulfill their earlier promises by providing prompt and just compensation and arranging counseling for alternative employment if possible.

Communications that direct are important as the actual merger begins to take place (the re-entry stage). While the previous types of communication have to continue, the best form of directive communication will be the modeling of the new culture by the leadership and management groups. If a significant gap is perceived then cynicism will emerge and put the merger at grave risk.

CASE STUDY

A Board Refuses to Set an Example

A non-profit system owned by a religious congregation and containing seven healthcare facilities had recently established a lay board of management. It was necessary to reorganize the system substantially in order to maintain

---

[67] See Roger Martin, "Changing the Mind of the Corporation," *Harvard Business Review on Change* (Boston: Harvard Business School, 1998) 136–7.

its financial viability. When communicating with the staff the trustees and the board stated that difficult decisions had to be made. The system's employees were reminded that the future depended on building teamwork and returning to the founding values of the system.

However, although the board members were professionally qualified persons, they did not learn more in-depth about the founding values or develop into a team. As this was noted by the executive staff, and communicated through them to other employees, all future communications from the board were received with cynicism. This affected morale so negatively that the system was only able to survive when another non-profit system absorbed it under the leadership of its team-oriented and value-based board. Morale among the staff improved accompanied by creative energy for change.

---

(4) For the effective merging of cultures founded on the vision, mission, and values of the healing Jesus, the axiom "the new belongs elsewhere" (see Chapter 4) may need to be implemented. People committed to a refounding process need to be protected by appropriate structures from undue interference.

CASE STUDY

Applying the Axiom
"The New Belongs Elsewhere"

A small city in United States had two non-profit acute-care hospitals (one Catholic and the other Baptist), which for one hundred years had provided free medical care for the poor in their emergency departments. This also safeguarded their tax-exempt status. As changes rapidly developed in healthcare, such as the shift from focusing on illness to focusing on wellness, from acute to community care, the two hospitals hesitated for a long time to make appropriate adjustments. It meant a twofold revolution in their thinking and acting.

First, to move beyond concentrating exclusively on the treatment of acute illness to community-based programs in the poorer sections of the city; second, to merge the two traditional rival organizations into one culture in order to better serve the town's population. It also meant collaborating better with appropriate government agencies, something that both hospitals had been doing reluctantly up to then.

It was decided to begin the merger process by jointly establishing a comprehensive healthcare service in several poorer areas of the town. To do this, the merger's leadership team, following the axiom "the new belongs elsewhere," established a new department accountable directly to the team, citing as their reasons: the need to move fast because of the health needs in the community; the fear that existing departmental subcultures were too attached to the illness model of healthcare and would absorb too much of the leadership team's energy in order to change; and the need to model the new collaborative culture in action.

The joint leadership team chose people of refounding qualities, making them accountable directly to themselves and not to any existing department in the hospitals. Within two months, the new department had established a mobile life-saving mammography program supported by a publicity campaign. They also created a program targeting migrant Hispanic youth with anti-drug publicity, along with strategically placed drug treatment centers with multilingual staff. The ongoing success of the project helped to break down resistance to the merger within both hospitals.

Guideline 8

Given the chaos that mergers can cause, together with the tumultuous environment of healthcare, refounding leaders are necessary as myth-revitalizers or myth-makers.

As explained earlier chaos is the norm in the ever-moving environment of organizational cultures, so that strategic management based solely on rational or linear models of decision-making will be ineffective (see Chapter 4). Leaders capable of acting in unpredictable surroundings are required to foster teamwork marked by the values of interdependence, mutuality, dialogue, collaboration, and community (see Chapter 5).

The ultimate stabilizing force in the chaos, and the foundation of these values, is the vision, mission, and values of the healing Christ (i.e., the *strange attractor* in chaos theory), the founding myth of all Christian healthcare ministry. Where this myth is only weakly present in the existing cultures or in the new culture formed through merging, these leaders are to be cultural *myth-revitalizers*. If no myth exists, then their task is to be *myth-makers* (see Chapters 6 and 7). Both tasks require people with a gift for refounding.[68]

Guideline 9

As groups and individuals experience grief because of cultural changes, there is need for this grief to be expressed; otherwise organizations and individuals will resist change.[69]

A culture is the emotional glue binding an organization together. However, since emotions do not lend themselves to evaluation by quantitative and analytic techniques the cost to people's feelings of grief during a merger can easily be overlooked.[70]

Example: Grief Follows a Decision to Merge

It was decided to merge one of Australia's best-known and loved health institutions, the 108-year-old Sacred Heart Hospice, with a nearby hospital conducted by the same religious congregation. There was an immediate reaction from the hospice's nurses, who claimed that the merger would

---

[68] See Paul Bate, *Strategies for Cultural Change* (Oxford: Butterworth Heinemann, 1995) 146–7, 240–5; William Bergquist, *The Postmodern Organization: Mastering the Art of Irreversible Change* (San Francisco: Jossey-Bass, 1993) 87–119. For a practical guide to help people unleash the power of myths as agents of cultural change see Michael Kaye, *Myth-Makers and Story-Tellers* (Sydney: Business and Professional, 1996).

[69] See James Hunt, "How People Get Overlooked in Takeovers," *Personnel Management* (July 1987) 24–6; William Mercer, "Costly Inattention: Ignoring Employee Impact Can Ruin Mergers," *Industry Week* (September 29, 1986) 28.

[70] See Paul J. Stonich, *Implementing Strategy* (Cambridge: Ballinger, 1982) 34–5.

cause the loss of "the special atmosphere and the personalised care that dying patients were given there."[71]

This incident is an example of what is happening throughout the Western world. On the one hand, the reality is that "healthcare providers must pursue strategies of integration, or they may fail to carry out their mission in the twenty-first century."[72] On the other hand, any form of integration—even for the right reason—commonly evokes a sense of grief, outrage, and sadness. In the above example the merger became a logical necessity because the hospice was under-used as terminally ill patients increasingly preferred to stay at home or in the community, but the consequent grief is understandable. If the nurses had not been able to express their grief publicly the process of merging would have been obstructed.

The art of leading organizational and individual grieving is the theme of the next chapter.

Summary

Mergers in healthcare are increasingly common for reasons such as the desire by would-be partners to improve a particular service or enhance their competitive position in the marketplace.[73]

Despite the popularity of mergers (and acquisitions) it is rare that they ever achieve their desired potential. Sometimes organizations merge in the hope that they will not have to change out-of-date structures, but no merger will protect them from the need to make radical changes. Sometimes there is a merger because one or both partners are so desperate to survive that they do not recognize the complexities involved. Disaster is inevitable.

When mergers succeed or fail, cultural compatibility has increasingly been looked to for an explanation. While a favorable financial result may be the primary attraction for a merger, whether it works may have more to do with how well the two organization's cultures match up. The culture of

---

[71] See Debra Jopson, "Nurses Fight Hospice Merger Plan," *The Sydney Morning Herald* (February 28, 1998) 17.

[72] Zuckerman and Coile, "Catholic Healthcare's Future," 30.

[73] See Alceste T. Pappas, *Reengineering Your Nonprofit Organization: A Guide to Strategic Transformation* (New York: John Wiley, 1996) 144–62.

an organization is what "personality" and "character" are to any individual.[74] As personalities clash or fit well together, so also with organizational cultures.

To assess cultural compatibility it is important to assess their philosophies of healthcare and to enter into the inner hearts of the cultures which are their operative myths. Myths are value impregnated felt beliefs that people hold, that they live by or live for, and that reside in the deepest recesses of their collective being (see Chapter 1). The operative story determines and sustains all the activities of an organization. These myths can be so radically diverse that mergers are rarely possible. Such is the case with Christian healthcare facilities and for-profit agencies.

If the myths of organizations are compatible mergers will succeed only when they are managed at every stage with cultural sensitivity. A merger, if undertaken for the right reasons, is such a complex process that people of refounding qualities are required to lead it.

A new organizational culture needs to develop in a merger. People must leave behind cherished attachments to risk the uncertainties of the new. It is virtually impossible to over-communicate in a merger process, simply because people are able to adjust to change more easily if they are able to face the known rather than the unknown. When communication is poor people will feel unnecessarily confused, manipulated, even viewing the other organization as an "invading enemy."

[74] See Harold J. Leavitt, *Corporate Pathfinders* (New York: Viking Penguin, 1987) 164–5.

Chapter 9

A Spirituality of Healthcare Ministry: Letting Go for Refounding

We too, then, should throw off everything that weighs us down . . . and with perseverance keep running the race which lies ahead of us.
—Heb 12:1-2

Ring out the grief that saps the mind.
—Alfred Tennyson, *In Memoriam,* cvi, st. 3

This chapter explains:

- the grief of healthcare cultures and individuals in the midst of rapid change;
- the need for rituals of grieving as a condition for institutional and personal holistic health;
- the helpful insights of traditional cultures about grieving;
- that examples of grieving rituals can be found in the Old and New Testaments;
- that a spirituality of letting go must permeate Christian healthcare, if refounding is to occur;
- guidelines to assist healthcare workers to be ritual leaders of organizational grieving.

All change involves loss and, therefore, grief. Grief, which is experienced by cultures as well as individuals, is the mixture of sadness, sorrow, denial, depression, guilt, and confusion that accompanies significant loss, such as the death of a friend, the loss of a job, the closure of an institution.

Today there are significant losses occurring throughout healthcare in Western societies as institutions and individuals struggle to make profound culture shifts and let go of traditional ways of responding to health needs (see Figure 4.1).

Change and loss may be intellectually accepted, but at the feeling level, where culture primarily resides, assent to change is far slower and more problematic. For this reason a process of grieving is imperative. Grieving is publicly approved ritual expression of loss within protected boundaries of sacred space where feelings can be freely expressed without condemnation or judgment. Unless individuals and cultures use such a ritual of mourning, which acknowledges loss and allows it to be let go of, they will remain haunted and paralyzed by grief. Suppressed grief is not healthy for society or for individuals. It suffocates creativity, holding people back from reimagining and initiating the new.

In addition to the turmoil in healthcare itself, Christians in healthcare services are confronted with stress in their own ministries; for this reason they require a particular spirituality to assist them. A spirituality is the way or style in which a person or community responds to Christ in the face of the challenges of everyday life in a given historical and cultural environment. A spirituality earths the Good News in the here and now. Spirituality for Christian healthcare ministers today emphasizes the abandonment of irrelevant ways of expressing the healing mission of Jesus, in order to embrace forms of ministry that respond to urgent holistic health needs.

The Grieving Imperative: Anthropological Insights

Cultures as well as individuals experience joy or grief. One has but to recall the nation-wide grief in the United States in response to the tragedy of the terrorist bombing in Oklahoma City in 1995. There was a feeling of collective sadness and shock that transcended the grief of individuals, but also affected them. The following case study illustrates a similar reality in a hospital culture confronted with dramatic losses.

CASE STUDY

Cultures of Hospitals in Grief

A state government in Australia unexpectedly announced that a central-city hospital of long-standing prestige was to close and be transferred to an existing hospital site in the suburbs. A few hours after the public announcement I walked into the hospital's foyer and immediately sensed the collective shock. No one had to say anything to tell me that the hospital culture was in grief, not just individual staff and patients.

Any pastoral response would require a two-level approach: one aimed at the collective or the culture itself and the other to the staff (and to a lesser degree the patients). Meanwhile, the hospital which was to be the site of the transferred city-center facility had similar collective feelings. Their identity would be destroyed by the government action because the relocated hospital was to keep its original name.

Grief and Grieving

Types of Grief

Individual and group grief may be described in various ways.[1]

Anticipated grief occurs when people fear loss that is to come, causing them to feel sad before the harm actually occurs. For example, a number of workers I interviewed in a hospital that had had a significant recent reduction in staff were experiencing anticipated grief. Though they still had their jobs they were sad, angry, and confused because they felt they also would eventually be unemployed.

Cumulative grief overload happens when loss is experienced from many quarters at the same time.

Example: Cumulative Grief Overload

A hospital department had been subjected to intense change over a year; it appeared to the CEO that they were coping well. However, one day she

[1] Gerald A. Arbuckle, *Change, Grief and Renewal in the Church* (Westminster: Christian Classics, 1991) 17–18.

sent word to the manager that one of the new doors into the unit was to be painted that day, a minor interruption by comparison with all that had happened over the year. The CEO described what then occurred:

> It was eventually reported to me that one unit staff member, on hearing what was to be done, verbally exploded with incredible rage, and banged the table with her fists, sending the coffee cups flying. Others were less dramatic, but verbally unrestrained in their anger against me, the board, and the trustees.

Suppressed grief occurs when people and cultures are not permitted to express their losses. Because they are constantly exposed to the suffering of patients and the anxieties of relatives, care-givers are culturally encouraged to suppress their feelings. They are ill-prepared then to acknowledge their own personal or institutional losses.

Examples: Suppressed Grief

Example 1: Depression Occurs

The manager of a cancer ward, on hearing it was to be closed, called his staff to tell them the news. He ended with this instruction: "We still have a job to do. We will work right to the day of closure as though nothing has happened! We must not show our sadness!" Following the unit's closing, several former staff members experienced significant depression and other signs of delayed grief.

Example 2: Silent Protest

A state government planned to build a new hospital in an economically poor American country town without consulting the people. This meant that the old facilities had to be destroyed. Politicians and bureaucrats assembled in the town hall to tell people their decision. The townspeople were angry because they liked the old building; their grandparents had helped to build it, with minimal government support at the time. However, the townspeople, most of whom were poorly educated and/or unemployed, felt they could not protest to the powerful visitors. During the period in which the hospital was being constructed the government was unable to obtain any voluntary assistance from the people. They remained, to quote a politician, "thoroughly uncooperative, sullen, and ungrateful for what we were doing for them!"

Chronic or *fatalistic* grief occurs when people sense there is no way for them to escape the implications of loss.

I sometimes find this among individual staff members or departmental subcultures in healthcare systems where changes are so rapid that people give up trying to cope. For example, a very successful hospital had decided to phase out its obstetric department; this subculture went into chronic grief because the staff could see no way to reverse the decision. "What's the use?" said a staff member. "We can't go back and no one is interested in listening to us!" Their grief was further exacerbated because other departments were flourishing and planning extensions. The CEO attempted several times to arrange for alternative employment opportunities, but very few responded. One staff member summed up the group's feeling: "We can trust no one now! We don't want to hear more words, because nothing can be done."

Cultures, like individuals, can develop defense mechanisms (e.g., repression, regression, or denial) against anxiety-creating loss. If defense mechanisms become chronically embedded in a culture people do not acknowledge grief.

For example, denial is the unconscious defense mechanism whereby reality is rejected because of its painful or threatening quality. In certain situations denial can be a healthy and necessary experience, for example, when it insulates people from receiving the full devastating impact of the shock of loss all in one moment. It gives them the space to begin the process of absorbing what has happened. The problem is when denial becomes chronic. Psychologist M. Scott Peck claims that the United States as a nation denies that the Vietnam War was morally and militarily a total failure, a "national sin." Only if the nation enters into the agony of reflection, with its accompanying doubts and pain, will it admit its mistakes and allow room for national revitalization.[2]

CASE STUDY ▰▰▰▰▰▰▰▰▰▰▰▰▰▰▰▰▰▰

Denial Causes Organizational Loss of Identity

For one hundred years a religious congregation had sponsored a hospital in a small American city, but its numbers had been so reduced that there remained only

[2] M. Scott Peck, *The Different Drum: Community-Making and Peace* (London: Rider, 1987) 223–4.

one representative on staff, the mission leader. The mission leader, on the verge of retirement, kept reminding her superiors that there was no adequate replacement for her and that the mission orientation programs were out-of-date in a secularized world. The congregational leader would not agree:

> The hour's orientation about our founding story which we offer new staff has worked in the past and will continue to do so. Moreover, we have devoted staff who believe in our values. Look at Dr. Y and Nurse X! Our primary duty now is to get the financial structures right so that the hospital can continue into the future.

On visiting the hospital I concluded that the culture had ceased to be visibly Catholic. There was no doubt about its technological efficiency after millions of dollars had been invested, but over the years the sponsors had employed senior administrative staff whose primary qualification was financial effectiveness. The sponsors were in chronic denial. It had been recommended to the sponsors that entirely new biblically-based orientation and in-service training programs were necessary, to be led by skilled educators, but nothing was done. The sponsors, as they were denying the chaos, had blocked off all chances for refounding their congregation and the hospital culture.

Responding to Grief: Grieving

Grieving or mourning is "the process whereby loss is acknowledged and the future with all its uncertainties, fears and hopes is confronted."[3] Cultures, like individuals, can avoid the painful experience of grieving but they do so at a cost, as Peter Marris observes: "If the process is aborted, from too hasty a readjustment or too unchecked a clinging to [that which is lost], the bereaved may never recover."[4]

---

[3] See Arbuckle, *Change, Grief, and Renewal,* 20–58; Gerald A. Arbuckle, *Refounding the Church: Dissent for Leadership* (Maryknoll, N.Y.: Orbis Books, 1993) 180–200; John Bowlby, *Grief Observed* (London: Faber and Faber, 1961) 7.

[4] Peter Marris, *Loss and Change* (London: Routledge & Kegan Paul, 1974) 31.

CASE STUDY

A Hospital Learns the Hard Way

For financial reasons the management board of a Catholic hospital had been forced to significantly reduce the staff in several departments. The decision was implemented with speed. Afterwards, the board arranged for celebratory parties to be held in the departments to reassure the remaining staff that the board believed in them and that all was now well. Despite the lavish preparations for the parties, only a small minority attended. One who did not attend commented:

> We were all so angry at what had happened. We lost our friends overnight. We felt guilty that we had survived. But the board had never listened either to their pain or our own. So we decided to protest as a group by not attending the parties. We hoped that this would force them to ask questions about their behavior, but to no avail.

For several months relationships between the board and these departments remained distant and confrontational. Finally, a newly appointed CEO arranged to meet with the staff of the departments and asked them to comment on the staff reduction. One said: "The flood-gates of anger and pain opened. The CEO listened. After the second meeting we felt better. Now we sense someone understands us and we can move forward."

Traditional Societies: Lessons for Healthcare

[Traditional peoples] faced [their] grief directly and worked out a system of personal social rituals and symbols that made it possible for [them] to deal with it directly. [Modern peoples do] not seem to know how to proceed in the expression of this fundamental emotion. [They have] no generally accepted social pattern for dealing with death (Edgar D. Jackson).[5]

---

[5] Edgar D. Jackson, *Understanding Grief* (New York: Abingdon Press, 1957) 57.

In the Western world we have lost the art of cultural grieving because our sense of community is weak. We need to re-learn this skill by studying traditional societies (including those of the Old and New Testaments).

The way in which a people's culture deals with physical bereavement sets the pattern for how the people cope with other significant losses. Earlier this century, when reflecting on his experience of traditional cultures, Emile Durkheim, a founder of sociology, wrote that: "Mourning is not a natural movement of private feelings wounded by a cruel loss; it is a duty imposed by the group."[6] No member of a traditional culture is permitted to be indifferent to a death in their midst because, when one person dies, in a sense the entire group dies; this needs to be formally acknowledged. A set of relationships has been destroyed by the death, and a new set must be established if the community is to hold together and survive. If death is unacknowledged the new order of relationships cannot emerge and the community is unable to return to good health. Durkheim's comment may appear to be rather cynical in denying mourners spontaneity of feeling, which must often be real enough, but he is right about the need for the community to mourn.

CASE STUDY

Traditional South Africa Shows the Way

Archbishop Tutu established the ritual of the "crying room" when he opened hearings of South Africa's Truth and Reconciliation Commission in 1996. It has become a very busy place. Many witnesses break down before they can finish their testimony, some scream with anguish, as they describe the atrocities and injustices. Traditional African cultures recognize that truth has curative power for people in grief, and this belief underpins this ritual of the commission. Rather than drive the races apart, this ritual of shared journey into a divided past seems to be bringing them together.

This was not the case with Yugoslavia. Talking about the atrocities committed by various ethnic factions during World War II was forbidden under Tito, who believed

---

[6] Emile Durkheim, *The Rules of Sociological Method* (New York: Free Press, 1965) 31.

that would have been bad for national unity and socialist brotherhood. Hence, when communism collapsed, all the suppressed grief with its bitter resentments burst into the open, leading to division and ethnic cleansing.[7]

Traditional societies accept that whenever there is significant loss there will be three stages in the grieving. Since the movement through these stages is not automatic, there need to be appropriate rituals under the direction of ritual leaders to ensure that people keep to the task of grieving. It is recognized that people can become trapped in one stage and even regress to an earlier one. In order for the group to survive this cannot be allowed to happen.

Stages of Grieving

The three stages of grieving are similar to the pattern of change as explained in Chapter 4 (see Figure 4.3). The first stage, that of reluctance, is marked by a stunned feeling of sadness or trauma together with resistance to acknowledging loss. There can be a yearning or nostalgia for what has been lost, a restlessness, despair, anger that may be directed indiscriminately, for example, against friends, God, another culture, or religious superiors as the assumed cause(s) of the enduring sadness (see Figure 9.1).

In the second stage, the liminality or chaos phase, a culture feels attracted by both the security of the past and the call to face the future. It is a period of anxious reflection, a search into mythological roots to regain a sense of identity and self-worth. This is a risky time because there is a temptation for the culture or organization to cling tenaciously to what has been lost and refuse to face the future. The group can even initiate a spectacular project that is totally out of touch with reality. For example, the trustees and board of a hospital, denying that it was in desperate financial problems, decided to build an expensive wing. They refused to believe that the suburb was already over-supplied with hospitals. This merely delayed the hospital's closure by a few months.

If resistance to the reality of loss continues in this stage, chronic grief takes hold and it is difficult, if not impossible, for people to move out of the escapist depression.

[7] See Marcus Gee, "Making Peace with the Past," *The Globe and Mail* (May 8, 1996) 15A.

The third stage is the recovery or re-entry phase. The bereaved culture or organization is able to look with detachment at what has been lost. It is realized that life must go on with the best of the past being carried over into the future.

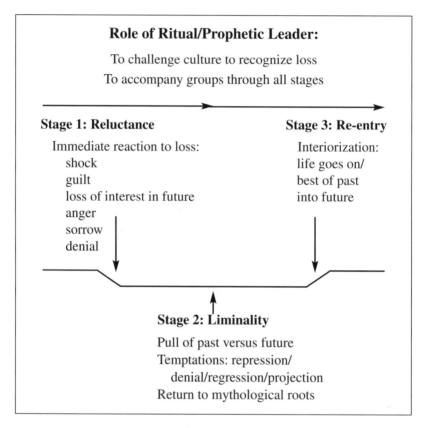

Figure 9.1: Cultural Grieving and the Role of Ritual Leader

Rituals of Grieving for a Healthy Society

By *ritual* I here mean "the stylized or repeated symbolic use of bodily movement and gesture within a social context to express and articulate meaning."[8] Ritual, therefore, is not confined to the religious aspects of life

---

[8] See Robert Bocock, *Rituals in Industrial Society* (Edinburgh: George Allen & Unwin, 1974) 37; Gerald A. Arbuckle, *Earthing the Gospel: An Inculturation Handbook for the Pastoral Worker* (Maryknoll, N.Y.: Orbis Books, 1990) 96–106.

but is integral to all human activity. Ritual action in many contemporary cultures occurs within a social context where there is the potential for conflict in social relations; it is undertaken to resolve or hide this conflict. For example, according to Western custom, when people resolve or hide a tension/conflict between them they may shake hands; it is a gesture of set form (stylized) that at least outwardly conveys the meaning that peace has been restored.

Rituals in traditional cultures, however, do not serve to hide reality but seek to name and resolve conflicts to allow new life to emerge. It is recognized that if conflict is covered up there is danger that it will eventually erupt and destroy the tribe.

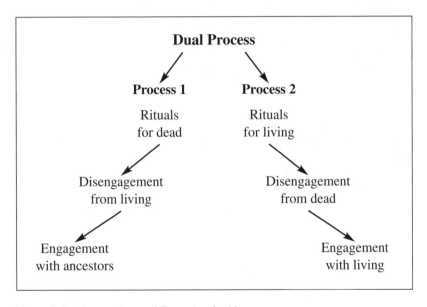

Figure 9.2: Disengaging and Engaging for Newness

There are normally two levels of oppositional, *disengagement/engagement* ritual processes at work, and they are operative in all three stages of grieving, but especially in the liminality stage (see Figure 9.2). First, there is a process directed at the deceased. The dead are formally *disengaged* from the living; they are given permission, as it were, to leave this world and to become *engaged* in relationships with other spirits elsewhere. They are assigned to a new, esteemed, and safe status: tradition. Among the Australian aborigines, for example, although the spirit is independent of flesh, in the sense of outlasting their disunion, a spirit is thought to haunt its former home. It must be formally encouraged to move on if it is to become an honored ancestor.

The second set of disengagement/engagement rituals relates directly to the living. They must formally become *disengaged* from the negative influences of the deceased and *engage* themselves in forming a new set of social relationships or culture.[9]

These ritual processes respond to needs of the bereaved at three levels: the psychological, mythological, and sociological. At the psychological level, people require a ritual that culturally permits or encourages them to express fully and openly their feelings of loss. They need also to see meaning in their loss, so in the ritual cultural myths are articulated that both console and challenge the bereaved to reflect on the purpose of life. At the sociological level, the bereaved need to feel that their grief is understood and shared by others, and that at the right moment they can return to society and be fully accepted by it.

The following case study illustrates the purpose and power of ritual grieving in a traditional culture.

CASE STUDY

Ritually Creating a Healthy Society

As is the custom in parts of New Zealand, when my father died his body was received into the church accompanied by Maori women wailing in a high-pitched stylized form. The wailing reminds people that it is their right and duty to express their personal and collective sorrow publicly and without embarrassment. Many in the Anglo-Saxon congregation whose culture discouraged public crying broke down into tears. By the end of the ritual, the congregation and I, as minister, were emotionally exhausted, which is precisely one of the objects of the formal wailing.

At the graveside a Maori elder, a ritual leader in his culture, spoke directly to the deceased, formally encouraging and commanding his spirit to move to the noble state of

[9] See Kenneth Maddock, *The Australian Aborigines: A Portrait of Their Society* (Harmondsworth: Penguin Books, 1974) 158–76.

ancestorhood: "Go friend, to your mother and father. Fare-well! Go to the belly of the land!" The spirit has the right to be an ancestor; as long as it remains on earth it cannot attain to this dignity and meanwhile endangers the living by not allowing them to get on with life. The living are also exhorted to let the spirit go and to form new relation-ships. In Maori tradition mourning continues for a year, ending with the blessing of the gravestone. The spirit is given its final encouragement to move on and the mourn-ers to build and adjust to new relationships.

Role of Ritual Leaders

In traditional cultures there are always ritual leaders, often chosen be-cause of their special gifts. They are culturally prophetic people in that, in the midst of grief, they call people to return to the founding myths of their cultures from which comes the energy to let go of the dead and to build new relationships. In a true sense they are not doers of ritual but are them-selves the ritual. This does make them vulnerable, however, to attack from people who dislike leaders reminding them that loss has taken place.

Ritual leaders concretize by their inner conversion and conviction the idea that a new world is possible. Myth specialist Joseph Campbell de-scribes such a ritual leader as a "hero," who "ventures forth from the world of common day into a region of supernatural wonder: fabulous forces are encountered and a decisive victory is won. The hero comes back from this mysterious adventure with the power to bestow boons on his fellow man."[10] The ritual leader is a hero who has visited, and been converted to, the vision of a new world. The leader's behavior gives hope that the journey through sadness can be successful and that new relationships can emerge.

Western Cultures: Unhealthy Denial

When I spoke to a CEO about the need for rituals of grieving in his hos-pital following some radical downsizing, he replied: "Rituals concentrate too much on the negative. We must not talk about what has been lost, but

---

[10] Joseph Campbell, *The Hero with a Thousand Faces* (Princeton, N.J.: Princeton University Press, 1949) 30.

318 Refounding Christian Healthcare

about the good things in this facility. Our way of life is one of hope, not death!" He was reflecting the cultural values of much of the Western world. Western cultures do everything they can to camouflage death and repress it; for many death has become form of planned obsolescence.

Geoffrey Gorer summarizes his own research into the decline of grieving rituals in Britain and the United States: "Mourning is treated as if it were a weakness, a self-indulgence, a reprehensible bad habit instead of a psychological necessity."[11] Most Western cultures do little to prescribe or foster any healthy mourning rituals. Philippe Aries writes of the widespread denial of death: "It is above all essential that society . . . notice to the least possible degree that death has occurred. . . . If a ceremony still marks the departure, it must remain discreet and must avoid emotion."[12] This is a frightening picture of a death-denying society, for just as we seek to deny physical death, so also we ignore all kinds of painful personal and social loss.

In order to develop a spirituality of refounding within this unhealthy cultural environment, we need first to know some reasons for this death-avoiding mythology:

Medicalization/Privatization of Dying

In the medical model the patient becomes increasingly passive in the act of dying, a "puppet" in a "play" in which the principal actors are the medical staffs and the relatives of the sick or dying person. Doctors and family members hesitate to tell the person that death is imminent or possible. Sometimes the services of religious ministers are discouraged lest they disturb the peace of the patient and get in the way of hospital staff.

The dying person's family and friends become progressively isolated, strained, and alienated from the patient. They are apt to feel, as they surround the dying person's bed, that they are trespassing on foreign territory. In an institution that is primarily concerned with healing the sick, dying and death are signs of institutional failure; many hospital staff find this difficult to adjust to.

Commercialization of Death

The occupation of funeral directors, particularly in North America, has become very big business, largely transforming the ritual and symbolism

---

[11] Geoffrey Gorer, *Death, Grief and Mourning in Contemporary Britain* (New York: Doubleday, 1965) 85.

[12] Philippe Aries, *Western Attitudes towards Death: From the Middle Ages to the Present* (London: Johns Hopkins University Press, 1974) 90.

of death to conform with the ethic of the consumer society. The terminology of death has been softened. Anything that is thought to convey morbidity or death is taboo.[13]

The covering-up of loss throughout society has become an art form. Through doublespeak, those who are powerful in society aim to hide to their advantage the reality of pain and loss in all areas of life. People who lose their jobs are "dehired," "downsized," or "selected out" by firms that are having "workforce adjustments." When Chrysler closed a plant, it "initiated a career alternative enhancement program" and some five thousand employees lost their jobs. Patients no longer experience "pain," just "discomfort."[14]

CASE STUDY

Revolt Against Denial

Princess Diana's death provided an occasion for spontaneous and communal grieving in a death-denying culture. Her death was followed by a steep drop in the number of people in Britain seeking help for depression; the unprecedented public mourning allowed people to release, psychiatrists claim,[15] deeply buried emotions about some of their own personal problems. And they did it together, finding in the ritual of mourning a focus for their own free-floating grief.[16]

Individualism Destroys Community Bonding

The culture of individualism has lost the sense of corporateness and thus the need to grieve the loss of its members. John Donne's famous

[13] See David W. Moller, *Confronting Death: Values, Institutions and Human Mortality* (New York: Oxford University Press, 1996) 25–39; David Dempsey, *The Way We Die: An Investigation of Death and Dying in America Today* (New York: McGraw-Hill, 1975) 167–73; Richard Huntington and Peter Metcalf, *Celebrations of Death: The Anthropology of Mortuary Ritual* (Cambridge: Cambridge University Press, 1979) 184–211.

[14] See William Lutz, *Doublespeak* (New York: HarperPerennial, 1990) 1–21; Jessica Mitford, *The American Way of Death* (New York: Simon & Schuster, 1963) 18–19.

[15] Reported in *The Sydney Morning Herald* (December 17, 1997) 12.

[16] See Nathan Mitchell, "The Amen Corner," *Worship* 72:1 (1998) 44–5.

comment that "any man's death diminishes me, because I am involved in Mankind" has little meaning left in a culture of individualism.

"Pornography" of Death

Gorer speaks of the "pornography" of death. By this he means that significant loss is not to be mentioned publicly; it is to be treated only as a private fantasy. We are acquainted with the impersonal, "phony phenomenon" of death on television and we are conditioned to regard death and mourning as strictly private issues. Consequently, we may react to the abstract idea of death with a kind of indifference that would have been out of place in earlier times. Confronted with death as a personal crisis, we seem able to do little but escape squeamishly into euphemism.[17]

Letting Go: Biblical Reflections

No need to remember past events,
no need to think about
     what was done before.
Look, I am doing something new,
now it emerges; can you not see it? (Isa 43:18-19)

The driving force in Western capitalist cultures is the secularized Judeo-Christian myth of death and resurrection reinvigorated by contemporary economic rationalism. It is a corrupted myth. A this-world resurrection is overemphasized, and the pain of death is downplayed or ignored.

The Christian creation myth, however, is that God, in Christ, calls us to communities of faith, in and through which we must struggle together to develop a world of love and justice (see Chapter 5). Our struggle for holistic health, though imperfect here, is itself the sign of the perfect world of love and justice that will exist at the end of time (2 Pet 3:13). The effectiveness of this struggle will depend on our own willingness to be "crucified with Christ" (Gal 2:19), that is, to disengage ourselves from all that is not of Christ. Then we are so dead to the past, and so engaged in Christ's life, that with St. Paul we may say, "And yet I am alive; yet it is no longer I, but Christ living in me" (Gal 2:20). The author of the letter to the Hebrews uses a sporting image to describe the grieving process: "We too, then should throw off everything that weighs us down . . . and with perseverance keep

---

[17] See Geoffrey Gorer, "The Pornography of Death," *Encounter* (October 1955) 49–52.

running in the race which lies ahead of us. Let us keep our eyes fixed on Jesus, who leads us in faith and brings it to perfection" (Heb 12:1-2).

Everything—healthcare structures, organizations, attitudes and customs, congregational charisms—is to be measured by this creation story that we are called daily to relive. Faithfulness to Christ the healer is determined by conformity to the urgings of his ever-renewing redemptive purposes, not to a particular institution or historical form of healthcare. The ongoing rejection of whatever does not conform to these purposes is an imperative for faithfulness. This is at the heart of a spirituality of letting go.

Grief and Grieving

Almost every chapter in the Scriptures, especially the Old Testament, refers to the symptoms and causes of death, either personal or metaphorical: personal and national alienation from God through sin, sickness, plagues, famine, wars, exile. Indeed, misery, death, and chaos are never absent in the Scriptures. Hence, feelings, physical symptoms, and behavioral patterns associated with loss are described frequently and often in vivid language.

Grief in the Bible: Symptoms

Sadness: The two disciples on the road to Emmaus are sad because Jesus, their longed-for revolutionary hero, is dead: "They stopped, their faces downcast" (Luke 24:17).

Anger: Jeremiah is angry with Yahweh because he has lost his family and friends: "A curse on the day when I was born!" (Jer 20:14).

Loneliness: "My God, my God, why have you forsaken me?" (Ps 22:1).

Hope: "So now, Lord, what am I to hope for? / My hope is in you" (Ps 39:7).

There are physical signs of grief, such as *weariness* (Job 3:7), *breathlessness* (Job 9:18), *dry throat:* "I am exhausted with calling out, my throat is hoarse" (Ps 69:3). There are sleep *disturbances* (Dan 2:1), *bowel problems,* and *heart palpitations:* "In the pit of my stomach / how great my agony! / Walls of my heart! / My heart is throbbing!" (Jer 4:19). *Loss of appetite* and *crying:* Hannah does not eat and cries because she has lost the capacity to bear children (1 Sam 1:7-8) and Jesus weeps at the death of Lazarus (John 11:35). *Anxiety* at loss: St. Paul writes: "I had no relief from anxiety, not finding my brother Titus there" (2 Cor 2:13).

Since Jewish people had a traditional way of life, with a strong sense of group identity, it is not surprising to find among them a pattern of coping with loss characteristic of traditional or group-centered cultures. The prophet Isaiah explains to the Israelites the following dynamic of grieving evident in both Testaments:

> No need to remember past events,
> no need to think about
>   what was done before.
> Look, I am doing something new,
> now it emerges; can you not see it? (Isa 43:18-19)

Hebrew Scriptures: Rituals of Letting Go

> Incurable sorrow overtakes me . . .
> "Prepare to call for the mourning women! . . .
> Let them lose no time
>   in raising the lament over us!" (Jer 8:18; 9:16).

From time to time for the Israelites, in vivid contrast to their frequent experience of personal and corporate distress and grief, there are eruptions of surprising, even dramatic, newness or joy in the midst of grieving. The three stages of ritual grieving are identifiable in these experiences; for example, the Exodus story is the archetypal event of letting go/initiation into newness (see Chapter 5).

David's response to grief is a model to the Israelites of how they need to grieve. David laments the loss of Saul and Jonathan: "By your dying I too am stricken, I am desolate for you" (2 Sam 1:25). Deep in the chaos of liminality he consults YHWH, who calls him to a startling new leadership role on condition that he lets go of the loss: "'Go up! . . . To Hebron.' . . . The men of Judah came, and there they anointed David as king of the House of Judah" (2 Sam 2:1, 4). However, David could take possession of the new status only because he openly acknowledged the depth of his loss and through YHWH's help let it go.

Grief must be expressed, but the common good requires that it not become chronic. Otherwise the community's health will suffer. David's mourning for his son Absalom had become too protracted and threatened to undermine his military leadership and the welfare of his soldiers and people. He had to be told bluntly by his friend Joab, a ritual leader, that the time for mourning was over and the future had to be faced constructively: "Today you have made all your servants feel ashamed. . . . Now get up, come out and reassure your soldiers; for if you do not come out, I swear

. . . not one man will stay with you tonight" (2 Sam 19:6, 8). David was brought back to reality and speedily did what he was asked, apparently with a renewed self-confidence: "The king got up and took his seat at the gate. . . . So the king started home and reached the Jordan" (2 Sam 19:9, 16). Once again, newness sprang from desolation.

Psalms: Grieving Rituals

The psalms provide a tripartite pattern for ritual grieving. Following Paul Ricoeur, Walter Brueggemann identifies three categories of psalms: hymns of *orientation* praising God's order in nature and society (e.g., Psalm 104), psalms of *dislocation* or lamentation that mark the liminal or chaos stage of mourning (e.g., Psalms 74 and 88), and psalms of *reorientation* or reentry (e.g., Psalm 23).[18]

Two functions of ritual are evident in the lamentation psalms. First, they legitimize public expression of the grief feelings of the community or individual, such as Psalm 137: "By the rivers of Babylon / we sat and wept / at the memory of Zion" (v. 1). The people felt deep in their hearts the loneliness and oppression that comes from being in a foreign and hostile land. The psalm allowed them to articulate this pain over and over again, reassuring them that it was fitting and necessary to do so openly. Second, the ritual structure or form of the lament song also prescribes the stages the people must follow in their mourning in order to attain a revitalized relationship with YHWH. They must struggle to let the loss go and be open to a vision of newness beyond all human comprehension.

Elizabeth Kubler-Ross's model[19] of the stages of grieving is well-known: denial, anger, bargaining, depression, acceptance. Brueggemann recognizes that there are some similarities between this model and that of the lamentation psalms. For example, both assume that those who grieve move from an experience of chaos to an inner peace and require a trusted person or group to accompany them on their journey. But there are significant differences in the lament psalms, in which there are six stages: an address to God, complaint (e.g., anger), expression of trust, petition, assurance, vow to praise.[20] In the psalms people want to make their problems YHWH's

---

[18] See Walter Brueggemann, "Psalms and the Life of Faith: A Suggested Typology of Function," *The Journal for the Study of the Old Testament* 17:1 (1980) 3–22; Arbuckle, *Change, Grief, and Renewal*, 64–76.

[19] Elizabeth Kubler-Ross, *On Death and Dying* (New York: Macmillan, 1969).

[20] See Walter Brueggemann, "The Formfulness of Grief," *Interpretation: A Journal of Bible and Theology* 31:3 (1977) 265–75.

problems in the hope that then YHWH will be obliged to do something constructive about them. This is not part of Kubler-Ross's model.

Also in contrast to the Kubler-Ross stage of denial and the feeling of isolation, a lament psalm starkly proclaims from the beginning that the psalmist or community is afflicted. There is no camouflaging loss. So miserable is the sufferer that there is nothing left but to trust YHWH. The declaration of trust sparks off a hope-filled petition to YHWH in lieu of the stage in Kubler-Ross's framework of bargaining leading to depression. In the grief psalms, no matter how horrible the situation may be, there is still the hope that YHWH will intervene, just as he has repeatedly done in the past.

The words of reassurance in the lament psalms and the stage of acceptance in Kubler-Ross's typology at first sight may appear to have identical functions. For her, "acceptance" seems to mean a stoic resignation in the face of the inevitable. This view is contrary to a fundamental assumption in the lament psalms that, while death is known to be inevitable, there is always the historically supported belief that YHWH can transform every chaos experience into a stunning new beginning. The task of the well-adjusted Israelite is never to give up hope. That is the mark of every true covenant member.

Brueggemann does not downplay the importance of Kubler-Ross's model as an aid to understanding what may happen when people are confronted with the fear of chaos, death, or significant loss. Rather, his aim is to show that those with faith similar to that of the Old Testament believers see things quite differently. They do not deny the reality of loss. On the contrary, they see chaos as the occasion to rediscover the historical fact that the God of surprises can intervene in human affairs to "create new heavens and a new earth . . . [where] no more will the sound of weeping be heard" (Isa 65:17, 19).

Example: Psalm 74—A Model for Healthcare Reformers

In Psalm 74 the pivotal symbol of YHWH's presence to the people, the Temple, has been sacrilegiously destroyed and YHWH gets the full blame! With its devastation the very identity of the Israelites as a people and their sense of power are shattered: "God, why have you finally rejected us, / your anger blazing against the flock you used to pasture? / . . . / The enemy have sacked everything in the sanctuary" (vv. 1, 3). And there is no indication that the situation will change: "We see no signs, no prophet any more,

/ and none of us knows how long it will last" (v. 9). Desolation reigns, but in the midst of this liminality of grief the writer looks back to the founding myth of creation when YHWH molded the world into an orderly shape out of the primeval chaos:

> You . . . turned primordial rivers into dry land . . .
> you caused sun and light to exist,
> you fixed all the boundaries of the earth,
> you created summer and winter (vv. 15-17).

When during the Exodus the chosen people were threatened with destruction from the pursuing Egyptians, YHWH "split the sea in two" (v. 13). Now with the Temple's destruction new chaos erupts. Yet Israel, encouraged by YHWH's previous dramatic interventions as retold by the psalmist, has hope that God will bring a new order and identity to the nation: "Do not let the downtrodden retreat in confusion, / give the poor and needy cause to praise your name. / . . . / Arise, God, champion your own cause" (vv. 21-22). After expressing anger against God, allowing it to go, and acknowledging the depth of powerlessness, Israel in the person of the psalmist is surprised to feel an energy for action, a newness that has no human origin.

This psalm speaks to religious congregations as sponsors of healthcare facilities in the Catholic Church today. Forty years ago it could not have been imagined that the supply of recruits to their communities would decline with such rapidity. Their hospitals looked so secure, pivotal symbols, like the Temple for the Israelites, of God's abiding love for their communities, but chaos has hit. Sponsors, in the footsteps of the exiled Israelites, must cry out: "Arise, God, champion your own cause" (Ps 74:22). There is a constant need to let go in the liminality of unknowing in order to be open to the radically new of refounding.

In brief, the Hebrew Scriptures are filled with calls to sorrow over what has been destroyed or broken down if there is to be new life; through the lamentation psalms we are even taught how to grieve. We are constantly reminded of the founding myth of the Israelite people: no matter how chaotic our condition may be, God has the power to do the humanly impossible: to lift us out of "the seething chasm, from the mud and mire." He can "set my feet on rock" and make "my footsteps firm . . . a fresh song in my mouth" (Ps 40:2, 3). Lament psalms, writes Claus Westermann, transform the experience of chaos into a way of approaching "God with

326 Refounding Christian Healthcare

abandonment that permits daring and visioning and even ecstasy."[21] We are called to search beyond chaos to the signs of newness God is offering us, not to be paralyzed in the chaos or to escape nostalgically into the past. Hope provides the vision (the "strange attractor" in chaos theory) inspiring us to keep journeying in the darkness:

> For thus says Yahweh
> ....
> he is God, who shaped the earth
> ....
> who set it firm;
> he did not create it to be in the chaos,
> he formed it to be lived in
> ....
> I did not say, 'Offspring of Jacob,
> search for me in chaos!' (Isa 45:18-19).

Christian Scriptures: Rituals of Letting Go

> Blessed are they who mourn:
> they shall be comforted (Matt 5:5).

Jesus both in words and actions invites his followers to let go to allow the new to enter their lives. At one point he denounces those who refuse to grieve in this world, despite all that he has done to call them to this: "we sang dirges, / and you wouldn't cry" (Luke 7:32).

Transfiguration: Model of Grieving

In the transfiguration of Christ the three-fold stages of grieving are clearly visible. First, there is the movement up the mountain, which is the *separation* stage. Then the events on the mountain itself, the *liminality* phase. In the presence of the disciples Jesus "was transfigured. . . . Elijah appeared to them with Moses" (Mark 9:2, 4). The impulsive Peter cannot rest quietly in this chaotic moment, so he seeks to control his anxiety and the situation by wanting to escape into a frenzy of building: "'let us make three shelters, one for you, one for Moses and one for Elijah.' He did not know what he was to say; they were so frightened" (Mark 9:5-6). A voice from the cloud speaks: "This is my Son, the Beloved. Listen to him" (Mark

---

[21] Claus Westermann, *Elements of Old Testament Theology* (Atlanta: John Knox Press, 1982) 103.

9:7). With that Moses and Elijah disappear. The message is this: let the old covenant, as symbolized by Moses and Elijah, go and follow the prophetic dynamic of Jesus and his teachings.

The third stage, the re-aggregation phase, is symbolized by the movement down the mountain, but it rapidly becomes clear that the disciples have not abandoned their desires for power over people (Mark 9:14-29, 33-37). They have to experience more rituals of letting go for inner conversion to occur.

Passion and Resurrection: Letting Go in Stages

Matthew's account of Christ's passion and resurrection reminds us that following Jesus necessitates an ongoing struggle to let go.[22] The ritual stages are precisely defined, and at each point Jesus is called by the Father to walk with hope further into the unknown. There are several steps to the separation stage, each marking a further movement of Jesus away from a world of security he had established as a preacher of the kingdom: the anointing in anticipation of his burial (26:6-13); the drama of the Last Supper (26:17-19, 26-29); the anticipated and actual loss of friends— Judas and Peter (26:14-16, 20-25, 30-35). One senses in the narrative an ever-deepening sadness in Jesus as he begins the pilgrimage of letting go of a world of loving crowds and supportive friends, and an exciting ministry of preaching and healing.

In the second phase of grieving, the liminality stage, there are many scenes, each one a further experience for Jesus of deepening loss. It begins with the trial of the agony in the garden where Jesus wrestles with the rising fear of facing death; there is a harrowing inner struggle, for he does not want to die. And there is the yearning to revive the bonding relationship with his three closest disciples, but in this he fails. Having subordinated his will to God's, he lets the relationship go and in its place discovers an invigorating new bonding with his Father and his mission (26:36-46).

The crucifixion, death, and burial of Jesus conclude this stage of letting go: mocked, stripped, crucified between two thieves, with a few remaining friends "watching from a distance" (27:55). Yet in the midst of this darkness, the humanly impossible new begins to break through. Jesus recites the lamentation Psalm 22 which, though it recounts the sadness of total

---

[22] See Mark McVann, "One of the Prophets: Matthew's Testing Narrative as a Rite of Passage," *Biblical Theological Bulletin* 23:1 (1993) 14–20; Gerald A. Arbuckle, *From Chaos to Mission: Refounding Religious Life Formation* (Collegeville: The Liturgical Press, 1996) 121–3.

disaster, also expresses its opposite: the vision of the saving power of God. In the chaos of his dramatic letting go in dying, Jesus is already being initiated into the new life of hope that comes only from God, in whom he has total trust.

The reentry phase occurs when Jesus joins his disciples, but as the resurrected one, commissioning them as evangelizers to relive his own experience of letting go into newness (28:16-20).

Emmaus: From Chaos to Hope

On the road to Emmaus the two disciples mirror the sadness of the wider community of disciples (Luke 24:13-35). Their journey predictably has the three stages of grieving. The separation stage occurs when the companions freely express to Jesus their anger and sadness because things have not turned out as they had desired: Jesus, their hoped-for revolutionary leader against the Roman oppressors, is dead. They then enter the liminality stage of their ritual journey and here Jesus, having won their trust, recounts the founding story of their salvation and strongly challenges them to recognize and accept their loss. This will open them to a community and personal newness beyond human imagination as a result of Jesus' death and resurrection (Luke 24:25-32).

On interiorizing this message they experience a dramatic newness and energy, expressed by the words "Did not our hearts burn within us?" (24:32). Immediately they want to share their joy with others—the re-aggregation stage: "They set out at that instant and returned to Jerusalem" where "they told their story of what had happened on the road" (Luke 24:33, 35).

Ritual Leaders of Grieving

In a traditional culture the community's leaders exercise a pivotal role in challenging the culture to acknowledge loss and the dangers of chronic denial in all its devious forms. So also in both biblical Testaments. Brueggemann writes that the ritual ministry of prophetic leaders "consists of offering an alternative perception of reality and in letting people see their own history in light of God's freedom and his will for justice." Grieving, he says, "is a precondition. . . . Only that kind of anguished disengagement permits fruitful yearning and only the public embrace of deathliness permits newness to come."[23]

---

[23] Walter Brueggemann, *The Prophetic Imagination* (Philadelphia: Fortress Press, 1978) 110, 113.

The Hebrew prophets are skilled ritual leaders of grieving but the Israelites do not always want to acknowledge their grief; this makes the task of the prophet as ritual leader more difficult. The prophets refuse to be seduced into the denial of the grief of the people, no matter the personal cost to themselves. "Do not prophesy the truth to us," the Israelites shout, "tell us flattering things" (Isa 30:10). On the contrary, the prophets passionately call the people to acknowledge their losses and to reject their attachment to them.

The denial of the people causes the prophets personal grief, yet they ceaselessly challenge the people to name the grief and move on, inspired by a vision of a new world (Jer 4:19-20). Whenever the Israelites admitted their anger and their complete dependence on YHWH they experienced signals of a newness beyond all their dreams; they found not a God of anger but one of "tenderness and compassion" (Exod 34:6).

It is the same dynamic in the New Testament:

The angel Gabriel is a ritual leader for Mary, calling her to let go of her security in order to experience a newness beyond imagination. While being "deeply disturbed" (the chaos stage) she responds in hope to the angel's ritual initiative (Luke 1:26-38).

On many occasions Jesus assumes the same role, calling his disciples to let go of the past to be open to the new:

Unless a wheat grain falls into the earth and dies,
it remains only a single grain;
but if it dies
it yields a rich harvest (John 12:24).

As a ritual leader Jesus is what he calls others to be and do. He is the grain that "yields a rich harvest."

St. Paul calls the Philippians to grieve over their attachments to worldly things to be open to the resurrected Christ, but he can assume this ritual leadership role because he has himself been through death to life: "For him I have accepted the loss of all other things, . . . that I may come to know him and the power of his resurrection" (Phil 3:8, 10).

CASE STUDY

Ritual Leadership at the Ascension

After the ascension of Jesus, his disciples were in grave danger of denying the fact that he was no longer with them. Their loss and denial had to be publicly

articulated and dealt with otherwise they would not be
open to the dramatic, transforming newness of the Spirit.
Luke describes the role of the two angels as ritual community leaders: the disciples "were still staring into the
sky as he went, when suddenly two men in white were
standing beside them, and they said, 'Why are you Gali-
leans standing here looking into the sky?'" (Acts 1:10-
11). Jesus had disengaged himself from his followers,
achieving a new status beside his Father. The disciples
had to be encouraged to journey to the next stage of their
grieving. They left for the upper room in Jerusalem—
their liminality experience—in order to pray over and
ponder the loss and the vision of the promised, fear-
creating newness to be realized at Pentecost (Acts 1:14).

Qualities of Ritual Leaders

Biblical leaders of grieving have the same qualities as refounding
people.[24]

They Are Good Listeners. Moses, like the other prophets, is open to
hearing YHWH and the people's sufferings; he keeps contact with people
by wandering around the camps and speaking informally to them outside
their tents.[25]

Christ's ministry is one of listening, both to the Father and to the people,
toward whom he is never remote. Their pain is his pain. On one occasion,
as Jesus approaches Jerusalem, he pauses and looks out over the city,
breaking into a powerful lament: "Jerusalem, Jerusalem. . . . How often
have I longed to gather your children together, as a hen gathers her chicks
under her wings, and you refused!" (Matt 23:37). The city's official leaders decline to lead the city in a lament for their failings and sins (Luke
19:39-40). Jesus knows the city is to be destroyed after his death, so he
grieves and openly weeps about the calamity (Luke 19:41): "They will
leave not one stone standing on another . . . because you do not recognise
the moment of your visitation" (Luke 19:44).

[24] See Arbuckle, *From Chaos to Mission,* 190–201.
[25] See Arbuckle, *Grieving for Change: A Spirituality for Refounding Gospel Communities* (Westminster: Christian Classics, 1991) 151–6.

They Recognize the Need for Community Healing. Moses, like all prophets who followed him, shrewdly understands the need for the people to express the pain of loss openly and without judgment, as well as the necessity for them to experience the chaos (Deut 8:2, 5).

Moses also appreciates the need for people in the chaos stage to maintain contact with their collective roots in Egypt and to be constantly reminded of the vision of a promised land ahead (Exod 8:7-8). Thus he encourages them to collect the bones of Joseph and to carry them into the wilderness (Exod 13:19).

They Mourn Their Own Losses. A ritual leader needs to be comfortable with the chaos in their own journey. Unless one is able to mourn one's failings and losses and so to experience inner healing, it will be impossible to have empathy for the grief of others. This means regular structuring of time and space to be with oneself and with God; feverish busyness is no atmosphere for contemplation, self-knowledge, letting go, and visioning for the future.

Moses could never have kept to the role of ritual leader, if he was not at the same time grappling with his own inner journey of faith and conversion. A naturally impatient man with a powerful temper (Exod 2:12; 32:19), he could never have survived without constantly praying to YHWH from the anguish of his own inner chaos. The stories of Jeremiah (Jer 20:7-18) and, of course, Jesus (Mark 14:35-42) were similar.

They Acknowledge the Need for Visioning. In the midst of the people's grieving Moses would re-articulate the visionary newness of the time ahead of them (Deut 8:7). Jesus would do the same (John 16:6-7).

They Avoid Creating Dependency. The task of the ritual leader, as exemplified in the ministries of Moses and Jesus, is to empower the group or culture to assume responsibility for its own grieving. The temptation to allow people to become overly dependent is to be resisted by the ritual leader. Neither Moses nor Jesus succumbed to this temptation.

As the re-entry stage—the entrance into the Promised Land—is about to begin for the Israelites, Moses slips away, with remarkable patience and detachment, to die alone on a mountain and to rest in an unmarked grave (Deut 32:1-7). When the two disciples at Emmaus are in danger of becoming overly dependent on Jesus' presence, Jesus withdraws to allow them to test their newfound apostolic strength by returning to Jerusalem—the re-entry phase of their ritual of loss (Luke 24:30-35).

They Have Down-to-Earth Humanity. The life of Jesus was a paradox of divine proportions! He, King of Kings, was born in a stable and died on a cross. Nothing could be more incongruous, yet nothing was more powerful in conveying the truth of the words: "I have come / so that they may have life / and have it to the full" (John 10:10). The source of Christ's humor is in his detachment from self, his humility, his total faith in the Father:

> Who, being in the form of God,
> did not count equality with God
> something to be grasped.
> But he emptied himself
> taking the form of a slave (Phil 2:6-7).

This inner detachment was the ultimate source of his ability to call others to let go of the dead or dying and embrace the new.[26]

Practical Guidelines: Leading Organizational Grieving

> The management of change depends upon our ability to articulate the process of grieving. . . . When loss cannot be articulated, its suppressed tensions will in the end prove more profoundly disruptive than the social conflicts which relieve them (Peter Marris).[27]

This conclusion by Marris makes perfect sense in line with this chapter's explanations: whoever fails to acknowledge organizational grief cannot lead effectively. Since the art of facilitating mourning through rituals has virtually disappeared in the Western world, the task of ritual leadership is a difficult one for trustees, boards, CEOs, and managers. Hence, the following summarizes in practical steps the material of this chapter.

Guideline 1

The refounding of healthcare ministries is essential, which means abandoning methods of the past that are no longer relevant. What Philip Keane writes on healthcare reform describes the challenge to change for Christian healthcare ministries:

---

[26] See Arbuckle, *Earthing the Gospel,* 214–5; and Arbuckle, *From Chaos to Mission,* 198.

[27] Marris, *Loss and Change,* 91, 103.

[The] revision of the U.S. health care delivery process is truly a matter of "revisioning," of forming a whole new vision. . . . To accomplish such revisioning, all . . . need to let go of some of our treasured idols. . . . We need to become truly free to think new thoughts, hope new hopes, and dream new dreams.[28]

Guideline 2

Grief is the inevitable consequence of change. Do not be alarmed at the strength with which grief can be expressed. To those not experiencing grief, its symptoms may appear to be over-reactions. Pathological reactions to significant loss can be expected if organizational and individual grief are ignored.[29]

People experiencing the same loss, such as layoffs and technological changes, do not necessarily feel or express grief precisely at the same time or in the same way. For example, grief can be anticipated by some but not by others; it may be delayed or suppressed by some while others immediately show its symptoms. Grief may come in waves from different people and groups, and on occasions when leaders may least expect.

Guideline 3

Cultures, like individuals, experience grief. Cultures have lives of their own, and therefore they also grieve when change occurs; they affect the feelings, attitudes, and behaviors of individuals.

Guideline 4

Rituals legitimize and give order to the grieving process. As grieving is primarily about the adjustment of feelings, intellectual discussion or arguments by themselves are of little or no assistance. There is no instant solution to grief, but rituals of grieving help people to manage their loss in ways that contribute to personal and cultural holistic health.

Cultural and personal adjustment to significant loss may take years, rather than months or weeks. It is beneficial to recall how difficult and slow it is for nations to gaze into the dark recesses of their past to admit

[28] Philip Keane, *Health Care Reform: A Catholic View* (New York: Paulist Press, 1993) 67.

[29] See Colin M. Parkes, *Bereavement* (New York: International University Press, 1972) 142.

losses: Americans about slavery and the near-genocide of their country's indigenous peoples, Australians about their murderous treatment of their aboriginal peoples, Germans about the Holocaust and the carnage of the war, the British about the racial arrogance and cruel excesses of empire.[30]

Guideline 5

Since the task of the ritual leader is to call people prophetically to a "perception alternative to the consciousness and perception of the dominant culture around"[31] *them, leaders of healthcare will (a) be aware of the negative cultural forces within themselves and (b) know and be committed to the founding myth of Christian healthcare.*

Trustees, boards, and CEOs are the people primarily responsible for the ongoing vitality of the founding story in their organizations. In calling their healthcare cultures to grieve, they need first to return as ritual leaders to this myth as the source of their own energy and capacity to direct others. Second, they must liberate themselves from values of the surrounding culture that are contrary to this myth, such as economic rationalism, secularism, and the denial of loss.

Guideline 6

Healthcare leaders, in order to be ritual leaders, must first be mourners themselves. Though loss can only be shared partly, nonetheless cultures/people in grief readily sense those able to empathize with them. The empathetic listener is sensitive not only to the other's feelings, but also to how that person is experiencing them. Trustees, boards, and CEOs can be seduced into a medical model of behavior which, with its emphasis on scientific, depersonalized detachment, encourages them to remain emotionally uninvolved in the grief of their staffs. As mere managerial technicians they are incapable of leading their organizational cultures and staffs toward holistic health. Management consultant Jeanie Daniel Duck comments:

> In most corporate settings, it is strictly taboo for a senior executive to cry, to show tenderness or grief.[32] [That's] a big mistake. . . . Change is funda-

---

[30] See "Sorry Isn't Enough," *The Economist* (July 25, 1998) 21.

[31] Brueggemann, *The Prophetic Imagination,* 13.

[32] Jeanie Daniel Duck, "Managing Change," *Harvard Business Review: On Change* (Boston: Harvard Business School, 1991) 67.

mentally about feelings; companies that want their workers to contribute their heads and hearts have to accept that emotions are essential to the new management style.[33]

Moses warns the Israelites: "be very careful what you do . . . see that you do not corrupt yourselves by making an image in the shape of anything whatever" (Deut 4:15-16). To prevent the corrupting clinical aloofness of the medical model, and at the same time to avoid undue emotional involvement in the grief around them, leaders will need to find a place in their inner selves that provides sanctuary—a safe haven for personal reflection and renewal where they are able to heal their wounds from the past and prepare for new ventures. If they are struggling with their own inner chaos, as the prophets did, then they have the credibility to be ritual leaders of healing for others.

Guideline 7

Since loss results in the breakdown of meaning, leaders are to help their organizational cultures and staffs create new meaning systems through appropriate rituals. Every official communication by organizational leaders is an effort to create a shared meaning with others. Since ritual aims to convey meaning within a particular social context, each official reporting is a ritual. The keys to morale maintenance are the systematic and appropriate ritual communications by trustees, boards, and CEOs. Employees, if they are to reconstruct a pattern of meaning in their lives in the midst of organizational cultural turmoil, need to know the reasons why the changes are important for the organization's mission; that their grief will be sensitively acknowledged by their leaders; and how they fit into the new culture, that is, what retraining is required, what values will be guaranteed.

Leaders respond to these needs in a twofold way: through *formal* communications directed to the organizational culture as a whole, and through *informal* communications focused on particular individuals and groups, such as managers or individual departments.

Formal Ritual Communications

Examples of formal ritual communications are the announcement of changes to the organization, such as rebuilding programs or department

---

[33] Ibid., 66.

closures. These interventions must be made with the tripartite process and the different needs of each stage in mind.[34]

Separation Stage: Communicating Impending Change. First, communication at public meetings needs to be led by the appropriate leader (e.g., the CEO) and as much detail of the changes as possible should be given. Be clear and unambiguous in conveying information and consistent in what is said. If mistakes have been made in communicating, they need to be honestly admitted.[35]

There needs to be acknowledgment of the pain people will experience in adjusting to the changes, and assurance that supports are already planned, such as fair severance payments or retraining programs. The leader will avoid argument and assure participants that their reactions will be responded to as soon as possible. Participants must feel that they can speak without becoming victimized.

Second, the leader should situate the changes in the context of the vision, mission, and values of the healing mission of Jesus Christ.

CASE STUDY

Leaders React to Grief

The CEO of a major Australian hospital asked me to assist in leading the culture through the first stage of grieving, directly after the announcement of radical changes to the hospital and site. It was officially communicated to the hospital that I would be available at two levels: to groups, such as departments, and to individuals. The aim was to provide a safe environment for groups and individuals to express their feelings of loss. The sessions were no longer

---

[34] See also the following titles by William Bridges: *Transitions: Making Sense of Life's Changes* (Reading, Mass.: Addison-Wesley, 1980); *Managing Transitions: Making the Most of Change* (London: Nicholas Brealey, 1995); *JobShift: How to Prosper in a Workplace without Jobs* (London: Nicholas Brealey, 1995). William Bridges also emphasizes three stages of transition necessitating an internal psychological process through which individuals come to terms with a new situation. Bridges, however, does not develop the cultural aspects of these three stages.

[35] See Delorese Ambrose, *Healing the Downsized Organization* (New York: Three Rivers Press, 1996) 74.

than an hour and I began by briefly reassuring people of confidentiality and the purpose of the gatherings. Following the opportunity for people to express their feelings, I would help them to see that humanly and culturally feelings of grief were normal and to be expected. If they remain suppressed it was dangerous to them personally and to the culture. The evaluations were positive. One respondent summarized: "These sessions tell us the administration cares. We felt safe to express how we felt."

Liminality Stage: Creative Responses. As Moses communicated with the Israelites in the desert through frequent ritual interventions—for example, by re-articulating the vision, what had to be done to get there, what needed to be left behind—so also should leaders in healthcare facilities. Meetings are needed at regular periods to keep people publicly informed of developments, with time for them to express their feelings.

As these formal communication sessions will be taking place during the liminal phase there needs to be deliberate effort to identify opportunities or plans that are emerging and details about retraining programs. People are to be encouraged to contribute to the change; they must feel that their ideas will be taken seriously. This is also the time to refer more forcefully to the philosophy and values of Christian healthcare.

At suitable moments the leader can officially delegate to another person, such as to the mission leader, the role of directing the organization through biblically-based rituals of grieving, though people should never feel compelled to attend. These rituals must be well prepared and follow the dynamic of naming the loss, letting it go, and articulating some signs of newness.[36]

Re-entry Stage: Celebrating Newness. Each significant sign of newness needs to be acknowledged in a public way: the opening of a new facility, the creative actions of departments and individuals.

Informal Ritual Interventions

This type of communication is directed to particular groups and individuals. Promises made earlier are to be fulfilled: those to be laid-off must be

---

[36] For an example of a structured ritual of grieving see Gerard Whiteford as cited by Arbuckle, *Refounding the Church,* 197–8.

treated with justice and compassion and offered immediate compensation and counseling services to help them find alternative work. Those who remain require particular assistance either at the group or individual level. Some examples follow.

Employees as Survivors. David Noer notes:

> Survivors become increasingly resigned, fatigued, and depressed; they experience a deepening sense of loss of control; and they get angrier. Layoff sickness is probably the primary reason that downsizing has seldom resulted in increased productivity. . . . [Survivors need to move] from being victims to being adventurers in control of their own identity, happiness, and creative powers.[37]

Survivors can feel guilty that they remain while their co-workers have lost their jobs, and they must also adjust to new co-workers, all of which adds to their sense of lostness. One survivor of hospital downsizing commented to me: "I have a job. I feel guilty. Why me? All my friends of years have gone. It's going to take years to build new friendships, I am too old. I feel betrayed by the hospital. Perhaps I will lose my job next."

Middle-managers/Supervisors. Since traditionally managers have been recruited to maintain the status quo, not to lead in the building of a new culture, they are ill-prepared to cope with radical change. For example, they may escape to their offices to avoid the pain of their departments, thus encouraging more rumors and anxiety in their organizational subcultures. The CEO must be sensitive to their needs, offering them the requisite training and support to be ritual leaders of change in their departments.

Frontline Personnel. Employees who directly interact with the public, such as switchboard operators, front-desk staff, or publicity personnel, can be the recipients of the negative reactions of the public and even staff during radical organizational change. Not only do they need accurate information about what is happening, they also need the skills to relate positively to the grief around them.

---

[37] David M. Noer, "Leadership in an Age of Layoffs," *Issues and Observations* 13:3 (1993) 1, 3; David M. Noer, *Healing the Wounds: Overcoming the Trauma of Layoffs and Revitalizing Downsized Organizations* (San Francisco: Jossey-Bass, 1993); John E. Gutknecht and J. Bernard Keys, "Mergers, Acquisitions and Takeovers: Maintaining Morale of Survivors and Protecting Employees," *Academy of Management Executive* 7:3 (1993) 26–35.

Guideline 8

Congregational sponsors need to ritually grieve their loss of control over healthcare facilities. Religious congregations are called to grieve loss at two significant levels: first, their membership is in decline; second, they are losing control over, and sometimes ownership of, healthcare facilities that have been developed over generations.

The following case study illustrates how one congregational leader re-acted to organizational grief.

CASE STUDY

A Congregational Leader Acts as a Ritual Director

A congregational leadership team arranged for a large gathering of lay boards and CEOs from several of their hospitals to present their plans for the establishment of a public juridic person. The rapid decline of the congrega-tion's membership and consequent aging necessitated a pro-active approach.

The congregational leader explained this, and told the assembly that at a certain date the sisters would with-draw from all control. The assembly was stunned. A spokesperson for the employees stated: "The sisters will always be around. We trust in Providence. We cannot act without them!" The leader repeated the determination of the congregation to hand over ownership and control to a new body under lay leadership. Through a series of sub-sequent grieving rituals the congregational leadership led their religious communities, as well as the lay boards, through the stages of letting go.

However, a few sisters remained as mission leaders after the healthcare system had passed to lay people. Several found it difficult to let go of control. Hospital staff members, when in conflict with CEOs and man-agers, would ask these sisters to intervene "because you are sisters and things are not being managed correctly as before." The sisters would side with the staff. This made the task of the lay administrators difficult. Other mission

leaders, while publicly stating that lay people should succeed them, would subtly refuse to hand over authority.
When they retired there were no laity trained for the task.

Guideline 9

Since Western societies are death-denying, it is a Christian ministry to challenge this social ill. There are several ways to respond to this challenge:

- by campaigning to change public opinion through educational programs and political pressure groups;
- through educational programs in healthcare facilities in support of holistic health;
- by Christian healthcare workers struggling to be what their mission proclaims;
- by encouraging a Christian-based hospice and palliative care movement; the need is clear: about 80 percent of all deaths in the United States occur not in a family environment but in institutions such as hospitals, chronic care facilities, or nursing homes;[38]
- by "urging healthcare facilities . . . to form partnerships for healthy living with parish churches."[39] This would be an act of refounding, as parishes have tended to hand over most of the pastoral care of the sick to hospital chaplains.

Summary

Grief is the sadness that cultures and individuals experience as a consequence of significant loss; the sadness is due to the breakdown of a structure of felt meaning. Grieving is the ritual process whereby cultures and

---

[38] See Moller, *Confronting Death,* 43; Sandol Stoddard, *The Hospice Movement: A Better Way of Caring for the Dying* (New York: Vintage Books, 1992).

[39] Catholic Health Association of the United States, *Partners in Healing: Healthcare Organizations and Parish Communities* (St. Louis: CHA, 1995) v. See also Catholic Health Association of Saskatchewan, *Parish Home Ministry of Care Basics* (Saskatoon: CHAS, 1995).

individuals adjust to loss. There is a profound tension between the contradictory pressures to cling to that which is lost and to build new relationships in which loss is accepted. Grieving rituals help people to articulate this tension and adjust to the realities of life.[40] Because feelings are involved, this process cannot be rushed.

In contrast to traditional cultures, Western societies have lost a sense of community and the art of ritual grieving. This encourages all kinds of pathological individual and group reactions to loss. The past haunts us; we do not know how to exorcise its powerful grip on our emotions and memories. This holds us back from rediscovering ourselves in the chaos of loss, and inhibits our potential for holistic health.

Healthcare is experiencing grief-overload because change is so rapid and multifaceted; traditional cultures and the Scriptures provide models of how we are to grieve. Trustees, board members, CEOs, and managers, with the use of these models, are to be ritual leaders calling their organizational cultures to grieve, thus also giving permission to individuals to do so. However, to be effective ritual leaders of mourning these people must first be mourners of their own losses; without this they have no empathy for what others experience.

Christ's life, especially his agony, death, and resurrection, is a journey of grieving, in which he is at the same time that which is lost and the leader of the mourning ritual. Detachment, which is the letting go of all that hinders individuals and organizations from a committed healing relationship with God, is at the heart of all authentic grieving. Jesus is *the* model of detachment, for "he emptied himself, / taking the form of a slave / . . . / accepting death, / death on a cross" (Phil 2:7-8), in order that we might share the new fruits of his victory over death through his resurrection (John 16:20).

---

[40] See Marris, *Loss and Change,* 31.

Epilogue

They were astounded . . . and were filled with awe.

—Luke 5:24

To refound healthcare ministry requires people committed to a clear vision of Christian holistic healing and prepared to collaborate in ways that tackle the roots of contemporary healthcare problems, even though they risk being socially marginalized for their efforts. The incident in the ministry of Christ that succinctly summarizes this theme is the healing of the paralytic in body and spirit (Luke 5:17-26; Mark 2:1-12).

Through this event people had come to know of Jesus' concern for the sick and marginalized. Friends of the paralytic, however, had to overcome significant obstacles in order to reach Christ: the crowd blocked the entrance to the room where Jesus was speaking (Luke 5:19) and the Pharisees and scribes objected to Christ's healing ministry.[1] The sick person's companions were not deterred; with perseverance and ingenuity they collaboratively found a radically different way to bring their friend to Christ: "They went up onto the top of the house and lowered him and his stretcher down through the tiles into the middle of the gathering, in front of Jesus" (Luke 5:19).

This was a creative and courageous act. The people in the room would have been angry that the normal way of approaching a visitor like Jesus had not been followed. One can only imagine what they thought about the

---

[1] See Robert C. Tannehill, *The Narrative Unity of Luke-Acts* (Philadelphia: Fortress Press, 1986) 89–96.

343

noise being made by the care-givers as they dug through the roof and then lowered the stretcher to the floor in front of Jesus. Jesus was deeply moved by their faith-inspired innovative act and rewarded them by holistically healing their friend (Luke 5:20, 24-25).

Jesus himself as care-giver refused to be intimidated by the Pharisees and scribes who were vociferously opposed to what Jesus was to do. They were not evil people. They were committed to maintaining what they thought were the commandments and codes for religious speech and healthy behavior. But the problem was that "they had lost imagination, and so had become insensitive to the new ideas which [were] necessary to creative hope and faith."[2] In brief, for them the cultural status quo had to be upheld, no matter how oppressive it was to people. Jesus responded to this obstruction by immediately healing the man in mind and body, using the authority given him by the Father.

Today's care-givers must often labor in cultures that deny that the sick have need of holistic healing. However, in a collaborative way and with the authority of Christ himself they also can find imaginative ways to overcome any barrier. Then people "filled with awe" will say: "We have seen strange things today" (Luke 5:26).

[2] Walter R. Bowie and others, *The Interpreter's Bible,* vol. 8 (Nashville: Abingdon Press, 1980) 105.

Index

methods of communication, 335–38
rituals, 314–17, 322–28
role of ritual leaders, 317
stages, 313–14
traditional cultures, 311–13
Western cultures, 317–20
Gutierrez, Gustavo, 177

Handy, Charles, 119
Health
Biblical, xvii–xviii, 154
holistic
—definition, xvii–xviii, 22–23,
41, 154, 169–73
—principles, 52–55
—World Health Organization
definition, xvii, 154
medical model, 24–26, 206
premodern, 15–20
Health maintenance organizations
(HMOs)
growth, 67
impact on physicians, 67–68
profit-maximizing, 68
reactions to, 68–70
Healthcare policy
Beveridge, 63
Bismarckian, 63
consumer sovereignty, 63
holistic, 7, 22–23, 39–40, 52–55,
57, 154, 106–07
individual responsibility, 55–56
paramodern, 50–55
traditional public, 55
Hehir, Bryan, 97, 151, 236
Hospitality, 157
Hospitals
containers of anxiety, 126–27
decline, xix, 80–81
historical stages, 50
length of stay, 85–86

Illich, Ivan, 32

Illness, 14
Inculturation
characteristics, 183–88
history, 182–83
Intentional faith communities
definition, 256–57
First world, 259–60
healthcare, 264–70
necessity, 261–64
Third world, 257–59

Justice, 156, 158

Kauffman, Christopher, 23

Land and healthcare
Aborigines, 58–59
Israelites, 166–67
Maori, 166
Leadership
functions, 115–26
servant, 219–22
transforming, 76, 211–12
Liberation theology
history, 177–78
significant characteristics,
178–79
Locke, John, 112–13
Lyth, Isabel Menzies, 143

Managed care, 66–70
health maintenance organizations
(HMOs), 67–70, 84
integrated delivery networks, 67
Management
management and leadership, 90,
113, 123, 212–13
management language, 86–87,
88–90
managerialism, 74, 137
McCormick, Richard A., xiv, 77,
80–81, 91, 95
McKeown, Thomas, 24